MEYERHOLD ON THEATRE

REVISED EDITION

MEYERHOLD
ON THEATRE
REVISED EDITION

*translated and edited with
a critical commentary*

by

EDWARD BRAUN

Methuen Drama

Published by Methuen Drama

3 5 7 9 10 8 6 4 2

Copyright © 1969, 1991, 1998 by Edward Braun

Edward Braun has asserted his right under the Copyright, Designs and Patents Act, 1988 to be identified as the author of this work.

First published in the United Kingdom by Methuen and Co Ltd

Reprinted in a fully revised edition in 1991 by Methuen Drama

This edition, with revisions, published in 1998 by Methuen Drama,

A CIP catalogue record for this book is available from the British Library

ISBN 0 413 38790 9

Printed by Cox & Wyman Ltd, Reading, Berkshire

To the memory of
Alexander Fevralsky

'Call me what instrument you will, though
you can fret me, yet you cannot play upon me.'

Hamlet III, 2

CONTENTS

ILLUSTRATIONS

9

PREFACE

This book is intended as an introduction to the work and ideas of Meyerhold. Since it first appeared in 1969, numerous works have been published that together have restored him to his pre-eminence amongst Russian directors of the twentieth century. There have been collections of his writings and utterances in a number of languages, most notably *Meierkhold – statyi, pisma, rechi, besedy*, published in Moscow in 1968, which contains the original texts of most of the pieces that I have included in this volume. It remains representative of the full range of Meyerhold's career, but in revising the text I have drawn the reader's attention to additional source material available in English translation.

In particular, I would mention Paul Schmidt's useful collection *Meyerhold at work* (Manchester, 1981) and Mel Gordon's documentation of biomechanics in *The Drama Review* (Vol.18, No.3). Béatrice Picon-Vallin's exhaustive *Vsevolod Meyerhold – Ecrits sur le théâtre* (Lausanne, 1973–1992) is the most complete collection in translation to date.

I could not have completed this work without the encouragement of Professor Elizabeth Hill during my postgraduate years in Cambridge. Equally, I recall with deep gratitude the generous help and advice that I received in the Soviet Union from many scholars and theatre practitioners. In particular, I must mention Maria Ivanova, Irina Meyerhold, Isaac Schneidermann, Maria Valentei and, above all, Alexander Fevralsky, whose many invaluable comments and corrections have been incorporated in this new edition. For permission to publish visual material I am indebted to the British Museum, the Bakhrushin State Theatre Museum, Moscow, and the Lunacharsky State Theatre Museum, Leningrad. The late Jay Leyda kindly consented to the inclusion of his translation of Meyerhold's letters referring to *The Lady of the Camellias*.

Bristol, September 1997   EDWARD BRAUN

Part One

THE SEARCH FOR NEW FORMS

1902-1907

MEYERHOLD WAS BORN ON 28 January (old style) 1874 in the small trading centre of Penza, some 350 miles to the south-east of Moscow. He was the eighth child of German parents, his father being a prosperous vodka distiller. Christened Karl Theodore Kasimir, Meyerhold changed his name to Vsevolod Emilevich in 1895, when he was converted from the Lutheran to the Orthodox faith and took Russian nationality. After spending only one year reading law at Moscow University, he was admitted to the drama school of the Moscow Philharmonic Society, where one of the teachers was Vladimir Nemirovich-Danchenko. At the final examinations in February–March 1898 Meyerhold was one of only two students to be awarded the Society's silver medal for acting, the other being Olga Knipper, the future wife of Chekhov.

In that same year the 'Moscow Popular Art Theatre', as it was originally called, was founded by Stanislavsky and Nemirovich-Danchenko, and Meyerhold was invited to join the company. He appeared in three-quarters of all performances in the first season, his most memorable role being Konstantin Treplev in *The Seagull*, which he played at the historic première on 17 December 1898.

Meyerhold spent four years with the Art Theatre, during which time he appeared in eighteen roles ranging from character parts to juvenile leads, and also worked as an assistant director. He became very friendly with Chekhov,[1] who was most disturbed to learn that Meyerhold was not included in the list of shareholders when the theatre was reorganized as a joint stock company at the beginning of 1902.[2]

At the time, it was suggested that this is what forced Meyerhold to leave the company, but if that is so, he seems to have welcomed the opportunity. He was finding it difficult to reconcile his angular, grotesque style of acting with the muted naturalism demanded by Stanislavsky, and was being entrusted with noticeably fewer new parts than before (although he did play Tuzenbakh in the first production of *Three Sisters* in January

---

[1] For a French translation of the extant Meyerhold-Chekhov correspondence (only one letter from Chekhov survives) see Nina Gourfinkel's *Vsévolod Meyerhold – Le théâtre théâtral*, éd. Gallimard, 1963.

[2] Cf. Chekhov's letter to Olga Knipper, 10 February 1902.

1901). More than anything, it was this that persuaded him to leave Moscow rather than a desire to become a director.

However, with a Moscow Art colleague, Alexander Kosheverov, he assembled a company of twenty-seven artists under the modest title 'A troupe of Russian dramatic artists' and hired the municipal theatre at Kherson in the Ukraine for the 1902–3 season. From the start, Meyerhold let it be known that his company was a far cry from the provincial barn-stormers of previous years who seldom performed the same play twice in one season. He set aside five weeks for uninterrupted rehearsals, cut the repertoire to more manageable proportions, and more than doubled the customary seasonal budget. It seemed a foolhardy risk, for he had no assets of his own and practically all the money was borrowed.

The repertoire differed little from the Moscow Art Theatre's: It included Chekhov's *Seagull, Uncle Vanya* and *Three Sisters*, plus a number of works by Ibsen and Hauptmann. Likewise, the style of production was strictly naturalistic; in later years Meyerhold said:

> I began as a director by slavishly imitating Stanislavsky. In theory, I no longer accepted many points of his early production methods, but when I set about producing myself, I followed meekly in his footsteps. I don't regret this because it was a short-lived phase; besides, it served as excellent practical schooling. There is no danger in imitation for the young artist; it is an almost inevitable stage.[1]

But if Meyerhold's methods were well tried, they were a revelation to Kherson, and the season yielded a sufficient profit to finance a tour of neighbouring southern towns in the spring. Whilst at Sevastopol, the company gave a performance of Maeterlinck's *Intruder*, Meyerhold's first production of the Belgian symbolist.

As Meyerhold was later to observe,[2] the theatre was the last of the arts to respond to the symbolist movement in Russia. However, before the start of the second Kherson season he announced a change in the company's artistic policy, reflected in its new title, 'The Fellowship of the New Drama'.

This new policy was enthusiastically endorsed by the symbolist poet, Alexei Remizov, who now became the Fellowship's literary manager. The repertoire included plays by Maeterlinck and the young Polish decadent playwright, Stanislaw Przybyszewski (1868–1927). It was in Przybyszewski's *Snow* (19 December 1903) that Meyerhold took the first tentative

---

[1] Recorded by Alexander Gladkov in 'Meyerhold govorit' in *Tarusskie stranitsy*, Kaluga, 1961, p. 302.
[2] See *The New Theatre Foreshadowed in Literature*, pp. 34–39 below.

steps towards non-representational staging. Remizov described it as 'A symphony of snow and winter, of pacification and irrepressible longing'.[1]

This and other modest attempts to break away from the Moscow Art style had a mixed reception from the local critics, but again the season was a financial success, and Meyerhold's reputation was spreading, thanks, no doubt, to Remizov's link with *Vesy*, the influential Moscow symbolist organ.

The following season (1904–5), Meyerhold and his company moved to Tiflis, the capital of Georgia, where they were offered a secure engagement at the new, well-equipped theatre of the Artistic Society. The opening production was *Three Sisters*, the style of which set the predominant tone for the season. A local critic wrote:

> ... the public was intrigued by various rumours that the 'Fellowship of the New Drama' was going to give them something 'new', something which Tiflis had never seen before ... When the eagerly awaited 'new thing' was presented it turned out to consist mainly of an unusually painstaking production of the play, numerous minor details all inspired by the desire to achieve an effect of the greatest possible illusion.[2]

Meyerhold's solitary attempt at innovation was a revival of *Snow* in which the entire action seems to have been obscured by a violet-tinted murk, baffling public and critics alike, and for a time having an alarming effect on attendances. There were no further experiments, but soon Meyerhold was to have the opportunity to try out his ideas before a more sophisticated audience.

In 1904 the Moscow Art Theatre staged Maeterlinck's trilogy of one-act plays, *The Blind*, *The Uninvited Guest*, and *Inside*. The production was a failure and Stanislavsky was forced to concede the inadequacy of conventional representational methods when faced with the mystical abstractions of the 'new drama'. In his autobiography *My Life in Art*, he describes how in vain he sought a solution in the other arts:

> My God! – cried out a querulous voice within me – is it possible that we, artists of the stage, are doomed by the materiality of our bodies to eternal servitude and the representation of crude reality? Are we destined never to surpass the achievements (splendid though they were in their day) of our realist-painters?[3]

He resolved to form an experimental studio to help him find the solution to this dilemma, and it was Meyerhold whom he invited to become its

---

[1] In *Vesy*, 1904, no. 4.

[2] *Tiflissky listok*, Tiflis, 28 September 1904, p. 2.

[3] K. S. Stanislavsky, *Moya zhisn v iskusstve*, Moscow, 1962, p. 340.

artistic director. Stanislavsky believed that Meyerhold had already dis-covered a formula for the staging of symbolist drama, which he had been prevented from realizing only by the material limitations of the provincial theatre.[1]

Meyerhold's own history of the Theatre-Studio is contained in the pages that follow, whilst Stanislavsky describes it in *My Life in Art*. Meyerhold and his young company were left to work undisturbed at Pushkino, just as the original Art Theatre company had been in 1898. As Meyerhold says, from the very first meeting in May 1905 there was an ominous divergence of opinion over the organization and policy of the Studio, with Stanislavsky particularly apprehensive over the role of the actor in Meyerhold's projects. Stanislavsky was partially reassured after watching the first public rehearsal at Pushkino on 12 August. Indeed, he even said of *The Death of Tintagiles*: 'It caused a furore. It is so beautiful, so new, so sensational!'[2]

But his doubts persisted, and little reassurance was offered by the more conservative members of the parent company. The armed rising in Moscow forced the temporary closure of practically all theatres on 14 October 1905; this was sufficient pretext first to postpone the Studio's opening at the Povarskaya Street Theatre, and shortly afterwards to cancel it al-together.

Meyerhold was not slow to realize the hopeless incompatibility of his new ideas and the traditional style of acting of the artists at his disposal. Early in 1906, even though faced with a return to the uncongenial artistic climate of Tiflis and Kherson, he wrote: 'The collapse of the Studio was my salvation; it wasn't what I wanted, not what I wanted at all.'[3]

No sooner had Meyerhold rejoined the Fellowship of the New Drama in Tiflis than he was invited by Vera Komissarzhevskaya to join her Peters-burg company as an actor and director. Clearly he was now feeling his strength, for he had the confidence to bargain keenly over terms before agreeing to join an actress who was hailed as 'the Russian Duse' and had set up her own theatre to further the cause of the new drama.

Before the end of the Tiflis season in March, Meyerhold succeeded finally in staging the productions of Maeterlinck's *Death of Tintagiles* and Ibsen's *Love's Comedy*, which he had prepared at the Theatre-Studio. It was around this time that he first read Georg Fuchs's *Die Schaubühne der*

---

[1] K. S. Stanislavsky, op. cit., p. 341.

[2] K. S. Stanislavsky, *Sobranie sochinenii*, vol. 7, Moscow, 1960, p. 324.

[3] Letter (undated) in N. Volkov, op. cit., vol. 1, p. 221.

Zukunft (The Stage of the Future).[1] The extent of Meyerhold's quotations from Fuchs is proof of the influence which this work exerted on him. As well as corroborating his own rejection of naturalism and his efforts to reveal the hidden 'sub-text' os a play, it opened his eyes to the significance of the forestage, the lessons to be learnt from the Oriental theatre in the use of rhythmical movement, and the inherent contradiction between the two-dimensional scenic backcloth and the three-dimensional figure of the actor.

Meyerhold experimented with a number of these innovations during a season by the Fellowship at Poltava in June and July. In several productions (including Ibsen's *Ghosts*) he removed the front curtain, built a deep forestage and employed a single, constructed (not painted) setting. Also, he introduced the expressive dance-like movements of the Japanese theatre.[2]

From the accounts of Meyerhold's early productions for Komissarzhev-skaya,[3] it would seem that he reverted to Maeterlinck's concept of a static drama which had ruled his experiments in Moscow. It is true that there was now a stepped forestage, but the artists were confined mainly to expressive poses on a narrow strip of stage (2 metres deep in *Sister Beatrice*) against a flat decorative panel. If Meyerhold set too great store by the purely decorative aspect of the production, it was partly in an effort to camouflage the actors' persistent tendency to lapse into a crude, melo-dramatic style of delivery and gesture when confronted with a non-realistic task.

The production of Blok's *Fairground Booth* (30 December 1906)[4] marked a crucial stage in Meyerhold's development. First it initiated his rejection of static poses and flat settings; second it was his first acquaint-ance with the characters of the *commedia dell' arte*, which was to exert a life-long influence on him. As his own account shows,[5] the final production of that first season, Leonid Andreev's *Life of a Man*, demonstrated an even freer handling of scenic space, and it was probably the first time that area lighting was used in the Russian theatre. He employed the technique again the following year in Wedekind's *Spring's Awakening* (15 September 1907).

Meyerhold was anxious to open the second season with a production of Fyodor Sologub's *Gift of the Wise Bees* 'in the round', but this was resisted

[1] Published Berlin, 1904-5 (undated).
[2] See Meyerhold's description of *The Cry of Life*, p. 64 below.
[3] See notes on *Hedda Gabler* (p. 65) and *Sister Beatrice* (p. 68).
[4] See pp. 70-71, 139-140, and 141 below.
[5] See pp. 71-72 below.

by Fyodor Komissarzhevsky, Vera's brother, and at that time the company's head of design. First he objected that it infringed theatre regulations (which it did), then later confessed that he personally was opposed to the project. It was typical of the clashes which Meyerhold's dictatorial methods and intransigent opinions were provoking. Vera Komissarzhevskaya herself gradually yielded to the overwhelming opinion of the critics that Meyerhold's eccentric style was stifling her creativity and transforming her artists into a troupe of marionettes.

The breaking-point was the second production of the season, *Pelléas and Mélisande* (10 October 1907). Still attracted by the idea of theatre in the round, Meyerhold tried to compromise by setting the action on a raised platform in the middle of a conventional stage and surrounded by the orchestra. To make matters worse, he reverted to the static style of presentation and the decorative panel. Finally, Komissarzhevskaya, at the age of forty-three, was incongruously cast as the childlike Mélisande. Immediately after the performance she called a meeting of the theatre directors and announced that 'the theatre must recognize that everything it has done up to now has been a mistake, and [Meyerhold] must either renounce his production methods or leave the theatre altogether'.[1] Meyerhold protested that *Pelléas* marked the close of a cycle of experiments which had demonstrated the limitations of 'decorative stylization' and the need to explore further staging in depth. There was a brief rapprochement, but within a month Meyerhold received notice of summary dismissal and soon after was replaced as artistic director by Fyodor Komissarzhevsky.

Ironically, three days before his dismissal his production of Sologub's *Death's Victory* drew grudging praise from the harshest critics. What impressed them most was the plasticity achieved by deploying the actors on a broad flight of steps extending the full width of the stage from the line of the proscenium arch to the back wall. In fact, the effect would have been even more striking had Meyerhold overcome his colleagues' caution and extended the steps right down into the auditorium. It was a significant attempt to break the barrier of the footlights and establish a more direct relationship between performer and spectator. To this extent, it was prophetic of the course which Meyerhold's work was shortly to take.

[1] N. Volkov, op. cit., vol. I, p. 335.

1. The Naturalistic Theatre and the Theatre of Mood

The Moscow Art Theatre has two aspects: the Naturalistic Theatre[1] and the Theatre of Mood.[2] The naturalism of the Art Theatre is the naturalism adopted from the Meiningen Players; its fundamental principle is the *exact representation of life*.

Everything on the stage must be as nearly as possible *real*: ceilings, stucco cornices, fireplaces, wallpaper, stove-doors, air-vents, etc.

A real waterfall flows on the stage and the rain falling is real water. I recall a small chapel built out of real wood, a house faced with thin plywood, double windows with cotton-wool padding and panes coated with frost. Every corner of the set is complete in every detail. Fireplaces, tables and dressers are furnished with a mass of oddments visible only through binoculars, and more than the most assiduous and inquisitive spectator could hope to take in during the course of an entire act. The audience is terrified by the din of a round moon being dragged across the sky on wires. Through the window a real ship is seen crossing a fiord. On the stage not only is there a whole set of rooms but it is several storeys high, too, with real staircases and oak doors. Sets are both struck and revolved. The footlights glare. There are archways everywhere. The canvas representing the sky is hung in a semicircle. When the play calls for a farmyard the floor is strewn with imitation mud made out of papier mâché. In short, the aim is the same as that of Jan Styka's[3] panoramas: the merging of the picture and the actual. Like Styka, *the designer of the naturalistic theatre works in close co-operation with the joiner, the carpenter, the property-master and the model-maker*.

In productions of historical plays the naturalistic theatre works on the principle of transforming the stage into a display of authentic museum pieces of the period or, failing that, of copies from contemporary illustrations or museum photographs. The director and the designer attempt to fix as accurately as possible the year, the month and the day of the action. For example, it is not enough for them that the play is set in the 'periwig age'; fantastic topiary, fairy-tale fountains, winding, maze-like paths,

[1] Repertoire: Pisemsky's *Rule of Will*, Hauptmann's *Henschel*, Naidenov's *Walls*, Gorky's *Children of the Sun*, etc. [Meyerhold's note.]

[2] Repertoire: Chekhov's plays. [Meyerhold's note.]

[3] Jan Styka (1858–1925). Polish genre painter.

23

avenues of roses, clipped chestnuts and myrtle, crinolines and whimsical coiffures: the charm of all this is lost on the naturalistic director. He must establish the exact style of sleeve worn in the time of Louis XV and how the ladies' coiffures during the reign of Louis XVI differed from those of Louis XV's time. Ignoring Somov's[1] method of stylizing an epoch, he goes in search of fashion magazines of the very year, month and day on which, according to his calculations, the action took place.

That is how *the technique of copying historical styles* was born in the naturalistic theatre. With such a technique it is natural that the rhythmical construction of a play like *Julius Caesar* with its precisely balanced conflict of two opposing forces is completely overlooked and so not even suggested. Not one director realized that a kaleidoscope of 'lifelike' scenes and the accurate representation of the plebeian *types* of the period could never convey the synthesis of 'Caesarism'.

Actors are always made up *true to character* – which means with faces exactly like those we see in real life. Clearly, the naturalistic theatre regards the face as the actor's principal means of conveying his intentions, ignoring completely the other means at his disposal. It fails to realize the fascination of plastic movement, and never insists on the actor training his body; it establishes a theatre school, yet fails to understand that physical culture must be a basic subject if one has any hope of staging plays like *Antigone* or *Julius Caesar*,[2] plays which by virtue of their inherent music belong to a different kind of theatre.

One recalls many examples of virtuoso make-up, but not one example of poses or rhythmical movement. In *Antigone*, the director – seemingly unconsciously – felt an urge to group the actors after the style of frescoes and vase drawings, but he was unable to *synthesize, to stylize* the results of his research and succeeded only in representing it photographically. On the stage one saw a series of resurrected tableaux; they resembled a range of hills separated by ravines, for their inner rhythm clashed violently with the 'lifelike' gestures and movements of the intervening action.

The naturalistic theatre has created actors most adept in the art of 'reincarnation', which requires a knowledge of make-up and the ability to adapt the tongue to various accents and dialects, the voice being employed as a means of sound-reproduction; but in this plasticity plays no part. The actor is expected to lose his self-consciousness rather than develop a sense of aestheticism which might balk at the representation of externally ugly,

---

[1] Konstantin Somov (1869–1939).

[2] All the naturalistic productions criticized in this article were staged at the Moscow Art Theatre.

misshapen phenomena. The actor develops the photographer's ability *to observe the trifles of everyday life.*

In Khlestakov 'nothing is sharply indicated', to use Gogol's expression, yet his character is perfectly clear. *There is absolutely no necessity for sharpness of outline in the clear representation of character.*

'The sketches of great masters often produce a stronger impression than their finished paintings. . . .'

'Wax figures have no aesthetic impact even though they represent the closest imitation of nature. It is impossible to regard them as artistic creations, because they leave nothing to the imagination of the spectator.' (Schopenhauer.)

The naturalistic theatre teaches the actor to express himself in a finished, clearly defined manner; there is no room for the play of allusion or for conscious understatement. That is why one so often sees overacting in the naturalistic theatre; it knows nothing of the power of suggestion. Yet there were some artists who made use of it, even in the heyday of naturalism: Vera Komissarzhevskaya's Tarantella in *The Doll's House*[1] was no more than a series of expressive poses during which the feet simply tapped out a nervous rhythm. If you watched only the feet, it looked more like running than dancing. What is the effect on the spectator if a naturalistic actress trained by a dancing-master ceases to act and conscientiously dances every step of the Tarantella?

In the theatre the spectator's imagination is able to supply that which is left unsaid. It is this mystery and the desire to solve it which draw so many people to the theatre.

'Works of poetry, sculpture and the other arts contain a rich treasury of the deepest wisdom; through them speaks the very nature of things to which the artist merely gives voice in his own simple and comprehensible language. Of course, everyone who reads or looks at a work of art must further the discovery of this wisdom by his own means. In consequence, each will grasp it according to his latent and actual ability, just as a sailor can plumb his lead only to the depth which his line allows.' (Schopenhauer.)

Thus the spectator in the theatre aspires – albeit unconsciously – to that exercise of fantasy which rises sometimes to the level of creativity. Similarly, how can an exhibition of paintings possibly exist except as a spur to the imagination?

[1] 1904. Revived by Meyerhold, 1906.

It would seem that the naturalistic theatre denies the spectator's capacity to fill in the details with his imagination in the way one does when listening to music. But nevertheless, the capacity is there. In Yartsev's *In the Monastery*,[1] the first act is set inside the inn of a monastery with the sound of the evening chimes outside. There are no windows, but from the chiming of the bells the spectator conjures up a picture of the courtyard with mounds of bluish snow, pines (like a painting by Nesterov),[2] trampled paths from cell to cell, the golden domes of the church: one spectator sees this picture; another – something different; a third – something different again. The mystery takes hold of the audience and draws it into a world of fantasy. Then, in the second act the director introduces a window and reveals the monastery courtyard to the audience. Where are *their* fir-trees, *their* mounds of snow, *their* gilded domes? The spectator is not only disenchanted but angry, for the mystery has vanished, his dreams are shattered.

This constant insistence on the banishment from the stage of the power of mystery is further demonstrated by *The Seagull*. In the first act of the original production[3] one couldn't see how the characters left the stage; they crossed the bridge and vanished 'somewhere' into the black depths of the wood (at that time the designer was still working without the help of carpenters). But when the play was revived, every corner of the set was laid bare: there was a summer house with a real roof and real columns; there was a real ravine on stage and one could see clearly how the characters made their exits through this ravine. In the original production the window in the third act was placed to one side and the landscape was hidden; when the characters entered the hall in galoshes, shaking out their hats, rugs and scarves, one pictured autumn, a fine drizzle, and puddles in the court-yard covered with squelching boards. In the revival the windows in the improved set faced the spectator so that the landscape was visible. Your imagination was silenced, and whatever the characters said about the landscape, you disbelieved them because it could never be as they described it; it was painted and you could see it. Originally, the departure of the horses with their bells jingling (the finale of the third act) was simply heard offstage and vividly evoked in the spectator's imagination. In the second production, once the spectator saw the veranda from which the people departed, he demanded to see the horses with their bells, too.

'A work of art can influence only through the imagination. Therefore it must constantly stir the imagination.' (Schopenhauer.) But it must really

---

[1] At the Moscow Art Theatre, 1904.   [2] Mikhail Nesterov (1862–1942).
[3] At the Moscow Art Theatre, 1898. Revived 1905.

stir it, not leave it inactive through trying to show everything. To stir the imagination is 'the essential condition of aesthetic activity as well as the basic law of the fine arts. Whence it follows that a work of art must not give *everything* to our senses but only as much as is necessary to direct our imagination on the right track, letting it have the last word'. (Schopenhauer.)

'One should reveal little, leaving the spectator to discover the rest for himself, so that sometimes the illusion is strengthened even further; to say too much is to shake the statue and shatter it into fragments, to extinguish the lamp in the magic lantern.' (Tolstoy, *On Shakespeare and the Drama.*)

And somewhere in Voltaire: 'Le secret d'être ennuyeux, c'est de tout dire.'

If the spectator's imagination is not disillusioned, it becomes even sharper, and art – more refined. How did medieval drama succeed without any stage equipment? Thanks to the lively imagination of the spectator.

The naturalistic theatre denies not only the spectator's ability to imagine for himself, but even his ability to understand clever conversation. Hence, the painstaking *analysis* of Ibsen's dialogue which makes every production of the Norwegian dramatist tedious, drawn-out and doctrinaire.

It is in productions of Ibsen that one sees the *method* of the naturalistic director revealed most clearly. The production is broken up into a series of scenes and each separate part of the action is *analysed* in detail, even the most trifling scenes. Then all the carefully analysed parts are stuck together again.

The assembling of parts to form the whole is an essential aspect of the director's art, but in speaking of this *analysing* by the naturalistic director, I do not mean the combining of the contributions of the poet, the actor, the musician, the designer and the director.

In his didactic poem, *An Essay on Criticism* (1711), the celebrated eighteenth-century critic Pope enumerated the obstacles which prevent the critic from pronouncing true judgement. Amongst them he cited the habit of examining *in detail*, identifying the primary task of the critic as the attempt to place himself in the position of the author, in order that he might view the work *as a whole*. The same might be said of the stage-director.

The naturalistic director subjects all the separate parts of the work to analysis and fails to gain a picture of the *whole*. He is carried away by the filigree work of applying finishing touches to various scenes, the gratifying products of his creative imagination, absolute pearls of verisimilitude; in consequence, he destroys the balance and harmony of the whole.

Time is a very precious element on the stage. If a scene visualized by the author as incidental lasts longer than necessary, it casts a burden on to the next scene which the author may well intend as most significant. Thus the spectator, having spent too long looking at something he should quickly forget, is tired out before the important scene. The director has placed it in a distracting frame. One recalls how the overall harmony was disturbed in the Moscow Art interpretation of Act Three of *The Cherry Orchard*. The author intended the act's leitmotiv to be Ranevskaya's premonition of an approaching storm (the sale of the cherry orchard). Everybody else is behaving as though stupefied: they are dancing happily to the monotonous tinkling of the Jewish band, whirling round as if in the vortex of a nightmare, in a tedious modern dance devoid of enthusiasm, passion, grace, even lasciviousness. They do not realize that the ground on which they are dancing is subsiding under their feet. Ranevskaya alone foresees the disaster; she rushes back and forth, then briefly halts the revolving wheel, the nightmare dance of the puppet show. In her anguish, she urges the people to sin, only not to be 'namby-pambies'; through sin man can attain grace, but through mediocrity he attains nothing.

The following harmony is established in the act: on the one hand, the lamentations of Ranevskaya with her presentiment of approaching disaster (fate in the new mystical drama of Chekhov); on the other hand, the puppet show (not for nothing does Chekhov make Charlotte dance amongst the 'philistines' in a costume familiar in the puppet theatre – a black tail-coat and check trousers). Translated into musical terms, this is one movement of the symphony. It contains the basic elegiac melody with alternating moods in pianissimo, outbursts in forte (the suffering of Ranevskaya), and the dissonant accompaniment of the monotonous cacophony of the distant band and the dance of the living corpses (the philistines). This is the musical harmony of the act, and the conjuring scene is only one of the harsh sounds which together comprise the dissonant tune of the stupid dance. Hence it should blend with the dancing and appear only for a moment before merging with it once more. On the other hand, the dance should be heard constantly as a muffled accompaniment, but only in the background.[1]

---

[1] Similar instances of dissonant notes emerging fleetingly from the background and encroaching on the act's leitmotiv are: the station-master reading poetry; Yepikhodov breaking his billiard cue; Trofimov falling downstairs. And note how closely and subtly Chekhov interweaves the leitmotiv and the accompaniment:

The director at the Art Theatre has shown how the harmony of the act can be destroyed. With various bits and pieces of equipment, he makes an entire scene of the conjuring, so that it is long and complicated. The spectator concentrates his attention on it for so long that he loses the act's leitmotiv. When the act ends the memory retains the background melody, but the leitmotiv is lost.

In *The Cherry Orchard*, as in the plays of Maeterlinck, there is a hero, unseen on the stage, but whose presence is felt every time the curtain falls. When the curtain falls at the Moscow Art Theatre one senses no such presence; one retains only an impression of 'types'. For Chekhov, the characters of *The Cherry Orchard* are the means and not the end. But in the Art Theatre the characters have become the end and the lyrical-mystical aspect of the play remains unrevealed.

Whereas in Chekhov the director loses sight of the whole by concentrating on its parts, because Chekhov's impressionistically treated images happen to lend themselves to portrayal as clearly defined figures (or *types*), Ibsen is considered by the naturalistic director to require *explanation* because he is too obscure for the public.

Firstly, experience has convinced him that the 'boring' dialogue must be enlivened by something or other: a meal, tidying the room, putting something away, wrapping up sandwiches, and so on. In *Hedda Gabler*, in the scene between Tesman and Aunt Julie, breakfast was served; I well remember how skilfully the actor playing Tesman ate, but I couldn't help missing the exposition of the plot.[1]

In Ibsen, besides giving a clearly defined sketch of Norwegian *types*, the director excels in emphasizing all sorts of 'complicated' (in his opinion) dialogue. One recalls how the essence of *Pillars of the Community* was completely lost in this painstaking analysis of *minor* scenes. Consequently, the spectator who had read the play and knew it well witnessed a completely new play which he didn't understand because he had read something else. The director gave prominence to a number of secondary, parenthetic scenes and brought out their meaning. *But the truth is that the sum of the meaning of all the parenthetic scenes does not add up to the meaning of the whole play.* One decisive moment prominently presented

---

Anya (*agitatedly*): And just now someone said that the cherry orchard was sold today.
Ranevskaya: Sold to whom?
Anya: He didn't say who; he's gone now. (*Dances* with Trofimov)
                                                    [Meyerhold's note.]

[1] Cf. Meyerhold's production of *Hedda Gabler*, described on pp. 65–68 below.

decides the fate of the act in the mind of the audience, even though everything else slips past as though in a fog.

The urge to *show* everything, come what may, the fear of mystery, of leaving anything unsaid, turns the theatre into a mere illustration of the author's words. 'There's the dog howling again', says one of the characters, and without fail a dog's howling is reproduced. The spectator concludes the 'departure', not only from the retreating sound of the harness bells but from the thundering of hooves on the wooden bridge over the river as well. You hear the rain beating on the iron roof; there are birds, frogs, crickets.

In this connection, let me quote a conversation between Chekhov and some actors (from my diary). On the second occasion (11 September 1898) that Chekhov attended rehearsals of *The Seagull* at the Moscow Art Theatre, one of the actors told him that offstage there would be frogs croaking, dragon-flies humming and dogs barking.

'Why?' – asked Anton Pavlovich in a dissatisfied tone.
'Because it's realistic' – replied the actor.
'Realistic!' – repeated Chekhov with a laugh. Then after a short pause he said: 'The stage is art. There's a genre painting by Kramskoy in which the faces are portrayed superbly. What would happen if you cut the nose out of one of the paintings and substituted a real one? The nose would be "realistic" but the picture would be ruined.'

One of the actors proudly told Chekhov that the director intended to bring the entire household, including a woman with a child crying, on to the stage at the close of the third act of *The Seagull*. Chekhov said:

'He mustn't. It would be like playing pianissimo on the piano and having the lid suddenly crash down.'
'But in life it often happens that the pianissimo is interrupted quite unexpectedly by the forte,' retorted one of the actors.
'Yes, but the stage demands a degree of artifice,' said A. P. 'You have no fourth wall. Besides, the stage is art, the stage reflects the quintessence of life and there is no need to introduce anything superfluous on to it.'

One need hardly amplify Chekhov's indictment of the naturalistic theatre implicit in this dialogue. The naturalistic theatre has conducted a never-ending search for the fourth wall which has led it into a whole series of absurdities. The theatre fell into the hands of fabricants who tried to make everything 'just like real life' and turned the stage into some sort of antique shop.

Following Stanislavsky's dictum that one day it will be possible to show the audience a real sky in the theatre, every director has racked his brains to raise the roof as high as possible over the stage. Nobody realizes that instead of rebuilding the stage (a most expensive undertaking), it is the fundamental principle of the naturalistic theatre which needs to be broken down. It is this principle alone which has caused the theatre to commit such absurdities.

Nobody believes that it is the wind and not a stage-hand which causes the garland to sway in the first scene of *Julius Caesar*, because the characters' cloaks remain still. The characters in Act Two of *The Cherry Orchard* walk through 'real' ravines, across 'real' bridges, past a 'real' chapel, yet from the sky are suspended two big pieces of blue-painted canvas with tulle frills, which bear no resemblance at all either to sky or clouds. The hills on the battlefield in *Julius Caesar* may be constructed so that they decrease in size towards the horizon, but why don't the characters become smaller, too, as they move away from us towards the hills?

'The usual stage set depicts landscapes of great depth but it is unable to show human figures of corresponding size against these landscapes. Nevertheless, such a set pretends to give a true representation of nature! An actor moves ten or even twenty metres back from the footlights, but he still looks just as tall and is seen in just as much detail as when he was standing close to them. According to the laws of perspective governing decorative art one ought to move the actor as far back as possible and then, in order to relate him correctly to the surrounding trees, houses and mountains, show him considerably reduced in size – sometimes as a silhouette, sometimes as a mere dot.'[1]

A real tree looks crude and unnatural beside a painted one, because its three dimensions strike a discordant note with the two dimensions of art.

One could cite a host of such absurdities, brought about by the naturalistic theatre's policy of the exact representation of nature. The rational definition of a given object, the photographic representation and illustration of the text of a play by means of decorative art, the copying of a historical style: these are the tasks which the naturalistic theatre sets itself.

Whereas naturalism has involved the Russian theatre in complicated stage techniques, the theatre of Chekhov (the other aspect of the Art Theatre), by revealing the power of *atmosphere* on the stage, has introduced that element without which the Meiningen-style theatre would have

[1] Georg Fuchs, *Die Schaubühne der Zukunft*, cit., p. 28.

31

perished long ago. Yet still the naturalistic theatre has not availed itself of this new element, introduced by Chekhov's 'music', to stimulate its further development. Chekhov's art demands a theatre of mood. The Alexandrinsky Theatre's production of *The Seagull*[1] failed to catch the mood which the author demanded.

The secret lies not in the chirping of crickets, not in dogs barking, not in real doors. When *The Seagull* was performed by the Art Theatre in the Hermitage Theatre[2] the stage *machinery* was not yet perfected and technology had not yet extended its tentacles to all corners of the theatre.

The secret of Chekhov's mood lies in the *rhythm* of his language. It was the rhythm which was captured by the actors of the Art Theatre during the rehearsals of that first production of Chekhov; it was captured because of the actors' love for the author of *The Seagull*.

If the Art Theatre had not captured the rhythm in Chekhov's plays, it would never have succeeded in re-creating it on the stage, and would never have acquired that second aspect which secured for it the title of 'the theatre of mood'. This aspect was the Art Theatre's *own*, not a mask borrowed from the Meiningen players.

I am firmly convinced that Chekhov himself helped the Art Theatre to succeed in accommodating under one roof both the naturalistic theatre and the theatre of mood; he helped by being present at rehearsals of his plays during which not only frequent discussions with the actors but the sheer fascination of his own personality influenced their taste and their conception of the purpose of art.

The new aspect of the theatre was created by a definite group of actors who became known as 'Chekhov's actors'. The key to the performance of Chekhov's plays was held by this group which almost invariably acted in them, and which may be regarded as having created Chekhov's rhythm on the stage. Every time I recall the active part which the actors of the Art Theatre played in creating the characters and the mood of *The Seagull* I understand why I believe firmly in the actor as the principal element in the theatre. The atmosphere was created, not by the *mise en scène*, not by the crickets, not by the thunder of horses' hooves on the bridge, but by the sheer musicality of the actors who grasped the rhythm of Chekhov's poetry and succeeded in casting a sheen of moonlight over their creations.

In the first two productions, *The Seagull* and *Uncle Vanya*, when the actors were still free, the harmony remained undisturbed. Subsequently,

[1] In 1896.
[2] The company performed in this theatre from 1898 to 1902.

the naturalistic director first based his productions on 'the ensemble' and then lost the secret of performing Chekhov.

Once everything became subordinated to 'the ensemble', the creativity of every actor was stilled. The naturalistic director assumed the role of a conductor with full control over the fate of the *new tone* which the company had discovered; but instead of extending it, instead of penetrating to the heart of the music, he sought to create atmosphere by concentrating on external elements such as darkness, sound effects, properties and characters.

Although he caught the speech rhythms, the director lost the secret of conducting (*The Cherry Orchard*, Act Three), because he failed to see how Chekhov progresses from subtle realism to mystically heightened lyricism.

Having found the key to Chekhov, the theatre sought to impose it like a template on other authors. It began to perform Ibsen and Maeterlinck 'à la Chekhov'.

We have already discussed Ibsen at the Art Theatre. Maeterlinck was approached, not through the music of Chekhov but through the same process of rationalization. Whilst the people in *The Blind* were broken down into *characters*, Death in *The Intruder* appeared as a gauze cloud. Everything was most complicated, as is customary in the naturalistic theatre, but not in the least stylized – even though everything in Maeterlinck is stylized.

The Art Theatre had the remedy in its own hands: it could have progressed to the New Theatre through the lyrical power of Chekhov, the musician; but it subordinated his music to the development of all manner of techniques and stage devices; finally it even lost the key to its 'own' author – just as the Germans lost the key to Hauptmann once he began to write plays other than domestic dramas, plays which demanded a completely different approach (*Schluck and Jau, And Pippa dances!*).

[First published in *Teatr, kniga o novom teatre*, Petersburg, 1908. Reprinted in Meyerhold's *O Teatre*, Petersburg, 1913, pp. 14–28.]

NOTE   Written in 1906. An earlier version of Meyerhold's interpretation of *The Cherry Orchard* is contained in a letter to Chekhov dated 8 May 1904:

Your play is abstract, like a Tchaikovsky symphony. Before all else, the director must get the 'sound' of it. In the third act, against a background of the stupid stamping of feet – this 'stamping' is what he must hear – enters Horror, completely unnoticed by the guests.

'The cherry orchard is sold.' They dance on. 'Sold.' Still they dance. And so on to the end. When one reads the play, the third act produces the same effect as the ringing in the ears of the sick man in your story *Typhus*. A sort of irritation. Jollity with overtones of death. In this act there is something terrifying, something Maeterlinckian . . .

> [*Literaturnoe nasledstvo, tom* 68 – *Chekhov*,
> Moscow, 1960, p. 448.]

2. The New Theatre Foreshadowed in Literature

I read somewhere that 'the stage inspires literature'. This is not true. If the stage is influencing literature, then it is in one respect only: it is tending to arrest the progress of literature by creating a group of writers who are influenced by the prevailing tendency (Chekhov and his imitators). The growth of the New Theatre is rooted in literature. Literature has always taken the initiative in the breaking down of dramatic forms. Chekhov wrote *The Seagull* before the Art Theatre appeared and staged it. It was the same with Van Lerberghe[1] and Maeterlinck. Where are the theatres capable of producing Verhaeren's *Dawn*, Bryusov's *Earth*, Vyachislav Ivanov's *Tantalus*, or any of Ibsen's plays? The theatre is prompted by literature, not only by playwrights who create a new form which demands a fresh technique but by critics who reject the old forms.

If one were to read all the dramatic notices written about our theatres from the time of the opening of the Moscow Art Theatre up to 1905, when the first attempts were made to develop a stylized theatre, one recurring theme would remain firmly in the memory: *the campaign against naturalism*.

Of all the opponents of naturalism the most unrelenting has been the dramatic critic Kugel[2] ('Homo Novus'). His articles have shown him consistently to be a considerable authority on stage technique with a firm grasp of the historical development of the drama and an exceptional love

---

[1] Charles Van Lerberghe (1861–1907). Belgian poet and dramatist.

[2] Alexander Kugel (1864–1928), editor of the influential Petersburg theatrical weekly *Teatr i iskusstvo*, and a bitter critic of Meyerhold throughout the prerevolutionary period.

of the theatre. Through his critical articles Kugel has contributed greatly to the growth of the theatre by helping the new audience and the pioneers of the New Theatre to recognize the pernicious consequences of the theatre's obsession with Russian 'Meiningenitis'. But although Kugel's articles have been so valuable for their vigorous attempts to eradicate every ephemeral and superfluous element from the theatre – everything which Chronegk (the director of the Meiningen Theatre) introduced – it has been impossible to guess what sort of theatre Kugel himself is advocating. What does he intend as a replacement for the complicated methods of the naturalistic theatre? Taking the actor as the basis of the theatre, Kugel dreams of the revival of 'inward feeling', but apparently he regards 'inward feeling' as something sufficient in itself. So his theatre remains chaotic, reminiscent of the nightmare of the provincial stage, the ultimate in taste-lessness.

The dramatic critics' campaign against naturalism has fostered a spirit of discontent within the theatre. But in their search for new forms the innovators of the stylized theatre are indebted above all to those new poets[1] who have publicized the ideas of the New Drama through the pages of the various artistic journals, and to the plays of Maurice Maeterlinck. Over a period of ten years Maeterlinck has written a succession of plays[2] which have been greeted with nothing but bewilderment, especially when they have been performed on the stage. Maeterlinck himself has stated repeatedly that his plays have been produced in too complex a fashion. The extreme simplicity of his dramas, their naïve language, their frequently changing scenes clearly demand a new method of production. Van Bever,[3] describing a production of *Pelléas and Mélisande* carried out under the author's direct supervision, says: 'The properties were reduced to a minimum; Mélisande's tower, for example, was represented by a wooden framework covered with grey paper.' Maeterlinck demands extreme

---

[1] I shall deal in detail with only two poets, Valery Bryusov and Vyacheslav Ivanov, whose articles on art and the theatre I regard as the most valuable contributions to the realization of the breakaway. But this does not mean that I have forgotten the contribution of others; for how could I forget those such as Anton Krainy, who in his observations on the theatre (the periodicals *Voprosy zhizni* and *Novy put*) broke boldly with old theatrical tradition and turned his attention to the new movements in the dramatic field, or Przybyszewski, with his refined conception of art in general and the theatre in particular. Worthy of mention, too, is the splendid chapter 'The Old and the New Repertoire' in *The Book of Great Wrath* by A. L. Volynsky. [Meyerhold's note.]

[2] Maeterlinck's first play, *The Princess Maleine*, was written in 1889. [Meyerhold's note.]

[3] Adolphe van Bever, *Maurice Maeterlinck*, Paris, 1904.

simplicity of production so that the spectator's imagination can supply all that is left unsaid. Above all, he fears that actors accustomed to playing in the cumbersome surroundings of our theatres may be prone to over-externalize everything, with the result that the subtle, concealed, inner part of his tragedies will remain unrevealed. All of which leads him to the belief that his tragedies demand extreme immobility, almost to the point of resembling puppet plays (tragédie pour théâtre marionnette).

For years Maeterlinck's dramas have been performed unsuccessfully, and those who appreciate the art of the Belgian dramatist have been dreaming of a New Theatre with a new technique, of a theatre to be called the 'Stylized Theatre'.

In order to formulate a plan for this theatre, to master its technique, one must start with Maeterlinck's own remarks on the subject.[1] He maintains that tragedy is manifested not through extremes of dramatic action, not in heart-rending cries, but, on the contrary, in the most silent, immobile form and in the quietly spoken word.

The need is for a static theatre. This is not something new and unprecedented, for the greatest of the classical tragedies, *The Eumenides*, *Antigone*, *Electra*, *Oedipus at Colonus*, *Prometheus*, *The Choephorae* are all 'static' tragedies. Not only do they lack external action, but also psychological action – what is known as a 'plot'. They are examples of a static drama in which Fate and man's position in the universe form the tragic axis.

Tragedy in which there is no action in the exposition of the plot, and which is based on the interrelation of Fate and Man, requires a static theatre with a technique embodying movement as plastic music, as the external depiction of an inner experience (illustrative movement), so that restrained gestures and economy of movement are preferable to the gestures of public declamation. This technique shuns all superfluous movement, lest it distract the spectator's attention from the complex inner emotions conveyed by a rustle, a pause, a break in the voice, or a tear which clouds the eye of the actor.

Every dramatic work contains two levels of dialogue: one is the 'external, necessary dialogue', made up of words which accompany and explain the action; the other is the 'inner dialogue' which the spectator should over-hear, not as words but as pauses, not as cries but as silences, not as soliloquies but as the music of plastic movement.

Maeterlinck's 'external, necessary dialogue' is constructed so that his characters are required to speak a minimum of words and the action con-

[1] 'Le Tragique quotidien' in *Le Trésor des Humbles* (1896).

tains a maximum of tension. In order to reveal Maeterlinck's 'inner dialogue' to the spectator and to facilitate his comprehension of it, the dramatic artist must develop new means of expression.

I think I am right in saying that in Russia Valery Bryusov[1] was the first to stress the futility of the 'truth' which theatres have expended all their efforts in depicting in recent years. Equally, he was the first to indicate the new means of dramatic presentation. He demanded the rejection of the futile 'truth' of the contemporary stage in favour of *conscious stylization* (all the italics are mine).

In the same article Bryusov stresses the significance of the *actor* as the principal dramatic element. However, in this he differs from Kugel, who regards 'internal feeling' as self-sufficient and acting as a function totally unrestrained by self-discipline, quite remote from the overall conception of the director.

Although Bryusov's point concerning conscious stylization is closer to the basic theme of my article, I must stop to examine his conception of the actor's role before I can proceed to an examination of the stylized theatre and its new technique.

According to Bryusov, the fable, the idea of the work of art, is its *form*; the figures, colours and sounds are the means of expressing it. A work of art is of value only if the artist has imbued it with his own soul. A work of art's content is the artist's soul. Prose, verse, colour, clay, the fable: all these are the artist's means of expressing his soul.

Bryusov rejects the distinction between creative artists (poets, sculptors, painters, composers) and interpretative artists (musicians, actors, singers, theatre designers). True, he says, some produce lasting, permanent works of art whereas others are obliged to re-create their art each time they wish to render it accessible to their audience, but in both cases the artist is a 'creator'.

'The actor on the stage is just like the sculptor before a piece of clay, he has to embody in a recognizable form exactly the same subject-matter: *the impulses and sensations of his soul.* A pianist's means of expression are the sounds produced by his instrument, the singer employs his voice; the actor – his body, speech, mime and gesture. The work which the interpretative artist performs serves as the form for his own creation.'

'*The actor's creative freedom is unhampered by his receiving the form of his creation complete from the author of the play* . . . Artists create

[1] 'Nenuzhnaya pravda' (The unnecessary truth), in *Mir iskusstva*, Peterburg, 1902, no. 4. [Meyerhold's note.]

freely, depicting the great moments of biblical history, even though here too the form is supplied from without.'

'The task of the theatre is to create conditions under which the actor's creativity can be manifested most freely and can be most fully comprehended by the audience. *The theatre's sole obligation is to assist the actor to reveal his soul to the audience.*'

Rejecting the words 'the theatre's *sole* obligation', I would expand Bryusov's thoughts as follows: *the theatre must employ every means to assist the actor to blend his soul with that of the playwright and reveal it through the soul of the director.* And just as the actor's freedom is unhampered by the form of his creation being received complete from the dramatist, so it will not be limited by what the director gives him.

All theatrical means must be devoted to the service of the actor. The attention of the audience should be focused exclusively on him, for acting occupies the central position in the art of the stage.

According to Bryusov, the entire European theatre – with a few minor exceptions – is moving in the wrong direction. I shall not bother to mention all the absurdities perpetrated by the naturalistic theatre in its striving for the exact representation of life which support Bryusov's assertion – they are described quite adequately in the first chapter.[1]

Bryusov stands for the furtherance of stylization in the theatre, by which he does not mean the conventional stylization of actors who, desiring but lacking the ability to speak as in real life, resort to the unnatural emphasizing of words, ridiculous gestures, strange sighs and the like. Or the stylization of stage-designers who attempt to represent a room by building a three-sided box-set on the stage. Rejecting such thoughtless, stereotyped, anti-artistic stylization, he wishes to see the growth of *conscious stylization* in the theatre as a production technique with its own distinct flavour. 'There is stylization in the absence of colour in marble and bronze statues. An engraving with black leaves and a striped sky is stylized, yet it can yield pure aesthetic pleasure. Wherever there is art, there too is stylization.' Obviously it is not necessary to eradicate scenery completely and return to the time when the titles of the scenes were simply written on columns, but 'we must build stage sets which are comprehensible to everybody – just as any language needs to be comprehensible, just as white statues, flat pictures, and black engravings are comprehensible'.

Then Bryusov indicates the active role of the spectator in the theatre.

[1] In *The Naturalistic Theatre and the Theatre of Mood* (pp. 23–33 above).

'It is time for the theatre to stop imitating reality. A cloud in a painting is flat, stays motionless, does not change its shape or colour, yet it contains something which excites in us the same sensation as a real cloud in the sky. *The stage must supply that which is needed to help the spectator to picture as easily as possible in his imagination the scene demanded by the plot of the play.*'

I shall speak of Vyacheslav Ivanov when I discuss the repertoire of the Stylized Theatre.

[First published in *Teatr, kniga o novom teatre*, cit. Reprinted in Meyerhold's *O Teatre*, cit., pp. 28–35.]

NOTE Probably written in 1907. Maeterlinck was produced first in Russia in 1895 (*Inside* in Petersburg); Meyerhold's first production was of *The Intruder* at Sevastopol in Spring, 1903.

---

3. The Theatre-Studio

The so-called 'Theatre-Studio' was due to open in Moscow in 1905. Over a period of almost six months (in the spring at the model workshop of the Art Theatre, in the summer in Dupuy Park at the Mamontov Estate[1] on the Yaroslavl Road, and in the autumn at the theatre by the Arbat Gate) actors, directors, designers and musicians assembled by Konstantin Sergeevich Stanislavsky were preparing for the opening of the new theatre with extraordinary energy. But the work of the theatre was destined to remain unseen – not only by the general public but even by the close circle of those interested in this new dramatic undertaking.

But although the Theatre-Studio never opened its doors to the public, it still played a most significant part in the history of the Russian theatre. There is no doubt that everything which our leading theatres began subsequently to produce with such nervous excitement and extreme haste derived from that one source; all the motives underlying their various new interpretations were interrelated and were familiar to anyone who had

[1] The property of Savva Ivanovich Mamontov (1841–1918), wealthy industrialist and patron of the arts. Together with Stanislavsky and Meyerhold, he was a director of the Theatre-Studio.

been concerned in the work of the Theatre-Studio. But the historian is unable to record this phenomenon, because the theatre's work proceeded behind closed doors and only a few were fortunate enough to make the acquaintance of the new-born theatre.

Valery Bryusov wrote of the dress-rehearsal of *The Death of Tintagiles*: 'I was one of the few fortunate enough to see the dress-rehearsal of Maeterlinck's *Death of Tintagiles* at the Studio. It was altogether one of the most fascinating performances I have ever seen.'[1]

At the same time as the Theatre-Studio was seething with activity one could read the following in newspapers and periodicals:

1. 'This spring (1905) saw the third anniversary of the Fellowship of the New Drama (1902–1905), which turned out to be its last. The Fellowship of the New Drama no longer exists. Its manager, Meyerhold, is returning to Stanislavsky's Art Theatre in Moscow. Stanislavsky is assembling a new company headed by Meyerhold; it will have a "contemporary" repertoire of 10–15 plays. Provincial tours are planned, as well as a series of evenings in the auditorium of the History Museum with the participation of the company of the new theatre. These evenings will be devoted to Russian and foreign poets (Baudelaire, E. Poe, Verhaeren, Bryusov, Balmont, Vyachislav Ivanov, Andrei Bely and others).'

2. 'The subsidiary company of the Art Theatre (The Theatre-Studio), set up by Stanislavsky and under the immediate direction of Meyerhold, will be housed in the Girsh Theatre, Arbat Gate. The aim of this enterprise is the propagation of seriously directed and well-equipped companies and theatres in the provinces.'

3. 'The link with the Art Theatre will be mainly one of principle, in the sense that works will be produced on the same "artistic" basis. The repertoire, however, will differ to some extent.'

4. 'One wonders whether this theatre will uphold and further the tenets of the Art Theatre, or whether it will embody the new movements and experiments in drama and the art of the theatre.'

This last question remained open. There was no fathoming the nature of a theatre which could include in its repertoire Maeterlinck and Gorky, Przybyszewski and Ibsen, Verhaeren and Polevoy (*Russian Heroism*). Clearly, nobody knew whether the Theatre-Studio was really a branch of the Art Theatre; that is, whether the Art Theatre and the Studio were

[1] *Vesy*, Moscow, 1906, no. 1 (under pseudonym 'Avrely').

joined by the same ideological link, as say, the Moscow Maly and the Novy Theatre.[1]

The Theatre-Studio was founded by Konstantin Sergeevich Stanislavsky. It is true that I became the artistic director of a company made up of a nucleus of the best members of the Fellowship of the New Drama, but it is not true that the Theatre-Studio was a subsidiary of the Art Theatre, even though it was envisaged as such by Stanislavsky.

This correction is necessary if one is to understand that the Theatre-Studio functioned independently from first to last. In my opinion, this was why it broke away so quickly and so easily from the course of the Art Theatre, renounced perfected forms so readily and plunged headlong into a new world in order to start building on new foundations.

The first meeting of the members of the Theatre-Studio took place on 5 May, and at this very first meeting the following points were made:

1. Contemporary forms of dramatic art have long since outlived their usefulness.

2. The modern spectator demands fresh techniques.

3. The Art Theatre has achieved virtuosity in lifelike naturalism and true simplicity of performance, but plays have appeared which require new methods of production and performance.

4. The Theatre-Studio should strive for the renovation of dramatic art by means of new forms and new methods of scenic presentation.

Judging by the fact that an extract from Antoine's work was read out to the actors, it is evident that the young theatre was expected simply to develop those forms discovered already by the Art Theatre. But the desire for new forms of scenic presentation appropriate to the new spirit in dramatic literature did not in itself signify the abrupt break with the past which was to occur later in the work of the Theatre-Studio.

'Obviously the Art Theatre with its naturalistic style does not represent the last word and has no intention of remaining frozen to the spot; the young theatre, together with its parent company, the Art Theatre, must continue the process and move forward.' [Stanislavsky]

Thus it seemed that the Theatre-Studio was required only to 'evolve' and, perhaps, to evolve in the same manner as the Art Theatre. But as early as June, at the opening of the rehearsal room at the Mamontov

---

[1] A theatre in Moscow affiliated to the Bolshoi and the Maly, with both an operatic and a dramatic company. Closed in 1907.

Estate, one of those present expressed his reluctance to see the Studio imitating the Art Theatre.

In order to discover a technique of staging appropriate to the literary forms of the new drama, and to revise stage design by means of new technical devices, the artists and directors – the company had dispersed until June – retreated for a month to the model workshop which had kindly been made available by the Art Theatre.

May was a significant month for the Theatre-Studio; that spring was crucial in shaping the destiny of its directors.

In the model workshop plans were worked out for the following plays: Polevoy's *Russian Heroism*, Przybyszewski's *Snow*, Rachilde's *Salesman of the Sun*, Hauptmann's *Colleague Krampton* and *Festival of Thanksgiving*, Tetmayer's *Sphinx*, Maeterlinck's *Seven Princesses* and von Hoffmannsthal's *Woman in the Window*.

The following artists worked in collaboration with the stage-directors: Denisov, Ulyanov, Prince Gugunava and Golst.

But to an artist the construction of a model to determine the lines, angles and atmosphere of a setting seems unnecessary labour. If the director and the artist share the same views on painting, the director prepares a sketch of the setting which the artist uses to work out a colour scheme and the arrangement of the colour masses. This collaboration yields a series of designs. The director's outline sketch in pencil or charcoal or, if he has no aptitude for painting, the artist's coloured sketches, are in themselves almost sufficient for the construction of the settings without any recourse to models.

So after we had completed a whole series of models representing true-to-life interiors and exteriors, the atmosphere in the workshop became uneasy, with everyone waiting impatiently for someone else to give the order to burn or break up every model.

But there was no regret, for this labour had served a specific purpose: everyone realized that once the glue on the models had set, the entire machinery of the theatre was set with it. As we turned those models over we seemed to be holding the entire contemporary theatre in our hands. In our desire to burn and destroy them we were already close to the desire to destroy the obsolete methods of the naturalistic theatre.

The first move towards the final rejection of the model was made by Sapunov and Sudeikin. It was the very first step in the search for new, simple means of expression on the stage.

They were working on the designs for Maeterlinck's *Death of Tintagiles*. They approached this task with trepidation, since they both enjoyed designing for the stage and both loved Maeterlinck; but they promised only to prepare designs, refusing point-blank to glue together models. Only when the designs were finished did they agree to produce coloured models, and then only so that the stage-crew could see the stage-plan; in other words, so that the location of the flats, flooring, rostra and so on should be clear.

By the time it became known in the model workshop that Sapunov and Sudeikin had produced stylized designs for *The Death of Tintagiles* in *plan* form, the other artists were already stopping work.

Thus, out of dissatisfaction with models was born the technique of impressionistic plans. I stress 'plans' because those artists who had already agreed to compromise and produce models with architectural details (the task of the naturalistic theatre) were obviously reluctant to abandon their representational style. But no matter how close to life all their glued-together interiors and exteriors came, each artist now tried to vary this crude naturalistic job (the building of houses, gardens and streets on the stage) by introducing refined stylized colouring and trick lighting effects (in their painting).

The earlier models were discarded and the new work went ahead full swing. In the first act of *Krampton* (the artist's studio), instead of a full-sized room with all its furnishings, Denisov simply depicted a few bright areas characteristic of a studio. When the curtain rose, the atmosphere of the studio was conveyed by a single huge canvas occupying half the stage and drawing the spectator's attention away from all other details; but, in order that such a large picture should not distract the spectator with its subject, only one corner was completed, the rest being lightly sketched in with charcoal. In addition, there was the edge of a big skylight with a patch of sky, a step-ladder for painting the canvas, a large table, an ottoman (necessary to the action of the play) and a number of sketches strewn over the table. It marked the introduction of the principle of stylization.[1]

The main progress in this direction was achieved by Ulyanov in his work on Hauptmann's play *Schluck and Jau*. It was proposed to produce this play in the style of the 'periwig age'. The first version incorporated all

---

[1] With the word 'stylization' I do not imply the exact reproduction of the style of a certain period or of a certain phenomenon, such as a photographer might achieve. In my opinion the concept of 'stylization' is indivisibly tied up with the idea of convention, generalization and symbol. To 'stylize' a given period or phenomenon means to employ every possible means of expression in order to reveal the inner synthesis of that period or phenomenon, to bring out those hidden features which are to be found deeply embedded in the style of any work of art. [Meyerhold's note.]

sorts of complicated scenery. Funny as it may seem, we proposed to reconstruct the halls and gardens of 17th and 18th century France from photographs and sketches copied from rare albums of that glorious epoch.

But once the principle of stylization was finally established the problem was quickly and easily solved. Instead of a host of details, one or two bold brush-strokes sufficed:

Act One: the castle gates where the hunters find the drunken Schluck and Jau. On the stage one sees only the castle gates, with a circular revolving door surmounted by a bronze statue of Cupid. The gates are placed at the extreme front of the forestage. They are strikingly grandiose, huge and magnificent. The castle is not visible through the gates, but the spectator immediately grasps the style of the period and the wealth of those living beyond the gates from a series of *bosquets* which lead upstage. The figures of Schluck and Jau before the magnificent gates immediately establish the play's essential contrast and lead the spectator on to the plane of tragi-comedy and satire. (A further variant by the artist is simple in the extreme: there is no gate, no fence, but merely bosquet arches with suspended wicker baskets and flower-beds behind.)

The atmosphere of the royal bedchamber is synthesized by an absurdly elaborate bed of exaggerated proportions with an incredible canopy. The whole scale is exaggerated to give the impression of royal splendour and comically overblown extravagance. At the same time, there is a hint of satire (compare the drawings of Thomas Theodor Heine).

In the third scene the convention is pursued to its extreme. The mood of idleness and whimsy is conveyed by a row of arbours resembling wicker baskets and stretching across the forestage. The back curtain depicts a blue sky with fluffy clouds. The horizon is bounded by crimson roses stretching the entire width of the stage. Crinolines, white periwigs and the characters' costumes are blended with the colours of the setting into a single artistic design, a symphony in mother-of-pearl with all the charm of a painting by Somov. The rise of the curtain is preceded by a duet in the style of the eighteenth century. The curtain rises to disclose figures seated in each arbour: in the centre is the princess, on either side the ladies-in-waiting. They are embroidering a single broad ribbon with ivory needles – all in perfect time. In the background is heard a duet to the accompaniment of harpsichord and harp. Everything suggests musical rhythm: movements, lines, gestures, dialogue, the colours of the setting and costumes. Everything which needs to be hidden from the audience is concealed behind stylized flats, with no effort made to induce the spectator to forget that he is in the theatre.

In reply to the question raised by periodicals of the time – 'one wonders whether this theatre (the Theatre-Studio) will uphold and further the tenets of the Art Theatre or whether it will embody the new movements and experiments in drama and the art of the theatre' – there is only one conceivable answer.

It so happened that the Theatre-Studio had no desire to uphold and further the tenets of the Art Theatre, but preferred to devote itself to the construction of a new edifice, building from the foundations upwards.

A 'Literary Bureau' was created within the Theatre-Studio and attracted a number of prominent poets from the *Vesy*[1] and *Voprosy zhizni*[2] literary groups. The purpose of the Literary Bureau was to furnish the theatre with interesting new dramatic works from every country. The running of the Literary Bureau was entrusted to Valery Bryusov, who subsequently played a significant part in the running of the theatre.

The Theatre-Studio became a theatre of experiment, but it was not so easy for it to break away from the naturalism of the Meiningen school. When the fateful day came and our theatre 'shed its blooms before it had a chance to flourish', Valery Bryusov wrote in *Vesy* (January 1906):

'In the Theatre-Studio various attempts were made to break away from the realism of the contemporary stage and to embrace stylization wholeheartedly as a principle of dramatic art. In movement there was plasticity rather than impersonation of reality; groups would often look like Pompeian frescoes reproduced in living form. Scenery was constructed regardless of the demands of realism; rooms were made without ceilings; castle pillars were twined around with some sort of liana; dialogue was spoken throughout against a background of music, which initiated the spectator into the world of Maeterlinck's drama.

'But at the same time, theatrical tradition and the years of teaching of the Art Theatre exercised a powerful influence. Actors achieved a stylization of gesture worthy of the dreams of the Pre-Raphaelites, yet in their speech they still strove for the intonation of normal conversation; they attempted to express emotions in the same way as they are expressed in real life. Scenic design was stylized, but in its details it remained rigidly realistic. At the point where the skill of the director stopped the usual style of acting commenced, and at once it became clear that the actors were poor, lacked real training, and were incapable of true feeling. The

---

[1] *Vesy* ('The Balance'): leading Moscow symbolist monthly, of which Bryusov was joint-editor.
[2] *Voprosy zhizni* ('Questions of Life'): Petersburg monthly.

Theatre-Studio demonstrated to everybody who made its acquaintance that it is impossible to build a new theatre on old foundations. Either one must continue the construction of the Antoine-Stanislavsky theatre, or one must begin all over again.'

The full realization of these aims was frustrated because by May (the month of the abrupt breakaway from the Meiningen style) the company had been already engaged, most of the actors coming from the drama courses of the Art Theatre. As soon as rehearsals began after May, it was clear that the requirements of the Theatre-Studio demanded fresh acting material, more malleable and less enamoured of the charms of the established theatre. The Theatre-Studio was without a company. Two or three actors from the Art Theatre School and two or three from the Fellowship of the New Drama understood the new style. But the majority were from the drama courses of the Art Theatre, and the directors of the Theatre-Studio, before starting to create a repertoire, were faced with the task of preparing the actors by means of a series of discussions and experiments designed simply to familiarize them with the new style. It was then that it struck me that an acting school attached to a theatre is death for the actors studying there. An acting school must exist *independently* and must not teach the current style of acting. It must be organized so that a new theatre arises out of it, so that there is only one possible path leading from it: if the pupils do not go into the new theatre which they have created for themselves, they go nowhere. For if such a school not only maintains the strength of its 'own' theatre, but also replenishes with its surplus of pupils the companies of other theatres, it will cause only harm, because its actors will be regarded everywhere as alien, no matter how good they may be when judged by the standards of their own school.

The Theatre-Studio was a theatre in search of new scenic forms. One might have expected this fact to attract the special attention of drama critics. By commenting on the theatre's progress they would have helped it to advance along the correct path. But all the theatre's work went unnoticed; everything it tore down and everything it built up went unpublicized. The theatre never opened its doors to the public and history was deprived of the opportunity of assessing the value of the lessons which the theatre had learnt.

However, the extent of the Theatre-Studio's influence on the course of the Russian theatre may be judged by the fact that since its death, whenever there has been an important new production in Moscow or St Petersburg, people have compared it with the Theatre-Studio.

46

When *The Drama of Life*[1] was presented at the Art Theatre one Moscow newspaper remarked that the play was produced according to the principles of the Theatre-Studio. *Teatr i iskusstvo*[2] observed that the origin of the entire production (the attempt at stylization) could be traced back to the Theatre-Studio. Likewise, everything I did at Vera Komissarzhevskaya's Dramatic Theatre was (according to the theatre critic, Kugel) based on my work in the 'laboratory' attached to the Art Theatre. He, too, has claimed that the source of all new experiments and trends was the same Theatre-Studio.

My aim is to help the future theatre historian assess accurately the significance of the Theatre-Studio, to help directors who are painstakingly seeking fresh means of expression, to help the spectator fathom what it is that inspires the theatre of the New Drama, what sustains it and what it is seeking. To this end I will try to describe in as much detail as possible the work of the Theatre-Studio, to reveal as fully as possible the lessons learnt there.

It is essential to describe as completely as possible the evolution of the new principles of production which formed the basis of the stylized theatre, and to trace the historical development of those forces which swept away the principles of naturalistic drama and replaced them with the principles of the stylized theatre.

Before all else one ought to mention the services rendered to the Theatre-Studio by the provincial 'Fellowship of the New Drama', which was the first to turn a critical eye on the tenets of naturalistic drama. Thanks are due to Alexei Remizov, the director of the Fellowship's Literary Bureau, who gave most active encouragement to the work of the young champions in the new field. But this goes beyond the bounds of my task. I must limit myself to dealing with the contribution of the Theatre-Studio to the revolution of the contemporary stage (not its evolution, as was anticipated) and with the influence it had during its search for new paths on the work of existing theatres and on those theatres which came into being after its death.

Work on one play (Ibsen's *Love's Comedy*) led to criticism of the 'theatre of types' and revealed the possibility of a theatre of synthesis; work on another (*The Death of Tintagiles*) suggested the disposition of figures on the stage after the style of bas-reliefs and frescoes, the revealing of inner dialogue by means of the music of plastic movement, the possibility of examining the impact of *aesthetic*, as opposed to traditional *logical* effects –

[1] By Knut Hamsun (staged by Stanislavsky in 1907).
[2] The leading Petersburg theatrical periodical.

and much more besides which I shall discuss below. Work on the third play *Schluck and Jau* taught us to depict on stage nothing but the most important, 'the quintessence of life', as Chekhov put it; it revealed the difference between *the representation of a style on stage and the stylization of scenic situations*. And in all this work, the further it progressed, the more it uncovered the errors of our 'elder brother', the Art Theatre.

As the principal director of the Fellowship of the New Drama and the Theatre-Studio, I cannot describe the search for new dramatic forms without criticizing those forms which seemed to me not merely obsolete but positively harmful.

The principles of the Meiningen school became our chief enemies, and since in one area of its activities the Art Theatre followed the Meiningen principles, I was forced to recognize it, too, as my enemy in the struggle for new dramatic forms.

Before proceeding to an exposition of the principles of the stylized theatre I feel obliged to describe how I gradually became aware of the deficiencies of the Meiningen style during my search for new forms, and to explain what I felt necessary to overcome in the methods of the director of the Art Theatre.

Highly as I esteem the part played by the Art Theatre, not only in the history of the Russian theatre but in the field of contemporary European drama as a whole, I would still be doing a disservice both to myself and to those to whom this work is dedicated if I made no mention of those of its errors which helped us develop our new dramatic style.

I shall relate my thoughts on the Art Theatre as they were when I was working with the Fellowship of the New Drama and the Theatre-Studio.[1]

[First published in *Teatr, kniga o novom teatre*, cit. Reprinted in Meyerhold's *O Teatre*, cit., pp. 3–14.]

NOTE   Probably written in 1907. Of the designers mentioned, Denisov, Sapunov and Sudeikin continued to work with Meyerhold when he joined Vera Komissarzhevskaya in Petersburg in 1906.

It is interesting to compare the description of *Schluck and Jau* with Meyerhold's later discussion of the grotesque (see *The Fairground Booth*, pp. 137–142 below).

[1] See *The Naturalistic Theatre and the Theatre of Mood*, pp. 23–33 above.

Meyerhold as Treplev in *The Seagull*. Moscow Art Theatre, 1898.

Ulyanov's projected setting for *Schluck and Jau*. Theatre-Studio, 1905.

Komissarzhevskaya as Sister Beatrice, 1906.

The Ball Scene in *A Man's Life*, 1907.

4. First Attempts at a Stylized Theatre

The first attempts to realize a Stylized Theatre as conceived by Maeterlinck and Bryusov were made at the Theatre-Studio. In my opinion, this first experimental theatre came very near to achieving ideal stylized drama with its first production, *The Death of Tintagiles*; so I think it is appropriate to describe the work of the directors, actors and designers on this play, and to consider the lessons learnt during its production.

The theatre is constantly revealing a lack of harmony amongst those engaged in presenting their collective creative work to the public. One never sees an ideal blend of author, director, actor, designer, composer and property-master. For this reason, Wagner's notion of a synthesis of the arts seems to me impossible.[1] Both the artist and the composer should remain in their own fields: the artist in a special *decorative* theatre where he could exhibit canvases which require a stage rather than an art gallery, artificial rather than natural light, several planes instead of just two dimensions, and so on; the composer should concentrate on symphonies like Beethoven's Ninth, for the dramatic theatre, where music has merely an auxiliary role, has nothing to offer him.

These thoughts came to me after our early experiments (*The Death of Tintagiles*) had been superseded by the second phase (*Pelléas and Mélisande*).[2] But even when we started work on *The Death of Tintagiles* I was plagued already by the question of disharmony between the various creative elements; even if it was impossible to reach agreement with the composer and the artist, each of whom was trying instinctively to delineate his own function, at least I hoped to unify the efforts of the author, the director and the actor.

It became clear that these three, the basis of the theatre, could work as one, but only if given the approach which we adopted in the rehearsals of *The Death of Tintagiles* at the Theatre-Studio.

In the course of the usual discussions of the play (before which, of course, the director acquainted himself with it by reading everything written on the subject), the director and actors read through Maeterlinck's verses and extracts from those of his dramas containing scenes corresponding in mood to *The Death of Tintagiles* (the play, itself, was left until we

[1] Cf. pp. 82 ff. below.
[2] First performed on 10 October 1907 at Komissarzhevskaya's Theatre.

49

understood how to treat it, lest it became transformed into a mere exercise). The verses and extracts were read by each actor in turn. For them, this work corresponded to the sketches of a painter or the exercises of a musician. The artist must perfect his technique before embarking on a picture. Whilst reading, the actor looked for new means of expression. The audience (everybody, not just the director) made comments and assisted the reader to develop these new means. The entire creative act was directed towards finding those inflections which contained the true ring of the author's own voice. When the author was 'revealed' through this collective work, when a single verse or extract 'rang true', the audience immediately analysed the means of expression which had conveyed the author's style and tone.

Before enumerating the various new aspects of technique developed through this intuitive method, and while I still retain a clear picture of these combined exercises of director and actors, I should like to mention two distinct methods of establishing contact between the director and his actors: one deprives not only the actor but also the spectator of creative freedom; the other leaves them both free, and forces the spectator to create instead of merely looking on (for a start, by stimulating his imagination).

The two methods may be explained by illustrating the four basic theatrical elements (author, director, actor and spectator) as follows:

1. A triangle, in which the apex is the director and the two remaining corners, the author and the actor. The spectator comprehends the creation of the latter two through the creation of the director. This is method one, which we shall call the 'Theatre-Triangle'.

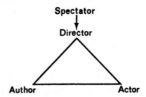

2. A straight, horizontal line with the four theatrical elements (author, director, actor, spectator) marked from left to right represents the other method, which we shall call the 'Theatre of the Straight Line'. The actor reveals his soul freely to the spectator, having assimilated the creation of the director, who, in his turn, has assimilated the creation of the author.

1. In the 'Theatre-Triangle' the director explains his *mise en scène* in detail, describes the characters as he sees them, prescribes every pause, and then rehearses the play until his personal conception of it is exactly reproduced in performance. This 'Theatre-Triangle' may be likened to a symphony orchestra with the director acting as the conductor.

However, the very architecture of the theatre, lacking any provision for a conductor's rostrum, points to the difference between the two.

People will say that there are occasions when a symphony orchestra plays without a conductor. Let us consider Nikisch[1] and the symphony orchestra which has been playing under him for years with scarcely a change in its personnel; take a composition which it has played several times a year over a period of ten years. If Nikisch were absent from the conductor's rostrum on one occasion, would the orchestra play the composition according to his interpretation? Yes, it is possible that the listener would recognize it as Nikisch's interpretation. But would the performance sound exactly as though Nikisch were conducting? Obviously, it would be worse, although we should still be hearing Nikisch's interpretation.

So I contend this: true, a symphony orchestra without a conductor is possible, but nevertheless it is impossible to draw a parallel between it and the theatre, where the actors invariably perform on the stage without a director. A symphony orchestra without a conductor is possible, but no matter how well rehearsed, it could never stir the public, only acquaint the listener with the interpretation of this or that conductor, and could blend into an ensemble only to the extent that an artist can re-create a conception which is not his own.

The actor's art consists in far more than merely acquainting the spectator with the director's conception. The actor will grip the spectator only if he assimilates both the director and the author and then gives of himself from the stage.

By contrast, an orchestral musician is distinguished by his ability to carry out the conductor's directions precisely, by dint of his virtuoso technique and *by depersonalizing himself*.

In common with the symphony orchestra, the 'Theatre-Triangle' must employ actors with virtuoso technique, but at all costs lacking in individuality, so that they are able to convey the director's exact concept.

2. In the 'Theatre of the Straight Line', the director, having absorbed the author's conception, conveys his own creation (now a blend of the author

[1] Arthur Nikisch (1855–1922), celebrated conductor of the Leipzig Gewandhaus Orchestra.

and the director) to the actor. The actor, having assimilated the author's conception via the director, stands face to face with the spectator (with director and author behind him), and *freely* reveals his soul to him, thus intensifying the fundamental theatrical relationship of performer and spectator.

In order for the straight line not to bend,[1] the director must remain the sole arbiter of the mood and style of the production, but nevertheless, the actor's art remains free in the 'Theatre of the Straight Line'.

The director describes his plan during the discussion of the play. The entire production is coloured by his view of it. He inspires the actors with his devotion to the work, and imbues them with the spirit of the author and with his own interpretation. But after the discussion all the performers remain completely independent. Then the director calls a further general meeting to create harmony from all the separate pieces. How does he set about this? Simply by balancing all the parts which have been freely created by the various individuals involved in the collective enterprise. In establishing the harmony vital to the production, he does not insist on the exact representation of his own conception, which was intended only to ensure unanimity and to prevent the work created collectively from disintegrating. Instead he retires behind the scenes at the earliest possible moment and leaves the stage to the actors. Then, either they are out of accord with the director or the author (if, say, they are not of the new school)[2] and 'set fire to the ship', or they reveal their souls through almost improvisatory additions, not to the text but to the mere suggestions of the director. In this way the spectator is made to comprehend the author and

---

[1] Alexander Blok (*Pereval*, Moscow, 1906, no. 2) fears that the actors 'might set fire to the ship of the play', but to my mind, discord and disaster could occur only if the straight line were allowed to become crooked. This danger is eliminated if the director accurately interprets the author, accurately transmits him to the actors, and if they accurately understand him. [Meyerhold's note.]

[2] The 'Theatre-Triangle' requires non-individualistic actors who none the less are outstanding virtuosi, regardless of their school. In the 'Theatre of the Straight Line' individual flair is most important, for without it free creativity is inconceivable. It needs a new school of acting, which must not be a school where new techniques are taught, but rather one which will arise just once to give birth to a free theatre and then die.

'The Theatre of the Straight Line' will grow from a single school as one plant grows from one seed. As each succeeding plant needs a new seed to be sown, so a new theatre must grow every time from a new school.

'The Theatre-Triangle' tolerates schools attached to theatres which provide a regular stream of graduates, who imitate the great actors who founded the theatre, and fill vacancies in the company as they occur. I am convinced that it is these schools which are to blame for the absence of genuine, fresh talent in our theatres. [Meyerhold's note.]

the director through the prism of the actor's art. *Above all, drama is the art of the actor.*

If you read any of the works of Maeterlinck, his poetry or his drama, his preface to the last collected edition,[1] his book *Le Trésor des Humbles*, where he speaks of the Static Theatre in a tone embodying all the colour and atmosphere of his works, you will see that he has no desire to evoke horror on the stage; nor does he seek to drive the spectator to such hysteria that he wants to flee in terror. On the contrary, he aims to provoke a fearful yet reasoning acceptance of the inevitability of life, to move the spectator to tears and suffering, and yet to soothe and console him. His first task is 'to alleviate our grief by implanting that hope which flags and then springs to life again'.[2] When the spectator leaves the theatre, life with all its pain resumes its course, but the pain no longer seems in vain; life flows on with its joys, its sorrows and its exigencies, but everything acquires meaning because we have seen that it is possible to emerge from the gloom, or at least to endure it without bitterness. Maeterlinck's art is healthy and life-giving. It summons people to a wise acceptance of the might of fate, and his theatre acquires all the significance of a temple. Pastore has good reason for extolling Maeterlinck's mysticism as the last refuge of apostates who refuse to recognize the temporal power of the Church yet cannot bring themselves to discard their free belief in another world. Such a theatre is fit for the presentation of religious subjects. No matter how sombre the colours of a work, so long as it is a *mystery*, it contains an indefatigable affirmation of life.

To us it seems that the whole mistake of our predecessors lay in their attempts at frightening the spectator instead of reconciling him with the inevitability of fate. 'At the foundation of my dramas' – writes Maeterlinck – 'lies the idea of a Christian God together with the ancient concept of Fate.' The author hears the words and lamentations of men as a muffled sound, as though they were falling into a deep abyss. He sees men from a vantage-point beyond the clouds as faintly glittering sparks. All he desires is to overhear in their souls a few words of humility, of hope, of compassion, of terror, and to show us the might of the fate which guides our destiny.

Our aim was to ensure that our production of Maeterlinck produced the same effect of reconciliation in the spectator's mind as the author himself intended. A performance of Maeterlinck is a *mystery*; either there is a

[1] Published in Russian in six volumes in Moscow, 1903–9.
[2] Hannibale Pastore, 'Maurice Maeterlinck', in *Vestnik inostrannoy literatury*, September 1903.

barely audible harmony of voices, a chorus of soft weeping, of muted sobs and a stirring of hope (as in *The Death of Tintagiles*), or there is an ecstasy which is transformed into a universal religious festival with dancing to the music of organ and trumpets, or a bacchanalia to celebrate a great miracle (as in Act Two of *Sister Beatrice*). The dramas of Maeterlinck are 'above all else a manifestation and purification of the spirit'. They are '. . . a chorus of souls singing *sotto voce* of suffering, love, beauty and death'. They have a *simplicity* which transports one to the realms of fantasy, a harmony which brings calm, a joy bordering on the ecstatic. It was with this understanding of the spirit of Maeterlinck's theatre that we began work on the rehearsal exercises.

What Muther[1] said of Il Perugino, one of the most fascinating painters of the Quattrocento, seems to me true of Maeterlinck: 'The contemplative lyrical character of his subjects, the quiet grandeur and archaic splendour of his pictures could only be achieved by a composition whose harmony is unmarred by the slightest abrupt movement or the merest harsh contrast.'

Proceeding from this general evaluation of Maeterlinck's art, our directors and actors intuitively established the following principles during the course of preliminary rehearsals:

A. Diction

1. The words must be coldly 'coined', free from all tremolo and the familiar break in the voice. There must be a total absence of tension and lugubrious intonation.

2. The sound must always be 'reinforced'; the words must fall like drops into a deep well, the fall being clearly audible without any vibration in space. There must be no diffusion of sound, no drawing out of word-endings (as in the reading of the Decadents' verses).

3. The internal mystical vibration is more powerful than the histrionics of the old theatre, which were invariably uncontrolled and ugly to look at, with flailing of arms, beating of breasts and slapping of thighs. The internal mystical vibration is conveyed through the eyes, the lips, the sound and manner of delivery: the exterior calm which covers volcanic emotions, with everything light and unforced.

4. In the expression of the tragic sorrows of the soul the form is dictated by the content. Maeterlinck prescribes one form and no other in order to convey that which is so simple and so long-familiar.[2]

---

[1] Richard Muther, German art historian.

[2] In practice, a question arose which I shall not attempt to answer, but content myself by merely stating: should the actor seek to discover the inner content of

5. The dialogue should never be gabbled; this is permissible only in those *neurasthenic* dramas where much play is made with lines of dots. Epic calm does not exclude tragic emotions, which always possess a certain grandeur.

6. Tragedy with a smile on the lips. I did not grasp fully the need for this until I happened to read the following words of Savonarola:

'Do not assume that Mary cried out at the death of her Son and roamed the streets, tearing her hair and acting like a madwoman. She followed Him with great humility. Certainly she shed tears, but her appearance revealed not so much sheer grief as a combination of *grief and joy*. Even at the foot of the Cross she stood in grief and joy, engrossed in the mystery of God's great mercy.'

If an actor of the old school wished to move the audience deeply, he would cry out, weep, groan and beat his breast with his fists. Let the new actor express the highest point of tragedy just as the grief and joy of Mary were expressed: with an outward repose, almost *coldly*, without shouting or lamentation. He can achieve profundity without recourse to exaggerated tremolo.

B. Plasticity

1. Richard Wagner reveals inner dialogue through the orchestra; the sung musical phrase lacks the power to express the inner passions of his heroes. Wagner summons the orchestra to his assistance, believing that only the orchestra is capable of conveying what is ineffable, of revealing the mystery to the spectator. Like the singer's phrase in the 'Musikdrama', the actor's word in the drama is an insufficiently powerful means of conveying inner dialogue. Surely if the *word* were the sole means of conveying the essence of tragedy, everybody would be capable of acting in the theatre. But merely by declaiming words, even by declaiming them well, one does not necessarily *say* anything. We need some new means of expressing the ineffable, of revealing that which is concealed.

---

his part right from the start, give play to his emotions, and then shape it later into some form or other, or vice versa? At the time we adopted the procedure of restraining the emotions until the form was mastered, and that still seems to me the correct order. People will object that this only leads to the form fettering the emotions. This is not so. Our teachers, the actors of the old naturalistic school, used to say: if you do not want to ruin the part, start by reading it over to yourself, and do not read it aloud until it sounds right in your heart. One should approach a role in a realistic drama by first reading through the text to oneself; in a non-realistic drama one should master first the rhythm of the language and the movement – the same method is right for both. [Meyerhold's note.]

Just as Wagner employs the orchestra to convey spiritual emotions, I employ *plastic movement*. But the old theatre, too, regarded plasticity as an essential means of expression; one has only to consider Salvini[1] in *Othello* or *Hamlet*. Plasticity itself is not new, but the form which I have in mind is new. Before, it corresponded closely to the spoken dialogue, but I am speaking of a *plasticity which does not correspond to the words*. What do I mean by this?

Two people are discussing the weather, art, apartments. A third – given, of course, that he is reasonably sensitive and observant – can tell exactly by listening to this conversation, which has no bearing on the relationship between the two, whether they are friends, enemies or lovers. He can tell this from the way they gesticulate, stand, move their eyes. This is because they move in a way unrelated to their words, a way which reveals their relationship.

The director erects a bridge between actor and spectator. He depicts friends, enemies or lovers in accordance with the author's instructions, yet by means of movement and poses he must present a picture which enables the spectator not only to hear the spoken dialogue but to penetrate through to the *inner* dialogue. If he has steeped himself in the author's theme and grasped the music of this inner dialogue, he will suggest plastic movements to the actor which will help the spectator to perceive the inner dialogue as the actors and he, himself, understand it.

The essence of human relationships is determined by gestures, poses, glances and silences. Words alone cannot say everything. Hence there must be a *pattern of movement* on the stage to transform the spectator into a vigilant observer, to furnish him with that material which the two people in conversation yielded to the third, the material which helps him grasp the true feelings of the characters. Words catch the ear, plasticity – the eye. Thus the spectator's imagination is exposed to two stimuli: the oral and the visual. The difference between the old theatre and the new is that in the new theatre speech and plasticity are each subordinated to their own separate rhythms and the two do not necessarily coincide. However, it does not follow that plasticity has always to contradict speech; a phrase may be supported by a wholly appropriate movement, but this is no more natural than the coincidence of the logical and the poetic stress in verse.

2. Maeterlinck's images are archaized; the names are like the names on icons; Arkel[2] is like a picture by Ambrogio Borgognoni; Gothic arches;

[1] Tommaso Salvini: leading Italian Shakespearian actor. He toured in Russia on several occasions from 1880 to 1901.

[2] In *Pelléas and Mélisande*.

56

wooden statues, carved and polished like palissander. One senses the need for symmetrical groupings in the manner of Perugino, for thus do they resemble most closely the divine nature of the universe.

'Women, effeminate boys and harmless, weary old men best express the gentle, dreamlike thoughts' which Perugino was striving to convey. Is not the same true of Maeterlinck? It is this which prompted an iconic style of portrayal.

The unsightly clutter of the naturalistic stage was replaced in the New Theatre by constructions rigidly subordinated to rhythmical movement and to the musical harmony of colour masses.

An iconic style was employed, too, in the construction of scenery – before scenery was abolished altogether. And since plastic movement acquired primary importance as a means of revealing inner dialogue, it was essential that scenery should do nothing to distract attention from this movement. It was necessary to focus the spectator's entire attention on the actors' movements. Therefore, we employed only one backdrop in *The Death of Tintagiles*. When rehearsed against a plain canvas drop, the tragedy produced a powerful impression because the play of gestures was seen in such sharp relief. But when the actors were transferred to a stage with scenery and space in which to move about, the play suffered. Hence we developed the decorative panel. But when we tried it out in a number of plays (*Sister Beatrice, Hedda Gabler, The Eternal Story*[1]) it was a failure.[2] We found that it was no more effective than suspended scenery, against which the effect of plastic movement is dissipated because it is not seen in firm relief. In Giotto, nothing detracts from the fluidity of his lines, because all his work has a decorative rather than a naturalistic basis. But just as the theatre must not revert to naturalism, equally it must not become merely 'decorative' (unless the word be interpreted in the same sense as in the Japanese theatre).

Like symphonic music, the decorative panel serves its own specialized purpose, and if figures are necessary – as in a painting – they must be painted figures, or in the case of the theatre, cardboard marionettes – but not wax, wooden, or flesh-and-blood figures. A two-dimensional decorative panel demands two-dimensional figures.

The human body and the objects surrounding it – tables, chairs, beds, cupboards – are all three-dimensional; therefore the theatre, where the main element is the actor, must find inspiration in the plastic arts, not in painting. The actor must study *the plasticity of the statue*.

These were the conclusions reached at the close of the first cycle of

[1] By Przybyszewski.   [2] All staged at Komissarzhevskaya's Theatre in 1906.

experiments in the New Theatre. A historically vital circle was completed and yielded a fund of experience in stylized production, which gave rise to a new view of the role of decorative art in the theatre.

On learning that the theatre intends to reject the decorative principle, actors of the old school will be delighted, interpreting this as no less than a return to the old theatre. Surely, they will argue, the old theatre was the theatre of three dimensions. So this means – down with the stylized theatre!

My answer is that the placing of the decorative artist firmly in the decorative theatre and the musician in the concert hall signifies not the death of the stylized theatre but its adoption of an even bolder course.

In rejecting the decorative panel the New Theatre has not discarded the technique of stylized production; neither has it rejected the presentation of Maeterlinck in iconic terms. The means of expression must now be architectural, rather than pictorial as they were before. All our plans for stylized productions of *The Death of Tintagiles*, *Sister Beatrice*, *Hedda Gabler* and *The Eternal Story* have been preserved intact, but they have been translated into the terms of the liberated stylized theatre. Meanwhile, the painter has retired to a realm where actors and concrete objects are not admitted, because the aims of the actor and the non-theatrical painter are quite distinct.

[First published in *Teatr, kniga o novom teatre*, cit. Reprinted in Meyerhold's *O Teatre*, cit., pp. 33–47.]

NOTE   Written late in 1907. According to Volkov, Meyerhold was well acquainted with Wagner's music from an early age. In July 1907 he staged two extracts from *Tristan and Isolde* at Terioki in Finland, just over the border from Petersburg. Later, in October 1909, he produced the full opera at the Marinsky Theatre. The article on *Tristan and Isolde* (pp. 80–98 below) contains a fuller exposition of his views on Wagner and Georg Fuchs.

---

5. The Stylized Theatre

'I call for the calculated stylization of the theatre of antiquity to replace the irrelevant truth of the modern stage',[1] said Valery Bryusov. Vyacheslav

[1] In 'Nenuzhnaya pravda' (1902), see p. 37 above.

Ivanov, too, awaits its revival. Bryusov makes only a passing reference to the phenomenon of stylization in the antique theatre; Ivanov however reveals a coherent plan for a Dionysian festival.

It is taking an excessively narrow view of Ivanov's project to interpret it as a repertoire composed exclusively of Greek tragedies and plays written in the style of Greek tragedy, such as his *Tantalus*. In order to demonstrate that Ivanov has a far broader repertoire in mind, we should need to examine everything which he has written. Unfortunately we are not concerned primarily with him; I want to draw on his insight in order to show more clearly the advantages of the stylistic technique, and to show that it alone makes it possible for the theatre to embrace the diverse repertoire advocated by Ivanov and the variegated bouquet of plays which our modern dramatists are presenting to the Russian stage.

Drama proceeded from the dynamic to the static pole.[1] Drama was born 'of the spirit of music, out of the dynamic energy of the choric dithyramb'. . . . 'The Dionysian art of the choric drama arose from the ecstasy of the sacrificial ritual.'

Then 'there began the separation of the elements of the primordial drama'. The dithyramb emerged as a distinct form of the lyric. Attention became focused on the hero-protagonist; his tragic fate became the centre of the drama. The spectator was transformed from a participant in the sacred ritual into an onlooker of the festive 'spectacle'. The chorus became separated both from the populace which occupied the orchestra and from the hero; it became a distinct element which illustrated the peripeteia of the hero's fate. Thus the theatre as 'spectacle' came into being.

The spectator experienced *passively* that which was presented on the stage. 'There arose that magic barrier which even today, in the form of footlights, divides the theatre into two opposed camps, the performers and the onlookers; no artery exists to unite these two separate bodies and preserve the unbroken circulation of creative energy.' The orchestra kept the spectator close to the action; when it was replaced by footlights the spectator became isolated. In the theatre of spectacle the stage resembles 'a stern, remote iconostasis which repels the desire to merge into a single festive throng'. The iconostasis has replaced 'the former low altar-rostrum' which the spectator could surmount in one ecstatic bound to join in the ritual.

Having originated in the dithyrambic homage paid to Dionysus, drama

[1] See Ivanov's *Po Zvyozdam* ('By the stars'), Petersburg, 1909, on the evolution of the drama, the theatre as spectacle and the fate of the mask [Meyerhold's note.]

gradually receded from its religious origins. The mask of the tragic hero, the recognizable embodiment of the spectator's own fate, the mask of a single tragic fate which embodied the universal 'I', became slowly objectivized over the course of centuries. Shakespeare explored characterization. Corneille and Racine made their heroes dependent on the morality of a particular age, thereby transforming them into materialistic formulae. The stage has become estranged from its communal-religious origins; it has alienated the spectator by its objectivity. The stage is no longer *infectious*, it no longer has the power of *transfiguration*.

But thanks to such dramatists as Ibsen, Maeterlinck, Verhaeren and Wagner,[1] the theatre is moving back towards its dynamic origins. We are rediscovering the precepts of antiquity. Just as the sacred ritual of Greek tragedy was a form of Dionysian *catharsis*, so today we demand of the artist that he heal and purify us.

In the New Drama external action, the revelation of character, is becoming incidental. 'We are striving to penetrate *behind* the mask, *beyond* the action into the character as perceived by the mind; we want to penetrate to the *inner mask*.'

The New Drama rejects the external in favour of the internal, not in order to penetrate man's soul and thus renounce this earth and ascend to the heavens (*théâtre ésotérique*), but to intoxicate the spectator with the Dionysian cup of eternal sacrifice.

'If the New Theatre is once again dynamic, then let it be totally dynamic.' If the theatre is finally to rediscover its dynamic essence, it must cease to be 'theatre' in the sense of mere 'spectacle'. We intend the audience not merely to observe, but to participate in a *corporate* creative act.

Ivanov asks: 'What is a fit subject for the drama of the future?' – and

[1] Why group Maeterlinck with Ibsen, or Verhaeren's *Dawn* with *The Death of Tintagiles*? The suffering god has two aspects: he is the drunken Dionysus and the dreaming Apollo. Ivanov inclines instinctively towards plays which are Dionysian in the sense of being intoxicating. But, he says, this does not mean that the Dionysian drama must necessarily be 'orgiastic' in its outward form. He sees the choric origin in two separate pictures:

'The orgiastic madness of wine
Laughs as it rocks the whole world,
But sober, and peacefully still,
It too occasionally rests.
Silent it hangs in pendulous loops,
Alert in its avaricious lair.'
                                        Fyodor Sologub.

'Equally Dionysian' – says Ivanov – 'are the dance of the wood Satyr and the immovable silence of the Maenad lost in contemplation and awareness of the god.'
                                        [Meyerhold's note.]

replies: 'Everything must be on a grand scale: tragedy, comedy, the mystery, the popular tale, the myth and the social drama.' The symbolical drama which is no longer obscure but 'strikes an answering chord in the popular soul'; the exalted, heroic tragedy which resembles the tragedies of antiquity (not, of course, a resemblance in dramatic structure – we are referring to Fate and Satire as the fundamental elements of Tragedy and Comedy); the mystery which is broadly analogous to the medieval mystery play; comedy in the manner of Aristophanes – this is the range of plays envisaged by Vyacheslav Ivanov.

Could the naturalistic theatre possibly cope with such a varied repertoire? No! The leading exponent of the naturalistic style, the Moscow Art Theatre, tried to embrace Greek classical theatre (*Antigone*), Shakespeare (*Julius Caesar* and *The Merchant of Venice*), Ibsen (*Hedda Gabler, Ghosts,* etc.), and Maeterlinck (*The Blind,* etc.). Even though it had Stanislavsky, the most talented director in Russia, at its head, plus a host of outstanding actors and actresses (Knipper, Kachalov, Moskvin, Savitskaya), it was powerless to cope with such a wide repertoire.

I maintain that its efforts were frustrated by its obsession with the Meiningen style, with the *naturalistic* method. The Moscow Art Theatre succeeded in mastering only Chekhov, and remained finally an 'intimate theatre'. The intimate theatres and all those which rely on the Meiningen method or on the 'atmosphere' of Chekhov's theatre have proved incapable of broadening their repertoire, and consequently have been unable to attract a wider audience.

With the passing of each century the antique theatre has become progressively transformed, and the intimate theatre represents its ultimate guise, its last offshoot. The theatre today is split into tragedy and comedy, whereas the antique theatre was a single, unified theatre.

I regard this fragmentation of the theatre into intimate theatres as the obstacle which is obstructing the rebirth of the universal theatre, the truly *dramatic* theatre, the festive theatre.

The offensive launched against naturalistic methods by certain theatres and directors[1] is no coincidence, but a direct outcome of historical evolution. Experiments with new theatrical forms have been provoked not by an idle whim of fashion, by the desire to introduce a new production method (stylization), nor by the need to satisfy the taste of the crowd for more and more acute sensations. The experimental theatres and their directors are

---

[1] The Theatre-Studio (Moscow), Stanislavsky (from *The Drama of Life* onwards), Gordon Craig (England), Max Reinhardt (Berlin), myself (Petersburg). [Meyerhold's note.]

seeking to create a stylized theatre in order to arrest the dissolution of the stage into *intimate* theatres, and in order to restore *the unified theatre*.

The stylized theatre embodies a technique so simplified that it will be possible to stage Maeterlinck as well as Wedekind,[1] Andreev as well as Sologub, Blok as well as Przybyszewski, Ibsen as well as Remizov.

The stylized theatre liberates the actor from all scenery, creating a three-dimensional area in which he can employ natural, sculptural plasticity. Thanks to stylization, we can do away with complicated stage machinery, and mount simple productions in which the actor can interpret his role free from all scenery and specifically *theatrical* properties – free from all purely incidental trappings.

In Ancient Greece at the time of Sophocles and Euripides, the competition amongst tragic actors gave rise to the art of the creative actor. Later, with the development of technical devices, the creative powers of the actor declined; with the further refinement of technical devices in our day, the independent function of the actor has declined still further. In this connection, Chekhov is right when he says – 'nowadays there are few outstandingly gifted actors, but the average actor has improved enormously' (*The Seagull*). By freeing the actor from the haphazard conglomeration of irrelevant stage properties, and by reducing technical devices to the minimum, the stylized theatre restores prominence to the creative powers of the actor. Concentrating on the restoration of tragedy and comedy (as manifestations of Fate and Satire), the stylized theatre avoids the 'mood' of Chekhovian theatre, which transforms acting into the passive experiencing of emotions and reduces the actor's creative intensity.

Having removed the footlights, the stylized theatre aims to place the stage on a level with the auditorium. By giving diction and movement a rhythmical basis, it hopes to bring about the revival of the *dance*. In such a theatre, dialogue can easily merge into melodic declamation and melodic silence.

The task of the director in the stylized theatre is to direct the actor rather than control him (unlike the Meiningen director). He serves purely as a bridge, linking the soul of the author with the soul of the actor. Having assimilated the author's creation, the actor is left *alone*, face to face with the spectator, and from the friction between these two unadulterated elements, the actor's creativity and the spectator's imagination, a clear flame is kindled.[2]

[1] Meyerhold produced *Spring's Awakening* at Komissarzhevskaya's Theatre in September 1907.
[2] Cf. pp. 50–53 above.

Just as the actor is freed from the director, the director is freed from the author. The author's stage directions are determined by the technical limitations of the theatre of the period when the play was written. Once the director has grasped the play's inner dialogue, he can interpret it freely, using the rhythm of the dialogue and the plasticity of the actor, and heeding only those stage directions which were not dictated by technical expediency.

Ultimately, the stylistic method presupposes the existence of a fourth *creator* in addition to the author, the director and the actor – namely, the spectator. The stylized theatre produces a play in such a way that the spectator is compelled to employ his imagination *creatively* in order *to fill in* those details *suggested* by the stage action.

In the stylized theatre 'the spectator should not forget for a moment that an actor is *performing* before him, and the actor should never forget that he is performing before an audience, with a stage beneath his feet and a set around him. When one looks at a painting, one is always aware that it is composed of paint, canvas and brush strokes, but none the less it creates a heightened and clarified impression of life. Frequently, the more obvious the artifice, the more powerful the impression of life.'[1]

Stylization is opposed to the techniques of illusion. It does not need the illusion of Apollonian fantasy. The stylized theatre employs statuesque plasticity to strengthen the impression made by certain groupings on the spectator's memory, so that the fatal notes of tragedy sound through the spoken dialogue.

The stylized theatre makes no attempt to emulate the variety of *mises en scène* of the naturalistic theatre, in which an abundance of scene changes creates a kaleidoscope of rapidly changing tableaux. It aims at a deft mastery of line, grouping and costume colour, which even when static creates an infinitely stronger impression of movement than the naturalistic theatre. Stage movement is achieved not by movement in the literal sense, but by the disposition of lines and colours, and by the ease and cunning with which these lines and colours are made to cross and vibrate.

Since the stylized theatre wants to abolish scenery which is located on the same plane as the actor and the stage properties, to remove the footlights, to subordinate acting to the rhythm of dialogue and plastic movement; since it anticipates the revival of the dance and seeks to induce the active participation of the spectator in the performance, then clearly the stylized theatre is leading to a revival of the Greek classical theatre.

Architecturally, the Greek classical theatre is the very theatre which

[1] Leonid Andreev, in a letter to me. [Meyerhold's note.]

modern drama needs: it has three-dimensional space, no scenery, and it demands statuesque plasticity. Obviously, its design will need to be modified in minor respects to meet modern requirements, but with its simplicity, its horseshoe-shaped auditorium, and its orchestra, it is the only theatre capable of accommodating such a varied repertoire as Blok's *Fairground Booth*, Andreev's *Life of a Man*, Maeterlinck's tragedies, Kuzmin's dramas, Remizov's mysteries, Sologub's *Gift of the Wise Bees*, and all the other fine new plays which have yet to find their theatre.

> [First published in *Teatr, kniga o novom teatre*, cit. Reprinted in Meyerhold's *O Teatre*, cit., pp. 48–55.]

NOTE Written in 1907. In this crucial article Meyerhold introduces two concepts, the 'mask' and the forestage, which were to exert a vital influence on his subsequent development. Both are examined further in the articles *Don Juan* and *The Fairground Booth* below.

An interesting attempt to revive the corporate theatrical experience of the Greek classical theatre was made with the production of Verhaeren's *Dawn* at the R.S.F.S.R. Theatre No. 1 in 1920 (see pp. 163–4 below).

Meyerhold was encouraged to include Stanislavsky in his list of theatrical innovators (note, p. 61) by the Moscow Art productions in 1907 of Hamsun's *Drama of Life* and Andreev's *Life of a Man*, both of which derived much from his own experiments in stylization.

---

6. Notes on Productions

THE CRY OF LIFE *by Arthur Schnitzler, adapted by Meyerhold*
Settings by Kostin. Première: Poltava, Summer 1906.[1]

In staging this play we experimented with stage props of exaggerated dimensions. A long divan, extending parallel to the footlights across the entire stage (itself slightly reduced in width, of course), was meant to suggest with its giant proportions an interior which would make anyone entering it feel hemmed in and reduced to insignificance by the overpowering size of the surrounding objects. An abundance of carpets, tapestries and cushions served to intensify this impression. Chekhovian

[1] By the Fellowship of the New Drama.

(a)

(b)

(c)

Tristan and Isolde, 1909. (a) and (b) Prince Shervashidze's costume designs for Tristan and Isolde. (c) The setting for Act Three.

The final scene in *Orpheus*, 1911.

Dom Juan, 1910.

atmosphere was banished in the interests of the fatal and the tragic. There was no loud dialogue to destroy the nuances of the mystically charged atmosphere. Wherever it was necessary to convey the extremes of passion, resort was made to a device of the grotesque: in order to reinforce the impact of dramatically intense scenes, the passages of intervening narrative were delivered in an unusually cool style, almost devoid of feeling and emphasis. The actors' moves either preceded or followed their lines. All movements were treated like dance steps (a Japanese device), regardless of whether they were meant to express any emotion or not.

[Meyerhold, *O Teatre*, cit., p. 192.]

HEDDA GABLER *by Henrik Ibsen*

Settings by Sapunov. Costumes by Miliotti. Première: 10 November 1906 at Vera Komissarzhevskaya's Theatre, Petersburg.

The theatre has chosen to use a single backdrop as a setting, either representational or simply decorative. The costumes, instead of being naturalistically authentic, are intended to harmonize as colour-masses with the background and present a synthesis of the style of the period and society in question, the subjective view of the designer, and the externally simplified representation of the character's inner nature. For instance, in *Hedda Gabler* the costume of Tesman corresponds to no definite fashion; although it is somewhat reminiscent of the 1820s, one is reminded equally of the present day. But in giving Tesman a loose jacket with sloping shoulders, an exaggeratedly wide tie, and broad trousers tapering sharply towards the bottoms, the designer, Vassily Miliotti, has sought to express the essence of 'Tesmanism', and this has been stressed by the director in the way Tesman is made to move and the position he occupies in the general composition. To harmonize with the colours of Sapunov's painted backcloth, Miliotti has dressed Tesman in dull grey. The walls, the portières and the sky (seen through a vast ivy-fringed window) are all light blue; the tapestry which covers an entire wall and the openwork screens on either side of the stage are painted in pale gold autumnal tints. The colours of the costumes harmonize amongst themselves and with the background: green (Hedda), brown (Loevborg), pale pink (Thea), dark grey (Brack). The table in the centre, the pouffes and the long narrow divan standing against the wall under the tapestry are all covered in light blue fabric flecked with gold to give it the appearance of brocade. A huge armchair stage-left is covered entirely in white fur, the same fur being used to partly cover the divan; a white grand piano projects from behind the screen stage-right and has the same blue and gold fabric hanging from it.

Behind the left-hand screen is glimpsed the silhouette of a huge green vase encircled with ivy and standing on a pedestal also covered with blue and gold fabric. Behind it is supposed to stand the stove for the scene between Hedda and Tesman when Hedda burns Loevborg's manuscript. The stove is suggested by a reddish glow which appears at the appropriate moments.

In front of the divan stands a low square table with a drawer in which Hedda hides the manuscript. On it Loevborg and Brack lay their hats, and on it stands the green box containing the pistols when it is not on the big table.

In the small white and green vases on the piano and the table and in the large vase on the pedestal there are flowers, mostly white chrysanthemums. More chrysanthemums rest in the folds of the fur on the back of the armchair. The floor is covered with dark grey cloth, with a fine tracery in blue and gold. The sky is painted on a separate drop behind the cut-out window: there is a day sky, and a night sky with coldly glittering stars (for Act Four).

The stage comprises a long narrow strip, 33 feet wide and 12 feet deep, higher than the usual stage-level and as close as possible to the footlights. The lighting is from footlights and overhead battens.

This strange room, if indeed it is a room, resembles least of all the old-fashioned villa of General Falk's wife.[1] What is the significance of this setting which gives the impression of a vast, cold blue, receding expanse, but which actually looks like nothing whatsoever? Why are both sides (where there should be doors – or nothing, if the room is supposed to continue offstage) hung with gold net curtains between which the actors make their exits and their entrances? Is life really like this? Is this what Ibsen wrote?

Life is not like this, and it is not what Ibsen wrote. *Hedda Gabler* on the stage of the Dramatic Theatre is *stylized*. Its aim is to reveal Ibsen's play to the spectator by employing new unfamiliar means of scenic presentation, to create an impression (but only an *impression*) of a vast, cold blue, receding expanse. Hedda is visualized in cool blue tones against a golden autumnal background. Instead of autumn being depicted outside the window where the blue sky is seen, it is suggested by the pale golden tints in the tapestry, the upholstery and the curtains. The theatre is attempting to give primitive, purified expression to what it senses behind Ibsen's play: a cold, regal, autumnal Hedda.

[1] i.e. Prime Minister Falk's widow.

Precisely the same aims are adopted in the actual production of the play (the work of the director with the actors). Rejecting authenticity, the customary 'lifelikeness', the theatre seeks to submit the spectator to its own inspiration by adopting a barely mobile, stylized method of production with a minimum of mime and gesture, with the emotions concealed and manifested externally only by a brief lighting of the eyes or a flickering smile.

The wide stage, its width emphasized by its shallowness, is particularly suited to widely spaced groupings, and the director takes full advantage of this by making two characters converse from opposite sides of the stage (the opening of the scene between Hedda and Loevborg in Act Three), by seating Thea, Hedda and Loevborg wide apart on the divan in Act Two. Sometimes (particularly in the latter instance) there may seem to be little justification in this, but it arises from the director's attempt to create an overall impression of cold majesty. The huge armchair covered with white fur is meant as a kind of throne for Hedda; she plays the majority of her scenes either on it or near it. The spectator is intended to associate Hedda with her throne and to carry away this combined impression in his memory.

Brack is associated with the pedestal bearing the large vase. He sits by it with one leg crossed over the other and clasps his hands round his knee, keeping his eyes fixed on Hedda throughout their keen, sparkling battle of wits. He reminds one of a faun. Admittedly, Brack moves about the stage and occupies other positions (as do Hedda and the other characters), but it is the pose of a faun by the pedestal which one associates with him – just as one associates the throne with Hedda.

The table serves as a pedestal for the motionless figures which the theatre seeks to imprint on the spectator's memory. When Loevborg produces the manuscript in Act Two he is standing upstage by the portière near Hedda and Tesman; Brack is by the curtain stage-left; the centre of the stage (the table) is empty.

In order to look through the bulky manuscript more comfortably, Loevborg comes forward to rest it on the table and after the words 'This contains all of me',[1] he lapses into a thoughtful silence, straightening up and placing his hand on the open manuscript. After a few seconds' pause he starts to turn over the pages, explaining his work to Tesman, who has now joined him. But in those motionless few seconds Loevborg and the manuscript have impressed themselves on the spectator and he has an

---

[1] In Michael Meyer's translation (Hart-Davis, 1962; Methuen, 1967) – 'This is my real book. The one in which I have spoken with my own voice' (p. 67).

uneasy presentiment of the words' significance, of what Loevborg is really like, what links him with the manuscript, and what bearing it has on the tragedy of Hedda.

The first scene between Loevborg and Hedda also takes place at the table. Throughout the entire scene they sit side by side, tense and motionless, looking straight ahead. Their quiet, disquieting words fall rhythmically from lips which seem dry and cold. Before them stand two glasses and a flame burns beneath the punch bowl (Ibsen stipulates Norwegian 'cold punch'). Not once throughout the entire long scene do they alter the direction of their gaze or their pose. Only on the line 'Then you too have a thirst for life!'[1] does Loevborg make a violent motion towards Hedda, and at this point the scene comes to an abrupt conclusion.

Realistically speaking, it is inconceivable that Hedda and Loevborg should play the scene in this manner, that any two real, living people should ever converse like this. The spectator hears the lines as though they were being addressed directly at him; before him the whole time he sees the faces of Hedda and Loevborg, observes the slightest change of expression; behind the monotonous dialogue he senses the concealed inner dialogue of presentiments and emotions which are incapable of expression in mere words. The spectator may forget the actual words exchanged by Hedda and Loevborg, but he cannot possibly forget the overall impression which the scene creates.

[Meyerhold, op. cit., pp. 187–90.]

NOTE   This account is by Pavel Yartsev, the literary manager of Komissarzhevskaya's Theatre, who also worked as Meyerhold's assistant director. Since Meyerhold includes it in his book without comment, it may be regarded as an accurate reflection of his views.

SISTER BEATRICE *by Maurice Maeterlinck*
Designer: Denisov. Première: 22 November 1906 at Vera Komissarzhevskaya's Theatre, Petersburg.

Sister Beatrice was produced in the style of Pre-Raphaelite and early Renaissance painting, but it would be wrong to conclude that we were aiming to reproduce the colours and composition of any one artist of either of these periods. The critics tried to compare the production with the most disparate artists: they spoke of Memling, Giotto, Botticelli and many others. In *Beatrice* we borrowed only the means of expression employed

[1] In Meyer's version, p. 75 – 'It wasn't knowledge you wanted! It was life!'

by old masters; the movements, groupings, properties and costumes were simply a synthesis of the lines and colours found in the Primitives. There are descriptions of the production by Maximilian Voloshin[1] and Pavel Yartsev:[2]

'A Gothic wall in which the green and lilac-tinted stone blends with the grey tones of tapestries and glimmers faintly with pale silver and old gold . . . The Sisters in greyish-blue, close-fitting garments with simple bonnets framing their rounded cheeks. I was constantly reminded of Giotto's frescoes in the cathedral at Florence, the glorious *Assumption of St Francis* portrayed with unsparing realism and idealized beauty. I dreamt that I was in love with this Catholic Madonna who reminded me so strongly of the one I had seen in Seville; I felt the horror of the sinful body of the mortal Beatrice, glimpsed beneath her crimson rags.' (Voloshin.)

'The Sisters form a single group and intone in rhythmical unison the words: "The Madonna has vanished! The statue has been stolen! The walls will avenge the theft!" In the scene of Beatrice's ecstasy in Act Two the Sisters interweave then separate, prostrate themselves on the flag-stones of the chapel and join in the joyous cry: "Holy Sister Beatrice!" At the precise moment when the chorus offstage and the pealing of the bells fall silent, the Sisters drop to their knees in a single line and turn their heads toward the chapel. From the steps descends the Madonna, dressed in Beatrice's habit and bearing the golden pitcher in her hands. Simultaneously, from the other side appear three young pilgrims with faces reminiscent of figures from Vrubel, clad in brown and bearing tall staffs; they fall to their knees, with hands outstretched above their heads. Slowly, to the strains of an organ, the Madonna passes across the stage, and as she approaches the Sisters they bow their heads. Stopping before the pilgrims, she raises the pitcher above their upstretched hands . . . In a cut-out opening suggesting the convent gates stands a group of beggars close together, those in front kneeling with their hands raised in supplication. When the Madonna turns towards them, raising her hands in blessing and revealing beneath the cloak of Beatrice the raiment of the Madonna, the beggars make a primitive gesture of naïve wonder, raising their hands with the palms facing forward.

[1] 'Liki tvorchestva, I – Teatr sonnoe videnie', in the newspaper *Russ*, Petersburg, 9 December 1906.
[2] 'Spektakli Peterburgskogo Dramaticheskogo teatra', in *Zolotoe runo*, Moscow, 1907, nos. 7–9.

'In Act Three the grouping of the Sisters holding the dying Beatrice recalls the "descent from the cross" motif in the paintings of the Primitives.' (Yartsev.)

The rhythm of the production was achieved by precisely calculated, extended pauses and clearly articulated gestures. Above all, we tried to purge the primitive tragedy of Romantic fervour. The melodious style of delivery and movements in slow motion were designed to preserve the implicitness of expression, and every phrase was barely more than a whisper, the manifestation of an inner tragic experience.

The settings were placed almost on top of the footlights and the entire action took place so close to the spectator that he was reminded irresistibly of the ambo in an ancient church.

According to the director's original project, which for practical reasons had to be modified, the entire forestage and the steps down into the auditorium should have been covered with polished wood to look like palissander; in this way the actors would have been completely separated from the background decorative panel and free to murmur barely audibly the gentle yet thrilling lines of Maeterlinck's text.

Yartsev gives an indication of the stylized manner adopted by the actors in *Sister Beatrice*: 'Not only in the third act did the Mother Superior in the group of Sisters surrounding the dying Beatrice merely incline her cheek towards Beatrice's feet when kissing them, but in Act One Bellidor simply touched Beatrice with his lips.'

[Meyerhold, op. cit., pp. 195–6.]

THE FAIRGROUND BOOTH by *Alexander Blok*
Designer: Sapunov. Music: Kuzmin. Première: *30 December 1906 at Vera Komissarzhevskaya's Theatre, Petersburg.*

The entire stage is hung at the sides and rear with blue drapes; this expanse of blue serves as a background as well as reflecting the colour of the settings in the little booth erected on the stage. This booth has its own stage, curtain, prompter's box, and proscenium opening. Instead of being masked by the conventional border, the flies, together with all the ropes and wires, are visible to the audience; when the entire set is hauled aloft in the booth, the audience in the actual theatre sees the whole process.

In front of the booth the stage area adjacent to the footlights is left free. It is here that the 'Author' appears to serve as an intermediary between the public and the events enacted within the booth.

The action begins at a signal on a big drum; music is heard and the audience sees the prompter crawl into his box and light a candle. The curtain of the booth rises to reveal a box set with doors stage-left and centre, and a window stage-right. Parallel to the footlights is a long table, behind which are seated the 'Mystics' (for a description of the Mystics scene see my article *The Fairground Booth*);[1] by the window is a round table with a pot of geraniums and a slender gilt chair on which Pierrot is sitting. Harlequin makes his first entry from under the Mystics' table. When the Author runs on to the proscenium his tirade is terminated by someone hidden in the wings who pulls him off by his coat tails; it turns out that he is tethered with a rope to prevent him from interrupting the solemn course of the events onstage. In Scene Two 'the dejected Pierrot sits in the middle of the stage on a bench'; behind him is a pedestal bearing a statue of Eros. When Pierrot finishes his long soliloquy, the bench, the statue and the entire set are whisked aloft, and a traditional colonnaded hall is lowered in their place. In the scene where masked figures appear with cries of 'Torches!' the hands of stage-hands appear from both wings holding flaming Bengal lights on iron rods.

'All the characters are restricted to their own typical gestures: Pierrot, for instance, always sighs and flaps his arms in the same way.'[2]

[Meyerhold, op. cit., p. 198.]

THE LIFE OF A MAN *by Leonid Andreev*
Settings constructed according to Meyerhold's plans. Première: 22 February 1907 at Vera Komissarzhevskaya's Theatre, Petersburg.

I produced this play *without sets* as they are generally understood. The entire stage was hung with drapes, but not as in *The Fairground Booth*, where the drapes were hung in the places usually occupied by scenery . . . In *The Life of a Man* the drapes were hung on the walls of the theatre itself and against the back wall of the stage, where 'distant views' are normally depicted. We removed all footlights, borders and battens in order to achieve a 'grey, smoky, monochrome expanse. Grey walls, grey ceiling, grey floor.'[3] 'From an unseen source issues a weak, even light which is just as grey, monotonous, monochrome and ghostly, casting no hard shadows, no brilliant spots of light.' In this light the Prologue is read. Then the curtain parts to reveal a deep, gloomy expanse in which everything stands

[1] See p. 141 below.
[2] Andrei Bely, 'Simvolichesky teatr', in the newspaper *Utro Rossii*, Moscow, 28 September 1907.
[3] The quotations are from Andreev's stage directions.

71

motionless. After about three seconds the spectator begins to make out the shapes of furniture in one corner of the stage. 'Dimly visible are the grey forms of old women huddled together like a group of grey mice.' They are sitting on a big, old-fashioned divan flanked by two armchairs. Behind the divan is a screen, in front of it a lamp. The old women's silhouettes are lit only by the light falling from this lamp. The effect is the same in every scene: a section of the stage is seen in a pool of light from a single source, which is sufficient to illuminate only the furniture and the characters immediately adjacent to it. By enveloping the stage in grey shadow, using a single light source to illuminate one area of it (the lamp behind the divan and the lamp over the round table in Scene One, the chandelier in the ball scene, the lamps above the tables in the drunk scene) we managed to create the impression of actual walls which were invisible because the light did not reach them. On a stage free from conventional settings, furniture and other properties assume a fresh significance; the nature and atmosphere of a room is determined by them alone. It becomes necessary to use props of clearly exaggerated dimensions. And always very little furniture; a single typical object takes the place of a host of less typical ones. The spectator is forced to take note of the unusual contour of a divan, an elaborate column, a gilded armchair, a bookcase extending across the entire stage, a ponderous sideboard; given all these separate parts, the imagination fills in the rest. Naturally, the characters' features had to be modelled as precisely as sculpture, with make-up sharply accentuated, the actors were obliged to accentuate the figures of the characters they were playing in the manner of Leonardo da Vinci or Goya.

Unfortunately the designer had no control over the costumes; they were selected from the theatre wardrobe by Fyodor Komissarzhevsky, who was the head of design at Vera Komissarzhevskaya's Theatre. With the use of a single light source, costumes assume particular importance, since their cut can have considerable effect on a group seen in silhouette.

The point of departure for the whole production was the author's direction: 'everything is as in a dream'. ('The life of a man will pass before you like a distant, ghostly echo.')

This production demonstrated that the New Theatre is not dedicated exclusively to two-dimensional presentation. The majority were wrong to assume that our whole system consisted merely in reducing settings to a decorative panel with the figures of the actors blending with it to form a flat and stylized bas-relief.

[Meyerhold, op. cit., pp. 198–200.]

Part Two

AT THE IMPERIAL THEATRES

1908-1917

THE CRITICS' GLEE AT Meyerhold's dismissal by Komissarzhevskaya quickly gave way to consternation when they learned that he had been engaged as a stage-director and actor at the Imperial Alexandrinsky Theatre and as a stage-director at the Imperial Marinsky Opera. In a statement to the press, the Director of Imperial Theatres, Vladimir Telyakovsky, said:

> I consider that Meyerhold, with his propensity for stirring up people, will be very useful in the State theatres. As regards his excesses, I am confident that he will curb them with us . . . . I am even afraid that his new surroundings may turn him into a conformist.[1]

Anticipating the hostile reception he was bound to receive from the august veterans of the Alexandrinsky, Meyerhold sent a letter to *Zolotoe runo* (1908, no. 7–9), in which he admitted the error of treating Komissarzhevskaya's Theatre as a laboratory and promised that henceforth he would confine his experiments to studio theatres. He gave a similar assurance to the company before the opening rehearsal of his first production, Knut Hamsun's *At the Gates of the Kingdom* (première 30 September 1908). The work was staged against a single permanent setting, designed to convey the essence of the drama rather than the designated locations, and inevitably this provoked disparaging comparisons with earlier productions such as *Hedda Gabler*. Furthermore, Meyerhold's performance as Ivar Kareno was deliberately sabotaged by certain members of the cast who could scarcely bring themselves to act on the same stage with him. In the circumstances, the production was bound to fail, and it was of little significance in Meyerhold's development.

However, it initiated his partnership with the stage-designer, Alexander Golovin. Eleven years Meyerhold's senior, Golovin had been a prominent member of the 'World of Art' movement since its first exhibition in 1898. Having worked in the Imperial theatres with great success since 1902, he designed the settings and costumes for *Boris Godunov* in Diaghilev's Russian season in Paris during the summer of 1908, and again for the première of Stravinsky's *Firebird* in 1910. With the exception of *Tristan and Isolde*, he worked with Meyerhold on all his major productions at the Imperial theatres.

[1] *Peterburgskaya gazeta*, Petersburg, 24 April 1908.

True to his word, Meyerhold limited his experimental productions to a succession of private theatres and studios (described in Part Three below). There was an interval of more than a year before his next major production, Wagner's *Tristan and Isolde*, at the Marinsky Opera (30 October 1909). Part of this time was taken up with exhaustive study of Wagner's own writings and the revolutionary works on theatre production of Adolphe Appia and Georg Fuchs. As a result, his already-formed ideas on the role of rhythmical movement in the theatre and his conception of the actor and stage space in three-dimensional terms assumed a new coherence. Now consolidated in practice as well as in theory, his musical interpretation of drama with gesture, rhythm and movement co-ordinated to convey the underlying ideas and emotions of the characters was henceforth to dictate his approach to every production.

Despite the unsuitability of the conventional box-stage of the Marinsky Theatre, the production of *Tristan*, with its plastic groupings against relief settings, and the measured, eloquent movements of the characters, was a revelation to an operatic public inured to flat stages and stock gestures. The settings and costumes by Prince Shervashidze were less successful, and for this Meyerhold was largely to blame. He chose to draw his inspiration from the same source as Wagner himself, namely the epic poem of Gottried von Strassburg. The result was a series of settings and costumes based on thirteenth-century French miniatures which hovered uneasily between representation and stylization, and hardly matched the heroic scale of Wagner's score. However, the production earned the fulsome praise of no less an authority than the musical director of the Bayreuth Opera, Felix Mottl, who, after acting as guest conductor for one performance, told Meyerhold that he had not seen such a faithful rendering of Wagner on any stage.[1]

Meyerhold's production of Molière's *Dom Juan* (9 November 1910 at the Alexandrinsky Theatre) followed close on his adaptation of Schnitzler's pantomime *Der Schleier der Pierrette* for the Interlude House, and both works reflected his growing preoccupation with the *commedia dell' arte*. For all the magnificence of Golovin's settings, the most significant feature of *Dom Juan* was the confining of the action to the deep forestage. Properties were kept to a minimum in order that the balletic caperings of the actors might be seen to better advantage. The one stationary figure was the mountainous Sganarelle of Konstantin Varlamov, who spent most of the play ensconced on a stool close to one of the two ornamental prompter's screens flanking the stage. This feature of the setting was dictated by a

[1] Cf. Valery Bebutov in *Vstrechi s Meyerholdom*, Moscow, 1967, p. 74.

combination of Varlamov's immobility and his incorrigible memory, but Meyerhold turned this to triumphant advantage by allowing him a freedom to improvize which delighted the audience and was entirely in keeping with the mood of the production.

Dom Juan marked a stage in Meyerhold's career in another vital respect: it conquered the prejudices of all but the most obdurate members of the Alexandrinsky company. Yury Yuriev, who played Dom Juan, writes in his memoirs:

> I was enthralled by this work and I wasn't the only one; everyone surrendered to the inspiration of the director. The truth is that it was a holiday for us![1]

The production of Moussorgsky's *Boris Godunov* at the Marinsky in January 1911 is memorable only because it was the one occasion on which Meyerhold worked with Chaliapin. The settings were those which Golovin had designed for Paris, and Meyerhold did little more than revise the earlier production. He was prudent enough to defer to Chaliapin's wishes rather than risk a major scandal, but even the little that Chaliapin did see of Meyerhold – he sang at only two performances – was evidently more than enough, for in 1917 he flatly refused to work with him on Dargomyzhsky's *Stone Guest*.

Of all Meyerhold's operatic work the most widely acclaimed was Gluck's *Orpheus* (21 December 1911). Whilst retaining the division between forestage and main stage from *Tristan*, he abandoned the reconstruction of a definite historical period in favour of a stylized evocation of antiquity after the manner of the eighteenth century. In conception, the production bore a close resemblance to *Dom Juan*; it sought to create a festive atmosphere by framing the stage picture with rich hangings and by keeping the auditorium flooded with light throughout the performance. In contrast to *Tristan* there were an act-drop and a front curtain, but these were designed by Golovin especially for the production. With their elaborate embroidery and encrustation, they presaged the dazzling opulence of the series of curtains used in *Masquerade* in 1917. Meyerhold remained true to his conception of plastic movement to the extent of employing a separate chorus and *corps de ballet*.[2] In this, he was helped greatly by Mikhail Fokine, who worked with him as ballet-master for this one production.

Strauss's *Elektra* (18 February 1913) was a curious aberration, both for Meyerhold and for Golovin. Inspired by Meyerhold's visit to Mikonos three years earlier and by Arthur Evans's recent excavations at Knossos, they sought to achieve a degree of archaeological reconstruction which came

[1] Y. Yuriev, *Zapiski*, vol. 2, Leningrad-Moscow, 1963, p. 171.
[2] See p. 107 below.

close to the Meiningen naturalism long since condemned by Meyerhold. Against this setting Strauss's score and von Hoffmannsthal's libretto seemed merely a wilful distortion of the ancient myth. The work was performed only three times, its removal being due partly to protests in the reactionary press which considered that it was 'absolutely impermissible at the time of the 300th anniversary of the Romanov dynasty to put on an opera in which members of a royal house are beheaded'.[1]

In the summer of 1913 Meyerhold's work was seen for the first time abroad. He produced Gabriele d'Annunzio's *La Pisanelle* for Ida Rubinstein at the Châtelet Theatre in Paris. With settings by Bakst, choreography by Fokine and over 200 extras, the production was a spectacular success. For Meyerhold it was significant above all as a means of drawing the attention of the West to his talents; it afforded valuable practice in the handling of large-scale crowd scenes, but otherwise marked no particular advance in his technique. The alliance with his fellow collaborators (particularly Ida Rubenstein) was uneasy, and although he established many contacts in Paris – notably with Guillaume Apollinaire – it was seventeen years before Meyerhold's work was seen outside Russia again.

The year 1913 saw the opening of Meyerhold's own studio, and it was there that he conducted the experiments which eventually yielded a bewildering succession of innovations in Moscow after the Civil War. These experiments and his work in the cinema at that time are described in later sections. Meanwhile, his productions at the Imperial theatres were largely a consolidation of lessons already learnt. The atmosphere engendered by war was hardly conducive to serious theatrical enterprises; initially the surge of nationalistic fervour stimulated a flood of patriotic plays, but all too soon this was succeeded by a preference for escapist trifles which had little to offer the stage-director.

One production which foreshadowed a vital line in Meyerhold's development after the Revolution was Ostrovsky's *The Storm* (9 January 1916). In his opinion, the true nature of Ostrovsky had been distorted by the naturalistic school which saw him as a mere genre dramatist. Stressing Ostrovsky's affinity with Pushkin, Lermontov and traditional Spanish tragedy, Meyerhold reinterpreted *The Storm* as a Russian romantic tragedy. He rejected the conventional emphasis on the vernacular in Ostrovsky's dialogue and sought to capture the underlying poetry. In an attempt to bring out the predominant national character of the drama, Golovin based the settings and costumes on the strong colours and ornamentation of traditional weaving and carving. Although restrained by

[1] Quoted in Nikolai Volkov, op. cit., vol. 2, p. 273.

comparison with later productions such as *Tarelkin's Death*, *The Forest* and *The Government Inspector*, *The Storm* was a bold challenge to tradition and the first of Meyerhold's many invigorating reinterpretations of the Russian classics.

In 1917 the monumental production of Lermontov's *Masquerade* was revealed to the public. Although it was put on finally at eighteen days' notice, it had been in preparation and intermittently rehearsed for five years. The cast of over two hundred comprised the permanent Alexandrinsky company augmented by students from various drama schools, including Meyerhold's own Studio. Meyerhold's 'comédiens', as he called his pupils, were particularly suited to the production by virtue of their familiarity with the grotesque, which was so vital to the realization of the work as he conceived it.

Lermontov's verse drama tells of the cynical and dissolute Petersburg nobleman, Arbenin, who has become reformed by the love of his young wife, Nina. They attend a masked ball and through the intrigue of the society which he despises, Arbenin is persuaded that Nina has been unfaithful to him. Enraged with jealousy, he poisons her and finally goes mad himself. Meyerhold intended originally to emphasise Lermontov's denunciation of the corrupt society of the 1830's, but the action became dominated by the figure of 'The Stranger', who was portrayed as an emissary of the infernal powers, first driving Arbenin to murder and then punishing him for the crime with madness. This despairing vision of life as a phantasmagoria ruled by the whims of malevolent forces was not new to Meyerhold: it appeared first in Blok's *Fairground Booth* and later inspired the nightmarish pantomime of *Columbine's Scarf*; it is germane to the concept of the sinister ambiguity of the mask which Meyerhold examines at length in his essay, *The Fairground Booth*.

From start to finish Meyerhold worked on *Masquerade* in closest collaboration with Golovin. In order to speed the remorseless advance of the tragedy, Lermontov's cumbersome five acts were treated as ten episodes; each had its own lavish setting, but the forestage and a series of five act-drops were used to ensure no pause in the action. Critical scenes were played at the edge of the forestage and a series of borders and screens (similar to *Dom Juan*) was devised to frame the characters in the more intimate scenes. As well as the many settings and costumes, Golovin designed all the furniture, china, glassware, candelabra, swords, walking-canes, fans – everything down to the last playing-card. Not a single item was taken from stock and everything of significance was made slightly over life-size in order to produce the required impact on the spectator. As with

Dom Juan, the auditorium lighting was left on throughout the performance. Tall mirrors flanked the proscenium opening, in order to break down with their reflections the barrier between stage and audience, to establish the affinity between Golovin's settings and Rossi's auditorium, and above all to heighten the prevailing atmosphere of illusion.

The music for the production was composed by Glazunov and based on themes from Glinka. On this occasion the entire choreography was arranged by Meyerhold, who plotted every step, including the masked-ball scene in which over a hundred and fifty guests took part.

The première on 25 February 1917 was the theatrical event of the decade, but on that day the tsarist régime was forced to a final confrontation with the starving workers of Petrograd and the first shots of the Revolution were exchanged. Not entirely without justification, critics hostile to Meyerhold seized on this ironic coincidence and condemned the profligacy of this, the richest spectacle the Russian theatre had ever seen, representing it as typical of Meyerhold's own decadence and megalomaniac extravagance.

Despite this and repeated criticism after the Revolution of the production's 'mysticism', it was revived frequently and performed right up to 1941. The settings and costumes were destroyed by enemy action during the Second World War, but Meyerhold's legacy survived even that, for after the war *Masquerade* was revived for the last time as a production without décor at the Leningrad Philharmonic with Yurev, then over 70, in his original part of Arbenin.

Although Meyerhold retained his posts at the Imperial theatres for a further season after the October Revolution, it is *Masquerade* which must be regarded as the culmination of his Petersburg period. Before the year was out he had thrown in his lot with the Bolsheviks and pledged himself to the democratization of the new, Soviet theatre.

1. Tristan and Isolde

I

If an opera were produced without words it would amount to *a pantomime*.

In pantomime every single episode, each movement in each episode (its plastic modulations) – as well as the gestures of every character and the

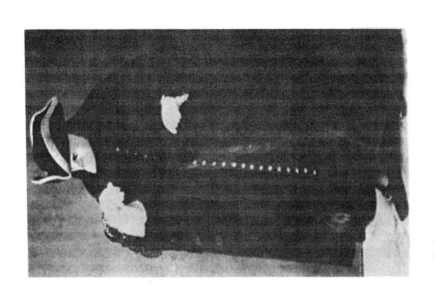

Two 'proscenium servants' from *Dom Juan*, 1910.

Illarion Pevtsov as 'The Stranger' in *Masquerade*, 1917.

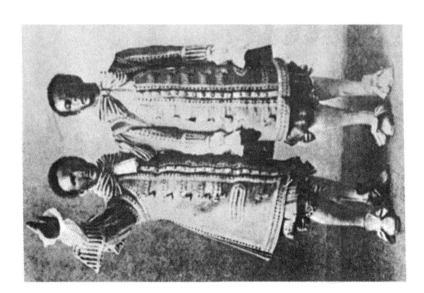

Costume designs by Alexander Golovin.
(a) and (b) *Dom Juan*, 1910 (Juan and Sganarelle).
(c) and (d) *Masquerade*, 1917.

groupings of the ensemble – are determined precisely by the music, by its changes in tempo, its modulations, its overall structure.

In pantomime the rhythm of the movements, gestures and groupings is synchronized precisely with the rhythm of the music; a performance may be regarded as perfect only if the rhythm of the music and the rhythm on the stage are perfectly synchronized.

So why don't operatic artists make their movements and gestures follow the musical tempo, the tonic design of the score, with mathematical precision?

Does the addition of the human voice to the art of the pantomime alter the relationship between music and stage action which exists in pantomime?

I believe it alters because the operatic singer bases his dramatic interpretation on the libretto rather than on the musical score.

In most cases the libretto is so *lifelike* that it induces the artist to adopt the acting style of the realistic theatre. The style varies with the period of the opera: if it is of the period when the dramatic theatre was dominated by graceful, stylized gestures, reminiscent of a puppet which moves in order to appear alive, then the artists perform in the style of French actors at the time of Racine and Corneille. But if it belongs to the age of naturalism the artists' style will closely resemble real life; stylized 'operatic' gestures will be replaced by highly realistic automatic movements, the reflex actions which accompany our everyday conversations.

In the first instance, the discrepancy between the rhythm of the orchestra and the rhythm of the gestures and movements is barely noticeable, for although the gestures are excessively cloying, prettified and ridiculously puppet-like, they are at least in time with the music. The fault lies simply in the gestures' lack of the logic and accuracy of expression which Wagner, for example, demands. In the second instance the discrepancy is intolerable: the music refuses to harmonize with everyday, automatic gestures, and the orchestra can do no more than furnish a ritornello, a refrain which is like the accompaniment to a bad pantomime. Furthermore the spectator's attention is fatally divided: the better the acting, the more naïve the very convention of opera appears; the situation of people behaving in a lifelike manner on the stage and then suddenly breaking into song is bound to seem absurd. Lev Tolstoy's bewilderment at the sight of people singing is easily explained: the singing of an operatic score to the accompaniment of realistic gestures inevitably reduces any sensitive onlooker to laughter. Stylization is the very basis of operatic art – *people sing*. Therefore no elements of real life should be introduced; as soon as stylization and reality are juxtaposed, the *apparent* inadequacy of stylization is revealed and the whole foundation of the art collapses. *Music drama must be performed in such a way that the spectator never thinks to question why the actors are singing and not speaking.*

The art of Chaliapin is an object lesson in this style of interpretation. He has the ability to balance, so to speak, on the ridge of the roof without slipping either to the side of naturalism or to the side of the operatic style which we inherited from the Italians of the sixteenth century when the main aim of a singer was to demonstrate the perfection of his 'roulades' and there was not the slightest connection between the libretto and the music.

Chaliapin's acting is always *true*: not true to life, but theatrically true. His is the slightly embellished truth of an art which is always elevated above life itself.

In *The Book on the New Theatre*,[1] Alexander Benois writes: 'The hero may perish, but even in his end one should be able to sense the sweet smile of a divine countenance.' One senses this smile in the denouement of several of Shakespeare's tragedies (*King Lear*, for instance); in Ibsen, Hilda hears 'harps in the air' at the death of Solness; Isolde 'melts into the breath of the boundless firmament'. One senses this 'sweet smile' again in Chaliapin's death of Boris. But is it only in the moment of death that it shines through Chaliapin's art? Consider the cathedral scene in *Faust* where Mephistopheles, not at all the triumphant spirit of evil, appears as the accusatory priest, the almost sorrowful confessor of Marguerite, the voice of her conscience. Here this unworthy, deformed, base (in Schiller's sense) creature is transformed by Chaliapin into an object of aesthetic pleasure.

Furthermore, Chaliapin is one of the few artists on the operatic stage who follows the composer's musical notation precisely, and imposes on his movements a design, a plastic design which is always in harmony with the tonic design of the score. As an illustration of this synthesis of plastic rhythm and musical rhythm, consider Chaliapin's interpretation of the Witches' Sabbath on the Brocken (in Boito's *Mephistopheles*); here, not only the movements and gestures of Mephistopheles as he leads the ritual dance are rhythmical – even the moments of tense, petrified *immobility* during the frenzy convey the rhythm which the orchestra is beating out.

The artistic synthesis which Wagner adopted as the basis for his reform of the music drama will continue to evolve. Great architects, designers, conductors and directors will combine their innovations to realize it in the theatre of the future. But there can be no complete synthesis before the advent of *the new actor.*

[1] *Teatr, kniga o novom teatre*, Petersburg, 1908.

It took the amazing Chaliapin to show the actor in the music drama the only possible way of scaling the towering edifice which was raised by Wagner. But that quality in Chaliapin which ought to serve as the ideal for every operatic artist has been completely misinterpreted by the majority; his theatrical truth has been interpreted as 'truth to life', as naturalism. This is because his début at the Mamontov Opera[1] coincided with the first ('Meiningen') period of the Moscow Art Theatre. The light from such a significant phenomenon as the Art Theatre was so strong that in its radiance the art of Chaliapin looked like the operatic equivalent of Meiningen naturalism.

Director and singers alike imagined they were following in Chaliapin's footsteps when, during the Ballad of the King of Thule in *Faust*, Marguerite was made to water a bed of flowers, although in the orchestral score a spinning wheel is expressly indicated.

For the actor in music drama, Chaliapin's art is as vital a source as the altar of Dionysus is for the tragedian. But he will not become a vital element in the Wagnerian synthesis until he learns to see Chaliapin's art not in the light of the Moscow Art Theatre, whose actors perform according to the laws of *mimesis*, but in the light of omnipotent rhythm.

Before proceeding to an examination of the characteristics of music drama and the role of movement in it, I should mention that I do not intend to make a close analysis of Chaliapin's style. I spoke of him simply to give some idea of the kind of operatic art under discussion.

I shall deal first with the movements and gestures of the actors because the *mise en scène* of a music drama must be created not on its own but with these movements in mind, just as the movements themselves can be worked out only by referring to the musical score.

One should distinguish between the two main operatic traditions. Taking Gluck as the father of music drama, we have two separate lines of development: one is Gluck-Weber-Wagner; the other is Gluck-Mozart-Bizet.

I should explain that the production method described below applies to Wagnerian music drama, that is, where the libretto and the music are composed free from mutual enslavement.

If the dramatic conception of a music drama is to come to life, it must not bypass the realm of music, for it is there that the mysterious world of our emotions finds expression. The world of the soul can express itself only through music; music alone has the power to express fully the world of the soul.

[1] The Moscow Private Russian Opera, owned and directed by Savva Mamontov. Chaliapin was principal soloist from 1896 to 1899.

The composer of the music drama mines his creation from the depths of music, and then gives it concrete shape by means of *words* and *harmony*; this is how he composes his score, a verbal-musical text.

Adolphe Appia (*Die Musik und die Inscenierung*)[1] considers that the only way of realizing a dramatic conception is to immerse oneself first in the world of the emotions, the realm of music.

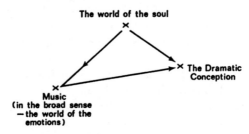

Appia rejects the direct approach; a dramatic conception not reached via music results in a worthless libretto.

Furthermore, see how graphically Appia determines the interrelation of the elements of the operatic theatre:

From MUSIC (in the broad sense)
is born
THE DRAMATIC CONCEPTION;

| the drama realized in time | this develops in images through word and tone \ into / the drama This drama becomes visible to the spectator with the help of | the score |
| the drama realized in space | the actor, reliefs, lighting, design Thus is born THE VERBAL-MUSIC DRAMA | the *mise en scène* |

[1] Munich, 1899. Published in English under the title *Music and the Art of the Theatre* by the University of Miami Press, 1962.

Music, which determines the tempo of every occurrence on the stage, dictates a rhythm which has nothing in common with everyday existence. The life of music is not the life of everyday reality. 'Neither life as it is, nor life as it ought to be, but life as we see it in our dreams.' (Chekhov.)[1]

The essence of stage rhythm is the antithesis of real, everyday life. Therefore, the actor's approach must be one of artistic invention, sometimes perhaps based on realistic material, but expressed ultimately in a form far from what we see in real life. His movements and gestures should be in accord with the stylized dialogue of his singing.

The skill of the naturalistic actor lies in his ability to observe life and to incorporate his observations in his acting; the actor in the music drama must never allow his experience of life to influence his performance.

In most cases the art of the naturalistic actor lies in surrendering to the dictates of his temperament. By prescribing a strict tempo, the musical score frees the actor in music drama from the demands of his own temperament.

The actor in the music drama must absorb the essence of the score and translate every subtlety of the musical picture into plastic terms.

For this reason he must strive for complete control over his body. Once the human body becomes supple and agile, it joins the orchestra and the *mise en scène* as *a means of expression*, and can begin to play an active part in the dramatic action. *Man*, performing in harmony with the *mise en scène* and the musical score, becomes *a work of art* in his own right.

Where does the human body, possessing the suppleness of expression demanded by the stage, attain its highest development? *In the dance*. Because the dance is the movement of the human body in the sphere of rhythm. The dance is to the body what music is to thought: form artificially yet instinctively created.

Richard Wagner defined the music drama as 'a symphony made manifest through visible and comprehensible action' ('ersichtlich gewordene Thaten der Musik').[2] To Wagner, the symphony, too, is indebted to the dance: 'The modern symphony is based on the harmonized dance', he says. Beethoven's Seventh Symphony in A major he called 'the apotheosis of the dance'.

Thus 'visible and comprehensible action' embodied by the actor implies choreographic action. Given that the dance is the source of gesture in the music drama, it follows that the operatic artist should learn gesture not

---

[1] A paraphrase of Treplev's words in Act One of *The Seagull*. Cf. Meyerhold's analysis of Act Three of *The Cherry Orchard* (pp. 28–29 above).

[2] All the quotations of Wagner are from his *Oper und Drama* (1851).

from the actor of the conventional theatre but from the ballet-master.[1]

'The art of music and poetry becomes comprehensible. . . only through the art of the dance.' (Wagner.)

At the point where the spoken word fails in its power of expression the language of the dance begins. In the Nō theatre of ancient Japan, whose plays resembled our operas, the performers were expected to be dancers as well as actors.

Apart from the agility which transforms an opera singer's movements into those of a dancer, another quality distinguishes him from the actor in the dramatic theatre. If the latter wishes to convey to the audience the pain which a memory causes him, he has to suggest it by means of mime. In the music drama the music has the power to suggest this pain. Therefore, the operatic artist must observe the principle of *economy of gesture*, because he need employ gestures only to supply what is missing from the musical score, or to complete what has been only half-said by the orchestra.

In the music drama the actor is not the only medium of contact between poet and audience. He is one of several means of expression, neither more nor less important than the rest, and it is his task to remain conscious of them all. But, of course, it is principally through the actor that the music translates the dimension of time into spatial terms.

Before music was dramatized it could create an illusory picture only in time; once dramatized, it was able to conquer space. The illusory became real through the mime and movement of the actor subordinated to the musical design; that which before had dwelt only in time was now manifested in space.

II

Speaking of 'the theatre of the future' which is destined to be 'a union of all the arts', Wagner calls Shakespeare (referring to the time when he was with the Lord Chamberlain's Company) 'the Thespis of the tragedy of the future': 'The theatre of Shakespeare will have the same relation to the theatre of the future as the wagon of Thespis had to the theatre of Aeschylus and Sophocles.' Beethoven, he says, was the one who discovered the language of the artist of the future.[2]

Wagner foresees the theatre of the future at the point where these two

[1] By this I mean the ballet-master of the new school. To me, the ideal ballet-master today is Fokine. [Meyerhold's note.]

[2] According to Wagner, Beethoven was the principal creator of the symphony based on the 'harmonized dance' which Wagner valued so highly. [Meyerhold's note.]

poets join hands. And then Wagner's precise evocation of his vision: 'The poet will be vindicated when the marble creations of Pheidias are clothed in flesh and blood.'

What Wagner valued above all in the Shakespearian theatre was firstly that the company was an ideal fellowship, 'thiasus' in the Platonic sense ('eine besondere Art von ethischer Gemeinschaftsform', in the words of Theodor Lessing).[1] Secondly, he considered that Shakespeare's theatre came close to the ideal of universal art: 'Shakespeare's drama is such a true representation of the world that it is impossible to identify the subjective aspect of the poet in the artistic representation of ideas.' In Wagner's opinion, Shakespeare's art reflects the soul of the people.

Since I began by considering the technical aspects of production, I feel I should note the following points in Wagner's advocacy of Shakespeare as a worthy model (bearing in mind Wagner's love of the Classical world).

Wagner admired the architectural simplicity of the Shakespearian stage and especially the situation of the actors performing with spectators on all sides. Most appositely, he calls the forestage of the old English theatre 'der gebärende Mutterschoss der Handlung'.[2]

But did Wagner not see the forestage of the Renaissance theatre, used so extensively by Italian singers, as a copy of this curious Old English phenomenon? Of course not. Firstly, Wagner honoured the design of the Greek Classical theatre, installing the orchestra in a concealed pit where our forestage ('orchestra') is located.[3] Secondly, in view of his proposed elevation of man to the level of a cult and his dream of the plastic transformation of man on the stage, he could not possibly regard our forestage as a fit place for groupings based on the *principle of plastic transformation*. This is how Wagner imagines this transformation:

'Having once attained perfect physical development, *living*, perfect man is destined to become a work of art in his own right. But the favourite art of man is *drama*. Therefore, plastic art shall be vindicated by the magic transformation of stone into the flesh and blood of living man, of the inanimate into the living, of the monumental into the art of the moment. Only when the dancer, the mime, the singer, and the actor are seized with this creative urge can we hope for the realization of these aims. True plastic art will come into being when sculpture is replaced by architecture,

[1] Th. Lessing, *Theater-Seele, Studie über Bühnenästhetik und Schauspielkunst.* [Meyerhold's note.]

[2] The pregnant womb of the action.

[3] See *Wagner and the Dionysian ritual* in Vyacheslav Ivanov's *Po Zvyozdam*, Petersburg, 1909. [Meyerhold's note.]

when the awful solitude of *one* man carved out of stone is replaced by a countless multitude of real living people, when dear-lamented sculpture is realized not in lifeless bronze or marble, but in the endlessly changing creations of flesh and blood, *when we use stone to construct stages for living works of art* and stop using it to represent living man.'

Wagner rejects not only sculpture, but portrait painting, too: 'There will be no place for it when splendid man, untrammelled by artistic limits, without resort to brush and canvas becomes a work of art in his own right.'

Then Wagner considers architecture. Let the architect devote himself to building a theatre in which man can become 'a work of art in his own right'. As soon as man's living form is recognized as a plastic unit we encounter the problem of what form the new stage should take (architecturally speaking). This is a problem which has arisen frequently since the beginning of the nineteenth century, especially in Germany.

Here is what Ludwig Tieck, one of the leaders of the Romantic school, said in a letter to Raumer (the following is a paraphrase of the letter):

'I have spoken with you several times of my belief in the possibility of rebuilding the stage so that it bears a closer architectural resemblance to the old English stage. But for this the stage would need to be at least twice as wide as those to which we are accustomed. We ought to have given up trying to increase its depth long ago, since deep stages are both inartistic and anti-dramatic.

'Entrances and exits should be made not from the rear of the stage, but via the wings. In other words, the stage should be turned round to face side-on to the audience, so that everything which at present is seen in profile would be seen full face. Instead of being broad and shallow like a bas-relief, theatres at present are deep and high.'

Tieck saw a certain resemblance between the theatres of Old England and Ancient Greece. First, he liked the way in which both merely suggested everything; second, the fact that *the stage* (in the precise sense of the word) was *out in front*; everything which in our theatre is concealed by the wings was directly in front of the spectator, and the actors on the stage remained constantly in view, just like the performers in a circus ring.

The problem of how to locate painted scenery and human figures in different planes clearly preoccupied the famous classical architect, Schinkel (1781–1841); he proposed various new designs of stage, all of which corresponded to Wagner's dream of a landscape painting as a distant back curtain, replacing the Ancient Greek theatre's Hellenic landscape in the far background.

'The Greeks regarded nature simply as a setting for man; the gods, whom they regarded as personifications of the forces of nature, were in fact gods in human form. The Greeks strove to invest every natural phenomenon with a human form, for it was when seen in human form that nature exerted a boundless fascination over them. . . .

'Landscape painting must become the soul of architecture; it will teach us how to build a stage for the drama of the future in which it will furnish living, natural settings for living, *unsimulated* man.

'Everything which the sculptor and the historical painter have attempted to create in stone or on canvas will henceforth be created by the actor in himself: in his body and his limbs, in his features; he will create it for an aesthetically conscious age. The actor of today is inspired by the same motive which in the past has driven the sculptor to re-create the human form – the desire to imitate. The same eye which helped 'the historical painter to find the most beguiling and characteristic colours, costumes and compositions for his paintings, today determines the grouping of living people on the stage.' (Wagner.)

From what Wagner has to say about the role of painting in the theatre, about the forestage being entrusted to the architect, about the artist being employed not merely as a painter (painting provides only the 'Hintergrund') but as a director, too, about the importance of 'Stimmung' in everything concerning lighting, composition, colours, about the vital need for clarity in the actor's mimetic movements and gestures, about the acoustic conditions best suited to declamation: from all this it is clear that the Bayreuth stage could never have satisfied Wagner, because it had yet to sever the final link with the traditions of the Renaissance theatre, and, most important, because producers of Wagner failed to realize the necessity to take into account that reformer's fundamental conception of the stage as a *pedestal for sculpture*.

III

It was *Georg Fuchs* at the Munich Künstlertheater[1] who set about realizing the dream of Tieck, Immermann, Schinkel and Wagner, the reconstruction of the theatres of Ancient Greece and Old England.

[1] See *Yezhegodnik Imperatorskikh teatrov*, Petersburg, 1909, no. 3, 'Letters from Abroad, no. 3 – 'The Munich Artists' Theatre'; *Apollon*, 1909, no. 2, G. Fuchs, 'The Munich Artists' Theatre'. [Meyerhold's note.]

This type of stage is distinguished by the fact that the foreground is designed exclusively for *reliefs*. Broadly speaking, relief implies the French 'practicable' or the German 'praktikabel', meaning practicable and not purely decorative. Consequently, they are not used as a series of painted flats placed separately with the purely representational aim of improving the perspective or the lighting on the backcloth (by concealing floodlights behind the flats); nor is the term 'relief' used in the narrow sense of the Moscow Art Theatre, where it means a flat attached at an angle to the painted scenery in order to heighten the illusion of reality.

'Practicable reliefs' supplement a flat setting; they are not illusory, but serve purely practical ends; the actor can actually touch them, and they serve a similar purpose to a pedestal for sculpture. Thus the foreground is transformed into a 'relief-stage' and is quite separate from the painted background. In this way it becomes possible to avoid the unhappy juxtaposition of three-dimensional human forms with two-dimensional painting, which so often offends the spectator's aesthetic sensibility, and which is even more offensive when reliefs are introduced in order to camouflage the contradiction between the fictitious substance of the scenery and the concrete figure of the actor; that is, when painting is used not only as a 'Hintergrund' but in the foreground as well, in the same plane as the reliefs. 'The introduction of a relief into a picture is like the introduction of music into reading, of painting into sculpture; they all outrage "good taste" and jar on aesthetic sensibility.' (Benoi̇.)

In order to realize the principle of the relief-stage, Georg Fuchs had to rebuild the theatre completely. When one is obliged to work on a stage of Renaissance design, and tries to mount productions of Wagnerian dramas in the most appropriate manner (by dividing the stage into two separate planes: the relief-stage and the painted background), one straightway encounters an immense obstacle which renders the Renaissance stage an object of the most bitter hatred.

In the 'good old days' singers would step forward on to the forestage in order to perform their arias closer to the audience, as though on a concert platform where a singer sings a romance completely unrelated to the rest of the programme. After the disappearance of castrati and female exponents of vocal gymnastics (the coloratura soprano must forgive me for not finding a place for her in the theatre of the future) the forestage became superfluous. It is not used by modern opera singers because the libretto is no longer distinct from the score as it was in the old Italian operas, but requires the artists to play together in order to weave the pattern of the drama. Unfortunately, the Renaissance forestage projects so far that it is useless as a 'relief stage'; it stands in front of the curtain, so it is impossible to construct settings on it.

It was this which forced us to construct the relief-stage for Acts Two and Three of *Tristan* at the front of the main stage rather than on the forestage, which means that it is too far from the audience for the mime and plastic movements of the actors to be seen to their best advantage.

The Renaissance stage is a box with a 'window' cut in the side facing the audience (the bottom is the stage floor; the sides are the sides of the stage concealed by the wings; the lid is the roof of the stage invisible to the spectators). The sides of the box have to be hidden from the audience by drapes (side curtains), because it is not wide enough (the sides are too close to the edges of the opening), and a proscenium arch and borders have to be used because the top is too low.

Actors get lost on this box-stage, surrounded by daubed hangings above and around them and hemmed in by daubed pieces of scenery all over the stage; 'they are like miniatures in a gigantic frame' (E. T. A. Hoffmann).

If the forestage in front of the curtain is covered with a carpet which blends with the colour of the side curtains, if the stage immediately adjoining it is converted into a 'relief-stage' to serve as a pedestal for groupings, and finally, if the back curtain has the purely decorative task of furnishing a background to enhance the human figures and their movements, then the restrictions of the Renaissance stage can be largely overcome.

The proscenium stage at Bayreuth is considerably inferior to Fuchs's design for the Künstlertheater, but none the less it was praised by Wagner for the manner in which it made the figures on it appear over life-size.

It is this capacity for enhancing the apparent stature of figures that makes the relief-stage so suitable for Wagnerian drama – not because we want to see giants, but because it increases the plasticity both of single figures and of ensemble groupings.

The relief-stage is not an end in itself, but merely a means; the end is the dramatic action which the spectator pictures in his imagination, stimulated by the rhythmical waves of bodily movement; these waves must extend into space in order for the spectator to absorb the composition of movements, gestures, and poses.

Once the principle of bodily movement in space is accepted, the stage must be constructed so that the lines of rhythmical expression can stand out distinctly. Hence, everything which serves as a pedestal for the actor, everything on which he leans, everything he touches, must be constructed sculpturally, with the diffuseness of painting relegated to the background.

91

The greatest obstacle is the flat surface of the stage. If only one could mould it like a sculptor moulds his clay, the broad expanse of floor could be transformed into a compact series of surfaces on varying levels. Lines would be broken up, characters could be grouped more closely in delicate curves, beautiful chiaroscuro effects could be achieved, the sound would be more concentrated.

Stage action has been raised to a certain pitch of unity. It has become easier for the spectator to appreciate everything and everybody on the stage as one beautiful harmony. The listener-spectator's attention is no longer torn between auditory and visual impressions. Only thus is it possible to reveal the creative uniqueness of Wagner, his evocation of images with bold strokes and expressively simplified contours. Lichtenberger draws a telling comparison between Wagner's figures and the frescoes of Puvis de Chavannes.[1]

The figure of the actor is not allowed to merge with decorative canvases, which have been removed upstage, and so he becomes the centre of attention, a work of art in his own right. In order that the actor's gestures do not distract the spectators' attention from the musical picture, so that each one is profoundly significant, they must become more laconic; they must be simple, distinct, bold and rhythmical.

Usually, with the construction of scenic flats and 'practicables' the stage-designer's work is finished. But beyond that, it is important to establish harmony between the surfaces on which the actors' figures move and the figures themselves – not to mention harmony between the figures and the painted flats.

The artist is concerned in finding colours and lines for one part (the scenery) of the whole; the whole (the complete stage picture) he leaves to the director. But this is beyond the ability of a non-artist, of a director who lacks specialized artistic knowledge, either acquired in formal art classes or sensed intuitively. The director must embody the creativity of a sculptor and an architect.

I think Maurice Denis's words are of value: 'I watched as he (the sculptor, Maillol) employed in turn, almost systematically, spherical and cylindrical forms, attempting to satisfy Ingres' precept: "beautiful forms are flat surfaces rounded off." '

The director has a flat surface (the stage) and wood from which, like an architect, he constructs the essential practical stage fittings – plus the human body (the actor); his task is to combine these elements to form a harmonious, integrated work of art, a stage-picture.

[1] Henri Lichtenberger, *Richard Wagner, Poète et Penseur*, Paris, 1898.

The director's method corresponds closely to the architect's; the actor's method coincides exactly with the sculptor's: every gesture, every turn of the head, every movement contains the essence of the form and line of a sculptural portrait.

In Maurice Denis's opinion, of all the sculptors who might be invited by architects to embellish a palace of the future, Maillol above all could achieve a blend of sculpture and building which would avoid any impression of encumbrance.

Whose creative ideas are responsible for the form and colours of stage design? The artist's? If so, then he must also be an architect, for he must not only paint canvases but also transform the entire stage area into an harmonious whole. This architect should enlist a Maillol-like actor, so that the actor's sculpture (his body) breathes life into the dead stones (the practicables), transforming them into a mighty pedestal worthy of the great sculpture of the living body fashioned with rhythm.

'How few fashionable architects produce work worthy of the style and measure of Maillol!' – exclaims Maurice Denis.

The situation is the reverse in the theatre. We have our architects, but how few Maillols (actor-sculptors) there are. Whenever the stage area is transformed for the actor into a sculptural pedestal with a painted background, it is the work of architects. They will be either an artist and a director-architect in collaboration, or an artist who has gained control over a non-artist-director, or an artist, like Gordon Craig, who combines in his person director, architect and sculptor. But where are the Malliols, the actor-sculptors, who possess the secret of breathing life into dead stones, imbuing their bodies with the harmony of the dance? Chaliapin, Yershov[1] . . . who else can be added to the list? The stage knows nothing of the sorcery of Maillol.

When actors come to interpret Wagnerian roles, let them not dream of learning from German singers. Here is what Georg Fuchs (a German, be it noted, and so that much more reliable!) writes about them in his book *Der Tanz*:[2]

'The Germans' failure to recognize even today the beauty of the human body is revealed no more clearly than here, where its absurd distortions are unbearable to watch: Siegfrieds with tight corseted "Bierhaus" bellies; Siegmunds with sausage-shaped legs crammed into tights; Valkyries who appear to spend their leisure time in Munich beer halls

[1] Ivan Yershov (1867–1943). Russian tenor who sang Tristan in Meyerhold's production and later appeared at Bayreuth.

[2] Stuttgart, 1906.

93

over plates heaped with steaming offal and steins of foaming beer; Isoldes whose sole ambition is to play the part of fairground fat ladies and exercise their irresistible charms on the imagination of butchers' shop assistants.'

IV

As early as the 1840s Wagner, whilst searching through 'the pages of the great book of history', came across the story of the conquest of the Kingdom of Sicily by Manfred, the son of King Frederick II. Wagner had once seen an engraving of Frederick in his half-Arab court with his Arab dancing-girls. This engraving inspired him to write a dramatic composition of striking passion and brilliance, but he rejected the sketch simply because he considered the projected drama to be 'a magnificent historico-poetical fabric flashing with light and concealing as though with a magnificent cloak, *the noble human form* which alone had the power to bewitch him'.[1]

Wagner rejected historical subjects; in his opinion, a play should not be the private, individual creation of a subjective poet shaping his material according to his personal impulses; he preferred his plays to bear as far as possible the stamp of inevitability which all works inspired by popular legend reveal. And so, rejecting historical subjects, Wagner turned exclusively to mythology.

Lichtenberger expounds Wagner's thoughts on the superiority of the myth over the historical subject as follows:

'*Myths do not bear the stamp of a strictly defined historical period*;[2] the deeds which they recount belong to the distant buried past. The heroes whose praises they sing *are too simple and straightforward to require portrayal on the stage*; they are already alive in the popular imagination which created them *and a few broad strokes are sufficient to bring them to life*; their thoughts are ruled by unbridled, elemental passions which have stirred men's hearts from time immemorial; their spirits are youthful and *primitive*, determined by the principle of action and lacking all inhibitions and inherited prejudices. These are the heroes whose exploits are fit stuff for dramatists.'

When an artist and director approach the production of a work they must take into account whether it is based on a historical subject or on a myth, because obviously the two require quite distinct methods of production. The gap between a historical play in the theatre and a historical

---

[1] Henri Lichtenberger, op. cit.   [2] Meyerhold's italics throughout.

interior in a museum should be wide, but the gap between a historical play and a mythical play should be even wider.

The universal acceptance of Bayreuth as the model for the staging of Wagner has given rise to the custom of giving all his works the external appearance of so-called 'historical drama'. All those helmets and shields gleaming like samovars, clinking chain-mail, and make-up reminiscent of Shakespearian histories, all that fur on costumes and properties, all those actors and actresses with their arms bared . . . And then the tedious, colourless background of historicism – which is completely devoid of mystery and forces the spectator to try to fathom the precise country, century and year of the action – clashes with the orchestra's musical picture which is wrapped in a mist of fantasy. For whatever the stage looks like, Wagner's operas force one to listen to the music. Surely it was because of all this that Wagner, according to his intimates, once came up to some friends during a performance at Bayreuth and covered their eyes with his hands, so that they might concentrate more fully on the wonders of his pure symphonic music.

Wagner indicates how the goblet in his drama resembles the torch of the Ancient Greeks' Eros. What is interesting in this comparison is not the composer's emphasis on the profound symbolism of the torch – who could fail to see that? – but his intuitive concern with the creation of a whole atmosphere in which the torch, the sorcery of Isolde's mother, the perfidy of Melot, the golden goblet containing the love potion, and all the other elements ring true on the stage instead of being a mere collection of banal operatic devices.

Although Wagner 'in full consciousness' immersed himself in the spiritual world of his heroes, although he concentrated all his attention on the purely psychological aspect of the myth, the designer and the director of *Tristan and Isolde* must aim at a production which preserves the element of fantasy, and which will draw the spectator unfailingly into its fantastical ethos. This need detract in no way from Wagner's fundamental aim of extracting the spiritual element from the legend. Only a small part of existence can be conveyed by everyday objects; much more is revealed by the rhythm of poetry, the lines and colours of painting. For this reason the designer's principal task is to create a fantastic background, to clothe the characters with loving care in garments which are the pure products of his imagination and whose colours recall the crumbling pages of ancient tomes. Like Giotto, Memling, Brueghel and Fouquet, who succeed far more than any historian in transporting us into the atmosphere of an epoch, the designer must exercise his imagination to create costumes and objects which persuade us that at *some* time in the past everything was like this. This he must do with far more conviction than the designer who aims merely to reproduce on the stage costumes and interiors copied from museum exhibits.

A number of Wagner's biographers stress that the young Richard must have been influenced by the drawing lessons which he received from his stepfather, Ludwig Geyer. It is suggested that Wagner developed his artist's imagination as a result of lessons in painting and drawing: 'He pictures each act as a series of vast tableaux.' The reception in the Hall of the Wartburg, Lohengrin's arrival and departure in the boat pulled by a swan, the three Rhinemaidens at play in the depths of the river . . . all these are pictures 'which have yet to find their equal in art'.

But what distinction Geyer possessed as an artist lay only in portrait painting. One should not forget that he was also an actor. Wagner's brother and sister were also on the stage. Obviously Wagner went to plays in which Geyer, his brother and his sister were playing. It is more likely to have been the backstage atmosphere which influenced the imagination of the young Wagner, already rich in artistic ideas. In Lohengrin's departure on a boat pulled by a swan I see not so much 'a picture which has yet to find its equal in art' as the imprint of life behind the scenes of a mediocre German provincial theatre.

The artist, Anselm Feuerbach, left us the following lines on the theatre of Wagner's time: 'I hate the contemporary theatre because my eyes are sharp and I cannot help noticing all the trumpery properties and daubed make-up. From the depths of my soul I hate excess in decorative art. It corrupts the public, killing whatever instinct for beauty they still possess, and encourages barbaric tastes. Art finds such a theatre repugnant and shakes its dust from its feet.'

'The talent of a fresco painter' so often attributed to Wagner is exposed as spurious if one looks closer at his stage directions; they reveal him as an artist whose ear was more creative than his eye.

'The essence of the German spirit lies in its power to create from within: the one eternal god dwelt there even before He raised up a temple to his own glory.' (Wagner.)

Wagner's dramas were composed from within. His most profound inspiration was drawn from this 'eternal god' and poured into the creation of the inner content of his works, the libretto and the musical score. The external output, the form of the drama (here I am referring to its conception as a production on the stage), remained uninspired by any god. Böcklin could never agree with Wagner over the staging of *The Ring of*

Golovin and Meyerhold in 1923.

Masquerade, 1917.

Costume designs by Nikolai Sapunov for *Columbine's Scarf*, 1910.

(*a*) A Musician. (*b*) Gigolo.

The Fairground Booth (second version: 1914).

the Nibelungs and finally gave him nothing but one sketch for Fafner's make-up.

Having demanded a theatre of new design for his Bühnenfestspiele, Wagner buried the orchestra out of sight, but finally accepted a stage which technically was just as imperfect as it had ever been.

An author's stage directions depend on the level of stage technique at the time when the play is written. Stage techniques change, and an author's directions should be considered in the light of modern developments.[1]

Let the designer and director of *Tristan* take the cue for their stage pictures from the orchestra. What extraordinary medieval colouring there is in Kurwenal's song, in the shouts of the sailors' chorus, in the mysterious death leitmotiv, in the calls of the hunting-horns, and in the fanfares when Mark meets the ship in which Tristan has brought Isolde home to him. Yet Wagner places equal emphasis on the traditional operatic couch where Isolde is supposed to recline in the first act, and where Tristan lies dying in Act Three. In Act Two he stipulates a 'Blumenbank' where Tristan is supposed to place Isolde during the intermezzo of the love duet; yet the garden with the rustling of leaves blending with the sound of the horns is miraculously evoked by the orchestra. The mere contemplation of real foliage on the stage would be as flagrantly tasteless as illustrating Edgar Allen Poe. In the second act our designer depicts a huge towering castle wall and in front of it, right in the centre of the stage, there burns the mystical torch which plays such an important part in the drama.

Karl Immermann writes of *Wallenstein's Camp*: 'In productions of such plays, the secret is to exploit the spectator's imagination to the point where he believes in that which is not there.'

A huge stage may be packed with every conceivable detail, yet still you refuse to believe that there is a ship in front of you. Oh, what a problem it is to depict the deck of a moving ship in the theatre! All you need is one sail filling the entire stage to build a ship in the spectator's imagination.

'To say a lot with a little – that's the secret. The task of the artist is to use the greatest riches with the most prudent economy. The Japanese have only to draw one blossoming twig to evoke an entire spring. We draw the entire spring, and it doesn't add up to a single blossoming twig!' (Peter Altenberg.)

---

[1] I refer only to directions concerning the *mise en scène*, not to those directions in Wagner which reveal so superbly the essence of his orchestration. [Meyerhold's note.]

97

In the third act Wagner calls for a stage crammed with lofty battlements, a parapet with a central watch-tower, castle gates in the background and a spreading linden tree; all our artist gives is a cheerless expanse of horizon and the bare desolate cliffs of Brittany.

[First published in *Yezhegodnik Imperatorskikh teatrov*, Petersburg, 1910, no 5. Reprinted in Meyerhold's *O Teatre*, cit., 1913, pp. 56–80]

NOTE Meyerhold collected the material for this aritcle during the twelve months' work on his production of *Tristan and Isolde*. It furnished the text of a lecture delivered in November 1909. As mentioned above (p. 58), Meyerhold produced two extracts from the opera in the summer of 1907.

Having first encountered the ideas of George Fuchs in 1906 (see pp. 20–21 above), Meyerhold adpts his conception of the relief-stage, which was employed first at the Munich Art Theatre in the summer of 1908. For Fuchs's exposition of his theories, see *Die Revolution des Theaters*(Munich and Leipzig, 1909). Mordecai Gorelik discusses Wagner, Appia and Fuchs at some length in his *New Theatres for Old* (New York, 1940; London, 1947).

Meyerhold's interest in the Japanese theatre was stimulated by reports of Otodziro Kawakami's company on tour in 1902, even though he seems never to have seen them.

---

2. Dom Juan

When I spoke[1] of the possible means of re-creating the stage conventions of the exemplary ages of drama, and of the two ways to stage plays of the theatres of the past, I omitted to mention one possible exception to the suggested rules. I said that in producing a work from a past age of the theatre it is by no means obligatory to stage it *according to the archaeological method*; in the process of reconstruction there is no need for the director to bother with the exact re-creation of the architectural character-

[1] In *Starinny teatr v S. Peterburge* (The Ancient Theatre in Petersburg), written 1907 and published in *O Teatre*, cit., pp. 117–20.

istics of the stage of the period in question. An authentic play of the old theatre may be staged as a *free composition* in the spirit of the theatre in which it was originally staged, but on one inflexible condition: from the old theatre one *must* select those architectural features which best convey the spirit of the work.

In staging, say, Molière's *Dom Juan*, it would be a mistake to move heaven and earth to achieve an exact copy of a theatre of Moliere's time, such as the Palais-Royal or the Petit-Bourbon.

If we go to the heart of Molière's works, we find that he was trying to remove the footlights from the contemporary stage, since they were better suited to the heroic drama of Corneille than to plays with their origins in the popular theatre.

The academic theatre of the Renaissance failed to take advantage of the projecting forestage, keeping actor and audience at a mutually respectful distance. Sometimes, the front rows of the orchestra stalls were moved right back to the middle of the parterre, sometimes even further.

How could Molière accept this segregation of actor and public? How could his overflowing humour have its proper effect under such conditions? How could the whole range of his bold, undisguisedly authentic characterization be accommodated within such a space? How could the waves of accusatory monologue of an author outraged by the banning of *Tartuffe* reach the spectator from such a distance? Surely the actor's ability and freedom of gesture were hemmed in by the wings?

Molière was the first amongst the stage-masters of the Roi-Soleil to attempt to shift the action from the back and centre of the stage forward to the very edge of the proscenium.

Neither the antique stage nor the popular stage of Shakespeare's time had any need for the scenery which the striving for illusion demands nowadays; nor was the actor merely a unit of illusion in those days. With his gestures, his mimicry, his plasticity and his voice, the actor was *all* that the dramatist had and all that he needed to express his entire conception.

It was the same in medieval Japan. In the Nō plays, with their refined ceremony in which movement, dialogue and singing were all rigidly stylized, where the chorus filled a role similar to that of the Greek chorus, and where the outlandish sounds of the music were designed to transport the spectator into a world of hallucination, the director placed his actors on a stage close enough to the spectator for their dances, movements, gesticulations, grimaces and poses to be clearly visible.

It is no coincidence that I refer to the ancient Japanese theatre whilst discussing a production of Molière's *Dom Juan*. From descriptions of Japanese theatrical performances of approximately the same period as Molière, we know that special stage-assistants, known as 'kurogo' and clad in special black costumes resembling cassocks, used to prompt the actors in full view of the audience. When the costume of an actor playing a woman's part[1] became disarranged at a tense moment in the drama, one of the kurogo would quickly restore the graceful folds of the actor's train and attend to his coiffure. In addition, they had the task of removing from the stage any objects dropped or forgotten by the actors. After a battle the kurogo would remove fallen helmets, weapons and cloaks. If the hero died on the stage, the kurogo would quickly cover the corpse with a black cloth, and under the cover of the cloth 'the dead actor' would run off the stage. When the course of the action required darkness on stage the kurogo would squat down at the hero's feet and illuminate his face with a candle on the end of a long stick. To this day the Japanese preserve the acting style of the days of the creators of the Japanese drama: Onono Otsu (1515–81), Satsumo Joun (born 1595) and Chikamatsu Monzaemon (1653–1724), the Japanese Shakespeare.

Isn't the Comédie Française trying now to resurrect the traditions of Molière's 'comédiens' in the same way?

At one and the same time (in the second half of the sixteenth century and throughout the seventeenth century) the theatres of the far West (France, Italy, Spain and England) and the far East were jingling with the bells of pure theatricality.

Is it a coincidence that every single trick in every one of the theatres of this glorious age was performed on that magic area called the proscenium?

But what of the proscenium? Like a circus arena hemmed in on all sides by a ring of spectators, the proscenium projects right out to the audience so that not a single gesture, not a single movement, not a single grimace of the actor is lost in the dust of the wings. And note the conscious adroitness of every gesture, movement, pose and grimace of the proscenium actor. No wonder! How could an actor with pompous affectations and awkward movements survive so close to the audience as the proscenium of the Old English, Spanish, Italian and Japanese theatres?

The proscenium, in the artful hands of Molière, was the best means of counteracting the studied aloofness of the Corneillian style dictated by the

---

[1] Kvan-yei (1623–1724) banned the appearance of women in the theatre; previously they had been the principal performers. Subsequently youths played the female parts, but an edict of 1652 banned their appearance as well. [Meyerhold's note.]

whims of Louis XIV's court. And how it profited Molière when he was performed on a proscenium contrived in face of all the conventions of the contemporary stage! How his grotesques sprang to life once they were free to perform without hindrance on a deep, projecting stage area. The atmosphere which fills this space is not stifled by the wings, and the light projected into the dust-free atmosphere falls directly on to the lithe figures of the actors so that the entire surroundings seem to be designed for the intensification of the play of bright light – both from the stage lighting and from the lights in the auditorium which are left on throughout the performance.

By rejecting certain details typical of the stage of Louis XIV's time (such as a slit in the curtain for the head of the 'annonceur'), does the director run the risk of overlooking that which is essential to the style of Molière?

There are plays such as Sophocles' *Antigone* and Griboedov's *Woe from Wit* which may be perceived by the modern spectator in the light of his own time. It is even possible to perform both these plays in modern dress; the hymn to freedom in the first and the conflict of generations in the second are expressed with a clear, persistent leitmotiv and retain their tendentiousness, whatever the setting.[1]

On the other hand, there are works which cannot be understood properly by the modern spectator unless he is able both to grasp all the subtleties of the plot and to penetrate the intangible atmosphere which enveloped both the actors and the audience of the author's day. There are plays which cannot be appreciated unless they are presented in a form which attempts to create for the modern spectator conditions identical to those which the spectator of the past enjoyed. Such a play is Molière's *Don Juan*. The audience will not appreciate the full subtlety of this enchanting comedy unless it is acquainted straight away with all the minute details of the age

[1] Of the three great Greek tragedians it is in Sophocles that we find the greatest degree of rationality. In Aeschylus the chorus plays an *active* part and the entire tragedy is musically motivated and related to the dance rhythms of plastic culture. In Euripides, who was concerned with the depiction of passions, it is emotionality which predominates (*vide Phoenissae*), and in spite of the author's obvious attempts to separate the theatre from religion, his tragedies remain infused with the customs of his time. In Sophocles' *Antigone* the chorus is transformed into a *raisonneur* and becomes tediously rational. The main thread of the plot is almost cut off from its religious origins and the centre of gravity is shifted to the theme of the struggle for freedom. It is these defects in Sophocles' *Antigone* which make it possible for the modern spectator to comprehend a production which owes nothing to the properties of the antique stage. I should add that my criticism of the rational element in Sophoclean tragedy is limited to *Antigone*; in his other plays this deficiency is less prominent. [Meyerhold's note.]

which gave rise to the play. Therefore, when a director sets about staging *Dom Juan*, his first task is to fill the stage and the auditorium with such a compelling atmosphere that the audience is bound to view the action through the prism of that atmosphere.

When one reads Griboedov's *Woe from Wit* every page seems to reflect some aspect of modern life, and it is this which makes the play so significant for the modern public. If Molière's *Dom Juan* is read without any knowledge of the age which shaped the genius of its author, what a dull play it seems! How tedious is the exposition of its plot compared with even Byron's *Don Juan*, to say nothing of Tirso de Molina's *El Burlador de Sevilla*. If one reads Elvira's great speeches in Act One, or Dom Juan's long attack on hypocrisy in Act Five, one soon gets bored. If the spectator is not to get bored, too, if whole passages are not to strike him as simply obscure, it is essential somehow to remind him constantly of the thousands of Lyonnais weavers manufacturing silk for the monstrously teeming court of Louis XIV, the 'Hôtel des Gobelins',[1] the whole town of painters, sculptors, jewellers and carpenters under the supervision of the celebrated Le Brun,[2] all the craftsmen producing Venetian glass and lace, English hosiery, Dutch mercery, German tin and bronze.

Hundreds of wax candles in three suspended chandeliers and two candelabra on the proscenium, little blackamoors floating about the stage sprinkling intoxicating perfumes from crystal bottles on to red-hot platinum; little blackamoors darting about the stage picking up a lace handkerchief dropped by Dom Juan, offering a stool to a tired actor; little blackamoors fastening Dom Juan's shoelaces as he argues with Sganarelle; little blackamoors appearing with lanterns for the actors when the stage is plunged into semi-darkness; little blackamoors removing cloaks and rapiers from the stage after Dom Juan's desperate fight with the brigands; little blackamoors crawling under the table at the appearance of the Commander's statue; little blackamoors summoning the public with tinkling silver bells and announcing the intervals (in the absence of a curtain): all these are not merely tricks designed for the delectation of snobs, but serve the central purpose of enveloping the action in a mist redolent of the perfumed, gilded monarchy of Versailles.

The more grandiose and colourful the costumes and properties (only remember to keep the design of the stage itself as simple as possible!) the

---

[1] Tapestry weavers, established in the fifteenth century in Paris by the Gobelin family from Rheims. Granted a royal charter by Louis XIV in 1667.

[2] Charles Le Brun (1619–90), 'peintre du roi' who supervised the interior decoration of Versailles.

more clearly the 'comédien' in Molière stands out in contrast with the stiff formality of Versailles.

Was it his provincial wanderings, a life spent in hastily erected fairground booths, that lent such forthrightness to Molière's character? Or perhaps the struggle against hunger? Or did he acquire his vehement tone in the company of the actress-mistresses who brought him such wretched disillusionment? Evidently Louis XIV had good reason to cool towards Molière after his short-lived affection for him.

Surely the discord between the Roi-Soleil (whose aspect is suggested to the spectator by the rich decoration of the proscenium) and the poet who makes Sganarelle in these glittering surroundings speak of stomach disorders, the contrast between the refinement of the setting and the harshness of Molière's grotesque, strikes the modern spectator as so artfully contrived that he cannot help but surrender wholeheartedly to the theatre of Molière. And does a single detail of his genius pass unnoticed now?

Molière's *Dom Juan* is played without a front curtain. Since this was the case neither at the Palais-Royal nor at the Petit-Bourbon, why has the curtain been removed? Usually, the spectator is left cold by the sight of the curtain, no matter how beautifully decorated it might be by some great master. The spectator has come to the theatre to look at what is behind the curtain, and until it rises he looks idly at whatever is depicted on it. Once the curtain rises, what a time it takes for the spectator to absorb all the many wonders surrounding the characters on stage. This is not the case with a stage which is open from start to finish; it is not the case when we have a special pantomime of extras preparing the stage in full view of the audience. Long before the actors appear on the stage the spectator is breathing in the atmosphere of the period. And then everything which seemed either tedious or superfluous when he read the play suddenly strikes him in a new light.

And there is no need to plunge the auditorium into darkness, either in the intervals or during the play itself. Bright light infects the spectators with a festive mood as they enter the theatre. When the actor sees a smile on the lips of a spectator he begins to admire himself, as though looking in a mirror. The actor wearing the mask of Dom Juan will conquer the hearts not only of the actresses in the masks of Mathurine and Charlotte, but also the heart of the owner of those beautiful eyes which he sees flashing in the audience in response to the smile he is acting.

[Published in Meyerhold's *O Teatre*, cit., pp. 121–8.]

NOTES ON THE SETTINGS FOR *Dom Juan*

The stage to be divided into two parts:

1. The proscenium, constructed according to architectural principles, intended exclusively for 'reliefs' and the figures of the actors (who perform only on this area). The proscenium to have a forestage projecting deep into the auditorium. No footlights. No prompt box.

2. The upstage area, intended exclusively for painted backdrops, is not used by the actors at all, except in the finale (downfall and immolation of Juan), and even then they will appear only on the dividing line between the two areas.

Act One

In the text: 'The theatre represents a palace'. Set: downstage: gobelins. Row of armchairs. Candelabra (for decorative purpose). Upstage: hidden.

At the end of the act Dom Juan says: 'Now we must see about our new amorous enterprise', showing that Act Two follows immediately after Act One; since Act Two takes place in the daytime, so must Act One. Besides, I want very much to make Act One joyous, bright, festive, and sunny; I should like to utilize the effect of stylized candelabra on the forestage, to see them burning from the very beginning of the performance. Perhaps we could do it like this: when the spectator enters the auditorium, he sees the stage in half-darkness with candles flickering in tall gilded candelabra and the designs of the gobelins faintly visible. The signal for the act to begin is a quiet overture: six to eight little blackamoors run on and swiftly extinguish the candles; the stage is filled with light; the blackamoors disappear; the act begins on a joyful, exhilarating note.

Act Two (Day)

In the text: 'The theatre represents a village by the sea.' Set: downstage same as Act One, only with the gobelins drawn aside; upstage: Sicilian landscape to illustrate the line: 'Can such a lady really live in this place, amidst these woods and rocks . . .'

Act Three (Evening and Night)

In the text: 'The theatre represents a wood.' Set: foreground as before; background: i. a wood, and ii. a sepulchre (held in readiness for a quick change). We divide the act into two scenes.

In this act one character again refers to 'these trees and rocks'.

I should like to divide the lighting into four phases:

   i. At the beginning, evening (effect concentrated on the background).

  ii. Gradual dimming of the proscenium lighting in order to heighten the effect of the silhouettes cast on the backdrop by the foliage of the trees centre-stage. A genuine 'Schattenspiel' after the manner of the old travelling theatres.

 iii. Complete darkness (the light shining through the foliage disappears in Scene Six when Dom Juan and Sganarelle are alone on stage. The entire stage is lit by a single lantern held by Juan.

 iv. Juan conceals lantern under his cloak, quick change in total darkness, phosphorescent light on the sepulchre after the change of scene.

Act Four (Night)

This act follows straight on from Act Three (quick change).

In the text: 'Dom Juan's room'. Set: Dom Juan's room with left-hand side hidden by large curtain (characters appear from behind it); right-hand side: large window revealing starlit night.

All action on forestage. Only starlit night in background.

Act Five (Evening)

In the text: 'Pastoral landscape'. Set: forestage empty; upstage: pastoral scene (painted screens and practicable props). On the line dividing the two stage areas a place ready for the Statue to lead Dom Juan down to his immolation.

Towards the end of Scene Three the sky on the backdrop is darkened (perhaps it clouds over) to make a more effective scene of the immolation and the flash of lightning which coincides with the thunder in the finale.

A decorated screen stands on the line dividing the two stage areas and is unfolded or removed to satisfy the varying requirements of each scene . . .

> [From a letter from Meyerhold to Golovin, 30 May 1909.
> Quoted in *Alexander Yakovlevich Golovin*,
> Leningrad and Moscow, 1960, pp. 159–60.]

NOTE   The first passage, published in *O Teatre*, is dated 1910.

    The Ancient Theatre, headed by Nikolai Yevreinov and Baron Driesen, opened in Petersburg in 1907 with a repertoire containing medieval miracles, moralities and farces, together with Adam de la Halle's pastorale,

Robin and Marion. A second season (1911–12) was devoted mainly to the Spanish theatre of the seventeenth century (Calderon, Lope de Vega, Tirso de Molina). In his article (see footnote p. 98 above) Meyerhold praised the project, but deplored the parodistic style of the productions and the failure to preserve the essential conventions of the theatres in question.

Meyerhold's proposals in his letter to Golovin differ only in certain details from the eventual production. In its final form the setting comprised a series of borders, decreasing in aperture and framing a backdrop placed just beyond the proscenium arch. The backdrop changed to convey the place of action (see illustration facing p. 65). The 'Schattenspiel' idea was abandoned. Two candelabra on the forestage were lit by the blackamoors some time before the start of the performance.

The play was accompanied by music from Rameau's *Hippolyte et Aricie* and *Les Indes galantes*.

The notion of the 'mask' was explored by Meyerhold for the first time in this production. He expounds it with special reference to the character of Dom Juan in his essay, *The Fairground Booth* (see pp. 132–3 below).

---

3. *Orpheus* at the Marinsky Theatre

The opera was performed in the version published in 1900 by A. Durand et Fils. This version was based on Gluck's revision for the Paris Opera written ten years after its first performance in Vienna (1762), with the role of Orpheus, composed originally for contralto, adapted for tenor. (The first performance of this version took place in the presence of the composer in 1774 with Le Gros singing the part of Orpheus. A further version with the part of Orpheus again scored for contralto dates from 1859.) . . .

We might have staged the opera in costumes identical to those used in Gluck's time, or alternatively we might have created a perfect illusion of Classical antiquity. Both approaches seemed wrong to the designer and the director, since Gluck himself had contrived a skilful blend of realism and stylization. At the Marinsky Theatre the work was viewed, so to speak, through the prism of the age in which the composer lived and worked. Everything was designed in the style of antiquity as it had been conceived by artists in the eighteenth century.

Technically speaking, the stage was divided rigidly into two planes: the proscenium, which remained devoid of painted scenery and was decorated exclusively with embroidered hangings; and the main stage, which was given over entirely to painted sets. Particular attention was paid to the so-called 'planes of action': practicable rostra deployed in such a way as to dictate the groupings and movements of the characters. For example, in Scene Two the descent of Orpheus into Hades takes place on a path descending steeply across the stage from a considerable height with two sheer cliffs falling away to either side and downstage of it. This arrangement of the planes of action ensures that the figure of Orpheus dominates the chorus of Furies and does not become confused with them. With these cliffs on either side of the stage, the only possibility is to have the chorus and the *corps de ballet* in two groups straining upwards from the wings towards Orpheus. In this way, the scene at the Threshold of Hades is not chopped up into a number of episodes but becomes a synthesis of two directly opposed movements: Orpheus descending, and the Furies first meeting him menacingly then retreating before him.

For the scene in Elysium the chorus was placed offstage in order to avoid the customary disharmony of movement between those two still disparate elements, the chorus and the *corps de ballet*. Had the chorus remained on stage, the spectator would immediately have noticed the one group dancing and the other singing, whereas in Elysium the homogeneous group of 'les ombres heureuses' demands of the performers a uniform degree of plasticity.

In Act Three, Scene Two, after Eros has resurrected Eurydice and sung the final line of his recitative 'je viens vous retirer de cet affreux séjour, jouissez désormais des plaisirs de l'amour!' he leads Orpheus and Eurydice from the rocky heights upstage (constructed from practicable rostra) forward on to the stylized carpet of the proscenium. When Orpheus, Eurydice and Eros step on to the forestage, the landscape behind is hidden by the main curtain and the final trio is sung as a concert piece. During the trio the setting for the 'Ascent from Hades' is replaced behind the curtain with the setting for the Apotheosis, which is revealed on a signal from Eros immediately following the conclusion of the trio.

[Meyerhold's *O Teatre*, cit., pp. 203-5.]

NOTE   A second version of these notes which survives in manuscript form was published in *Alexander Yakovlevich Golovin*, cit., pp. 162-3. It does not differ materially from the text included here, and appears to have been written shortly before the première of *Orpheus* in 1911.

Part Three

DOCTOR DAPERTUTTO

1908-1917

MEYERHOLD WAS NOT LONG without a theatre in which to pursue his experiments with new dramatic forms. In December 1908 he was invited to collaborate in the opening of an intimate theatre housed in the Petersburg Theatre Club. Called 'Lukomore' ('The Strand'), it was modelled on Ernst von Wolzogen's 'Überbrettl' in Berlin[1] and Nikita Baliev's late-night theatre club, 'The Bat', which had opened in Moscow earlier that year. But the theatre was a failure; the lengthy programme of one-act pieces, which included an adaptation of Poe's *Fall of the House of Usher*, proved far too earnest for the informal club atmosphere and was taken off after less than a week. In a letter to Gurevich, the theatre critic of the newspaper *Slovo*, Meyerhold wrote:

> The group is forming an 'Intimate Theatre Society'. Our immediate task is to create an artistic 'balagan' [lit. 'fairground booth']. Away from the fug of the gaming-house – which is all the Theatre Club really is – our balagan will be able to flourish in an atmosphere unpolluted by the belches (pardon my vulgarity) of clubmen. Wait and see – our group will create a haven of rest for the cultured Petersburg theatregoer.[2]

It was to be two years before Meyerhold realized this ambition at the Interlude House, but the failure of the Lukomore did not inhibit his activities outside the Imperial theatres. On 19 February 1909 the Liteiny Theatre presented *The Lady from the Box*, a melodrama adapted by him from a story of circus life by the Danish writer, Herman Bang. With its portrayal of circus performers and its melodramatic conventions, it reflected Meyerhold's increasing interest in all forms of popular entertainment.

By this time, too, his literary output was growing. As well as the five pieces called collectively *On the History and Technique of the Theatre* which appeared in the anthology *Teatr – kniga o novom teatre* in 1908,[3] he published a review of Max Reinhardt's work at the Berliner Kammerspiele[4]

---

[1] See p. 136 below.
[2] 12 December 1908, quoted in Nikolai Volkov, op. cit vol. 2, p. 39.
[3] These pieces comprise Part One above.
[4] *Vesy*, 1907, no. 6. Also in Meyerhold's *O Teatre*, Petersburg, 1913, pp. 83–89.

and a short biographical sketch of Edward Gordon Craig.[1] In this latter
piece Meyerhold stresses that he was totally unaware of Craig's book,
The Art of the Theatre, at the time of the Theatre-Studio in Moscow
(Summer 1905).[2] It was in Berlin in April 1907 that he first encountered
Craig's theories in an article published in German as *Etwas über den
Regisseur und die Bühenausstattung* and identified their influence in Reinhardt's production of Maeterlinck's *Aglavaine and Selyzette*.[3] Together
with his article on Craig, Meyerhold published in the same journal translations from the German of *Etwas über den Regisseur und die Bühnenausstattung*[4] and *Uber Bühnenausstattung*.[5]

In the autumn of 1909 he was prompted by his interest in the Oriental
theatre to translate from German the Japanese Kabuki tragedy *Terakoya*,
which was performed subsequently at the Liteiny Theatre (but not produced by Meyerhold). At this time, Meyerhold added to the work of
stage-director, writer and translator the task of teaching acting technique
at the Pollak School of Music, Drama and Opera. In November 1909 his
pupils presented a programme of extracts from eight plays; they employed
mime and movement to emphasize the salient points of the scenario to
which each extract was reduced, whilst dialogue played only a subordinate
role.

The method which Meyerhold adopted to revive the spirit of Molière in
Dom Juan at the Alexandrinsky Theatre was explored by him first in a
private production of Calderon's *Adoration of the Cross* in April 1910. It
was performed by a cast of poets and writers at the makeshift 'Tower
Theatre' in the home of the poet Vyacheslav Ivanov. Meyerhold's aim was
not to depict thirteenth-century Siena as prescribed in the text, but rather
to evoke the primitive theatre of Calderon's day. To this end, Sudeikin,
the designer, improvised a setting from the rich hangings provided by
Ivanov. The front curtain was operated by two little liveried blackamoors,
prototypes for the 'proscenium servants' in *Dom Juan*. The stage, on the
same level as the auditorium, was well suited to the calculated naïvete of
Meyerhold's production, and enabled the cast to make their exits and
entrances through the auditorium. In the same naïve manner the actors
used the curtains to conceal themselves and simulated a field by spreading

---

[1] *Zhurnal Literaturno – khudozhestvennogo obshchestva*, Petersburg, 1909–10,
no. 9. Also in *O Teatre*, cit., pp. 90–93. For a short appraisal of Meyerhold by
Craig, see his article 'The Russian Theatre Today' in *The London Mercury*,
October 1935 (vol. 32, no 192).
[2] *O Teatre*, p. 91.   [3] Ibid., p. 86.
[4] Published in *Deutsche Kunst und Dekoration*, 1904–5, July.
[5] Published in *Kunst und Künstler*, 1904, Heft II.

a carpet in full view of the spectators. It was Meyerhold's first essay in the style which became known as 'traditionalism'.

In Autumn 1910 the 'artistic balagan' where Meyerhold was hoping to stage his experimental productions finally opened; called the Interlude House and run by the 'Fellowship of Actors, Writers, Musicians and Artists', it was housed in the former Skazka Theatre. The footlights were removed, the tiny stage joined to the auditorium by a flight of steps, and the rows of seats replaced by restaurant tables. As well as a late-night cabaret, the organizers aimed to present a varied repertoire including ancient and modern farces, comedies, pantomimes and operettas. The Interlude House opened on 9 October 1910 with a programme comprising a musical comedy, *The Reformed Eccentric*, a pastorale, *Liza, the Dutch Girl*, a burlesque, *Black and White – a Negro Tragedy*, and a production by Meyerhold of Arthur Schnitzler's pantomime, *The Veil of Pierrette*, with music by Dohnany and costumes and settings by Sapunov. The first three items provoked reactions varying from indifference to derision, but Meyerhold's production remained a haunting memory for those present. Freely adapted by himself, the work bore scant resemblance to the original, and even the title was altered to *Columbine's Scarf*. The aim was to banish the cloying sweetness so often associated with pantomime and create a chilling grotesque in the manner of E. T. A. Hoffmann. The three scenes were broken down into fourteen fleeting episodes, in order that the spectator should be shocked by the constant switches of mood into an unquestioning acceptance of the play's own ghastly logic. This episodic structure, ideally suited to the disorientating effects of the grotesque, was used by Meyerhold again in *Masquerade* and in nearly all his productions in the twenties, most notably *The Forest* and *The Government Inspector*. As he later observed in his lecture *Chaplin and Chaplinism* (see p. 322 below), this method derives from the same psychological premise as cinematic montage.

Here is an eye-witness description of the scenario of *Columbine's Scarf*:

The frivolous Columbine, betrothed to Harlequin, spends a last evening with her devoted Pierrot. As usual, she deceives him, swearing she loves him. Pierrot proposes a suicide pact and himself drinks poison. Columbine lacks the courage to follow him and flees in terror to the wedding ball where the guests await her impatiently. The ball begins, then whilst an old-fashioned quadrille is playing, Pierrot's flapping white sleeve is glimpsed first through the windows, then through the doors. The dances, now fast, now slow, turn into an awful nightmare, with strange Hoffmanesque characters whirling to the time of a huge-headed Kapellmeister, who sits on a high stool and conducts four weird musicians. Columbine's terror reaches such a pitch that she can hide it no longer and she rushes back to Pierrot. Harlequin follows her and when he sees Pierrot's corpse he is convinced of his bride's infidelity. He forces her to dine before the corpse of the love-stricken Pierrot. Then he leaves, bolting the door fast. In vain Columbine tries to escape from her prison, from the ghastly dead body. Gradually, she succumbs to madness; she whirls in a frenzied dance, then finally drains the deadly cup and falls lifeless beside Pierrot.[1]

The rhythm of the entire production was dictated by the hideous Kapell-meister and his sinister band. When finally the corpses of Pierrot and Columbine were discovered he fled in terror through the auditorium, as though acknowledging his manipulation of the tragedy. Just as in *Masquerade* six years later, the luckless victims seemed to have been marked down by some devilish power from which there was no escape.

In making great play with objects as an aid to mime (a letter, a rose, a glove, the fatal cup), Meyerhold paid implicit homage to the *commedia dell' arte* from which the principal characters were drawn. Of similar traditional origin was the extension of the action into the auditorium when the strange figure of Gigolo,[2] the master of ceremonies, led the motley wedding guests in a nightmarish polka round the tables of the spectators.

Columbine's Scarf also saw the reappearance of the blackamoor proscenium servant who was soon to figure so prominently in *Dom Juan*. On this occasion there was one only, who came on during the play to invite the audience to take refreshment.

The second programme of the Interlude House (3 December 1910) included Meyerhold's production of Znosko-Borovsky's new comedy, *The Transfigured Prince* (designs by Sudeikin, music by Kuzmin). Meyerhold himself, in *The Fairground Booth* (p. 140 below), describes some of the devices used in this production to achieve what Pushkin called 'stylized improbability'. The play's author describes the battle scene:

> Sudeikin's setting in clashing fiery red and gold gave the spectator an impression of raging blood and fire, which was intensified by terrifying rumblings and explosions backstage. An actor dressed as a warrior crawled from underneath the set – thereby emphasizing that the theatre was only simulating a battle, and dispelling any illusion of a real battle that the audience might have – and began to give a graphic picture of a violent conflict between two vast armies. As he spoke, shots rang out and bullets and cannonballs flew; eventually he took flight, tumbled down the steps and hid under the first available table. Recovering his breath, he said: 'I should imagine I'll be safer here.' However, the continuing gunfire drove him from that refuge as well and finally he fled from the theatre, crying: 'Every man for himself!'[3]

This second programme of the Interlude House proved its last; yet in his two short-lived productions in that modest little theatre Meyerhold

[1] Yevgeny Znosko-Borovsky, *Russky teatr nachala XX veka*, Prague, 1925, pp. 311–12.

[2] For Meyerhold's description of Gigolo, see p. 140 below.

[3] Ye. Znosko-Borovsky, op. cit., p. 303.

achieved a synthesis of theatrical elements and an understanding of the spectator's role in the performance which spoke of a new awareness of the possibilities of 'total theatre'.

Whilst Meyerhold was working on *Columbine's Scarf* he was asked by Telyakovsky, Director of Imperial Theatres, to adopt a pseudonym for his private theatrical activities, as they constituted a breach of contract and might cause mutual embarrassment. At the suggestion of the composer and poet, Mikhail Kuzmin, he took the name of 'Doctor Dapertutto', a character from E. T. A. Hoffmann's *Adventure on New Year's Eve* (in *Fantasiestücke in Callot's Manier*, Part 2). Doctor Dapertutto was a real-life manifestation of the mask, a ubiquitous Doppelgänger who assumed responsibility for all Meyerhold's experiments in the eccentric and the supernatural for the rest of his time at the Imperial theatres.

In October 1911 an unsuccessful attempt was made to revive the Interlude House with a short season in Moscow. But rather than abandon his experiments in *commedia dell' arte*, Meyerhold formed a pantomime group with Vladimir Solovyov, whose harlequinade, *Harlequin, the Marriage Broker*, they performed in various versions throughout that winter.[1]

June 1912 saw the creation of a new Fellowship of Actors, Writers, Musicians and Artists at the seaside resort of Terijoki just over the Finnish border. Under the artistic directorship of Meyerhold, the young company performed at the Casino Theatre in a repertoire which ranged from Shaw's *You Never Can Tell* and Strindberg's *Crimes and Crimes* to comic interludes by Cervantes and new productions of *The Adoration of the Cross* and *Harlequin, the Marriage Broker*. The company gave only occasional performances and the easy regimen enabled Meyerhold to complete his essay *The Fairground Booth*, which, together with his earlier theatrical writings (published and unpublished), appeared in 1913 under the title *O Teatre* (On the Theatre). In his introduction (dated November 1912) Meyerhold names *The Fairground Booth*, *Columbine's Scarf* and *Dom Juan* as the decisive productions in his first ten years as a stage-director, and acknowledges the vital contributions of the two designers, Golovin and Sapunov. Unhappily, the summer at Terijoki was marred by the death of Sapunov from drowning – he was 32.

At the start of the 1913–14 season Meyerhold resumed his pedagogical activities, this time in a studio of his own on Troitskaya Street.[2] The organization, curricula and public performances of the Studio are described in the extracts from Doctor Dapertutto's journal, *Lyubov k tryom apel-*

---

[1] See Meyerhold's description on pp. 144–6 below.
[2] The following year the Studio moved to Borodinskaya Street.

sinam, included below. The publication took its name from Carlo Gozzi's 'fiaba teatrale', *The Love of Three Oranges,* of which a free adaptation by Meyerhold, Solovyov and Vogak appeared in the first number.[1] Meyerhold and his friends took Gozzi as their exemplar, since it was he who had revived the declining *commedia dell' arte* in the eighteenth century with fairy-tale plays which combined the conventions of the literary and the improvised theatres.

The editorial board of *The Love of Three Oranges* was responsible for the double bill comprising Blok's *Unknown Woman* and *Fairground Booth* which was performed seven times at the Tenishev Academy (now the Leningrad State Theatre Institute) in April 1914. Meyerhold denied that they were Studio productions, but the majority of the actors were pupils and even the scenery was prepared by them. The Academy amphitheatre was specially converted to resemble a Greek classical theatre with a semi-circular 'orchestra' and shallow 'skena'. On this occasion Meyerhold incorporated a number of devices from the Oriental theatre in order to blow the gaff of theatrical illusion. Here is an eyewitness account of *The Unknown Woman*:

> The opening scene takes place in a tavern. A number of actors with no parts in the play acted as 'proscenium servants' with the task of scene-shifting. Dressed in special unobtrusive costumes and moving rhythmically, they brought on tables, stools, a bar, and to the rear raised a green curtain on bamboo poles. Then in half-darkness the actors appeared, carrying bottles and glasses which they tried to place unobtrusively on the tables; they took their seats and after a momentary silence began to laugh softly, creating a buzz of conversation to draw the public into the atmosphere of a tavern. One of the servants sat down on the floor close at hand, ready to act as prompter if need be, but only if someone really forgot his lines. When the scene ended there was a roll of drums and the servants who had been holding up the curtain walked forward, stretching the curtain above the actors and then lowering it to hide them from the audience whilst they removed all the properties from the stage. Then the proscenium servants behind the curtain climbed on to stools and raised their end of it to expose the white, reverse side to the audience. Meanwhile, directly in front of the platform other servants rolled on from either side the two component parts of a wooden bridge, and on the platform a further group erected a new curtain of blue gauze with gold stars. So finally, when the white curtain was lowered, the audience saw a hump-backed bridge against a sky sprinkled with stars. As the actors mounted the bridge, the servants waved tarlatan veils in front of them to represent a snowy, starlit night. When a star was supposed to fall, all the chandeliers [in the hall] were extinguished and one of the servants lit a simple sparkler on a long pole which another raised right to the ceiling and then lowered for the first to extinguish in water; then the chandeliers came on again.

[1] It was Meyerhold who in 1918 gave Prokofiev the idea for the opera of the same name which is based on this translation. Cf. *Sergei Prokofiev 1953–1963,* Moscow, 1962, pp. 92–93.

The last scene, a 'grotesque' representation of a drawing room in varying shades of yellow, was enacted on the platform itself. In front of it knelt the proscenium servants, holding candles to parody footlights. On a table were exaggeratedly artificial fruits and flowers which the actor-guests themselves removed as they went off. There was also a door onstage leading nowhere (to an entrance hall?), through which the guests entered, throwing off their overcoats and joining in a conversation in which some were audible, others not.

When the time came for the Unknown Woman to disappear, she simply went off between the wing curtains whilst a proscenium servant lit a blue star on a pole and held it in the window. To a roll of drums, the curtain fell once more on the furniture and it was borne away like the sailing ships mentioned in the text. The play was over.[1]

In the tavern scene all the men had red false noses (some wore green or red and yellow striped wigs) and the women had bright, red-painted cheeks like wooden dolls. The Man in Blue's voluminous cloak was constantly arranged by one of the proscenium servants. The Unknown Woman had huge painted eyelashes.

For *The Fairground Booth* the booth was represented by blue canvas screens behind the platform and paper lanterns suspended from strings above the acting area. Meyerhold retained the device of the cardboard cut-out Mystics from his earlier production of the play (see p. 141 below). The same proscenium servants were used.

During the interval there was a performance by an itinerant troupe of Chinese jugglers which Meyerhold had come across in Petersburg, and the cast threw real oranges to the audience.

Blok, who had been enchanted by the original production of *The Fairground Booth* in 1906, was now out of sympathy with 'Meyerholdia', preferring 'healthy realism, Stanislavsky, and musical drama'.[2] But although he regarded the Tenishev productions merely as curious experiments, his plays, with their dizzy swoops from the exalted lyric of one line to the broad burlesque of the next, demanded a flexibility of interpretation which at that time Meyerholdian theatricalism alone could encompass. The productions demonstrated the full extent of Meyerhold's assimilation of the spirit and techniques of the Kabuki and Nō theatres, which lent his style at once a new freedom and a new discipline.

The coming of war did not halt the activities of the Studio, but its impact was reflected in the increasingly irregular appearances of *The Love of Three Oranges*. The combined sixth and seventh issue for 1914 (published in February 1915), contained a patriotic play by Meyerhold, Solovyov and Yury Bondi entitled *Fire*. Based on actual events on the Belgian front, the

---

[1] Ye. Znosko-Borovsky in *Sovremennik*, Petersburg, 1914, June, pp. 120–1.
[2] Alexander Blok, *Zapisnie knizhki* 1901–1920, Moscow, 1965, p. 209.

work is a scenario in eight scenes with an apotheosis, and is designed to leave full scope for improvisation. Although never performed, it bears a close resemblance to another agitatory work, *The Earth in Turmoil*, produced by Meyerhold in 1923. In particular, the stage directions for *Fire* ('a series of iron girders and beams, with the centre occupied by an observation platform joined by a system of catwalks to the invisible foundations of the whole structure. On the platform a series of levers for controlling a complex system of dykes . . .')[1] strikingly anticipate Popova's gantry construction for the later production.

The official public début of the Studio took place on 12 February 1915.[2] For the occasion the Borodinskaya Street auditorium was arranged to resemble in miniature the amphitheatre used for the Blok plays. The thirty-one Studio 'comédiens' were dressed in two uniform styles of costume, one for the actors and one for the actresses. The programme was repeated twice more in March before the season closed. That summer Meyerhold made his first film, *The Picture of Dorian Gray*, to be followed in 1916 by *The Strong Man*.

War forced the curtailment of the 1915–16 season and the Studio gave no further public performances. Consequently Meyerhold's dream of staging a full-length production of *Hamlet* with his pupils was never realized, and after one further season the Studio closed in Spring 1917. Although it never yielded the permanent company which Meyerhold had hoped for, the four seasons gave him the chance to consolidate his ideas in practice, and laid the basis for both the style and the company which he created in Moscow after the Civil War.

In 1915 Boris Pronin, the impresario of the old Interlude House, opened a new intimate cellar theatre called 'The Comedians' Rest', and it was there in April 1916 that Meyerhold presented a new version of *Columbine's Scarf*. However, Sudeikin's designs suffered badly in comparison with Sapunov's and the production was not a success, the one interesting feature being a rudimentary flying ballet performed by Harlequin on a wire suspended from the flies.

On this muted note the public career of Doctor Dapertutto closed, but unlike many of his kind he did not emigrate after 1917, and even in the most arid years of Socialist Realism he never strayed far from Comrade Meyerhold's elbow.

[1] *Lyubov k tryom apeisinam*, 1914, no 6–7, p. 50.
[2] For Meyerhold's account, see pp. 149–51 below.

1. The Fairground Booth

I

'The mystery-play in the Russian theatre' – thus Benois entitles one of his *Letters on the Arts*.[1] One might assume that he was writing about a production of one of Alexei Remizov's plays based on the tradition of the medieval spectacle, or perhaps that Scriabin had realized one of his dreams and Benois was hastening to announce to the world the greatest-ever event in the history of the Russian stage, the appearance of a new scenic form based on the mystery-rites of Ancient Greek culture.

However, it transpires that the Russian mystery-play has been achieved not by Remizov, not by Scriabin, but, according to Benois, by the Moscow Art Theatre with its production of *The Brothers Karamazov*.[2]

It is certainly not from the Greek 'mysterion' that Benois derives the word 'mystery'. Nobody is likely to suspect him of discerning the heritage of the marvellous Eleusinian mysteries in this production.

Perhaps Benois' mystery is closer to the 'ministerium'. But what traces of the medieval mystery are there to be found here? Perhaps the production of *The Brothers Karamazov* contains both the catharsis of the Ancient Greek mystery and the sermonizing and vivid illustrativeness of the medieval mystery?

There are elements of catharsis and sermonizing present in Dostoevsky's novel, but they are contained in the inspired structure of the thesis and antithesis (God and the Devil). Zosima and Karamazovism, the symbols of divinity and diabolism, are the two inseparable foundation stones of the novel. On the stage the plot's centre of gravity is transferred to Mitya. Dostoevsky's basic triad of Zosima, Alyosha and Ivan has disappeared, and with it their interrelationship. In this form *The Brothers Karamazov* is simply a dramatized fable of the novel, or, more precisely, of a few chapters from the novel. Such an adaptation of a novel into a play seems to us nothing less than blasphemous, not only with regard to Dostoevsky, but, if the adapters were aiming to write a mystery-play, with regard to the idea of the true mystery-play as well.

If we are really in search of a Russian mystery-play, from whom can we expect it if not from Remizov or Scriabin? But then the question arises: Is

[1] In the newspaper *Rech*, Petersburg, 27 April 1912. [Meyerhold's note.]
[2] Première: 12 October 1910; production: Nemirovich-Danchenko.

119

the time ripe? And a further question: Is the theatre able to accommodate the mystery-play?

Scriabin's first symphony sang a hymn of praise to art as a religion; his third revealed the power of the free spirit and the affirmation of self; in the *Poem of Ecstasy* man is consumed with joy at the realization that he has traversed the thorny path unscathed and his hour of creation has arrived. In these works Scriabin has gathered material of no small worth and fit for the grand ritual called the mystery in which music, dance, light and the intoxicating scent of field flowers and herbs all blend into a grand harmony. When one realizes the miraculous speed with which Scriabin has progressed from the first symphony to *Prometheus*, one feels confident that he is ready to present the mystery to the world.[1] But since *Prometheus* has failed to elicit a concerted response from the contemporary audience, why should Scriabin want to present a mystery-play to them? It is not surprising that the author of *Prometheus* is drawn to the banks of the Ganges. The audience for his mystery-play is lacking; he has yet to gather around him a circle of true believers and devotees.

Whenever the question of presenting mystery-plays to a wide public is raised I feel prompted to cite two examples from the history of the French theatre which we would do well to heed.

'Les Confrères de la Passion'[2] adhered strictly to the precepts of the original mystery, and so were obliged to remain within the closed community of the Holy Trinity, performing only before the initiated.

'Les Clercs de la Basoche'[3] resorted to the principles of mummery and went out into the streets. It was there, in the intimate relationship between the histrion and his public, that the true theatre was created.

The two forms of public performance, the mystery and the theatrical entertainment, have become totally divorced from each other. Yet in Russia there is stubborn refusal to admit the gulf which separates them.

Remizov's *Devil Play*[4] is put on in a theatre where only yesterday the audience was thrilled by that veritable wizard of theatricality, the author of *The Fairground Booth*.[5] Maybe a section of the audience hissed Blok and his actors, but his theatre was still theatre. And perhaps the very fact that the audience felt free to hoot so violently demonstrates better than any-

[1] Scriabin's mystery play, *The Preliminary Act*, which he dreamt of presenting by the side of the Ganges, remained uncompleted on his death in 1915.

[2] Founded in 1402.

[3] Founded in 1302.

[4] Produced by Fyodor Komissarzhevsky at his sister's theatre in December 1907.

[5] Produced by Meyerhold in 1906; see p. 21 above.

thing that the reaction was a reaction to a performance of true theatricality. Remizov's neo-mystery, like any mystery, demands an entirely different attitude on the part of the spectator, yet they behaved in exactly the same way as they did at *The Fairground Booth*. How could Remizov have risked exposing his *Devil Play* in the auditorium where with one wave of his magic wand Blok was able to create an atmosphere of true theatricality?

I am convinced that until the writers of neo-mysteries sever their connections with the theatre, until they quit the theatre altogether, the mystery will continue to obstruct the theatre, and the theatre – the mystery.

Andrei Bely is right. Reviewing the symbolist theatre of today, he comes to the conclusion: 'Let the theatre remain the theatre, and the mystery – the mystery.' Well aware of the danger of mixing two contrasting genres and of the total impossibility of reviving the mystery-play so long as religion remains in its present stagnant condition, he wants to see 'the restoration of the traditional theatre in all its humble dignity'.[1]

The restoration of the traditional theatre is hampered by the alliance which the public itself has formed with those so-called dramatists who turn literature for reading into literature for the theatre – as though the public's attitude to the theatre were not confused enough already. By describing the production of *The Brothers Karamazov* as a mystery-play, Benois is only adding to this confusion and obstructing the revival of the traditional theatre. Clearly he has been driven almost to distraction by the chaos from which the contemporary theatre is totally incapable of extricating itself for lack of energetic people capable of forcing the division of the theatre which took place in old Paris. How else can one account for his calling a performance which has nothing in common with the mystery 'a spectacle of a truly religious nature'?

However, a few more lines from the same letter contain the key – if not to Benois' conception of the mystery, then at least to his attitude towards the theatre as theatre. He writes: 'And so I repeat that, like Mitya, the Art Theatre cannot lie.' And further: 'Everything which the Comédie Française is doing, everything which Reinhardt and Meyerhold might yet do – that is all deception and "cabotinage", and is beyond the reach of the Art Theatre.'

Benois attaches a derogatory meaning to the word 'cabotinage'. He

[1] Andrei Bely, 'Teatr i sovremennaya drama' in *Teatr, kniga o novom teatre,* cit., pp. 288, 289.

seems to be reproaching somebody with the prevalence of some harmful element in the theatre. In Benois' opinion, those concerned in the reform of the contemporary stage are deceiving the public by creating some fictitious renovated theatre. The Moscow Art Theatre alone, in his opinion, 'cannot lie'. He regards the introduction of 'cabotinage' into the world of the theatre as a deception; 'it is all deception and "cabotinage" ', and is beyond their (i.e. the directors of the Moscow Art Theatre) 'reach' because 'they cannot lie'.

But is a theatre without cabotinage possible? And what is this cabotinage that is so detested by Benois? The cabotin is a strolling player; the cabotin is a kinsman to the mime, the histrion, and the juggler; the cabotin can work miracles with his technical mastery; the cabotin keeps alive the tradition of the true art of acting. It was with his help that the Western theatre came to full flower in the theatres of Spain and Italy in the seventeenth century. Whilst acknowledging the mystery and welcoming its revival on the Russian stage, Benois speaks disparagingly of cabotinage as some sort of evil; yet the mystery players themselves sought the help of the cabotins. The cabotin was to be found wherever there was any sort of dramatic presentation, and the organizers of mystery-plays relied on them to perform all the most difficult tasks. From the history of the French theatre we know that the mystery-player was incapable of performing without the help of the juggler. During the reign of Philippe le Bel[1] farce suddenly made an unexpected appearance amongst the religious subjects in the form of the bawdy adventures of Renart.[2] Who but the cabotins were capable of performing this farce? With the gradual development of processional mysteries there appeared more and more new plots which demanded of the performer an ever-widening range of technical accomplishments. The solution of the complex problems posed by the mystery-plays fell on the shoulders of the cabotins. Thus we see that cabotinage was common even in the mystery-plays and the cabotin played a decisive part in their development.

Having sensed its own inadequacy, the mystery began gradually to absorb the elements of popular entertainment as personified by the mummers, and was forced to go from the ambo, through the parvis into the churchyard, and thence out on to the market-place. Whenever the mystery play tried to come to terms with the theatre, it was bound to resort to the principles of mummery, and no sooner had it reached a

[1] Philippe IV, King of France 1285–1314.
[2] Renart the Fox, in *Le Roman de Renart*, a collection of poems written in the twelfth and thirteenth centuries in which all the characters are animals.

compromise with the art of the actor than it was absorbed by this art and ceased to be a mystery-play.

Perhaps it has always been so: if there is no cabotin, there is no theatre either; and, contrariwise, as soon as the theatre rejects the basic rules of theatricality it straightway imagines that it can dispense with the cabotin.

Apparently, Benois regards the mystery as the means of arresting the decline of the Russian theatre, and cabotinage as the cause of it. I hold the opposite view: it is 'the mystery' (in Benois' sense) which is ruining the theatre and cabotinage which can bring about its revival. In order to rescue the Russian theatre from its own desire to become the servant of literature, we must spare nothing to restore to the stage the cult of cabotinage in its broadest sense.

But how can this be done? First of all, it seems to me that we should apply ourselves to the study and restoration of those theatres of the past in which the cult of cabotinage once held sway.

Our dramatists have no idea at all of the laws of true theatre. In the Russian theatre of the nineteenth century the old vaudeville was replaced by a flood of plays of brilliant dialectic, plays à thèse, plays of manners, plays of mood. . . .[1]

The story-teller employs fewer and fewer descriptive passages, enlivens his narrative by allocating more and more dialogue to his characters, and eventually invites the reader into an auditorium. Has the story-teller any need of the cabotin? Of course not. The readers themselves can go up on to the stage and read the dialogue of their favourite author role-by-role out loud to the public. This is what is meant by 'an affectionate rendering of the play'. No time has been lost in finding a name for the reader turned actor, for now we have the term 'the intellectual actor'. The same deathly hush prevails in the auditorium as in the reading-room of a library and it

---

[1] I mention the old vaudeville not because we must necessarily revive it in the theatre; rather, I quote it as a dramatic form which is linked on the one hand with theatrical – as opposed to literary – traditions, and on the other with the tastes of the people. Remember that the vaudeville came to us from France and that the French vaudeville (*vide* Victor Fournel, *Les Spectacles populaires et artistes des rues*, Paris, 1863, pp. 320–1) originated as follows: 'For a long time an improvised popular theatre was functioning near the Porte St Jacques; the crowds flocked there to enjoy the humorous songs and sketches of three indefatigable wits, whose fame far outlived them. All three were baker's apprentices from Normandy who had come to Paris to try their luck, bringing to the capital the bold lively style of genuine Norman folksinging and acting, from which all France was later to derive its vaudeville. The whole town knew and loved them, and the names they took, Gaultier-Garguille, Gros-Guillaume and Turlupin, hold a lasting place in the history of French humour.' Thus we see that the vaudeville originated in the art of the folk song and the folk theatre. [Meyerhold's note.]

sends the public to sleep. The reading-room of a library is the only proper place for such gravity and immobility.

In order to make a dramatist out of a story-teller who writes for the stage, it would be a good idea to make him write a few pantomimes. The pantomime is a good antidote against excessive misuse of words. Only let the new author not fear that we want to deprive him altogether of the right to speak on the stage. He will be permitted to put words into the actor's mouths, but first he must produce *a scenario of movement*. How long will it be before they inscribe in the theatrical tables the following law: *words in the theatre are only embellishments on the design of movement?*

I read somewhere: 'Drama in reading is primarily dialogue, argument and taut dialectic. Drama on the stage is primarily action, a taut struggle. The words are, so to speak, the mere overtones of the action. They should burst spontaneously from the actor gripped in the elemental progress of the dramatic struggle.'

The organizers of medieval festivals of mystery-plays appreciated only too well the magical power of pantomime. In the French mysteries at the end of the fourteenth and the beginning of the fifteenth century the most moving scenes were invariably mimed. The characters' movements explained the play's meaning far better than any amount of argument in verse or prose.[1] Significantly it was not until the mystery-play had progressed from the dry rhetoric of religious ceremony to the new forms of spectacle, full of the elements of emotionality (first to the miracle, then to the morality, and finally to the farce), that the juggler and the mime appeared simultaneously on the stage.

The mime stops the mouth of the rhetorician who belongs not on the stage but in the pulpit; the juggler reveals the total self-sufficiency of the actor's skill with the expressiveness of his gestures and the language of his movements – not only in the dance but in his every step. Most important

---

[1] The question of the power and significance of mime recalls an episode from an earlier age: 'According to a certain Roman writer, a foreign monarch once witnessed at the court of Nero a pantomime in which a famous actor enacted all twelve labours of Hercules with such clarity and expression that the foreigner understood everything without a word of explanation. He was so amazed by this that he asked Nero to make a present to him of the actor. Nero was extremely surprised at such a request, but the guest explained that on the border of his kingdom there lived a savage people whose language nobody could understand and who, in their turn, could not understand what their neighbours wanted of them. By means of mime this famous actor could convey the king's demands to the savages without any risk of misunderstanding.' (*Dances, their history and development from antiquity to the present day*, Gaston Charles Vuillier, St Petersburg, 1902, p. 15.) [Meyerhold's note.]

to the juggler is a mask, then a few rags to brighten his costume, a little braid, a few feathers, a few bells, a little of everything to give the performance plenty of glitter and plenty of noise.

No matter how piously inclined the organizers of the religious shows were, they still had to have three naked girls to represent the sirens at the celebrations of the arrival of Louis XI; at the arrival of Queen Isabella of Bavaria the religious performance was accompanied by the good citizens enacting the great battle of King Richard against Saladin and the Saracens. At the arrival of Anne of Bavaria an actor representing the prologue addressed the crowd in verse.

Do we not see in all this the tendency to subordinate every spectacle to cabotinage? Symbolic figures, processions, battles, prologues, parades: they are all elements of that pure theatricality which even the mysteries could not do without.

It is to the heyday of cabotinage that one must look for the origins of the theatre. For example, the theatre at the Hospice of the Holy Trinity[1] developed not from the mystery-plays but from the street mummery performed during the processional arrivals of kings.

Nowadays the majority of stage-directors are turning to pantomime and prefer this form to verbal drama. This strikes me as more than a coincidence. It is not just a question of taste. In their attempts to propagate pantomime, directors are not merely attracted by the peculiar fascination which the genre possesses. In order to revive the theatre of the past contemporary directors are finding it necessary to begin with pantomime, because when these silent plays are staged they reveal to directors and actors the power of the primordial elements of the theatre: the power of the mask, gesture, movement and plot.

However the mask, gesture, movement and plot are ignored by the contemporary actor. He has lost sight of the traditions of the great masters of the art of acting. He no longer listens to what his elder colleagues have to say about the self-sufficiency of the actor's art.

In the contemporary theatre the comedian has been replaced by 'the educated reader'. 'The play will be read in costume and make-up' might as well be the announcement on playbills today. The new actor manages without the mask and the technique of the juggler. The mask has been replaced by make-up which facilitates the exact representation of every feature of the face as it is observed in real life. The actor has no need of the juggler's art, because he no longer 'plays' but simply 'lives' on the stage.

[1] The first permanent theatre of the Confrérie de la Passion, in which farce and mummery gradually encroached on the original mystery plays.

'Play-acting', that magic word of the theatre, means nothing to him, because as an imitator he is incapable of rising to the level of improvisation which depends on infinite combinations and variations of all the tricks at the actor's command.

The cult of cabotinage, which I am sure will reappear with the restoration of the theatre of the past, will help the modern actor to rediscover the basic laws of theatricality. Those who are restoring the old theatre by delving into long-forgotten theories of dramatic art, old theatrical records and iconography, are already forcing actors to believe in the power and the importance of the art of acting.

In the same way as the stylistic novelist resurrects the past by embellishing the works of ancient chroniclers with his own imagination, the actor is able to re-create the technique of forgotten comedians by consulting material collected by scholars.[1] Overjoyed at the simplicity, the refined grace, the extreme artistry of the old yet eternally new tricks of the histrions, mimi, atellanae, scurrae, jaculatores and ministrelli, the actor of the future should or, if he wishes to remain an actor, *must* co-ordinate his emotional responses with his technique, measuring both against the traditional precepts of the old theatre.

Whenever one speaks of the restoration of the old theatre one is told how tedious it is for contemporary dramatists to have to imitate the works of the past in order to compete with the entr'actes of Cervantes, the dramas of Tirso de Molina and the theatrical tales of Carlo Gozzi. But if the modern dramatist chooses not to copy the traditions of the old theatre, if

---

[1] Just consider what we can surmise from the stage direction: 'Enter Don Gutierre, as though jumping over a fence' (in Calderon's *Doctor of his own honour*). This 'as though' gives the actor a clear picture of the agility of his Spanish counterpart's entrance, whilst it helps the director to visualize the primitive stage setting of the time. Similarly, the director is helped by the following theatrical inventory dating from 1598:

Item: one cliff, one dungeon, one hell-mouth, one Dido's tomb.
Item: eight pits, one ladder for Phæton to ascend to heaven.
Item: two sponge-cakes and one city of Rome.
Item: one golden fleece, two gibbets, one laurel tree.
Item: one wooden vault of heaven, one head of the prophet Mahomet.
Item: three heads of Cerberus, snakes from *Faustus*, one lion, two lion's heads, one big horse with legs.
Item: one pair of red gloves, one papal mitre, three king's crowns, one scaffold for the execution of John.
Item: one pot for boiling the Jew.
Item: four sets of vestments for Herod, one green cloak for Mariamne, one jacket for Eve, one costume for the Holy Spirit and three Spanish noble's hats. [Meyerhold's note.]

for a while he withdraws from the theatre which is seeking its inspiration in antiquity, it will be all the better for the contemporary stage. The actor may get bored with perfecting his craft in order to perform in outdated plays; soon he will want not only to act but to compose for himself as well. Then at last we shall see the rebirth of *the theatre of improvisation*. Should the dramatist wish to help the actor in this, his role might seem at first glance to amount to very little; but he will quickly find that he is faced with the intricate task of composing scenarios and writing prologues containing a schematic exposition of what the actors are about to perform. Dramatists will not, I trust, feel degraded by this role. After all, Carlo Gozzi lost nothing at all by providing Sacchi's[1] troupe with scenarios which left the actors free to compose their own improvised monologues and dialogues.

I am asked why the theatre needs all these prologues, parades and so on. Isn't the scenario sufficient in itself?

The prologue and the ensuing parade, together with the direct address to the audience at the final curtain, so loved both by the Italians and Spaniards in the seventeenth century and by the French vaudevillistes, all force the spectator to recognize the actors' performance as pure play-acting. And every time the actor leads the spectators too far into the land of make-believe he immediately resorts to some unexpected sally or lengthy address *a parte* to remind them that what is being performed is only *a play*.

Whilst Remizov and Scriabin search for a place on market-squares ready to receive the new theatre, whilst their mysteries wait for the faithful to assemble, the theatre of the juggler will be waging a bitter struggle with the comedy of manners, the dialectic play, the play *à thèse* and the theatre of mood; the new *theatre of masks* will learn from the Spaniards and the Italians of the seventeenth century and build its repertoire according to the laws of the fairground booth, where entertainment always precedes instruction and where movement is prized more highly than words. Not for nothing was pantomime the favourite dramatic form of the Clercs de la Basoche.

Schlegel claims that the Greek raised pantomime to the ultimate level of perfection. M.K.[2] adds that 'only a people which practised the plastic arts with such success, only a country which contained so many statues,

---

[1] Antonio Giovanni Sacchi (1708–88), the last great exponent of *commedia dell' arte*. His company had great success performing Gozzi's fiabe in Venice in the 1760s.
[2] *Opyt istorii teatra*, Moscow, 1849, p. 136. [Meyerhold's note.]

where everything spoke of grace, could develop the pantomime to perfection'.

Even though we lack the sun and the sky of ancient Attica, surely we, too, can aspire to similar wonders of grace through the constant exercise of the art of pantomime?

II
TWO PUPPET THEATRES

The director of the first wants his puppets to look and behave like real men. Like an idolator who expects the idol to nod its head, this puppet-master wants his dolls to emit sounds resembling the human voice. In his attempts to reproduce reality 'as it really is', he improves the puppets further and further until finally he arrives at a far simpler solution to the problem: replace the puppets with real men.

The other director realizes that his audience enjoys not only the humorous plays which the puppets perform but also – and perhaps more important – their actual movements and poses which, despite all attempts to reproduce life on the stage, fail to resemble exactly what the spectator sees in real life.

Whenever I watch contemporary actors performing I am reminded of the sophisticated puppet theatre of the first director, that is, the theatre in which man has replaced the puppet. Here man strives just as hard as the puppet to imitate real life. The reason he is summoned to replace the puppet is that in copying reality he can do something which is beyond the puppet: he can achieve an exact representation of life.

The other director wanted to make his puppets imitate real people, too, but he quickly realized that as soon as he tried to improve the puppet's mechanism it lost part of its charm. It was as though the puppet were resisting such barbarous improvements with all its being. The director came to his senses when he realized that there is a limit beyond which there is no alternative but to replace the puppet with a man. But how could he part with the puppet which had created a world of enchantment with its incomparable movements, its expressive gestures achieved by some magic known to it alone, its angularity which reaches the heights of true plasticity?[1]

I have described these two puppet theatres in order to make the actor

[1] Cf. the comment on the cubist painter André Lhote in *Apollon*, 1912, no 6, p. 41: 'Having paid tribute to the florid, two-dimensional style of stained glass, the young artist became absorbed in *the rhythmical angularity of wood sculpture.*' [Meyerhold's note.]

consider whether he should assume the servile role of the puppet, which affords no scope for personal creativity, or whether he should create a theatre like the one where the puppet stood up for itself and did not yield to the director's efforts to transform it. The puppet did not want to become an exact replica of man, because the world of the puppet is a wonderland of make-believe, and the man which it impersonates is a make-believe man. The stage of the puppet theatre is a sounding board for the strings of the puppet's art. On this stage things are not as they are because nature is like that but because that is how the puppet wishes it – and it wishes not to copy but to create.

When the puppet weeps, the hand holds the handkerchief away from the eyes; when the puppet kills, it stabs its opponent so delicately that the tip of the sword stops short of the breast; when one puppet slaps another, no colour comes off the face; when puppet lovers embrace, it is with such care that the spectator observing their caresses from a respectful distance does not think to question his neighbour about the consequences.

When man appeared on the stage, why did he submit blindly to the director who wanted to transform the actor into a puppet of the naturalistic school? Man has yet to feel the urge to create *the art of man* on the stage.

The actor of today will not understand that the duty of the comedian and the mime is to transport the spectator to a world of make-believe, entertaining him on the way there with the brilliance of his technical skill.

The imaginary gesture valid only in the theatre, the stylized theatrical movement, the measured tones of theatrical declamation: they are all condemned by public and critics simply because the concept of 'theatricality' still bears the traces of the style of acting which was developed by the so-called 'inspirational actors'.

The inspirational actor is content to rely exclusively on his own mood. He refuses to bend his will to the discipline of technique. The inspirational actor proudly claims to have rekindled the flame of improvisation in the theatre. In his naïveté he imagines that his improvisations have something in common with the improvisations of traditional Italian comedy. He does not realize that the improvisations of the *commedia dell' arte* had a firm basis of faultless technique. The inspirational actor totally rejects technique of any kind. 'Technique hinders creative freedom' is what he always says. For him the only valid moment is the moment of unconscious creativity born of the emotions. If such a moment comes, he succeeds; if not, he fails.

Does the display of emotion really diminish the self-discipline of the actor? Real live men danced in plastic movements around the altar of Dionysus; their emotions seemed to burn uncontrollably, inflamed to

129

extreme ecstasy by the fire on the altar. Yet the ritual in honour of the god of wine was composed of predetermined rhythms, steps and gestures. That is one example of the actor's self-discipline unaffected by the display of emotion. In the dance the Greek was bound by a whole series of traditional rules, yet he was at liberty to introduce as much personal invention as he wished.

It is not just that the modern actor has no comprehension of the rules governing the art of comedy (art being, after all, that which is subject to laws or as Voltaire said: 'the dance is art because it is bound by laws');[1] he has reduced his art to the most alarming chaos. As if that were not enough, he considers it his bounden duty to introduce chaos into all the other art forms as soon as he lays hands on them. He takes music and violates its fundamental principles by inventing 'melodeclamation'.[2] When he reads poetry from the stage he heeds only the content of the verse, rearranging the logical stresses and ignoring completely every consideration of metre, rhythm, caesura, pause and musical intonation.

In his search for verisimilitude the actor of today concentrates on eliminating his 'self' and tries to create an illusion of life on the stage. Why do they bother to write actors' names on the playbills? In its production of Gorky's *Lower Depths*,[3] the Moscow Art Theatre brought a real tramp on to the stage in place of an actor. The pursuit of verisimilitude reached such a point that it was considered better to free the actor from the impossible task of creating a total illusion of life. Why did they print the name of the man playing Teterev[4] on the posters? Can a man who plays *himself* on the stage really be called a 'performer'? Why mislead the public?

The public comes to the theatre to see the art of man, but what art is there in walking about the stage as oneself? The public expects invention, play-acting and skill. But what it gets is either life or a slavish imitation of life. Surely the art of man on the stage consists in shedding all traces of environment, carefully choosing a mask, donning a decorative costume, and showing off one's brilliant tricks to the public – now as a dancer, now as the intrigant at some masquerade, now as the fool of old Italian comedy, now as a juggler.

---

[1] I quote from Levinson's brilliant article 'Noverre and the aesthetic of the ballet in the eighteenth century', *Apollon*, Petersburg, 1912, no 2. [Meyerhold's note.]

[2] The reading of verse and prose to musical accompaniment, popular in Russia in the second half of the nineteenth century.

[3] Première: 18 December 1902; production: Stanislavsky and Nemirovich-Danchenko.

[4] In Gorky's *Philistines* (1902). The part was played by a real church chorister.

If you examine the dog-eared pages of old scenarios such as Flaminio Scala's anthology,[1] you will discover the magical power of the mask.

Arlecchino, a native of Bergamo and the servant of the miserly Doctor, is forced to wear a coat with multicoloured patches because of his master's meanness. Arlecchino is a foolish buffoon, a roguish servant who seems always to wear a cheerful grin. But look closer! What is hidden behind the mask? Arlecchino, the all-powerful wizard, the enchanter, the magician; Arlecchino, the emissary of the infernal powers.

The mask may conceal more than just two aspects of a character. The two aspects of Arlecchino represent two opposite poles. Between them lies an infinite range of shades and variations. How does one reveal this extreme diversity of character to the spectator? With the aid of the mask.

The actor who has mastered the art of gesture and movement (herein lies his power!) manipulates his masks in such a way that the spectator is never in any doubt about the character he is watching: whether he is the foolish buffoon from Bergamo or the Devil.

This chameleonic power, concealed beneath the expressionless visage of the comedian, invests the theatre with all the enchantment of chiaroscuro. Is it not the mask which helps the spectator fly away to the land of make-believe?

The mask enables the spectator to see not only the actual Arlecchino before him but all the Arlecchinos who live in his memory. Through the mask the spectator sees every person who bears the merest resemblance to the character. But is it the mask alone which serves as the mainspring for all the enchanting plots of the theatre?

No, it takes the actor with his art of gesture and movement to transport the spectator to the fairy-tale kingdom where the blue-bird flies, where wild beasts talk, where Arlecchino, the loafer and knave sprung from subterranean forces, is reborn as a clown who performs the most astonishing tricks. Arlecchino is an equilibrist, almost a tightrope-walker. He can leap with amazing agility. His improvised pranks astonish the spectator with a hyperbolical improbability beyond even our satirists' dreams. The actor is a dancer who can dance a graceful monferrina as well as a hearty English jig. The actor can turn tears to laughter in a few seconds. He bears the fat Doctor on his shoulders, yet prances about the stage with no apparent effort. Now he is soft and malleable, now he is awkward and inflexible. The actor can command a thousand different intonations, yet he never employs them to impersonate definite characters, preferring to use

[1] *Il Teatro delle favole rappresentative* (1611), the first published collection of *commedia dell' arte* scenarios.

them merely to embellish his range of gestures and movements. The actor can speak quickly when playing a rogue, slowly and sing-song when playing a pedant. With his body he can describe geometrical figures on the stage, then sometimes he leaps, happy and free as a bird in the sky. The actor's face may be a death mask, yet he is able to distort it and bend his body to such a pose that the death mask comes to life.

Since the appearance of Isadora Duncan, and now even more with the Jaques-Dalcroze's theory of eurhythmics, the contemporary actor has begun gradually to concede the importance of gesture and movement on the stage. Yet still 'the mask holds little interest for him. No sooner is the question of the mask raised than the actor inquires whether it is seriously proposed to restore the masks and buskins of the antique theatre. The actor always visualizes the mask as an accessory; to him it is merely that which once helped to establish the character of the role and to overcome acoustical difficulties.

The time has yet to come when the appearance of an actor without a mask will once again bring cries of disapproval from the audience, such as happened in the reign of Louis XIV when the dancer Gardel[1] first dared to appear without a mask. For the present the actor will not concede the mask as a symbol of the theatre at any price – and in this he is not alone.

I tried to interpret the character of Dom Juan according to the principles of the theatre of the mask.[2] But the mask on the face of the actor playing Dom Juan went undetected, even by a critic like Benois.

'Molière loves Dom Juan; Dom Juan is his hero, and like every hero, he is something of a portrait of his author. So to substitute a satirical type for the hero . . . is far worse than just a mistake.'[3] That is how Benois sees Molière's Dom Juan. He would like to see him as the 'seducer of Seville' of Tirso de Molina, Byron and Pushkin.

In his wanderings from one poet to another Don Juan preserved the basic features of his character, but like a mirror he reflected the different nature of each poet, the different way of life of each one's country, and the moral precepts of each one's society.

Benois has completely forgotten that Molière treated the figure of Don Juan not as an end but purely as a means to an end. He wrote *Dom Juan* after *Tartuffe* had raised a storm of indignation amongst the clergy and the nobility. He was charged with a whole list of malicious crimes, and his

[1] Maximilien Gardel (1741–87) first discarded the mask in 1772 as Apollo in Rameau's *Castor and Pollux*.

[2] In the 1910 production (see above, pp. 98–105).

[3] *Rech*, Petersburg, 19 November 1910. [Meyerhold's note.]

enemies lost no time in recommending suitable punishments. Molière had only his own weapons to combat this injustice. In order to ridicule the bigotry of the clergy and the hypocrisy of the nobility which he so detested, he clutched at Don Juan like a drowning man at a straw. Many of the scenes and isolated phrases which cut across the mood of the main action and the character of the hero were inserted into the play by Molière simply to gain suitable revenge on those who obstructed the success of *Tartuffe*. Molière intentionally exposes 'this leaping, dancing, posturing Lovelace'[1] to scorn and derision in order to make him a target for his own attacks on the pride and vanity which he abhorred. But then he puts into the mouth of the same shallow cavalier whom he has just ridiculed a brilliant account of the prevailing vices of the period, hypocrisy and bigotry.

Furthermore, one must not overlook the marital drama which engulfed Molière just before his anguish at the banning of *Tartuffe*. 'His wife, lacking the perception to appreciate the genius and integrity of her husband, rejected him in favour of the most unworthy rivals; she became enamoured of salon prattlers whose sole advantage was their noble descent. Molière had not shirked earlier opportunities to hurl gibes at these marquis ridicules.'[2] Now he employed the person of Don Juan to renew his attacks on his rivals.

Molière needed comic scenes like the one with the peasant-women, not so much to characterize Don Juan as to drown his sorrows in the stupefying wine of comedy, the sorrows of a man robbed of domestic bliss by those shallow egotistical 'devourers of women's hearts'.

It is only too clear that Don Juan is a puppet whom Molière employs to square accounts with his innumerable enemies. For Molière, Don Juan is no more than a wearer of masks. At one moment we see on his face a mask which embodies all the dissoluteness, unbelief, cynicism and pretensions of a gallant of the court of Le Roi-Soleil; then we see the mask of the author-accuser; then the nightmarish mask which stifled the author himself, the agonizing mask he was forced to wear at court performances and in front of his perfidious wife. Not until the very end does he hand his puppet the mask of *El Burlador de Sevilla*,[3] which he borrowed from the touring Italians.

The greatest compliment that the designer and the director of Molière's *Dom Juan* (Alexander Golovin and the author) could possibly imagine was

---

[1] *Rech*, Petersburg, 19 November 1910. [Meyerhold's note.]
[2] *Artist*, Moscow, 1890, no 9. [Meyerhold's note.]
[3] The title of Tirso de Molina's play, the first to be based on the legend.

paid to them by Benois when he described their production as 'a dressed-up fairground booth'.

The theatre of the mask has always been a fairground show, and the idea of acting based on the apotheosis of the mask, gesture and movement is indivisible from the idea of the travelling show. Those concerned in reforming the contemporary theatre dream of introducing the principles of the fairground booth into the theatre. However, the sceptics believe that the revival of the principles of the fairground booth is being obstructed by the cinematograph.

Whenever the question of the rebirth of the fairground booth is raised there are people who either completely reject its advantages or who extol the cinematograph and call for its enlistment in the service of the theatre.

Far too much importance is attached to the cinematograph, that idol of the modern city, by its supporters. The cinematograph is of undoubted importance to science as a means of visual demonstration; it can serve as an illustrated newspaper depicting 'the events of the day'; for some people it might even replace travel (horror of horrors!). But there is no place for the cinematograph in the world of art, even in a purely auxiliary capacity. And if for some reason or other the cinematograph is called a theatre, it is simply because during the period of total obsession with naturalism (an obsession which has already cooled off considerably) everything mechanical was enrolled in the service of the theatre.

This extreme obsession with naturalism, so characteristic of the general public at the end of the nineteenth and the beginning of the twentieth century was one of the original reasons for the extraordinary success of the cinematograph.

The romantics' vague dreams of the past excluded the strict limits of classical tragedy. In its turn, romanticism was forced to yield to the proponents of naturalistic drama. The naturalists proclaimed the slogan 'depict life as it really is', thereby confusing the two separate artistic concepts of form and content.

Whilst reproaching the classicists and the romantics with their obsession with form, the naturalists themselves set about perfecting form and in so doing transformed art into photography. Electricity came to the aid of the naturalists, and the result – a touching union of photography and technology – was the cinematograph.

Having once banished imagination from the theatre, naturalism, to be consistent, should have banished paint as well, not to mention the unnatural diction of actors. After all, the cinematograph took advantage of the development of verisimilitude, whilst replacing painted costumes and sets with the colourless screen and dispensing with the spoken word.

The cinematograph, that dream-come-true of those who strive for the photographic representation of life, is a shining example of the obsession with quasi-verisimilitude.

The cinematograph is of undoubted importance to science, but when it is put to the service of art, it senses its own inadequacy and tries in vain to justify the label of 'art'. Hence its attempts to free itself from the basic principle of photography: it realizes the need to vindicate the first half of its dual appellation' the theatre-cinematograph'. But the theatre is art and photography is non-art. So the cinematograph, in its hasty efforts to incorporate colours, music, declamation and singing, is pursuing elements which are totally alien to its mechanical nature.

Just as all the theatres which are still trying to propagate naturalistic drama and plays fit only for reading cannot stay the growth of truly theatrical and totally non-naturalistic plays, so the cinematograph cannot stifle the spirit of the fairground booth.

At the present time, when the cinematograph is in the ascendant, the absence of the fairground booth is only apparent. The fairground booth is eternal. Its heroes do not die; they simply change their aspects and assume new forms. The heroes of the ancient Atellanae,[1] the foolish Maccus and the simple Pappus, were resurrected almost twenty centuries later in the figures of Arlecchino and Pantalone, the principal characters of the *commedia dell' arte*, the travelling theatre of the late Renaissance. Their audience came not so much to listen to dialogue as to watch the wealth of movement, club blows, dizzy leaps, and all the whole range of tricks native to the theatre.

The fairground booth is eternal. Even though its principles have been banished temporarily from within the walls of the theatre, we know that they remain firmly embedded in the lines of all true theatrical writers.

Molière, France's greatest comic and 'grand divertisseur du Roi-Soleil', depicted many times in his ballet-comedies what he had seen as a child in the booth of Gaultier-Garguille and his famous *collaborateurs*, Turlupin and Gros-Guillaume, and in the other booths of the fair at Saint-Germain.

The crowd there was entertained by puppets. 'Judging by the puppet plays which survive (regrettably few) and by the numerous contemporary eyewitness accounts, the humble puppet theatre was remarkable for the boldness of its attacks and the universality of its satire; France's political reverses, the squalid intrigues of the court, the ugly contortions of high

[1] The improvised rustic farces of Atella in Campania, dating from the third century B.C. or earlier.

society, the rigid stratification of the caste system, the manners of the nobility and the tradespeople, were all exposed to the ridicule of the nimble marionettes.' (Alexei Veselovsky.)

It was here that Molière acquired the power of denunciation which he later employed to fight authority and the nobility.

At the fair of Saint-Germain, Molière watched full-blooded performances of popular farce under a canvas awning, acrobats twirling to a cacophony of drums and tambourines, the itinerant surgeon, the conjurer and the quack, all competing for the attention of the thronging crowd.

Molière studied with the players of the Italian strolling troupes. Whilst with them he encountered the figure of Tartuffe in the comedies of Aretino[1] and borrowed the character of Sganarelle from the Italian buffoni. *Le Dépit amoureux* is an outright imitation of the Italians. *Le Malade imaginaire* and *Monsieur de Pourceaugnac* are based on all those scenarios of the Italian travelling theatre featuring doctors (*Arlecchino, medico volante*, etc.).

Banished from the contemporary theatre, the principles of the fairground booth found a temporary refuge in the French cabarets, the German Überbrettl, the English music halls and the ubiquitous 'variétés'.[2] If you read Ernst von Wolzogen's Überbrettl manifesto,[3] you will find that in essence it is an apologia for the principles of the fairground booth.

The manifesto stresses the significance of the art of the variétés, whose roots extend far below the surface of our age, and which it is wrong to regard as 'a temporary aberration of taste.' We prefer variétés, continues von Wolzogen, 'to the bigger theatres where the play takes up a whole evening with its ponderous, bombastic exposition of depressing events. We prefer them not because our spirit has grown barren, as certain pseudo-Catonians and "laudatores temporis acti" allege. On the contrary, we aim for conciseness and profundity, for clarity and the vigorous extract.

'The great discoveries and the many changes in the spiritual and tech-

---

[1] Pietro Aretino (1492–1556), Italian dramatist best known for his satirical comedies and his tragedy *Orazio* (1546).

[2] Obviously, I do not mean the 'variétés' ridiculed by Georg Fuchs, which he described as 'Simplicissimus-Stil' (transferred to the stage from the pages of the Munich periodical). But I should add a general qualification: although two-thirds of the acts in any of the better theatres of this type have no right to be called art, there is more art in the remaining third than in all the so-called serious theatres which purvey 'literary drama'. [Meyerhold's note.]

[3] Ernst von Wolzogen (1855–1934) founded the first literary cabaret in Germany in 1901, the Berlin 'Buntes Theater' or 'Überbrettl'. The 'manifesto' referred to is contained in Karl von Levetzow, *Ernst von Wolzogen's offizielles Repertoir. Erster Band. Buntes Theater*, Berlin, 1902.

nological life of our age have led to a quickening of the universal pulse; we are short of time. For this reason we seek conciseness and precision in everything. We oppose decadence and its inherent diffuseness and obsession with detail, with brevity, clarity and depth. And always in everything we seek broad dimensions.

'It is not true that we don't know how to laugh. Granted, we no longer laugh the meaningless, *amorphous* laugh of the cretin; we have replaced it with the brief, precise laugh of the cultured man who knows how to view things from all angles.

'Depth and extract, brevity and contrast! No sooner has the pale, lanky Pierrot crept across the stage, no sooner has the spectator sensed in his movements the eternal tragedy of mutely suffering mankind, than the apparition is succeeded by the merry Harlequinade. The tragic gives way to the comic, harsh satire replaces the sentimental ballad.'[1]

Wolzogen's manifesto contains an apologia for the favourite device of the fairground booth – *the grotesque.*

'Grotesque (Italian – grottesca) is the title of a genre of low comedy in literature, music and the plastic arts. Grotesque usually implies something hideous and strange, a humorous work which with no apparent logic combines the most dissimilar elements by *ignoring their details and relying on its own originality, borrowing from every source anything which satisfies its joie de vivre and its capricious, mocking attitude to life.*'[2]

This is the style which reveals the most wonderful horizons to the creative artist. 'I', my personal attitude to life, precedes all else. Everything which I take as material for my art corresponds not to the truth of reality but to the truth of *my* personal artistic whim.

'Art is incapable of conveying the sum of reality, that is, all concepts as they succeed one another in time. Art dismantles reality, depicting it now spatially, now temporally. For this reason, art consists either in images or in the alternation of images: the first yields the spatial forms of art, the second – the temporal forms. *The impossibility of embracing the totality of reality justifies the schematization of the real (in particular by means of stylization).*'[3]

Stylization involves a certain degree of verisimilitude. In consequence,

[1] It is not clear from Meyerhold's text whether the whole of this passage is a direct quotation.
[2] *Bolshaya Entsiklopedia*, 1902. [Meyerhold's note.]
[3] Andrei Bely, *Simvolism*, Moscow, 1910, section 2, 'Formy iskusstva'.

the stylizer remains an analyst *par excellence* (Kuzmin,[1] Bilibin[2]).

'Schematization' – the very word seems to imply a certain impoverishment of reality, as though it somehow entailed the reduction of its totality. The grotesque is the second stage in the process of stylization, when the final link with analysis has been severed. Its method is strictly synthetical. Without compromise, the grotesque ignores all minor details and creates a totality of life 'in stylized improbability' (to borrow Pushkin's phrase). Stylization impoverishes life to the extent that it reduces empirical abundance to typical unity. The grotesque does not recognize the *purely* debased or the *purely* exalted. The grotesque mixes opposites, consciously creating harsh incongruity and *relying solely on its own originality*.

In Hoffmann, ghosts take stomach pills, a bunch of flaming lilies turns into the gaudy dressing-gown of Lindhorst, the student Anselmus is fitted into a glass bottle. In Tirso de Molina, the hero's monologue has no sooner attuned the spectator to an air of solemnity – as though with the majestic chords of a church organ – than it is followed by a monologue *gracioso* whose comic twists instantly wipe the devout smile from his face and make him guffaw like some medieval barbarian.

On a rainy autumn day a funeral procession crawls through the streets; the gait of the pall-bearers conveys profound grief. Then the wind snatches a hat from the head of one of the mourners; he bends down to pick it up, but the wind begins to chase it from puddle to puddle. Each jump of the staid gentleman chasing his hat lends his face such comic grimaces that the gloomy funeral procession is suddenly transformed by some devilish hand into a bustling holiday crowd. If only one could achieve an effect like that on the stage!

Contrast. Surely the grotesque is not intended simply as a means of creating or heightening contrasts! Is the grotesque not an end in itself? Like Gothic architecture, for example, in which the soaring bell-tower expresses the fervour of the worshipper whilst its projections decorated with fearsome distorted figures direct one's thoughts back towards hell. The lusts of the flesh, the sin of lasciviousness, the insurmountable bestiality of life: all these seem to be designed to prevent excessive idealism from turning into asceticism. Just as in Gothic architecture a miraculous balance is preserved between affirmation and denial, the celestial and the terrestrial, the beautiful and the ugly, so the grotesque parades ugliness

[1] Mikhail Kuzmin (1875–1936), poet, critic and composer who wrote the music for a number of Meyerhold's productions.

[2] Ivan Bilibin (1876–1942), artist and stage-designer.

138

in order to prevent beauty from lapsing into sentimentality (in Schiller's sense).

The grotesque has its own attitude towards the outward appearance of life. The grotesque deepens life's outward appearance to the point where it ceases to appear merely natural.

Beneath what we see of life there are vast unfathomed depths. In its search for the supernatural, the grotesque synthesizes opposites, creates a picture of the incredible, and invites the spectator to solve the riddle of the inscrutable.

Blok (in Acts One and Three of *The Unknown Woman*), Fyodor Sologub (*Vanka, the Butler, and Jean, the Page*), and Wedekind[1] (*The Earth Spirit, Pandora's Box, Spring's Awakening*) have all succeeded in remaining within the bounds of realistic drama whilst adopting a new approach to the portrayal of life. They have achieved unusual effects within the bounds of realistic drama by resorting to the grotesque.

The realism of these dramatists in the plays mentioned is such that it forces the spectator to adopt an ambivalent attitude towards the stage action. Is it not the task of the grotesque in the theatre to preserve this ambivalent attitude in the spectator by switching the course of the action with strokes of contrast? The basis of the grotesque is the artist's constant desire to switch the spectator from the plane he has just reached to another which is totally unforeseen.

'Grotesque is the title of a genre of low comedy in literature, music and the plastic arts.' Why '*low* comedy'? And why only 'comic'? It is not only humorous artists who for no apparent reason have synthesized the most diverse natural phenomena in their works. The grotesque need not necessarily be comic (the aspect examined by Flögel in his *Geschichte des Groteskkomischen*); it can as easily be tragic, as we know from the drawings of Goya, the horrific tales of Edgar Allen Poe, and above all, of course, from E. T. A. Hoffmann.

Our own Blok in his lyrical dramas has followed the path of the grotesque in the spirit of these masters.

'Greetings world! You're with me again!
So long your soul has been close to me!
And now once more I shall breathe your spring
Through your window of gold!'

[1] Unfortunately Wedekind suffers greatly from his lack of taste and his constant tendency to introduce elements of literature on to the stage. [Meyerhold's note.]

Thus cries Arlecchino to the cold starry sky of Petersburg and leaps through the window. But 'the distance seen through the window turns out to be painted on paper'. The injured clown with his convulsed body hanging across the footlights cries to the audience that he is bleeding cranberry juice.[1]

The ornamentation employed in the fifteenth century by the artists of the Renaissance was based on examples found in the catacombs ('grotti'), baths and palaces of Ancient Rome, shaped into symmetrical garlands of stylized plants with animals and imaginary figures like satyrs, centaurs and other mythological beasts, with masks and garlands of fruit, birds, insects, weapons and vessels.

Was it not this particular form of grotesque which was reflected in Sapunov's costume designs for the pantomime, *Columbine's Scarf*, by Schnitzler-Dapertutto?[2] For the sake of a grotesque effect, Sapunov transformed Gigolo into a parrot by combing his wig from back to front to resemble feathers, and by arranging the tails of his frock-coat in the form of a real tail.

In Pushkin's short play set in the age of chivalry the mowers flail with their scythes at the legs of the knights' horses: 'some horses fall injured and others run wild'. Pushkin, who drew particular attention 'to the ancients with their tragic masks and their dualistic portrayal of character',[3] who welcomed such 'stylized improbability', is hardly likely to have expected real horses, previously schooled to fall injured and run wild, to be brought on to the stage.

In writing this stage direction Pushkin might almost have foreseen the actor of the twentieth century riding on to the stage on a wooden steed, as was the case in Adam de la Halle's pastorale, *Robin and Marion*,[4] or on the caparisoned wooden frames with papier maché horses' heads on which the Prince and his entourage embarked on their long journey in Znosko-Borovsky's *Transfigured Prince*.[5] The designer gave the horses' necks deep curves and stuck prancing ostrich feathers into their heads, which alone sufficed to make the clumsy frames covered with caparisons look like horses lightly prancing and proudly rearing on their hind legs.

In the same play the youthful prince returns from his journey to learn

[1] *The Fairground Booth.*

[2] See pp. 113–14 above.

[3] See the rough draft of his letter to Raevsky in 1829. [Meyerhold's note.]

[4] At the Ancient Theatre in Yevreinov's production (Petersburg, 1907); designer – Dobuzhinsky. [Meyerhold's note.]

[5] See p. 114 above.

that his father, the king, has died. The courtiers proclaim the prince king, place a grey wig on his head, and attach a long grey beard to his chin. In full view of the audience the youthful prince is transformed into the venerable old man which a king in the realm of fairy-tales is supposed to be.

In the first scene of Blok's *Fairground Booth*[1] there is a long table covered with a black cloth reaching to the floor and parallel to the footlights. Behind the table sit the 'mystics', the top halves of their bodies visible to the audience. Frightened by some rejoinder, they duck their heads, and suddenly all that remains at the table is a row of torsos minus heads and hands. It transpires that the figures are cut out of *cardboard* with frock-coats, shirt-fronts, collars and cuffs drawn on with soot and chalk. The actors' hands are thrust through openings in the cardboard torsos, and their heads simply rest on the cardboard collars.

Hoffmann's doll complains that she has a clockwork mechanism instead of a heart. The element of deception is important in the dramatic grotesque, just as it is in Hoffmann. The same is true of Jacques Callot. Hoffmann writes of this astonishing graphic artist: 'Even in his drawings from life (processions, battles) there is something in the appearance of the lifelike figures which makes them at once *familiar yet strange*. Through the medium of the grotesque the comic figures of Callot yield *mysterious allusions* to the perceptive observer' (my italics).

The art of the grotesque is based on the conflict between form and content. The grotesque aims to subordinate psychologism to a decorative task. That is why in every theatre which has been dominated by the grotesque the aspect of design in its widest sense has been so important (for example, the Japanese theatre). Not only the settings, the architecture of the stage, and the theatre itself are decorative, but also the mime, movements, gestures and poses of the actors. Through being decorative they become expressive. For this reason the technique of the grotesque contains elements of the dance; only with the help of the dance is it possible to subordinate grotesque conceptions to a decorative task. It was no coincidence that the Greeks looked for elements of the dance in every rhythmical movement, even in the march. It is no coincidence that the Japanese actor offering a flower to his beloved recalls in his movements the lady in a Japanese quadrille with her torso swaying, her head turning and slightly inclining, and her arms gracefully outstretched first to the left, then to the right.

[1] For a further description of this production, see pp. 70–71 above.

'*Cannot the body, with its lines and its harmonious movements, sing as clearly as the voice?*'

When we can answer this question (from Blok's *Unknown Woman*) in the affirmative, when in the art of the grotesque form triumphs over content, then the soul of the grotesque and the soul of the theatre will be one. The fantastic will exist in its own right on the stage; *joie de vivre* will be discovered in the tragic as well as in the comic; the demonic will be manifested in deepest irony and the tragi-comic in the commonplace; we shall strive for 'stylized improbability', for mysterious allusions, deception and transformation; we shall eradicate the sweetly sentimental from the romantic; the dissonant will sound as perfect harmony, and the commonplace of everyday life will be transcended.

[Published in Meyerhold's *O Teatre*, cit., pp. 143–73.]

NOTE   Probably started in 1911, but written mainly in the summer of 1912.

Meyerhold's criticism of Alexander Benois' evaluation of *The Brothers Karamazov* was one further encounter in a running fight between the two artists which originated when Meyerhold was with Komissarzhevskaya and Benois was drama critic for the Petersburg newspaper *Rech*. Meyerhold considers Benois' production methods at length in his article *Benois-regisseur*, where he examines the productions of Molière's *Malade Imaginaire* and Pushkin's *Little Tragedies* at the Moscow Art Theatre (*Lyubov k tryom apelsinam*, 1915, no 1–3, pp. 95–126).

Isadora Duncan appeared in Russia for the first time in 1904. Meyerhold saw her in January 1908 and wrote:

On the 9th I saw Duncan and her school. I was moved to tears. No trace of schooling. The dancer dances as joyfully as if she were in a green meadow. A happy flock. One would need dithyrambs to convey the picture. Poets will write songs in praise of Duncan. Citizens will erect golden monuments to this woman who wants to give back to children the joy which has been obliterated by the din of tramcars and automobiles.

[From a letter quoted in Volkov, op. cit., vol. I, p. 371.]

However, in 1915 he said: 'We cannot hope for a successful rendering of this extract [from *Hamlet*] until we have eliminated all traces of Duncanesque balleticism . . .' (see p. 152 below).

Emile Jaques-Dalcroze demonstrated his 'eurhythmic' exercises with a group of his pupils in Moscow and Petersburg in January 1911.

2. Notes on Productions

THE ADORATION OF THE CROSS *by Pedro Calderon*
First production: settings by Sudeikin. Première: 19 April 1910 at Vyacheslav Ivanov's Tower Theatre, Petersburg. Second production:[1] *settings by Bondi. Première: Summer 1912 at Terioki, Finland, by Fellowship of Actors, Writers, Artists and Musicians.*

This production was remarkable mainly for its external features: the treatment of the settings and the *mise en scène*. Everything was extremely simplified with virtually no sets at all. The aim was to create a setting which would show off the actors to best advantage and faithfully convey the spirit of Calderon.

The stage was decorated to resemble a large white tent, with the back wall divided into narrow vertical strips between which the actors made their exits and their entrances. The white curtain had a border of painted blue crosses and represented the symbolic boundary between the setting of the religious drama and the hostile outside world. The triangles formed by the roof inside the tent were decorated with stars. On either side of the stage stood tall white lanterns with small lamps burning behind matt paper, but these were merely symbolic lanterns, the stage being lit by battens overhead and to either side (there were no footlights). There were no scene changes; in the second *'jornada'* [act], in order to indicate that the action takes place in a monastery, two boys entered to the monotonous chiming of bells and erected large white triptych screens bearing simple likenesses of Catholic saints. Everything was austere and simple so that the predominant feature was the whiteness. The ornamentation on the tent walls and the screens was simply outlined in blue. The spectator was left in no doubt that the settings had no pictorial significance, and all attention was focused on the actors. The setting is no more than the page on which the text is inscribed; consequently everything connected with the setting was deliberately stylized.

[1] Described here. For a note on the 1910 production, see p. 110 above.

When the actors were meant to be tied to trees, in the absence of trees they leaned against two pillars on the forestage which were part of the permanent theatre structure; the rope which was supposed to secure them was simply hung round their arms. When the peasant was supposed to hide in a bush, he simply draped himself with a curtain. At the end of the play Eusebio is mortally wounded and crosses the stage crying, 'The way is barred by the Cross.' This was depicted quite literally: a boy dressed in black entered, carrying a blue wooden cross, and placed it in Eusebio's path.

[Meyerhold's *O Teatre*, cit., pp. 202–3.]

HARLEQUIN, THE MARRIAGE BROKER *by Vladimir Solovyov*
First production:[1] *settings by Yevseev; music by Spiess von Eschenbruch; première: 8 November 1911 at the Assembly Rooms of the Nobility, Petersburg. Second production: settings by Kulbin; music by de Bourg (adaptations of Haydn and Araja); première: Summer 1912 at Terioki, Finland, by Fellowship of Actors, Writers, Artists and Musicians.*

This harlequinade, written with the specific aim of reviving the theatre of masks, was staged according to traditional principles and based on our studies of the scenarios of the *commedia dell' arte*. Rehearsals were conducted jointly by the author and the director; the author, in accordance with his aim of reviving the traditional theatre, would outline the *mise en scène*, moves, poses and gestures as he had found them described in the scenarios of improvised comedies; the director would add new tricks in the style of these traditional devices, blending the traditional with the new to produce a coherent whole. The harlequinade was written in the form of a pantomime because, more than any dramatic form, the pantomime is conducive to the revival of the art of improvisation. In the pantomime the actor is given the general outline of the plot and in the intervals between the various key moments he is free to act *ex improviso*. However, the actor's freedom is only relative because he is subject to the discipline of the musical score. The actor in a harlequinade needs to possess an acute sense of rhythm, plus great agility and self-control. He must develop the equilibrist skills of an acrobat, because only an acrobat can master the problems posed by the grotesque style inherent in the fundamental conception of the harlequinade.

Instead of conventional sets there are two decorated screens, placed some distance apart to represent the houses of Pantalone and the Dottore

[1] Described here.

144

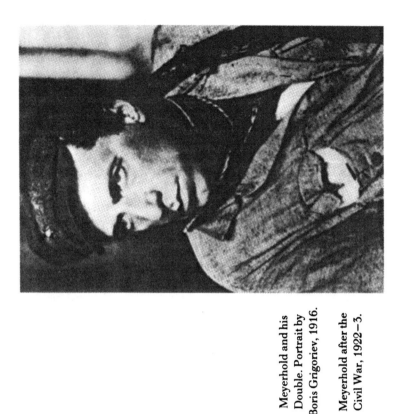

Meyerhold and his
Double. Portrait by
Boris Grigoriev, 1916.

Meyerhold after the
Civil War, 1922–3.

The Dawn, 1920.

The setting for *Mystery-Bouffe*, 1921 (model).

(standing on stools, they appear above these screens and motion to one another in a mimed discussion of the Dottore's marriage to Aurelia). The stage groupings are invariably symmetrical and the actors' movements acrobatic. All the jokes (whether prescribed or improvised) conform to the style of a traditional buffonade: striking one's rival across the face with a glove; a character transformed into a magician with the aid of the traditional pointed cap and false beard; one character carrying off another pick-a-back; fights, blows with clubs, cutting off of noses with wooden swords; actors jumping into the auditorium; dances, acrobatic numbers, Harlequin somersaulting; thumbing of noses from the wings; leaps and kisses; the final curtain with the actors forming up in a line and bowing comically to the audience; masks; shouts and whistles at the final exit; the introduction of short spoken phrases at moments of dramatic tension.

Before deciding finally on a satisfactory *mise en scène*, we experimented with a number of variants. One variant, later rejected but worth mentioning, consisted in dividing the stage arbitrarily into three planes: the proscenium, plus two further levels, respectively one and two steps higher than the proscenium; both levels were narrow, like pavements stretching the width of the stage and parallel to the proscenium opening. Each level had its own particular role in the action. For example, during the parade the author recited the prologue, introducing each character in turn; the actor in question stepped forward whilst the others remained standing on the highest level. Another variant resulted from replacing the music of Spiess von Eschenbruch with that of de Bourg (based on Haydn and Araja). Whereas the music of the first composer hampered the art of improvisation, the music of the second actually helped the actors to bring out the subtleties of the plot. Since both author and director were concerned exclusively in presenting a typical harlequinade, firmly rooted in the traditions of the Theatre of Masks, it was of utmost importance to choose music which would facilitate the movements of such a harlequinade.

On one occasion we altered the *mise en scène* because the performance took place in a concert hall where the sides of the square concert platform did not extend to the walls of the hall; this made it possible for Harlequin to leap off the sides of the stage and to materialize on stage rather like a *deus ex machina*.

One further variant: the harlequinade was performed on one occasion with the characters in tails, dinner jackets and evening gowns (at the home of Fyodor Sologub); to these modern clothes we added only the

145

essential props of the *commedia dell' arte*: a mask, a tambourine, a stick for Harlequin, a hat – just enough to suggest the character in question.

[*O Teatre*, cit., p. 200–2.]

3. The Meyerhold Studio

MEYERHOLD'S CLASS IN STAGE MOVEMENT 1914–1915

The members of the Studio are divided into groups according to their inherent styles and predilections for a particular theatrical genre or method of production.

Those who have performed in accordance with the old conventions before joining the Studio are grouped to form a separate '*Actors' Class*'. In this class they are given the opportunity to practise on the vaudevilles of the 1830s and 1840s and Spanish drama (Calderon's *Doctor of his own honour*) in order to learn those techniques of the new theatre which are closely related to the *commedia dell' arte* and the other truly theatrical ages of the theatre. Here, too, they will become familiar with the exemplars of modern drama who have been rejected, but who none the less constitute a powerful bulwark of the theatre . . . [A list follows which includes Blok, Bryusov, Sologub, Vyacheslav Ivanov, Remizov, Solovyov, Maeterlinck (first period), Claudel, Villiers de l'Isle-Adam – *Translator*.]

A *Grotesque Group* is developing not only completely new acting devices but also its own plays, composed in the Studio . . . [List follows – *Translator*.]

One of the classes of the Grotesque Group was attended by Marinetti. He suggested to a group which had just performed *Antony and Cleopatra* for him (three actors and four 'proscenium servants') the theme of *Othello* for improvisation. After a three-minute discussion on stage of the tragedy's salient features, the group performed a three-minute résumé of it.

Shortly, two further groups will be formed: a Classical Group and an Eighteenth-Century Group.

[*Lyubov k tryom apelsinam, Zhurnal Doktora Dapertutto*, Petersburg, 1914, no 2, pp. 62–63.]

The concept of movement is subject to the laws of artistic form. Movement is the most powerful means of theatrical expression. The role of movement is more important than that of any other theatrical element. Deprived of dialogue, costume, footlights, wings and an auditorium, and left with only the actor and his mastery of movement, the theatre remains the theatre. The spectator can understand the actor's thoughts and impulses from his moves, gestures and facial expressions. For the actor, the theatre is any stage which he can construct for himself – without the assistance of a builder, wherever and however necessary, and as quickly as his skill will allow (read about the Chinese travelling companies).

Concerning the differences between movement, gestures and facial expressions in the cinematograph and the pantomime: in the cinematograph an object appears on the screen for utilitarian reasons; in the Studio (in a pantomime) an object appears so as to afford the actor the chance to make use of it in order to make the spectator happy or sad. Thus the cinema actor is bound to differ from the actor in our Studio.

The cinematograph's principal aim is to grip the spectator by means of the plot. In the pantomime, the spectator is gripped not by the plot but by the manner in which the actor's free inspiration manifests itself through his sole desire *to dominate* the stage, which he himself has built, decorated and lit; to dominate, carried along by improvisations unexpected even to himself. What does it mean to transform oneself, to lose oneself in the character? What does it mean to reveal always oneself through a host of different characters? Pantomime excites not through what is concealed within it but by how it is created, by the framework which confines its heart, by the skill of the actor revealed through it. The actor's movements vary according to his costume, the properties and the setting. Far from arbitrary, costume is an integral part of the production; its cut and colour are of utmost importance. Make-up, too, is relative – there are masks and masks. Theatricality presupposes an inevitability of form.

Concerning the theatre's relationship with life: when the theatre aims at the photographic reproduction of life (the naturalistic theatre), movements serve to make clear to the spectator the various aims of the dramatist (the obligatory exposition; the underlying idea of the play; the psychology of the characters; conversations which satisfy the aims of the dramatist, not the demands of the spectator; the portrayal of background and 'life', etc. etc.). The theatre is art and everything in it should be determined by the laws of art. Art and life are governed by different laws.

An attempt to draw an analogy between the laws of the theatre and the laws of the plastic arts: to reveal the laws governing the art of the theatre one needs not merely to unravel the tangle, but to unravel it according to a most intricate system (the geometrical deployment of figures, etc.). The basis of the art of the theatre is acting. Even when the theatre is required to portray elements of real life, it re-creates its fragments by means which are exclusive to its own peculiar art, the means of which is 'play-acting'. To show life on the stage means *to perform* life; serious matters may become amusing and amusing matters appear tragic. Polonius' enumeration of the range of theatrical genres shows that in the actor's hands simple comedy becomes tragi-comedy; a series of ditties linked by actors' exits and entrances is transformed into a pastorale.

The actor of the new theatre must acquire a whole range of technical devices, which he can achieve only by studying the principles of acting from the truly theatrical ages of the theatre. There exists a series of axioms which hold good for the actor, regardless of the type of theatre in which he is performing.

Apropos to the study of the theatres of the past, it should be noted that this 'accumulation of treasures' is not done merely to flaunt them in their original form. Once he has learnt to cherish them, the actor should use them for adornment, should come thus 'endowed' on stage and know how to 'come to life' theatrically: to doff a beggar's cap as though it were pearl-encrusted, to hitch up a tattered cloak with the flourish of a *fidalgo*, to strike a tattered tambourine not merely to make a noise, but to convey through that one gesture all his skill and refinement, to strike it in such a way that the spectator forgets that it has no skin.

How do we aim to restore the traditions of the past in the present? Not simply by repeating the devices of the past – this we leave to the Ancient Theatre.[1] There is a difference between mere reconstruction and free composition based on the study and selection of traditional techniques.

The new actor's view of the stage as an area for the presentation of unprecedented events. 'Once I know – he says – that I am stepping on to a stage where the setting is not merely incidental, where the stage itself is joined directly to the auditorium, where the musical accompaniment is dominant, then I cannot help but know how to perform. Since my own performance will affect the spectator simultaneously with the setting and the music, my acting must be an integral part of the whole in order for every element to have a clear significance.' Knowing why his surroundings are as they are, knowing how the whole production has developed, the actor is transformed the moment he steps on to the stage, becoming himself a work of art. This new master of the stage, the actor, manifests his joy

[1] See pp. 105–6 above.

:hrough his melodious voice and his body malleable as wax. His movements, shaped by his regard for the law of Guglielmo ('partire di terreno'),[1] lemand almost the agility of an acrobat (the Japanese actor is both acrobat ind dancer). The dialogue forces the actor to become a musician. The pause reminds him to calculate rhythm as rigidly as a poet.

Concerning the differing attitudes towards music of Jaques-Dalcroze, Miss Isadora Duncan, Miss Loïe Fuller, the circus, the variety theatre, the Chinese and Japanese theatres. Music flows in time with the actor's moves ibout the stage and the moments when he is stationary. Sometimes the ictor's movements and the music do not coincide, but, initiated simul- :aneously, they constitute a peculiar form of polyphony. The birth of a new form of pantomime in which music dominates on its own level and :he actor's movements proceed parallel to it: without revealing to the ;pectator the metrical basis of the music and their own movements, :he actors attempt to weave a rhythmical pattern which is dictated by the metre. In the movements of an actor the pause signifies not an absence or :essation of motion, but, as in music, preserves an element of motion. Just because an actor is not in motion at a given moment it does not mean that he has relinquished the sphere of music. The actor remains constantly on ;tage, not only because there are no wings and hence no refuge offstage, but above all because once he has grasped the significance of the pause he :ontinues to participate in the action. It is during pauses that one sees most :learly the need for lighting, music, the glitter of props and the splendour)f costumes to sustain excitement. The two planes, the main stage and the proscenium, are of great importance to the actor who remains constantly)nstage, in the same way that music continues to be heard even when it is silent. (Cf. Ibsen's expression, 'to hear the silence'.)

[*Lyubov k tryom apyelsinam*, 1914, no 4–5, pp. 94–98.]

FIRST EVENING OF INTERLUDES, ÉTUDES AND PANTOMIMES *performed by members of the Studio on 12 February 1915. Maîtres de scène: Meyerhold and Vladimir Solovyov.*[2]

Street Conjurers

A pantomime in the manner of a Venetian popular show of the late eighteenth century (although the first version devised by Dzyubinskaya,)ne of the Studio's comédiennes, was closer in style to the quattrocento).

---

[1] See p. 156 below.
[2] The programme also included Solovyov's production of Cervantes's interlude, *The Cave of Salamanca.*

The pantomime was performed on two levels, the proscenium and the elevated main stage. The latter was occupied by the principal conjurer, together with his assistant and his acrobat. On the proscenium stands the audience which has gathered to watch the show (as prescribed by the plot), and which acts as a claque to rouse the enthusiasm of the modern audience (and to assist the principals in the pantomime). The proscenium also provides the setting for a number of scenes: the meeting of the Cavalier with the Lady in the Mask, the duel between the Cavalier and the Acrobat, and the final exit which proceeds up on to the main stage.

Properties: a curtain held by proscenium servants and serving as a backcloth for the juggling scene, a mat for the acrobat; a basket containing the juggler's equipment: a magic wand, a flying butterfly, a golden orange, a magic veil, a collapsible stick, a tambourine, two plates, a little violin with a long bow, a second pair of plates, two rapiers, a fan, a rose, capes, a snake, a bouquet of flowers, a clown's trumpet, a cap for collecting money.

Traditional theatrical jokes:

1. After the duel the musician chases the acrobat who has just killed his rival; they remain at a constant distance of about a foot from each other and run on the spot, concentrating more on making the spectators admire the rattling of their tambourines and their dazzling smiles than sustaining the psychology of the play.

2. The slain rival not only comes to life but even musters enough strength to hit the four others who had dared rob him when he was lying lifeless.

The story of the page who was faithful to his master and of other events worthy of presentation

An étude treated in the style of a sentimental story of the late seventeenth century. The action of the comedians is restricted to the main stage.

Properties: four bamboo poles and a veil representing a portable canopy. A length of tulle waved by the proscenium servants to emphasize moments of tension. A small stick representing a dagger.

The aim of the étude is to afford training in slow motion.

The Mousetrap scene from 'The Tragedy of Hamlet, Prince of Denmark' (*pantomime*)

Any dramatic work which is imbued with the quality of true theatricality is amenable to total schematization, even to the extent of temporarily removing the dialogue with which the skeleton of the scenario is embellished. In this form, schematically and mimetically performed, a genuinely theatrical play can still stir the spectator, simply because the scenario is constructed from traditional, truly theatrical elements.

The Lady, the Cat, the Bird and the Snake (Fragment from a Chinese play)
This fragment is meant to be neither stylized nor ethnographical. The pantomime resembles such dramatic works as Gozzi's *Turandot*. China is China as seen by the Venetians of the eighteenth century.

The entire play is performed on the forestage with the exception of the final scene when (1) the young Chinese prince goes on a long journey across a desert seated on the shoulders of the comedians who play the parts of warriors, but who temporarily represent a horse; (2) the entire cast goes off to war against an unseen enemy bearing long spears (the effect of a host of vertical lines is to deceive the spectator into seeing more people on stage than there really are (cf. Jacques Callot, Velasquez).

[*Lyubov k tryom apelsinam*, 1914, 6–7, pp. 105–15.]

AN ATTEMPT TO PROGRESS FROM EXERCISES IN STAGE MOVEMENT TO WORK ON DRAMATIC EXTRACTS WITH DIALOGUE. *Ophelia's mad scene from Hamlet*.
We took last year's pantomime scenario and adapted it for performance with dialogue.

The actress performing Ophelia is struggling to overcome the pretentious staging and the sugary gestures which were so admired by the critics at last year's performances; she is trying to recapture the naïve simplicity of the original strolling players.

The songs have not yet been set to music and for the present we are using a board struck with a bamboo stick as an accompaniment (you must not forget that you are speaking verse and that there can be none of the freedom enjoyed by the actor who 'lives' his part and is subject to no formal discipline; observe what freedom there is to be enjoyed even within the limits of formal discipline). The actor-musician has no difficulty with that which is beyond the reach of the actor whose musicality has yet to be awakened.

We shall work on this extract twice: in September and then again in December. One should become accustomed to working at such intervals; a break helps to smooth out the rough patches of one's initial attempt, because once the imagination has been fired it does not cease to function when the work is laid temporarily aside.

The tenseness caused by so-called 'experienced emotions' has been replaced by the free play of imagination and a stage technique has been liberated which brooks no obstacles. We cannot hope for a successful rendering of this extract until we have eliminated all traces of Duncanesque balleticism, until the actor takes the stage with all the dexterity of a juggler, manipulating his lines as the juggler does his balls, which fly back and forth above his head in intervals and patterns similar to the rhythm and rhyme of spoken verse. Remember the theatrical expression 'to project one's lines'; ask yourself whether you can control your breathing; don't your 'experienced emotions' disrupt the measure of your breathing? Perhaps you should consult some Hindu expert on the art of respiration.

It is time we reached some conclusion about the question of experienced emotions on the stage. Admirers of Oscar Wilde will have found the answer already in the words of Sybil Vane in *The Picture of Dorian Gray*: 'I might mimic a passion that I do not feel, but I cannot mimic one that burns me like a fire.'

The Studio has set itself the task of staging *The Tragedy of Hamlet, Prince of Denmark* without any cuts, either of complete scenes or of individual lines. Such a production can be achieved only if we succeed in finding the key to the performance of Shakespearian tragedy by experimenting with two or three extracts from the play, studying its form and then re-creating it on the stage.

I remember reading about the success in the London theatre of the 1560s of Thomas Preston's tragedy, *Cambyses*; what was so significant was the description of the play as a 'lamentable tragedy mixed full of pleasant mirth'. May one not consider the tragedy of Hamlet as a play in which the tears are glimpsed through a series of traditional theatrical pranks? Should we not forget once and for all the arguments of scholars about the strength or weakness of Hamlet's will, ignore all the various intentions which are attributed willy-nilly to the author? The same may be said of Shakespeare's age as of the theatre which preceded him: 'The whole gamut of artistic expression was played on two notes – the merry and the sad; moreover, the sad was frequently intermingled with the horrific and the merry with the caricatured; the intermediate notes expressing the more refined emotions were of little significance. Of music, singing, plays, etcetera, the public demanded that it be either deeply moved or made to laugh until it cried; if one and the same song or play achieved both ends, so much the better.' (N. Storozhenko, *Shakespeare's Predecessors*, St Petersburg, 1872.)

In the tragedy of *Hamlet* the elements of high drama and low comedy alternate not only in the play as a whole but within individual characters (particularly in the title role). In order to reveal this characteristic fully on the stage, we must construct the one kind of building where the actor will find it both easy and rewarding to *perform*.

[*Lyubov k tryom apelsinam*, 1915, no 4–7, pp. 208–11.]

STUDIO PROGRAMME FOR 1916–1917

Basic Course of Study:

1. The technique of stage movement. Members of the Studio must aim at perfection in dancing, music, athletics and fencing (the Studio directors will recommend specialist instructors in these fields). Recommended sports: lawn tennis, throwing the discus, sailing.

2. Practical study of the technical aspects of production: stage equipment, décor, lighting, costumes, hand-props.

3. The basic principles of Italian improvised comedy (*commedia dell' arte*).

4. The application in the modern theatre of the traditional devices of the theatres of the seventeenth and eighteenth centuries.

5. Musical recitation in drama.

N.B. (Items 3 and 4). The establishing of a formal canon must depend not on academic dogmatism but on the genetic study of traditional forms, and any divergence towards lifeless, academic imitation is regarded as dangerous.

Subjects for Discussion:

All subjects for discussion serve a clear purpose: to demonstrate the value of the essentially *theatrical* elements of the art of the theatre.

1. Mimesis: at its lowest level – imitation devoid of creative idealization; at its highest – the mask; its most profound variations – the comic, tragic and tragi-comic grotesque.

2. Analysis of acting devices together with the characteristics of outstanding actors and the ages when they were performing.

In any work of art it is essential that the *material* should express its agreement, so to speak, with the form which the artist has imposed upon it. It is a vital condition of the theatre that the actor manifests his art *through his technique alone*; through his acting he interprets the material placed at his disposal by employing those means which are consistent with the properties of the human body and spirit. Therefore, we should note that as well as refining his material (by achieving maximum

153

bodily flexibility) the actor must discover as soon as possible his own identity as an artist-histrion.

In order to help the instructor spot the merest idiosyncrasy of any actor who is engaged in establishing his *emploi*, every Studio member must complete by the end of the first month a kind of *curriculum vitae* recording every occasion on which he or she has performed as an amateur in childhood or adolescence and later as a conscious professional (where applicable), and defining his or her views on the theatre then and now.

3. Analysis of Russian dramatic works of the 1830s and 1840s (Pushkin, Gogol, Lermontov).

4. The influence of the popular theatre on the theatrical innovations of Molière, Shakespeare, Hoffmann, Tieck, Pushkin, Gogol, Remizov, Blok, etc.

5. The circus and the theatre.

6. Count Carlo Gozzi and his theatre.

7. The Spanish theatre.

8. The conventions of Hindu drama (Kālidāsa).

9. Stage and acting conventions in the Japanese and Chinese theatres.

10. Survey of recent theatrical theories (Edward Gordon Craig, Vsevolod Meyerhold, Nikolai Yevreinov, Fyodor Komissarzhevsky, Mikhail Gnesin, Emile Jaques-Dalcroze).

11. The roles of the stage-director and the designer in the theatre.

12. The programmes of other theatre schools (the projects of A. N. Ostrovsky, S. Yuriev, Voronov, Ozarovsky, etc.).

13. Theatre discipline compared with shipboard discipline. Those works prescribed as essential reading by the Studio Director and staff must be completed within the periods stipulated. The Studio journal, *The Love of Three Oranges. The Journal of Doctor Dapertutto*, is considered an indispensable textbook. Members of the Studio are required to attend all classes. Members of the Studio must be prepared at all times to perform the test exercises which are set periodically.

Candidates for entry into the Studio for the academic year 1916–17 will be classified as follows:

1. Past members of the Studio who have yet to gain graduation certificates.

2. New entrants.

Candidates in both categories will be subject to an entrance examination. Candidates in category 1 will be debarred from examination if:

1. they have failed to satisfy the Studio Director at their periodic examination;

2. they have failed to submit a *curriculum vitae* within the specified time;

3. their work has diverged consistently from the fundamental aims of the Studio.

Such candidates are invited to discuss their case personally with Vsevolod Emilevich Meyerhold. Those who have gained the title of 'Studio Comedian' are admitted to the new course without examination.

Candidates for examination are required to demonstrate the following:

1. Musical proficiency (as instrumentalist or singer).

2. Physical agility (gymnastic or acrobatic exercises; improvised pantomime extract containing acrobatic tricks).

3. Mimetic ability (performance of act without words on command; a *mise en scène* and the basic devices will be demonstrated by the Director).

4. Clarity of diction (reading from text).

5. Familiarity with theories of prosody.

6. Knowledge (if any) of other arts forms (painting, sculpture, poetry, dance), and own work if available.

7. Knowledge of dramatic history within limits of higher school course (questions and answers).

Those who are prevented by pathological shyness from doing themselves justice at the entrance examination will be given the opportunity of joining the Studio for a probationary period of one month, during which they will have the chance to show their theatrical ability in 'test classes'.

A pupil may gain the title of 'comedian' by passing a series of tests in accordance with a specified programme and after completing a period of Studio membership of a duration to be determined by the Director.

The period of study in the Studio is not limited in duration. However, periodically the membership is reduced by excluding those whose work no longer accords with the Studio's aims.

Any comedian who displays exceptional ability may be invited to participate in the formation of a new theatre which is under consideration at the moment.

The following are incompatible with Studio membership:

1. Participation in any public theatrical performances not organized by the Director.

2. Membership of other artistic schools without the authority of the Director.

[*Lyubov k tryom apelsinam*, 1916, no 2–3, pp. 144–8.]

NOTE These extracts are taken from the chronicle of the Studio's activities which was contained in each number of *The Love of Three Oranges*. Beginning in January 1914, Meyerhold's journal appeared at irregular intervals until the ninth and last number in late 1916. Its contents included articles on the history and theory of the theatre (with particular emphasis on the *commedia dell' arte*, Carlo Gozzi, and the Spanish theatre), translations of plays (Gozzi, Plautus, Tieck, etc.), reviews of contemporary productions and books on the theatre, and the works of modern Russian poets (Akhmatova, Blok, Sologub, etc.). The poetry section was run by Alexander Blok. As well as being editor, Meyerhold himself was among the contributors, all of whom were of a similar theatrical persuasion.

Apart from Meyerhold's classes in stage movement, the Studio curriculum comprised instruction in verse and prose speaking, voice-production, and the techniques of the *commedia dell' arte*. There were also lectures on theatre history (with particular reference to improvized comedy).

Guglielmo (p. 149) or Guglielmo Ebreo of Pesaro (*c.* 1400–75) was a celebrated Italian dancing-master and the author of a treatise on the dance entitled *De pratica seu arte tripudii vulghare opusculum*, in which he discusses the six indispensable qualities of the dancer. One of these, 'partire di terreno' (lit. 'the apportionment of the terrain') concerns the dancer's ability to judge the area in which the dance is being performed and adjust his steps accordingly.[1]

[1] Cf. Mabel Dolmetsch, *Dances of Spain and Italy 1400–1600*, London, 1954.

Part Four

OCTOBER IN THE THEATRE

1917-1921

DURING A VISIT TO Petersburg with the Moscow Art Theatre in March 1901 Meyerhold witnessed the brutal suppression of a student demonstration by the police and military. Soon afterwards he described his reaction to the event in a letter to Chekhov:[1]

> I want to burn with the spirit of the times. I want all servants of the stage to recognize their high destiny. I am irritated by those comrades of mine who have no desire to rise above the narrow interests of their caste and respond to the interests of society. Yes, the theatre is capable of playing an enormous part in the transformation of the whole of existence!

But neither then nor in 1905, when he was an avid observer of the armed rising in Moscow, did he attempt to exploit the theatre as a means of propaganda.

In 1913 he said in an interview:

> A theatre which presents plays saturated in 'psychologism' with the motivation of every single event underlined, or which forces the spectator to rack his brains over the solution of all manner of social and philosophical problems – such a theatre destroys its own theatricality. . . . The stage is a world of marvels and enchantment, it is breathless joy and strange magic.[2]

This remained Meyerhold's theatrical philosophy right up to 1917, despite the disdain for tsarist obscurantism which he shared with many other intellectuals of the time.

His disdain was greatly exacerbated by the languid indifference of the Alexandrinsky stalls patrons, which no production of his ever succeeded in stirring. When in November 1914 one of the rehearsals at his Studio was attended by an audience of wounded soldiers, he was moved to write: '. . . in the way they responded to the performance of the comedians, they constituted the very audience for which the new theatre, the truly popular theatre, is intended.'[3] Two months after the fall of the monarchy, at a debate entitled 'Revolution, Art and War', Meyerhold castigated 'the silent, passionless parterre where people come for a rest cure', and asked:

---

[1] Letter dated 18 April 1901, published in *Literaturnoe nasledstvo-Chekhov*, vol. 68, Moscow, 1960, p. 442.

[2] *Teatr*, Moscow, 24 October 1913, p. 5.

[3] *Lyubov k tryom apelsinam*, Petrograd, 1915, no 1–3, p. 140.

'Why don't the soldiers come to the theatre and liberate it from the parterre public?'[1]

In November 1917 the Bolsheviks transferred all theatres to State control and Lunacharsky, the People's Commissar for Education, invited 120 leading artists to a conference to discuss the reorganization of the arts. Only five accepted the invitation, and they included Blok, Mayakovsky and Meyerhold. It can be argued that Meyerhold was merely exploiting the Revolution to propagate his own reforms. But the caution displayed by the majority is significant: Bolshevik power was far from secure at that time and a declaration of solidarity amounted to a hazardous act of faith. This act Meyerhold committed and soon affirmed it in 1918 by joining the Bolshevik Party.

Whilst retaining his posts at the former Imperial Theatres, Meyerhold organized courses in production technique in Petrograd. These courses, the first of their kind in Russia, were held under the auspices of the Theatrical Department of the Commissariat for Education, of which Meyerhold was deputy head in Petrograd. The first, which ran from June to August 1918, was attended by nearly a hundred students with ages ranging from 14 to 53, and consisted of evening lectures designed to give a 'polytechnical education in the theatre arts'. There was a certain resemblance to Meyerhold's earlier Studio, with instruction in movement and mime; but of greatest significance was the stress laid on the need for co-operation between the stage-director and the designer. Meyerhold continued to direct the course until ill health forced him to move south in May 1919. After a further term, the course was discontinued.

In September 1918 plans were made to stage the first-ever Soviet play, Mayakovsky's *Mystery-Bouffe*, to mark the first anniversary of the October Revolution. It was to be produced by Meyerhold with the assistance of Vladimir Solovyov and Mayakovsky himself. However, the Petrograd theatres were still maintaining a position of cautious neutrality and the production was boycotted by the vast majority of professional actors. Consequently, the organizers were forced to make a public appeal in order to complete casting. Eventually all but a few main parts were played by students, with Mayakovsky himself filling three roles in the opening performance at the Petrograd Conservatoire on 7 November 1918.

The Bolshevik Government was more than a little embarrassed by the

[1] Report of a debate on 14 April 1917 in *Teatr i iskusstvo*, Petrograd, 1917, no 18, p. 297.

The Magnanimous Cuckold, 1922 (from left: Dobriner, Zaichikov, Ilinsky, Babanova).

The 1928 revival (from left: Zaichikov, Ilinsky, Kelberer).

(*a*) The 1922 production.

(*b*) The 1928 revival.

The Magnanimous Cuckold.

enthusiastic support it was receiving from the Futurist artists, fearing that their uncompromising brutalist vision of the new mechanized age might prove insufficiently beguiling for the masses. Lunacharsky, himself a critic of considerable liberality and perception, published an article in *Petrograd Pravda* championing *Mystery-Bouffe* and excusing in advance the worst aberrations of the production:

> As a work of literature, it is most original, powerful and beautiful. But what it will turn out like in production I don't yet know. I fear very much that the Futurist artists have made millions of mistakes . . . But even if the child turns out deformed, it will still be dear to us, because it is born of that same Revolution which we all look upon as our own great mother.[1]

The play parodies the biblical story of the Ark, with the flood representing world revolution, the seven 'clean' couples who survive – the exploiters, and the seven 'unclean' couples – the international proletariat. Having overthrown the 'clean', the 'unclean' are led by 'simply Man' through an innocuous hell and a tedious paradise to the promised land which is revealed as the utopian mechanized state of Socialism where the only servants are tools and machines.

Meyerhold treated this allegory with all the rigid schematization of the propaganda poster. In order to stress the solidarity of the 'unclean', they were dressed in identical grey overalls and spoke in the uniform elevated style of political oratory. The 'clean' were played in the broad, knockabout manner of the popular travelling show. The costumes and settings by Malevich (a huge blue hemisphere for the world, a few cubes for the ark, geometrical backcloths) made little concession to representation and were widely condemned. Clearly, they did not accord with Mayakovsky's conception, for he produced his own set of caricature costume designs, highly individualized and brightly coloured. *Mystery-Bouffe* attracted violent criticism both from the left and the right, and it was taken off after the three scheduled performances. Despite Mayakovsky's strenuous efforts it was nearly three years before the play was revived in a new version in Moscow, again with Meyerhold directing.

In May 1919, weakened by undernourishment and overwork, Meyerhold was forced to leave Petrograd for convalescence. He entered a sanatorium in Yalta, where he spent the summer receiving treatment for tuberculosis. When the Whites entered the town he fled by sea to Novorossisk, but there his Bolshevik sympathies were revealed and in August 1919

---

[1] 'Kommunistichesky spektakl'' in *Petrogradskaya pravda*, 5 November 1918, p. 2.

he was arrested. Meyerhold spent four months in prison and narrowly escaped execution for alleged subversive activities. Shortly after his release on parole, the town was reoccupied by the Red Army, whose political department Meyerhold now joined. For the remainder of his stay in the South he participated in regular military training and spoke at both political and theatrical debates, as well as producing one play, Ibsen's *Doll's House*, in Novorossisk.

As soon as Lunacharsky learnt of Meyerhold's vicissitudes, he summoned him to Moscow to take charge of the Theatrical Department for the entire Soviet Republic. The actor Igor Ilinsky describes Meyerhold's appearance at that time:

> He was wearing a soldier's greatcoat and on his cap there was a badge with Lenin's picture. . . . In spite of its apparent simplicity, his appearance was somewhat theatrical, because although he was dressed modestly and without any superfluous 'Bolshevik' attributes, the style was still *à la Bolshevik*: the carelessly thrown on greatcoat, the boots and puttees, the cap, the dark red woollen scarf – it was all quite unpretentious, but at the same time effective enough.[1]

Meyerhold's actions were no less dramatic than his appearance: he transformed the Theatrical Department into a military headquarters and proclaimed the advent of the October Revolution in the theatre. Assuming the editorship of the department's organ, *The Theatre Herald* (Vestnik teatra), he conducted a violent polemic on behalf of the proletarian, provincial, non-professional and Red Army theatres, and demanded a ruthless redeployment of the manpower and material resources concentrated in the small group of 'Academic Theatres' in Moscow. This group comprised the Bolshoi, the Maly, the Moscow Art and its first and second studios, Tairov's Kamerny, and the Moscow Children's Theatre. These the State considered the most worthy custodians of Russian theatrical traditions and rewarded them with its financial support. They were the true objective of Meyerhold's offensive, and his tirades soon resolved into an undisguised assault on their anachronistic styles and repertoires. Judged by his criteria at that time, he was largely justified. By 1920 the Revolution had left no impression on the Russian theatre and not one Academic Theatre had attempted to stage a Soviet play. Whilst the repertoire abounded in such works as Byron's *Cain* (Moscow Art Theatre), Wilde's *Salome* and Claudel's *Tidings brought to Mary* (Kamerny), and Lecocq's operetta, *The Daughter of Madame Angot* (Moscow Art Musical Studio), not one serious attempt had been made to exploit the professional theatre for propaganda purposes

[1] Igor Ilinsky, *Sam o sebe*, Moscow, 1962, p. 106.

since the three performances of *Mystery-Bouffe* in 1918. Tairov summed up the prevailing attitude: 'A propagandist theatre after a revolution is like mustard after a meal.'[1]

Not content with mere exhortation, Meyerhold took control of the Free Theatre Company, renamed it the 'R.S.F.S.R. Theatre No. 1', and augmented it with his own young and inexperienced nominees. The play chosen to inaugurate the new theatre was *The Dawn*, an epic verse drama written in 1898 by the Belgian symbolist poet Verhaeren, depicting the transformation of a capitalist war into an international proletarian uprising by the opposing soldiers in the mythical town of Oppidomagne. It was hurriedly adapted by Meyerhold and his assistant Valery Bebutov to bring out its relevance to recent political events.

The first performance, timed to coincide with the third anniversary of the October Revolution, took place on 7 November 1920 at the former Sohn Theatre. The derelict, unheated auditorium with its flaking plaster and broken seats was more like a meeting-hall; this was wholly appropriate, for it was in the spirit of a political meeting that Meyerhold conceived the production. Admission was free, the walls were hung with hortatory placards, and the audience was showered at intervals during the play with leaflets. Also derived from the meeting was the declamatory style of the actors, who mostly remained motionless and addressed their speeches straight at the audience. Critics rightly compared the production with Greek tragedy, which, as Meyerhold himself said (see p. 173), furnished the precedent for the chorus in the orchestra pit commenting on the peripeteia of the drama. The chorus was assisted in the task of guiding and stimulating audience reaction by a claque of actors concealed throughout the audience. At a fixed point in the play the character of the Herald would enter and deliver a bulletin on the progress of the real Civil War still being waged in the South. Meyerhold's highest aspirations were gratified on the night when the Herald announced the decisive break into the Crimea at the Battle of Perekop and the entire theatre rose in a triumphant rendering of the 'Internationale'. However, such unanimity of response did not occur every night but usually only when military detachments attended *en bloc* – as they sometimes did, complete with banners flying and bands ready to strike up.

Whilst the more sophisticated spectator was likely to find the conventions crude and the acting maladroit (not to mention the political message oversimplified or even repugnant), the proletariat at whom ostensibly the

[1] At a public debate on 20 December 1920, reported in *Vestnik teatra*, Moscow, 1920, no 78–79, p. 16.

163

production was aimed could not help but be puzzled by its appearance. The young designer, Vladimir Dmitriev, who had attended Meyerhold's theatre arts course in Petrograd, favoured the geometrical schematization of the Futurist school. His assembly of red, gold and silver cubes, discs and cylinders, cut-out tin triangles and intersecting ropes blended uneasily with the occasional recognizable object such as a graveyard cross or the gates of a city, to say nothing of the soldiers' spears and shields, or the curious 'timeless' costumes of daubed canvas. Furthermore, the overall picture looked merely tawdry in the harsh white light with which Meyerhold sought to dispel all illusion.

As with *Mystery-Bouffe*, the Party was discomfited by this manifestation of the style of its Futurist supporters. Lenin's wife, Nadezhda Krupskaya, had no complaint against the 'timelessness' of the production, but she objected violently to the ill-considered adaptation which showed the hero, Hérénien, as a traitor to his class who comes to terms with a capitalist power. She also repudiated the whole conception of a production which presumed to manipulate the responses of the audience:

> A hero divorced from time and space is not so bad, but to cast the Russian proletariat as a Shakespearian crowd which any self-opinionated fool can lead wherever the urge takes him is a sheer insult.[1]

As a direct consequence of her criticism, the work was rewritten to render it dialectically more orthodox, but all the original theatrical devices were retained.

For all its imperfections, *The Dawn* was a major success which ran for well over a hundred performances to packed houses. It proclaimed an epoch in the Soviet theatre and is rightly considered a *locus classicus* in the history of the political theatre.

Whilst criticizing the 'pretentiousness of the Futurist elements' in *The Dawn*, Lunacharsky considered it was a reasonable price to pay for the production's revolutionary fervour.[2] However, he refused point-blank to surrender the Academic Theatres to Meyerhold's demolition squad, saying:

> I am prepared to entrust Comrade Meyerhold with the destruction of the old and bad and the creation of the new and good. But I am not prepared to entrust him with the preservation of the old and good, the vital and strong, which must be allowed to develop in its own way in a revolutionary atmosphere.[3]

[1] *Pravda*, Moscow, 10 November 1920, p. 2.
[2] At the first debate on *The Dawn*, 22 November 1920. *Vestnik teatra*, 1920, no 75, p. 12.
[3] A. V. Lunacharsky, 'To my opponents' in *Vestnik teatra*, 1920, no 76–77, 14 December, p. 4.

All Academic Theatres in Moscow and Petrograd were brought under the aegis of the Commissariat for Education, thereby rendering Meyerhold's Theatrical Department innocuous in the one sector it truly coveted. His ambitions were realized to the extent that the Academic Theatres began now to stage Soviet works, but it was in their own good time and in their own well-tried manner. Briefly, the Korsh and Nezlobin Theatres rallied to Meyerhold and were renamed R.S.F.S.R. Theatres Nos. 2 and 3, but they enjoyed only a brief existence in this guise and yielded no productions of note. On 26 February 1921 Meyerhold resigned as Head of the Theatrical Department, and in May he severed his last effective connection with it.

May Day 1921 saw the second production at the R.S.F.S.R. Theatre No. 1. It was *Mystery-Bouffe*, completely rewritten to make it relevant to the course of events since 1917. As a playwright Mayakovsky was accorded unique status by Meyerhold, who in 1933 said of him:

> In his work with me, Mayakovsky showed himself to be not only a remarkable dramatist but a remarkable director as well. In all my years as a director I have never permitted myself the luxury of an author's co-operation when producing his play. I have always tried to keep the author as far from the theatre as possible during the period of actual production, because any truly creative director is bound to be hampered by the playwright's interference. In Mayakovsky's case I not only permitted him to attend, I simply couldn't begin to produce his plays without him.[1]

Mayakovsky was present from the first read-through of *Mystery-Bouffe* and added numerous topical couplets right up to the final rehearsal. The published text of this revised version is prefaced by the following exhortation:

> Henceforth everyone who performs, stages, reads or prints *Mystery-Bouffe* should alter the contents in order to make it modern, of the day, up to the minute.[2]

Amongst his amendments were the inclusion in the ranks of 'The Clean' of Lloyd George and Clemenceau, and the creation of a new central character 'The Conciliator' or Menshevik, who was brilliantly portrayed by the nineteen-year-old Igor Ilinsky in red wig, steel gig-lamps and flapping coat-tails, and with an open umbrella to symbolize his readiness for flight. His performance set the key for the whole production, an hilarious, dynamic, caricaturist rough-and-tumble, a carnival celebration of victory

---

[1] Meyerhold, 'A Word about Mayakovsky', address to the Meyerhold Theatre company on 25 February 1933. Published in *Sovetskoe iskusstvo*, 11 April 1936, p. 3.

[2] V. V. Mayakovsky, *Polnoe sobranie sochinenii*, vol. 2, Moscow, 1956, p. 245.

in the Civil War in total contrast to the still, hieratic solemnity of *The Dawn*. 'The Clean', in costumes by Victor Kisselyov, had something of the pith and vigour which made the ROSTA Satirical Windows[1] the most telling political posters of the early Soviet period, and were close in spirit to Mayakovsky's own sketches. However, once again 'The Unclean', clad this time in blue overalls, were of a uniform dullness which not even Mayakovsky's rhetoric could hide. Meyerhold was quick to realize that the portrayal of virtue – even Socialist virtue – untarnished and triumphant is inherently tedious and, as we shall see, his avoidance of it at all costs was to cause him unending trouble in the years to come and ultimately to contribute in large measure to his downfall.

The proscenium which had been bridged by the use of the orchestra pit in *The Dawn* was demolished once and for all in *Mystery-Bouffe*.[2] The stage proper was taken up by a series of platforms of differing levels, interconnected by steps and vaguely suggestive of the various locations in the action. In front a broad ramp sloped right down to the first row of seats, bearing a huge hemisphere over which the cast clambered and which revolved to expose the exit from 'Hell'. In this scene, one of the devils was played by a circus clown, Vitaly Lazarenko, who entered by sliding down a wire and performed acrobatic tricks. In the final act, which depicted the new, *electrified* promised land, the action spilled into the boxes adjacent to the stage, and at the conclusion the audience was invited to mingle with the actors onstage.

In this production Meyerhold dispensed finally with the front curtain and flown scenery. The theatre was bursting at the seams, unable to accommodate the kind of popular spectacle which Meyerhold was striving to achieve and it was now that the questions arose whose answers he was shortly to seek in Constructivism.

Despite the charges of Futurist obscurity and a boycott by all but three newspaper critics, *Mystery-Bouffe* was an even greater success than *The Dawn*, and was performed daily until the close of the season on 7 July. In the five months up to the end of May 1921, 154 performances of the two plays were watched by roughly 120,000 spectators.[3]

In Spring 1921, Soviet Russia was on the verge of bankruptcy as a consequence of the privations and chaos wrought by the Civil War. In order to

[1] A series of strip cartoons on social and political themes issued by the Russian Telegraph Agency (ROSTA). Mayakovsky was a regular contributor.
[2] The settings were by Anton Lavinsky and Vladimir Khrakovsky.
[3] *Vestnik teatra*, Moscow, 1921, no 93–94, p. 23.

restore the economy Lenin introduced his New Economic Policy, or 'NEP' as it was known. Under its provisions, considerable sectors of the economy reverted to private control and the ban on the investment of foreign capital was lifted. Its effects were quickly felt in the theatre, where many companies reverted to private ownership and were required once more to yield their investors a realistic profit.

In June 1921 the Moscow Soviet ordered the closure of the Theatre R.S.F.S.R. No. 1 on the questionable grounds of overspending. Thanks largely to Lunacharsky's intervention, the theatre continued to live a precarious existence throughout the summer, managing to stage one more production, Ibsen's *League of Youth* (17 August). A 'revolutionized' version of Wagner's *Rienzi* was abandoned after the second dress rehearsal. On 6 September 1921 the theatre closed for good and Meyerhold, the first Bolshevik director, was left with nowhere to work.

---

1. On the Contemporary Theatre

At the present time there are two possible types of theatre:
1. The non-professional proletarian theatre, whose roots are in the culture of the new ruling class.
2. The so-called professional theatre.

The first type, which demands the greater attention, is established so far only in outlying regions, in spite of the craze for theatricalization which has gripped almost the entire territory of the Russian Soviet Republic. There are reports of villages with as many as five theatres.

I need to devote most of my attention and the resources at my disposal to the establishment in the centre of Moscow of a theatre of the International Proletkult. I am required to do this by a resolution passed by the Second Congress of the Third International.[1] The Proletkult has increased in scope from All-Russian to International.

Because of this, but partly for autobiographical reasons, I have vowed to have as little as possible to do with the professional theatres.

At the request of Comrade Bebutov and the company I am here to help you in the difficult task of staging *The Dawn* (a play whose key has yet to

[1] July–August 1920.

be found and which invariably has been a failure) in the relatively short time left before the October celebrations.

So let us return to the question of the professional theatres and their only possible and – for the present – legal form. One characteristic of the professional actor is his imagined (for he alone believes in it) apolitical attitude.

In fact, it is utter nonsense to speak of an apolitical attitude. No man (no actor) has ever been apolitical, a-social; man is always a product of the forces of his environment. And is it not this which determines the nature of an actor throughout all his individual, social and historical metamorphoses? It is this law which shapes the interpretation of any character by any actor.

Take two Hamlets: Rossi[1] and Mounet-Sully.[2] The first, a true representative of the Italian popular tradition, possessed all the qualities of the rebel; the second, a product of the tradition of French comedy, a court actor, was a Hamlet of the age of feudalism.

Now about the theatre. What theatre has a right to the title 'exemplary'? The so-called 'State Exemplary Theatre'[3] has proved that it is not exemplary for our age, since it is not in accord with modern society. It has devoted itself to the pursuit of sugary, outmoded romanticism.

The only theatre which in its day could be regarded as exemplary (but only for a limited section of Russian society) was the Moscow Art Theatre. What was striking about its productions of Chekhov? The technique? No, the actors who first played Chekhov were totally deficient in technique; many of them were straight out of school. The reason why the Art Theatre's productions of Chekhov came to be regarded as models and inspired so many imitations was because the mood of the performers corresponded to the general mood of the Russian intelligentsia at that time.

Equally, the only theatre which can become exemplary in this age of mighty revolution is a revolutionary theatre. However, it is wrong to imagine that the repertoire of such a theatre must consist exclusively of Verhaeren's *Dawn* and Vermishev's *Red Truth*.[4] It could just as easily include Wilde's *Salome* and Shakespeare's *Hamlet*; everything depends on

[1] Ernesto Rossi (1827–96) appeared frequently in Russia, from 1877 to 1896.
[2] Jean Mounet-Sully (1841–1916) appeared in Russia in 1894 and 1899.
[3] The State Exemplary Theatre functioned in Moscow from 1919 to 1920 under the directorship of Vassily Sakhnovsky. Its repertoire consisted mainly of classical works.
[4] Alexander Vermishev, born 1879, died in 1919 at the hands of the Whites. *The Red Truth* (1919) was one of the first revolutionary plays and was performed widely in army and proletarian theatres during the Civil War.

the interpretation. The actress playing Salome might unconsciously draw material for her portrayal of perverted sensuality from the familiar and graphic example of Alix of Hesse.[1]

If the actor playing Herod could get right away from the contrived, sickly gaudiness of the Kamerny Theatre[2] in his portrayal of that depraved despot, then the figure of Jokanaan might stand out quite differently as a genuine revolutionary, bent on destroying a corrupt society.

After all, Mochalov conveyed a hint of Bakunin in Hamlet. In the same way, before running the King through, the New Actor could flick the crown from his head with a deft movement of his slender, steel rapier.

This is the only form which is permissible for the professional theatre, and it will depend on the company of the Free Theatre whether it is to remain a theatre divorced from modern life or whether it will become the theatre of those five magical letters – *The First Theatre of the R.S.F.S.R.*

[*Vestnik Teatra*, Moscow, 1920, no 70, pp. 11–12.]

NOTE   A transcript of Meyerhold's address to the company of the Free Theatre before the first rehearsal of *The Dawn* at the beginning of October 1920.

---

2. Inaugural Speech to the Company of the R.S.F.S.R. Theatre No. 1

The artistic Soviet of the R.S.F.S.R. Theatre has compiled a repertoire plan which includes *The Dawn* (Verhaeren), *Mystery-Bouffe* (Mayakovsky), *Hamlet* (Shakespeare), *Great Catherine* (Bernard Shaw), *Golden Head* (Claudel) and *Women in Parliament* (Aristophanes). But since all this is merely literature, let it lie undisturbed in the libraries. We shall need scenarios and we shall often utilize even the classics as a basis for our theatrical compositions. We shall tackle the task of adaptation without fear,

---

[1] Alexandra Fyodorovna, the wife of Nicholas II. Presumably Meyerhold is alluding to her relationship with Rasputin, although there is no proof of any impropriety between them.
[2] Tairov's production of *Salome* had its première at the Kamerny Theatre on 9 October 1917.

fully confident of its necessity. It is possible that we shall adapt texts in co-operation with the actors of the company, and it is a great pity that they were not able to help Valery Bebutov and me with *The Dawn*. Joint work on texts by the company is envisaged as an integral part of the theatre's function. It is possible that such team-work will help us to realize the principle of improvisation, about which there is so much talk at the moment and which promises to prove most valuable.

· The psychological make-up of the actor will need to undergo a number of changes. There must be no pauses, no psychology, no 'authentic emotions' – either on the stage or whilst building a role. Here is our theatrical programme: plenty of light, plenty of high spirits, plenty of grandeur, plenty of infectious enthusiasm, unlaboured creativity, the participation of the audience in the corporate creative act of the performance. And these are not merely technical requirements – far from it. Comrade Kerzhentsev is wrong when he writes in his book *The Creative Theatre*[1] that Vsevolod Meyerhold, in introducing the proscenium stage, is concerned purely with the technical reform of the theatre. For me, the proscenium is far more than just a technical refinement: it is the first step towards the unification of the stage with the auditorium which Comrade Kerzhentsev himself dreams of.

[*Vestnik teatra*, 1920, no 72–73, pp. 19–20.]

NOTE   Report of a speech made by Meyerhold on 31 October 1920.

---

3. On the Staging of Verhaeren's *The Dawn*

Mankind has reached a stage where all relationships, all concepts are changing. Whereas before 1917 we treated a literary work with a certain degree of care and consideration, today we are no longer such fetishists, we do not fall on to our knees and cry reverently: 'Shakespeare! . . . Verhaeren! . . .'

The audience has changed so completely, that we, too, need to revise our opinions. We have a new public which will stand no nonsense – each

[1] V. M. Kerzhentsev's *Tvorchesky Teatr* (Petrograd, 1918) was an early formulation of Proletkult theatre policy. It was republished four times.

spectator represents, as it were, Soviet Russia in microcosm . . . Now we have to protect the interests not of the author but of the spectator. The interests of the audience have assumed a vital significance.

But – we are asked – why don't you create new drama yourselves instead of mutilating the classics? From each work we extract the scenario, sometimes retaining isolated moments of it. But isn't this just how those dramatists worked who since their deaths have become so revered. Wasn't this the method of Sophocles, Shakespeare, Schiller, Tirso de Molina, Pushkin? . . . Or were they imbued with holy reverence for dead canons?

And another question: Which is better, Mérimée's *La Jacquerie* or Pushkin's *Scenes from the Age of Chivalry*? *Wilhelm Tell* by Schiller or by Aegidius Tschudi?[1] Boccacio's novella or Shakespeare's *All's well that ends well*? Sophocles' *Oedipus* or the Oedipus myth as it was recounted by the people?

Any re-creation of a work justifies its existence if it springs from an inner necessity. Thus the authors of the new version of *The Dawn* were compelled by the urgent demands of the modern spectator. Besides, as we see it, by the very act of buying or accepting a ticket the spectator affirms his confidence in a production which he hopes to enjoy. In the case in question, the 'demand' takes on a particular urgency since the production marks the October celebrations.

If we examine what we have cut out of the text, weigh up that flabby material, we find that it is literature – sometimes good, sometimes poor – but still literature. And in order that these literary 'treasures' should not disappear of their own accord in the whirlpool of stage action, we decided to remove them ourselves, thereby improving the action.

Thus this scenario, this skeleton of *The Dawn*, in losing its surplus weight, has developed a lean body. And in order to ensure the survival of this lean body, it has been supplied with a nervous system in the shape of the *comedian* – to whose voice we are most attentive.

We realize that the comedian who dies on stage in the part of Hérénien the Elder is not going to tolerate his body decomposing for half an act whilst we listen to the orations of a prophet from the country, a prophet from the town, a worker, a peasant, a shepherd, Jacques Hérénien, and so on. It's a different matter when the corpse of Jacques Hérénien is lying on the Square of the Peoples; there it is the centre of attention, a dramatic phenomenon.

Neither will the comedian tolerate extras recruited from drama schools

[1] Aegidius Tschudi (1505–72), Swiss author of one of the versions of the Tell legend on which Schiller based his play.

and amateur dramatic groups crowding the stage and impeding his performance, included on the assumption that the spectator will take a group of ten for a crowd of two hundred.

Apropos of which we should like to take this opportunity to ask the lover of crowd scenes how many extras are needed to satisfy Verhaeren's stage direction, 'The crowd acts as a single person of multiple aspects'? If he answers one hundred, we shan't believe him; two hundred – still too few! If the stage will not admit 20,000, then we prefer a mere seven.

Furthermore, the comedian cannot stand characters who talk without acting and simply elucidate the events of the play. Solution: either remove them to the pages of the programme or put them in the orchestra pit. Having no programme, we have settled for the orchestra pit.

And the comedian playing the part of Haineau will not permit his big moment, the statement of his maximum programme, to take the form of a mere explanation to his sister within the family circle. As a tribune, he demands the right to engage in open debate with his opponents at a public meeting.

But how can we surround him with the army of extras whose support is vital? He is not likely to accept two hundred – he needs a thousand. But how is that possible? Here's how: from statistics we can assume that the vast mass of the population of Siberia obtains cultural sustenance by forming drama groups and performing its own plays. In Moscow there are more than a hundred and fifty theatres. So we, too, have come to the conclusion that it would help the spectator-actor to get in some practice before making his appearance on the stage (if only to develop a stage temperament). Therefore we shall invite the thousands of spectators who will crowd the auditorium of the R.S.F.S.R. Theatre No. 1 to take an active part in the performance by offering the support which is demanded by Hérénien, Le Breux, Haineau, Claire and Hordain in the course of the action. . . .

Now the question of footlights. Shameful to relate, in spite of all the attempts to abolish from the big theatre the abomination of subterranean lighting, in spite of all the experiments in this field by Craig, Meyerhold and others, not one theatre in Moscow (for so long the home of that sworn enemy of footlights, Vyacheslav Ivanov) has seen fit to throw out this outmoded theatrical remnant. Consequently we are left with that other remnant – bourgeois stage illusion.

In the intimate theatres the removal of footlights has still not led to the elimination of bourgeois illusion, because in place of footlights they have bored a keyhole to satisfy the curiosity of prying spectators (in which number our spectator is not included). For a more detailed account of this, see the article, 'The Cricket on the Hearth, or At the Keyhole', in Doctor Dapertutto's Journal.[1]

In earlier productions the footlights were removed to build a proscenium stage; similarly, in *The Dawn* they have been removed for the sake of a Grecian 'orchestra', but neither the proscenium nor the 'orchestra' is dictated by purely *technical considerations*, as Comrade Kerzhentsev maintains in his book *The Creative Theatre*.[2]

Now a word on the sets. For us, 'decorative' settings have no meaning; 'decoration' is for the Secessionists and restaurants in Vienna and Munich; spare us 'The World of Art', 'Rococo' and the painstaking detail of museum exhibits. . . .

We have only to talk to the latest followers of Picasso and Tatlin to know at once that we are dealing with kindred spirits . . . We are building just as they are building . . . For us the art of manufacturing is more important than any tediously pretty patterns and colours. What do we want with pleasing pictorial effects?

What the *modern* spectator wants is the placard, the juxtaposition of the surfaces and shapes of *tangible materials*!

To sum up, both we and they want to escape from the box of the theatre on to the wide-open stage – and our artists will be delighted to throw away their brushes and take up axes, picks and hammers to hack stage sets out of the materials of raw nature.

[*Vestnik teatra*, 1920, no 72–73, pp. 8–10.]

NOTE   Article by Meyerhold and Bebutov dated 7 November 1920. It also contains an account of the disposition of the forces in Verhaeren's play (omitted here).

---

4. Speech at an Open Debate on *The Dawn*[3]

We have been accused today of distorting Verhaeren's amazing work. My reply is: no, Comrade Bebutov and I did not go far enough in our revision,

[1] Article by Meyerhold on Benois' production of *The Cricket on the Hearth* at the Moscow Art Theatre in *Lyubov k tryom apelsinam*, Petrograd, 1915, no 1–3.
[2] See p. 170 above.   [3] 22 November 1920.

the reason being that there was not enough time. We are too busy to spend one or two years on a single play; on our clock the second hand is all important. We can't afford to spend two or three years concocting a play which after all that time will be no more than run-of-the-mill popular propaganda. I have no doubt that at the rate we are working we are bound to go on making mistakes, but we shall make sure that we don't make the mistake of losing touch with contemporary reality as we build our theatre. We are right to invite the Cubists to work with us, because we need settings which resemble those we shall be performing against tomorrow. The modern theatre wants to move out into the open air. We want our setting to be an iron pipe or the open sea or something constructed by the new man. I don't intend to engage in an appraisal of such settings; suffice to say that for us they have the advantage of getting us out of the old theatre.

Today it has been suggested that *The Dawn* be taken away from us and given to another theatre. Long live the new R.S.F.S.R. Theatre which forces theatres to stage plays other than *Madame Angot* and trash by Rostand.[1] We shall be only too pleased to surrender *The Dawn* to the Moscow Art Theatre, but let them re-examine their own repertoire. If they agree to revise it and accept our play, we shall find others; we shall employ more and more Cubists and Suprematists and do away completely with the barrier of the footlights.

Perhaps we'll erect a trapeze and put our acrobats to work on it, to make their bodies express the very essence of our revolutionary theatre and remind us that we are enjoying the struggle we are engaged in.

I agree – maybe meetings and political harangues are no use, but I am delighted that we have got *our* spectator who says to us: this is *our* theatre. I don't think there is much likelihood of the Red Army taking its banners along to *Uncle Vanya* when it can come to productions which it looks on as its own. More than anyone, the Moscow Art Theatre is to blame for the passivity of the spectator whom it held in thrall for so long; at one time he was not even allowed to applaud when a surge of enthusiasm demanded applause. A theatrical performance should be a joyous event which rouses the public's emotions.

[*Vestnik teatra*, 1920, no 75, p. 14.]

[1] Lecocq's operetta *The Daughter of Madame Angot* was produced at the Musical Studio of the Moscow Art Theatre in May 1920. Rostand's *Cyrano de Bergerac* was put on by the former Korsh Theatre in October 1920.

5. The Solitude of Stanislavsky

'With martial stalk hath he gone by our watch.' (HAMLET, 1.i.)

In the last number of *Vestnik teatra*,[1] in our various references to the Moscow Art Theatre, we had no wish whatsoever to undermine the prestige of that great master, the founder and leader of the theatre, Stanislavsky. And at a time when the Moscow theatre world is like a garish bazaar, it would cause us great pain if anybody should think us too shortsighted to identify the solitary figure of Stanislavsky standing head and shoulders above the hurly-burly.

Nevertheless, what a tragedy! Stanislavsky, gallic by nature, pupil of the Paris Conservatoire, pupil of Fedotov, contemporary of Shumsky, lover of every comic situation and joke native to the theatre, of 'love potions' and 'little weaknesses', of everything which nourished the talent of Shchepkin, a brilliant Tutor[2] wielding his rapier like a master, with a tirelessly supple body, a voice of enormous range, a face with amazing mimetic properties (without resort to make-up), eyes described by Lensky as the most riveting in the theatre, a love of rich and stately costumes, a predilection for Shakespeare, Molière, Pushkin, Schiller – this man, born for the theatre of extravagent grotesque and enthralling tragedy, was forced year after year by the pressures of a philistinism inimical to him to break and distort his gallic temperament in catering to the tastes of the patrons of [fashionable restaurants], the proprietors of shops on Kuznetsky Most, and the owners of banking-houses and coffee-shops.

Having escaped from the family home at Krasnie Vorota when hardly more than a child, he exchanged his mercantile surname for a more resounding stage-name. However, in the interests of his theatre, he was obliged to submit to the will of dictators of fashion interested only in the flashy second-rate. Those private box and orchestra stalls patrons could not be bothered with the art of some market-place 'cabotin'. What they needed was solid reliability – something tangible! No fancy tricks! – only what they were familiar with.

This was the original reason for the propagation of 'Meiningenism' on Russian soil. But it was bombarded with so much criticism that in

[1] *Vestnik teatra*, 1921, no 87–88, pp. 2–3, 16–17.
[2] In Victor Dyachenko's comedy, *The Tutor*, produced in 1894 by Stanislavsky.

1905[1] Stanislavsky tried to root it out. *The Drama of Life*[2] was the first sign of his recovery from the ailment of 'Chronegkitis'. We will speak not of his 'failures', but rather of the *deviations* of his true nature towards enforced anomalies.

What an effort it must have cost this lover of cloak-and-sword drama to sit through long hours in an empty auditorium in order to check squeakers and tin-whistles, night-watchmen tapping, hooves drumming over bridges, curtains blowing in the wind, thunder crashing, a tub echoing weirdly as it dropped into a quarry, peas dropping to simulate hailstones, tarpaulins dragged across the floor to give the sound of waves, a gramophone recording of a child crying or dogs barking in the country, silk rustling to suggest the wind, ships' sirens, a crowd growling angrily reinforced by the bass notes of an accordion, church bells pealing melodiously, ancient doors creaking, the musical sound of a key turning in a lock, the jingling bells of a departing troika, a metronome for the ticking of a clock . . .

The form was set, but the capricious consumer demanded an ever richer variety of content. 'Alexander Ivanovich, write us a play, would you?' idly remarks some businessman to his dramatist-partner at chemin de fer in the English Club.

And the administration of the theatre in Karetny Row[3] acts like a seismograph. 'What's this quixotic nonsense about seeking the theatre through "theatricality"?' says the theatre manager to the artistic director. 'Back into the archives with *The Merchant of Venice*, *The Rule of Will*[4] and *Twelfth Night*, and let's find some literature!' cries the literary manager.[5]

And off they went: first Hauptmann, then Ibsen, then Dostoevsky, then Chirikov, then Gorky, then Surguchev, then Nemirovich-Danchenko . . . Once they reached Surguchev it was but one step further to Sumbatov. Amidst all this babel Stanislavsky contrived somehow to scale the heights of melodrama in the role of Loevborg,[6] to wear the rags of the vagabond Satin[7] as though they were the cloak of Don César de Bazan,[8] a Russian Sacchi. He revealed true theatrical style (which didn't escape Edward Gordon Craig's notice) even as a country doctor(!),[9] when for some reason

---

[1] i.e. by founding the Theatre-Studio.
[2] By Knut Hamsun (produced 1907).
[3] The home of the Moscow Art Theatre from 1898 to 1902.
[4] Written in 1866 by Alexei Pisemsky.   [5] Nemirovich-Danchenko.
[6] *Hedda Gabler* (1899).   [7] *The Lower Depths* (1902).
[8] Title of melodrama by Dennery and Dumanoir.
[9] Astrov in *Uncle Vanya* (1899).

he was required to appear in dubbined boots, complete with gun-dog and double-barrelled shotgun. And again he achieved all the brilliance of a Pantalone in the character comedy which the Moscow Art Theatre decided to make out of *Woe from Wit*;[1] and as Rakitin[2] he displayed an exquisite elegance, an almost Wildean refinement.

But the might of the literary theatre prevailed in the end. Stanislavsky was forced to take leave of Got, Coquelin and Judic. No longer could he be his true self in works like *The Drama of Life*, Maeterlinck's one-act plays or Molière's farces; and what other chance did he have, always creating symphonies of noises or non-dramatic works for the stage?

Once the management demanded a theoretical justification for its enterprises he had no alternative but to concoct his notorious *system* for a whole army of actors, psychologically 'experiencing' the parts of all those characters who do nothing but walk, eat, drink, make love and wear jackets.

Then, of course, the inevitable hangers-on appear and obligingly stack the master's shelves with loathsome textbooks of French experimental psychology. And conscientious pupils fill their notebooks with the acute paradoxes tossed off at random by the visionary and hurry off to hawk them about the theatrical market-place without pausing to seek the author's approval.

And nobody stops to think whether the moment will come when the master, exhausted with work alien to him, tired of forever sewing up the threadbare patchwork of worn-out phrases, will follow Gogol's example and hurl the oft-amended pages of his 'system' into the stove.

But it is not enough for his pupils that they have seized his treasure, divided up his cloak. They have taken possession of his entire being, removed him from the big theatre and put him to work in a theatre with no more room than a tram-car[3] on plays like *Cricket on the Hearth* (after Dickens), *The Deluge* (Berger), *The Wreck of the Good Hope* (Heijermans), *Youth* (Leonid Andreev), *The Green Ring* (Zinaida Gippius), *The Pattern of Roses* (Fyodor Sologub).

Thus, this 'maître des grands spectacles' with the theatrical range of a Michelangelo is reduced to fiddling around with little bits of clockwork. With *Cain*[4] he made a violent effort to free himself from this sugary idyll. It was a tragic failure – and it won't be the last. The dreamer's path will

---

[1] As Famusov (1906).   [2] *A Month in the Country* (1909).
[3] The First Moscow Art Studio, which from 1913 to 1921 functioned in premises seating one hundred spectators.
[4] Byron's *Cain*, produced at the Moscow Art Theatre by Stanislavsky in 1920.

go on being thorny until he realizes that he must tread it *alone* – not with those who want to concoct 'alkoholfrei' operetta in the style of *Cain* . . .

But, they will object, *Cain* was an attempt to create a theatrical 'synthesis'. What pretentious rubbish! Gluck's *Orpheus*, Mozart, Wagner, Aristophanes: anything but *Cain* and we might have taken it seriously. A fusion of music and spoken drama might have produced a sort of tragedy, or perhaps a comedy with music. Pure pantomime, Gnessin's theory of musical reading, a Hoffmanesque harlequinade: take your pick! Anything but these tawdry Directoire drawing-room engravings. . . .

It is a mistake to attempt a revival of *The Government Inspector*.[1] That theatre has no right to lay its hands on *The Government Inspector*. This alliance of the bloated factory-owning bourgeoisie and the Eichenwald-style[2] intelligentsia has done its utmost to speed the decay of the truly theatrical theatre. This is the atmosphere in which the apolitical school of acting has flourished. So how could *The Government Inspector*, that most tendentious of plays, possibly be within their range?

Do you remember the Moscow Art's first production[3] of this sublime comedy, when Khlestakov chose to crush cockroaches on the wall with his foot whilst recounting his tall stories, ignoring Gogol's direction for him to rest his feet on the table? Yet that one stage direction contains a prescription for the whole character and the whole work.

Recalling the paradoxical bursts of invention of Stanislavsky the innovator, we are convinced that *The Government Inspector* would receive a true interpretation if it were not ruined by the Moscow Art Theatre management and consultants who have been thrown up by the corrupt alliance of businessmen and intelligentsia. It was the same in Gogol's day; the actors' minds were so stuffed with notions of vaudeville that they were unable to comprehend the grimaces of Gogol's capriccio.

Like Tolstoy leaving Sofia Andreevna – lantern in hand – we see Stanislavsky stealing off to the Habima.[4] It's a strange potion the old man's taking: this nightmarish conglomeration of tongues: ancient Hebrew, Armenian[5] and Russian!!! We are on the verge of a tragic event. Just one drop more and – horror of horrors! – our beloved master will be

---

[1] Stanislavsky's second production of *The Government Inspector* was presented on 25 May 1921.

[2] Yuly Eichenwald, Russian critic.

[3] In 1908, directed by Stanislavsky, Nemirovich-Danchenko and Moskvin.

[4] The Hebrew Theatre Studio, founded in Moscow in 1918, was affiliated to the Moscow Art Theatre. Stanislavsky taught there.

[5] Vakhtangov was Armenian.

lost to the stage for ever; he is about to dissolve into the mists of an early Moscow spring, just as Gozzi once vanished from the Italian stage, swallowed up in the vapours of the canals of Venice.

But happily an alchemist is preparing a powerful antidote against the effects of the management: Vakhtangov, true henchman that he is, has not forsaken his knight. In these ancient Hebrew and Armenian surroundings the fanatics of the Moscow Art Third Studio are present to a man when Stanislavsky gives his lessons:

'No "authentic emotions"! Let your voices resound! Walk theatrically! Suppleness! The eloquent gesture! Dance! Bow! Duel with rapiers! Rhythm! Rhythm! Rhythm!' – the insistent shouts of Stanislavsky resound.

The gallic blood has caught fire.

The ornamental roses have withered; the green rings have broken, the flood is dammed; Rakitin's youth has faded; the 'Good Hope' has foundered.

Enter Eric XIV.[1] Listen to the clicking of Castillian castanets (Cervantes);[2] observe the masks of Italian improvised comedy (*Princess Turandot*);[3] now they are about to approach the tragic farce of Sukhovo-Kobylin via Maeterlinck's *Miracle of St Anthony*.[4]

In Moscow there is only one guardian of genuine traditions – the ever solitary Stanislavsky. The gates of the house of Shchepkin[5] stand wide before him!

In his solitude, he alone has the power to restore the desecrated rights of theatrical traditionalism with its '*conventional improbability*', '*enthralling action*', '*masks of exaggeration*', '*authenticity of passion*', '*verisimilitude of experience in a given situation*', '*critical freedom of the market-place*' and '*crude directness of common passions*'.[6]

[*Vestnik teatra*, 1921, no 89–90, pp. 2–3.]

NOTE Written in 1921 by Meyerhold and Valery Bebutov. Meyerhold never missed an opportunity to emphasize that his condemnation of the Art Theatre did not embrace Stanislavsky. Alexander Gladkov recalls that in 1936 he insisted on including *The Solitude of Stanislavsky* in a projected

---

[1] Strindberg's *Eric XIV* was produced at the First Moscow Art Studio by Vakhtangov in March 1921.
[2] Stanislavsky's proposed production of six Cervantes interludes was not realized.
[3] Produced by Vakhtangov at the Third Studio in February 1922.
[4] Vakhtangov's production, revived January 1921.
[5] The Maly Theatre.
[6] Quotations from Pushkin's pronouncements on the theatre.

179

collection of his articles.[1] The mutual respect of the two great directors was conclusively demonstrated by their professional rapprochement in 1938 (see pp. 250–1 below).

[1] Alexander Gladkov, 'Vospominania, zametky, zapisy o V. E. Meyerholde' in *Tarusskie stranitsy*, Kaluga, 1961, p. 298.

Part Five

BIOMECHANICS-CONSTRUCTIVISM-
ECCENTRISM-CINEFICATION

1921-1925

IN THE AUTUMN OF 1921 Meyerhold became Director of the newly formed State Higher Theatre Workshop in Moscow. In the first year the courses in theatre history, theory and practice were attended by about eighty students, some of whom had belonged to the company of the R.S.F.S.R. Theatre No. 1.

It was now that Meyerhold was able to develop the system of practical exercises for actors called 'biomechanics' which he demonstrated for the first time in public in June 1922. Initially, Meyerhold advanced biomechanics as the theatrical equivalent of industrial time-and-motion study and compared it to the experiments in the scientific organization of labour by the American Frederick Winslow Taylor and his Russian follower Gastev. However, the resemblance was superficial and was exaggerated by Meyerhold in order to show that his system was devised in response to the demands of the new mechanized age, as opposed to those of Stanislavsky and Tairov, which were unscientific and anachronistic. Although Meyerhold's initial claims were quickly seen to be specious, biomechanics became accepted as a thoroughly viable system of theatrical training which he employed to school his actors for all his subsequent productions. Eventually, its practical success was largely responsible for the introduction of some form of systematized physical training into the curriculum of every Soviet drama school.

In February 1922 the former Sohn Theatre reopened under the new title of 'The Actor's Theatre' with a company composed of the former Nezlobin troupe plus a number of students from Meyerhold's workshop. Meyerhold's first production, Ibsen's *Doll's House* (20 April 1922), caused a scandal. It was rushed on after five rehearsals and performed against a background of flats taken straight from stock and propped back to front against the stage walls, symbolizing – or so Meyerhold claimed – 'the bourgeois milieu against which Nora rebels'.[1] This was more than the 'Nezlobintsy' could stand and they fled after the one production, leaving Meyerhold and his company as sole tenants of the dilapidated theatre which they were to occupy until it closed for renovation in 1932.

[1] Meyerhold quoted by Sergei Yutkevich in *Vstrechi c Meyerholdom*, cit., p. 212.

Popova's portable construction for *Earth Rampant*, 1923 (with screen for projected titles).

The 'moving walls' for *Give us Europe*, 1924.

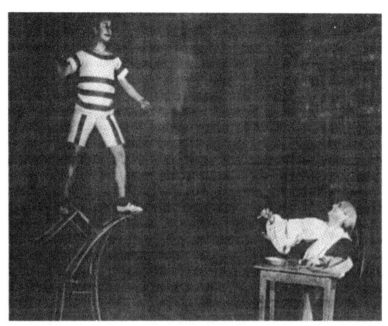

(*a*) With Pyriev as Bulanov and Mukhin as Neschastlivtsev.

(*b*) The finale.

The Forest, 1924.

Igor Ilinsky as Schastlivtsev in *The Forest*, 1924.

agility, 'a spring-board for the actor which quite rightly was compared to the apparatus of a circus acrobat'.[1] Crommelynck's tragi-farce tells of Bruno, a village poet who is so infatuated with his beautiful young wife, Stella, that he convinces himself that no man could conceivably resist her. Deranged with jealousy, he forces her to share her bed with every man in the village in the hope of unmasking her true lover. Faithful to the last, Stella flees with a man who at least is sure to trust her. Some critics, notably Lunacharsky, were scandalized by what they regarded simply as a salacious bedroom farce, but the majority were agreed that the risqué plot was completely redeemed by the brio, the style, and the good humour of Meyerhold's production. He transformed the play into a universal parable on the theme of jealousy, with the style of the performance furnishing a constant implicit commentary on the dialogue and situations. The actor's attitude to his part was conveyed through an eloquent succession of poses, gestures and acrobatic tricks, all accomplished with the casual dexterity of a circus clown. Boris Alpers describes Igor Ilinsky's performance:

> Bruno . . . stood before the audience, his face pale and motionless, and with unvarying intonation, monotonous declamatory style and identical sweeping gestures he uttered his grandiloquent monologues. But at the same time this Bruno was being ridiculed by the actor performing acrobatic stunts at the most impassioned moments of his speeches, belching, and comically rolling his eyes whilst enduring the most dramatic anguish.[2]

One need only compare this with Meyerhold's disquisition on the comedy of masks in his essay *The Fairground Booth* to see that *The Magnanimous Cuckold*, for all its modernist exterior, was a revival of the spirit, and in good measure, the letter, too, of the *commedia dell' arte*. It was fitting that Meyerhold should choose this production to commemorate the tercentenary of Molière.

Despite the spectacular success of *The Magnanimous Cuckold*, Meyerhold was faced once more in June 1922 with the possible loss of his theatre; this was averted only after violent protests from the theatrical Left and the Constructivists[3] and an open letter from himself in which he threatened 'to cease work in the Republic altogether'.[4] Not only did Meyerhold retain the use of the Actor's Theatre, he soon became Artistic Director of the newly formed 'Theatre of the Revolution' as well. At the same time he

[1] Alexei Gvozdev, *Teatr imeni Vs. Meyerholda* (1920–26), Leningrad, 1927, p. 28.
[2] Boris Alpers, *Teatr sotsialnoy maski*, Moscow-Leningrad, 1931, p. 34.
[3] See *Ermitazh*, Moscow, 1922, no 8, pp. 11–12.
[4] *Teatralnaya Moskva*, 1922, no 46, p. 8.

assumed overall control of the State Institute of Theatrical Art, formed by an amalgamation of the former Theatre Workshop, the State Institute of Musical Drama and nine smaller autonomous theatre studios. So disparate were the various factions that violent friction was bound to be generated, and this quickly led to the formation of an unofficial but quite separate Meyerhold Workshop within the Institute. Without State recognition and with only the box-office to support it, this Workshop ran the Actor's Theatre, with its young students discharging every function from door-keeper to scene-shifter. On 24 November 1922 *The Magnanimous Cuckold*, was joined in the repertoire by Sukhovo-Kobylin's *Tarelkin's Death*.

This 'comedy-jest', which Sukhovo-Kobylin completed in 1869, is a barely concealed satire on tsarist police methods. He had to wait until 1900 to see it performed, and then only after he had been obliged to remove its edge with numerous amendments. It was Meyerhold who first staged the original version in October 1917 at the Alexandrinsky Theatre; conceived in the phantasmagorical, Hoffmanesque style of much of his earlier work, it was a great popular success.

In a note on the play, Sukhovo-Kobylin writes: 'In keeping with the play's humorous nature, it must be played briskly, merrily, loudly – *avec entrain*.'[1] Meyerhold's response was to employ once again the knockabout tricks of circus clowns and strolling players. Varvara Stepanova designed a series of drab, baggy costumes decorated with stripes, patches and chevrons which looked like nothing so much as convicts' uniforms. On the empty stage there was an assortment of white-painted 'acting instruments' ready to be shifted and used by the actors as required. Each one concealed a trap: the table's legs gave way, the seat deposited its occupant on to the floor, the stool detonated a blank cartridge. Most spectacular of all was the cage used to simulate a prison cell into which the prisoner was propelled head-first through a sort of giant meat-mincer. As though all this was not enough to tax the spectator's nerves and the actor's courage, an assistant director (or 'laboratory assistant' as they were called) seated in the front row announced the intervals by firing a pistol at the audience and shouting 'Entrrrr-act!'; there were helter-skelter chases with the pursuers bran-dishing inflated bladders on sticks; at the end Tarelkin escaped by swinging across the stage on a trapeze. Illusion was never given a chance to intrude: Ludmilla Brandakhlystova, 'a colossal washerwoman of about forty', was played by the slender, youthful Mikhail Zharov[2] with no make-up and

---

[1] A. V. Sukhovo-Kobylin, *Trilogia*, Moscow, 1966, p. 348.

[2] The playing of Brandakhlystova by a man is authorized by Sukhovo-Kobylin himself – loc. cit.

ridiculous padding under his skirts; Tarelkin, bound hand and foot in prison and frantic with thirst, tried in vain to reach a cup of water held by a warder – then suddenly he winked broadly at the audience and took a long draught from a bottle of wine he had concealed in his pocket.

For all the production's vigour and invention it failed to share the success of *The Magnanimous Cuckold*. This was partly because Sukhovo-Kobylin's grim satire was hardly amenable to burlesque. But mainly it was marred by practical deficiencies: the 'acting instruments' functioned so capriciously that the young performers soon lost all confidence in them; the shapeless costumes tended to camouflage rather than enhance their movements; and they frequently had to perform in half-darkness when the erratic military searchlights which served as stage lighting fluctuated in power.

Nevertheless, *Tarelkin's Death* remains one of the most celebrated products of the movement known as 'eccentrism' which flourished in Russia in the early twenties.[1]

One of Meyerhold's two 'laboratory assistants' for the production was Sergei Eisenstein. He had been a student at the Theatre Workshop from its beginning in 1921 and had worked as designer for Meyerhold's uncompleted production of Shaw's *Heartbreak House*, proposing to augment his settings with cages of wild animals. Shortly after *Tarelkin's Death* he left Meyerhold to work as a director at the Moscow Proletkult Theatre. It was there that in April 1923 he staged Sergei Tretyakov's free adaptation of Ostrovsky's *Enough Simplicity for Every Wise Man* (1668) as a 'montage of attractions' on an arena stage and complete with a tightrope act by one of the characters.

In his next production Meyerhold reverted to the agitatory style of *Mystery-Bouffe*. For want of suitable Soviet plays, Sergei Tretyakov was commissioned to rewrite Marcel Martinet's verse drama, *Night*, the story of an abortive mutiny during an imaginary imperialist war. As with Verhaeren's *Dawn*, the aim was to transform the play's vague universality into direct allusions to recent Soviet history. Tretyakov sought to strengthen the dialogue by translating it into the laconicism of the propaganda

---

[1] The term 'Eccentrism' was coined by Grigory Kozintsev, Georgy Kryzhitsky and Leonid Trauberg to describe their experiments at the theatre-studio which they opened in Petrograd in 1921 and called 'FEKS' or the 'Factory of Eccentrism'. The style is sometimes said to have originated with Yury Annenkov's production of Tolstoy's comedy, *The First Distiller*, in Petrograd (1919), when he staged a scene in hell with the aid of circus acrobats performing a flying ballet, but the influence of Meyerhold-Dapertutto cannot be discounted.

placard and by schooling the actors in an appropriately aggressive style of declamation. The action's relevance to familiar historical events was underlined by familiar slogans projected on to a screen above the stage during the performance; these titles also performed a formal function, replacing the long-discarded from curtain as a means of dividing the play up and announcing the theme of each episode.

In *The Dawn* and *Mystery-Bouffe* both characters and events were synthesized through the medium of costumes and settings; but arbitrary aestheticism rather than universality was the overriding impression created by the Futurist geometrical abstractions, and the topicality of the propaganda was obscured. In the two Constructivist productions which followed the intention was different but the results were similar. As Ivan Aksyonov wrote at the beginning of 1923:

> So-called 'stage constructivism' started out with a most impressive programme for the total abolition of aesthetic methods, but once it appeared on the stage it began to show signs of being only too ready to adapt itself to its surroundings and now it has degenerated almost to a decorative device, albeit in a new style.[1]

In *Night*, or *Earth Rampant* as it was retitled, Meyerhold and his designer, Popova, sought to eliminate all risk of aesthetic blandishment by resorting to purely utilitarian objects: cars, lorries, motor cycles, machine-guns, field telephones, a harvester, a mobile kitchen, an aeroplane – only that which was required by the dramatic events. The one exception was a huge, stark wooden model of a gantry-crane which towered up into the flies.[2] The sole sources of light were huge front-of-house searchlights. The costumes were wholly naturalistic and the actors wore no make-up.

Just as in *Mystery-Bouffe*, the negative characters were portrayed as grotesque archetypes. When the 'Emperor' received news of the mutiny he squatted down on a chamber-pot emblazoned with the Imperial eagle and relieved himself to the accompaniment of a band playing 'God save the Tsar', after which an orderly removed the pot, holding his nose. As Meyerhold wrote soon afterwards, 'The actor-tribune acts not the situation itself, but what is concealed behind it and what it has to reveal for a specifically propagandist purpose.'[3]

On this occasion the tedium of unalloyed virtue was completely overcome by the stirring evocation of civil-war heroism which struck to the hearts of many of the spectators. For them the receding throb of the lorry which had driven on to the stage with the coffin of a martyred Red solider seemed like the finest and the most fitting

---

[1] I. A. Aksyonov in *Zrelishcha*, Moscow, 1923, no 21, p. 8.
[2] Cf. the stage directions for *Fire* (p. 118 above).   [3] See p. 206 below.

requiem to their own fallen comrades. Dedicated 'to the Red Army and the first Red soldier of the R.S.F.S.R., Lev Trotsky', *Earth Rampant* was first performed on 23 February 1923 to mark the Army's fifth anniversary.[1]

Meyerhold conceived *Earth Rampant* in the spirit of a mass spectacle, using the theatre gangways for the passage of vehicles and troops. Subsequently it was performed on a number of occasions as an open-air spectacle, being freely adapted to various settings. The most memorable performance was that given in honour of the Fifth Congress of the Comintern in Moscow in June 1924 when infantry and horse cavalry took part and there was an audience of 25,000.

In its search for revolutionary drama the Russian theatre turned to the German Expressionists, and in the early twenties a number of works by Kaiser, Hasenclever, Toller and others were staged. Under Meyerhold's supervision the Theatre of the Revolution put on Toller's *Machine Wreckers* (November 1922) and *Mass-Man* (January 1923). What attracted Soviet directors was the left-wing Expressionists' portrayal of the inhuman oppression of the individual by capitalist industrialism, and their representation, through the revolt of the individual, of the world revolution soon to come. However, the Expressionist hero with his vague, utopian dreams of the universal brotherhood of man cut a pitiful figure in a country which knew the reality of civil war, and he inspired few significant counterparts in Soviet drama. In fact, of all extant Russian dramatic literature Meyerhold's own play, *Fire*, is probably as close as any, in form as well as spirit, to the early works of Kaiser and Toller.

Tretyakov's adaptation and Meyerhold's production of Martinet's *Night* together constituted the first significant attempt in Russia to relate Expressionist abstractions to political reality. Alexei Faiko's 'romantic melodrama', *Lake Lyul*, which Meyerhold presented at the Theatre of the Revolution on 7 November 1923, discarded the hero figure altogether and concentrated on the portrayal of Western capitalist decadence. Faiko summarizes the play:

> Location: somewhere in the Far West, or perhaps the Far East. Many characters. Crowd scenes. White, yellow and black races. Hotels, villas, shops. Advertisement hoardings and lifts. A revolutionary struggle on an island. An underground movement. Conspiracies. The basis of the plot – the rise and fall of the renegade, Anton Prim.[2]

[1] The public première took place on 4 March 1923.
[2] Alexei Faiko, 'Lake Lyul' in *Vstrechi s Meyerholdom*, cit., p. 298.

As with the Expressionists, the dialogue was terse and the structure episodic, designed to convey the breakneck tempo of life in the 'big city', the dominant motif of the whole production.

Faiko on the setting and costumes:

> The back wall of the theatre was bared. Girders stuck out and wires and cables dangled uncompromisingly. The centre of the stage was occupied by a three-storeyed construction with receding corridors, cages, ladders, platforms and lifts which moved both horizontally and vertically. There were illuminated titles and advertisements, silvered screens lit from behind. Affording something of a contrast to this background were the brilliant colours of the not altogether lifelike costumes: the elegant toilettes of the ladies, the gleaming white of starched shirt-fronts, aiguillettes, epaulettes, liveries trimmed with gold.[1]

The setting designed by Victor Shestakov was obviously derived from Popova's construction for *The Magnanimous Cuckold*, yet cheerfully representational and hardly 'constructivist' in the precise sense. Meyerhold exploited the construction to its limits, using area lighting to switch the action constantly from one level to another, sometimes playing two scenes simultaneously in different places. It afforded him the flexibility which he had sought through the episodic adaptation of such works as *Columbine's Scarf* and *Masquerade*, and led him on to further experiments in montage at a time when that technique had been scarcely exploited in the cinema.

The production of *Lake Lyul* was Meyerhold's last at the Theatre of the Revolution. He left to devote himself exclusively to his own theatre which now officially bore his name. In April 1923 he had been honoured with the title of 'People's Artist of the Republic' to mark the twentieth anniversary of his debut as a director. He was the first stage-director and only the sixth Soviet artist over-all to be so honoured.

The production of Ostrovsky's *Forest* (19 January 1924) was conceived as an illustration of Meyerhold's dictum that 'A play is simply the excuse for the revelation of its theme on the level at which that revelation may appear vital today'.[2] It was a resumption of his polemic against the Academic Theatres, and in particular was directed against the Maly's recent traditional version of the same play. Meyerhold interpreted Ostrovsky's genre portrait of bigoted country gentry in the terms of the class war, rejecting character development in favour of 'social masks' whose interplay was the production's true end.[3] The action was adapted to sharpen the conflict

[1] Faiko, op. cit., p. 306.
[2] 'Meyerhold o svoyom *Lese*' in *Novy Zritel*, Moscow, 1924, no 7, p. 6.
[3] Cf. Meyerhold's remarks on masks and Ostrovsky on pp. 314–16 below.

190

between Raissa Pavlovna Gurmyzhskaya, the autocratic mistress of the rich estate, 'Tree Stumps', and Aksyusha, her young impoverished relative who serves as a maid of all work. Gurmyzhskaya, who, according to Ostrovsky, 'dresses modestly, almost in mourning', appeared in riding-habit, a violent red wig, and brandished a riding-crop, whilst Aksyusha displayed all the buoyant energy and industry of a modern 'komsomolka'. Every principal character was costumed to reveal his essential nature: Bulanov, a foppish young wastrel, adorned the estate in striped sports kit; Milonov, an obsequious neighbour, was transformed into a parish priest complete with full regalia and attendant acolytes. Ostrovsky's two itinerant actors, Arkashka Schastlivtsev (lit. 'Fortunate'), the comedian, and Gennady Neschastlivtsev ('Unfortunate'), the tragedian, were decked out in an odd assortment of garments from the theatrical rag-bag; Schastlivtsev was played as a down-and-out music-hall comic dressed in baggy check trousers, a short toreador's jacket and jaunty, battered sombrero; his partner resembled a provincial ham in a voluminous dark cloak and broad-sleeved Russian shirt. In their relationship with each other, their remoteness from the petty everyday world and their romantic championing of the true love of Aksyusha and her sweetheart, this pair were a conscious evocation of Don Quixote and Sancho Panza.

Since the point of the mask is to identify the character completely at his first appearance, gradual development of character can be discarded; accordingly, Meyerhold largely ignored the play's original time sequence and rearranged Ostrovsky's text according to the principles of montage. Altering little of the actual dialogue, he divided the original five acts into thirty-three episodes, shuffling them into new order, and inserting pantomime interludes for the sake of effective contrasts of mood and tempo.

Each episode was announced by the now familiar title projected on to a screen above the stage. For instance, after the prologue in which Milonov led the rest of the local inhabitants in procession across the stage with ikons and religious banners, the play opened with the meeting of the two actors (the original Act Two, Scene Two). This long scene, in which they swap tales of their adventures on tour, was split into seven brief episodes and interspersed with the eight scenes at 'Tree Stumps' from Act One. From episode to episode Arkashka and Gennady gradually descended a catwalk suspended above stage-level, arriving finally at a turnstile (forestage left) representing the entrance to 'Tree Stumps'.[1] The intervening episodes

[1] The setting and costumes were devised by Meyerhold and executed by Vassily Fyodorov. Beginning with *The Forest*, the designs for practically all Meyerhold's productions were executed in accordance with his own precise instructions.

191

were played on the main stage, area lighting being used as in *Lake Lyul* to pick out first one location then the other. The leisurely tempo of the players' progress, further emphasized by the miming of fishing, catching of insects and the like, contrasted abruptly with the domestic bustle on the stage below in a manner which Meyerhold himself compares on the one hand to Eisenstein's use of 'collision montage' in the cinema, and on the other to the episodic structure employed by Shakespeare and Pushkin.[1]

The permanent setting with its dynamic function was a refinement of Meyerhold's earlier, more overtly constructivist manner. His use of properties in *The Forest* served a similar purpose. An assortment of real objects with no obvious relationship was assembled onstage to be utilized as required: the swinging of Aksyusha and her lover, Pyotr, on 'giant-strides'[2] was synchronized with the dialogue to convey their rising elation as they planned their escape; Aksyusha conveyed her disdain of Gurmyzh-skaya by rhythmically beating laundry whilst retorting to her strictures; Arkashka stressed the absurdity of the social pretensions of Ulita, the housekeeper, by see-sawing with her and suddenly leaving her sitting in mid-air singing a sentimental ballad; Bulanov betrayed his fatuity by discoursing with Gennady whilst balancing on two chairs. Every device served both an ironic and a rhythmical function, as well as sometimes helping to gloss over dialogue which was not consistent with Meyerhold's new interpretation of the play.

Inevitably, with this treatment many of the more subtle character refinements in Ostrovsky's text were obscured, not least in the tragi-comical clown figure of Arkashka. But even so, Ilinsky enjoyed his greatest success of all in this part and the production remained permanently in Meyerhold's repertoire, being performed over 1,700 times. Probably more than any other work, it was *The Forest* which inspired the host of ill-conceived 'reinterpretations' of the classics by Meyerhold's imitators, the disease of 'meyerholditis' which in later years he himself was charged with propagating.

With his next production, *Give us Europe!* (15 June 1924), Meyerhold showed that his disregard for authors' rights was not restricted to the classics. This 'agit-sketch' was an amalgam by Mikhail Podgaetsky of two novels, *The Give us Europe Trust* by Ilya Erenburg and *The Tunnel* by Bernhard Kellermann, with additional material from Upton Sinclair and Pierre Hamp. Podgaetsky's scenario bore little resemblance to Erenburg's novel from which the bulk of the material was taken, and after further

[1] See pp. 318–19, 322 below.   [2] Ropes with loops, suspended from a pole.

alterations in the course of rehearsals the connection was attenuated still further. Only two years before Erenburg had proclaimed: '*Away with the author!* Theatre shouldn't be written in the study, but built on the stage.'[1] Now he sprang to the defence of his novel, protesting 'I'm not some classic but a real, live person', and claiming to be working on a stage version himself.[2] In an open letter Meyerhold retorted:

> . . . even if you had undertaken an adaptation of your novel, *The History of the Fall of Europe* [he meant the same work], you would have produced the kind of play that could be put on in any city of the Entente, whereas in my theatre, which serves and will continue to serve the cause of the Revolution, we need tendentious plays, plays with one aim only: to serve the cause of the Revolution.[3]

Give us Europe! was even more fragmented in structure than Meyerhold's previous episodic productions. It took the form of a political revue in seventeen episodes, of which only two or three featured the same characters twice. The theme was the struggle for the control of a war-devastated Europe between American capitalist millionaires and a Soviet 'radio trust'. There were no less than ninety-five roles divided between forty-five performers, amongst whom the champion quick-change artist was Erast Garin, who appeared as seven different inventors in a scene lasting fifteen minutes.

The production was remarkable for its settings, which were composed entirely of 'moving walls'. Devised by Meyerhold himself, these 'walls' were a series of eight to ten red wooden screens, about 12 feet long and 9 feet high, which were moved on wheels by stage-hands concealed behind each one. With the addition of the simplest properties, they were deployed to represent now a set of rooms, now a Moscow street, now a sports arena. The action never faltered and in some scenes the walls played an active part, their motion emphasized by weaving spotlights. For example, a fugitive fled upstage to be confronted by two rapidly converging walls; managing to squeeze through the narrowing gap just before one crossed in front of the other, he seemed to have disappeared when they separated and moved on across the stage. In fact, he had simply concealed himself behind one wall and left the stage with it.

Again Meyerhold employed projected captions, this time on three screens. As well as the title and the location of each episode, there were comments on characters, information relevant to the action, and quotations

---

[1] I. Erenburg, *A vsyo-taki ona vertitsya*, Moscow-Berlin, 1922, p. 114.
[2] Letter from Erenburg to Meyerhold dated 5 March 1924 in *Novy Zritel*, Moscow, 1924, no 18, p. 16.
[3] Ibid., p. 16–17.

from the written works and speeches of Lenin, Trotsky and Zinoviev. The depravity of the Western world was portrayed in the customary grotesque style, whilst the vigour of the young Soviet state was expressed by marching and singing Red sailors and komsomols performing biomechanics routines. Critics were quick to condemn this crude schematization; not only were the scenes in 'foxtrotting Europe' far more energetic and diverting (helped greatly by the performance of the first jazz band to appear in Soviet Russia), but there was an obvious danger in representing a deadly political enemy as a collection of emasculated cretins, cowards and libertines. By all but his most devoted followers Meyerhold was accused either of 'urbanism', the term used to describe a preoccupation with the dubious attractions of the big city suspiciously close to nostalgia, or of 'infantile leftism' – a naïve conception of the social situation which was bound to encourage disastrous complacency. Either way, Meyerhold clearly needed to look for far more sophisticated dramatic material in future.

Bubus, the Teacher, by Faiko (29 January 1925), was hardly the response the critics were demanding. Yet another flimsy political farce depicting the exhausted last fling of the rulers of an imaginary capitalist country on the verge of revolution, it invited the very schematization of Western decadent types which Meyerhold had already exploited to its limits. The one exception was the character of Bubus himself, an intellectual idealist who vacillated ineffectually between two camps and found himself rejected by the revolution when it finally came. He was an individual embodying the conflict of class loyalties within himself instead of displaying in two dimensions the attitudes of one particular side. In conception at least he represented a significant advance on the placard style of earlier Soviet theatre, a shift from crude agitation to more reasoned propaganda.

But Bubus apart, Faiko's play was so insubstantial that it presented no intellectual challenge whatsoever to Meyerhold. Once more brushing aside the protests of a mere author, he adapted the text to suit his own ends and developed a whole new range of production tricks to invest it with heavy significance. There was no production by Meyerhold which did not reaffirm his conception of rhythm as the basis of all dramatic expression, but in *Bubus* he restored it to the pre-eminence it had enjoyed in such pre-1917 works as *Tristan and Isolde*, *Don Juan* and *Masquerade*. With only the occasional break, every movement was synchronized with a musical accompaniment, the text being spoken as a kind of recitative. As in *Give us Europe*, lascivious foxtrots and shimmies were danced to jazz accompani-

ment; but most of the music was taken from Liszt and Chopin and performed by a pianist at a concert Bechstein perched high above the stage
in a gilded alcove ringed with coloured lights. By revealing the source of
the music to the spectator, Meyerhold hoped to counteract its stupefying
effects and reinforce its ironical function.

In contrast to the aggressive angularity of recent productions, the setting
(executed by Ilya Shlepyanov) consisted of a semicircle of suspended
bamboo rods completely enclosing a stage area covered with a circular
green carpet. The back wall was adorned with flashing neon signs and the
whole picture framed by an ornate false proscenium arch. Properties were
few, the most striking being a gilded fountain in the first act. The mel-
lifluous tinkling of the bamboo curtain at the entrance of each character,
the soft splashing of the fountain, the rhythmical flashing of the neon all
played their part in Meyerhold's complex orchestration.

True to Guglielmo's precept of 'partire di terreno',[1] the languid
aristocrats moved in broad curves within the rounded confines of their
fragile stockade. Faultlessly costumed, their fans, cloaks, top hats and
walking-sticks were the pretext for much elegant by-play in the style of
Meyerhold's Petersburg period. Frequently this business took the form of
'pre-acting', a device whose traditional antecedents Meyerhold acknow-
ledged, whilst emphasizing the novelty of its application in the political
theatre.[2]

Projected titles were omitted from *Bubus*, since it was considered that
pre-acting enabled the 'actor-tribune' to convey the sub-text with far more
subtlety and dexterity. However, the constant interpolation of mime emphasized rather than made good the frailty of the text, and was seen by many critics
as a regression to the gratuitous aestheticism of Meyerhold's early Petersburg
days. But for Meyerhold and his company it was a valuable exercise in
rhythmical discipline which told strongly in subsequent productions. Above
all, it marked his 'rediscovery' of music, the vital component in so much of his
finest work.

By the spring of 1925, Lenin's New Economic Policy had restored the
Soviet economy to solvency and the time had come to revoke the alliance
with private enterprise. To mark the closing of this era, Meyerhold put
on Nikolai Erdman's *Warrant* (20 April 1925), a satirical fantasy in the
style of Gogol. It was directed against the 'internal emigrés' of the NEP
period who still dreamt of the restoration of the monarchy and preserved

[1] See p. 156 above.   [2] See pp. 205−6 below.

all the trappings and customs of the old order. Like Bubus, Erdman's characters oscillate pitifully between the old and the new, and the situation arises where a party card is deemed a handsome dowry by virtue of the protection it will afford against the shocks of Communism.

Again Meyerhold employed 'pre-acting', adding the device of sudden freezes to convey the characters' horrified subconscious awareness of their true dilemma. The effect was heightened by the use of a double revolve: the petrified group would silently retreat; a gap would materialize in the seemingly impassable panelled wall enclosing the stage area; and they would be 'hurled from the stream of life on to the rubbish dump of history'.[1] Once more, props were used sparingly but effectively 'both as an instrument for acting and as a symbolic generalization of a way of life'.[2] A domestic altar complete with votive candles and horn-gramophone, a wrought-iron treadle sewing-machine, a piano decorated with paper flowers, a banquet table with epergne and candelabra: these were the objects the doomed 'nepmen' relied on to preserve their delusion of permanency.

But Meyerhold's production was more than a merciless jest at the expense of a helpless foe; there was little laughter at the closing line 'What's the point of living, mama, if they don't even bother to arrest us?' It was a glimpse of the tragic aspect of the grotesque, which recalled the Mayor rounding on the audience at the close of *The Government Inspector* and Blok's Clown bleeding cranberry juice in *The Fairground Booth*.[3]

For all its tendentious hyperbole, *The Warrant*, which Meyerhold regarded as the first true Soviet comedy, marked his rejection of placard drama; as Pavel Markov wrote, 'The production makes you think. It questions premises and proceeds by deduction.'[4] Significantly, Stanislavsky was deeply impressed, remarking on the last act: 'In this act Meyerhold has accomplished what I myself am dreaming of.'[5]

The following season, for the first time Meyerhold entrusted a production – Sergei Tretyakov's *Roar, China!* – to one of his assistants (Vassily Fyodorov). His own time was divided between work on Pushkin's *Boris Godunov* at the Vakhtangov Studio (the Third Moscow Art Studio) and *The Government Inspector* at his own theatre. *Boris Godunov* was never

---

[1] Mikhail Zharov, *Zhizn, teatr, kino*, Moscow, 1967, p. 184.
[2] Pavel Markov in *Pechat i revolyutsia*, Moscow, 1925, no 5–6, p. 291.
[3] Cf. p. 140 above.
[4] *Pechat i revolyutsia*, Moscow, 1925, no 5–6, p. 291.
[5] Quoted in Pavel Markov, *Pravda teatra*, Moscow, 1965, p. 43.

completed and almost twenty months passed before an astonished Moscow public was confronted with Meyerhold's version of a classic which they thought they knew as well as the Kremlin itself.

1. Biomechanics

In the past the actor has always conformed with the society for which his art was intended. In future the actor must go even further in relating his technique to the industrial situation. For he will be working in a society where labour is no longer regarded as a curse but as a joyful, vital necessity. In these conditions of ideal labour art clearly requires a new foundation.

We are accustomed to the rigid division of a man's time into *labour* and *rest*. Every worker used to try to expend as few hours as possible on labour and as many as possible on rest. Whereas such a desire is quite normal under the conditions of a capitalist society, it is totally incompatible with the proper development of a socialist society. The cardinal problem is that of fatigue, and it is on the correct solution of this problem that the art of the future depends.

In America at the present time much research is being devoted to the possible methods of incorporating rest in the work process instead of regarding it as a separate unit.

The whole question boils down to the regulation of rest periods. Under ideal conditions (taking account of hygiene, physiology and comfort) a rest of as little as ten minutes is capable of completely restoring a man's energy.

Work should be made easy, congenial and uninterrupted, whilst art should be utilized by the new class not only as a means of relaxation but as something *organically vital* to the labour pattern of the worker. *We need to change not only the forms of our art but our methods too.* An actor working for the new class needs to re-examine all the canons of the past. The very craft of the actor must be completely reorganized.

The work of the actor in an industrial society will be regarded as a means of production vital to the proper organization of the labour of every citizen of that society.

However, apart from the correct utilization of rest periods, *it is equally essential to discover those movements in work which facilitate the maximum*

197

use of work time. If we observe a skilled worker in action, we notice the following in his movements: (1) an absence of superfluous, unproductive movements; (2) rhythm; (3) the correct positioning of the body's centre of gravity; (4) stability. Movements based on these principles are distinguished by their dance-like quality; a skilled worker at work invariably reminds one of a dancer; thus work borders on art. The spectacle of a man working efficiently affords positive pleasure. This applies equally to the work of the actor of the future.

In art our constant concern is the organization of raw material. Constructivism has forced the artist to become both artist and engineer. Art should be based on scientific principles; the entire creative act should be a conscious process. The art of the actor consists in organizing his material; that is, in his capacity to utilize correctly his body's means of expression.

The actor embodies in himself both the organizer and that which is organized (i.e. the artist and his material). The formula for acting may be expressed as follows:

$N = A_1 + A_2$ (where N = the actor; A_1 = the artist who conceives the idea and issues the instructions necessary for its execution; A_2 = the executant who executes the conception of A_1).

The actor must train his material (the body), so that it is capable of executing instantaneously those tasks which are dictated externally (by the actor, the director).

In so far as the task of the actor is the realization of a specific objective, his means of expression must be economical in order to ensure that *precision* of movement which will facilite *the quickest possible realization of the objective.*

The methods of Taylorism[1] may be applied to the work of the actor in the same way as they are to any form of work with the aim of maximum productivity.

The conditions (1) that rest is embodied in the work process in the form of pauses, and (2) that art has a specific, vital function and does not serve merely as a means of relaxation, make it obligatory for the actor to utilize his time *as economically as possible.* Art is allocated a specific number of time units in the worker's timetable which must be utilized to the maximum effect. This means that one must not fritter away $1\frac{1}{2}$–2 hours in making up and putting on one's costume.

The actor of the future will work without make-up and wear an overall, that is, a costume designed to serve as everyday clothing yet equally suited

[1] Term derived from the name of Frederick Winslow Taylor (see p. 183 above).

to the movements and concepts which the actor realizes on the stage.

The Taylorization of the theatre will make it possible to perform in one hour that which requires four at present.

For this the actor must possess: (1) *the innate capacity for reflex excitability*,[1] which will enable him to cope with any emploi within the limits of his physical characteristics; (2) 'physical competence', consisting of a true eye, a sense of balance, and the ability to sense at any given moment the location of his centre of gravity.

Since the art of the actor is the art of plastic forms in space, he must study the mechanics of his body. This is essential because any manifestation of a force (including the living organism) is subject to constant laws of mechanics (and obviously the creation by the actor of plastic forms in the space of the stage is a manifestation of the force of the human organism).

The fundamental deficiency of the modern actor is his absolute ignorance of the laws of *biomechanics*.

It is quite natural that with the acting methods which have prevailed up to now, the 'inspirational' method and the method of 'authentic emotions' (essentially they are one and the same, differing only in their means of realization: the first employs narcotic stimulation, the second – hypnosis), the actor has always been so overwhelmed by his emotions that he has been unable to answer either for his movements or for his voice. He has had no control over himself and hence been in no state to ensure success or failure. Only a few exceptionally great actors have succeeded instinctively in finding the correct method, that is, the method of building the role not from inside outwards, but vice versa. By approaching their role from the outside, they succeeded in developing stupendous technical mastery. I am speaking of artists like Duse, Sarah Bernhardt, Grasso, Chaliapin, Coquelin.

There is a whole range of questions to which psychology is incapable of supplying the answers. A theatre built on psychological foundations is as certain to collapse as a house built on sand. On the other hand, a theatre which relies on *physical elements* is at very least assured of clarity. All psychological states are determined by specific physiological processes. By correctly resolving the nature of his state physically, the actor reaches the point where he experiences the *excitation* which communicates itself to the spectator and induces him to share in the actor's performance: what we used to call 'gripping' the spectator. It is this excitation which is the very essence of the actor's art. From a sequence of physical positions and situations there arise those '*points of excitation*' which are informed with some particular emotion.

[1] See p. 201 below.

Throughout this process of 'rousing the emotions' the actor observes a rigid framework of physical prerequisites.

Physical culture, acrobatics, dance, rhythmics, boxing and fencing are all useful activities, but they are of use only so long as they constitute auxiliary exercises in a course of *'biomechanics'*, the essential basis of every actor's training.

['The Actor of the Future and Biomechanics',
a report of Meyerhold's lecture in the
Little Hall of the Moscow Conservatoire, 12 June 1922;
in *Ermitazh*, Moscow, 1922, no 6, pp. 10–11.]

. . . When Jaques-Dalcroze invented his system of eurhythmics he was concerned primarily with the musical aspect, but the *question of rhythm* has proved vital for *everybody*. If we cannot handle a saw, if we are clumsy with a knife and fork, if we walk badly on the stage, we can learn from Dalcroze. Every craftsman – the blacksmith, the foundry-worker, the actor – must have rhythm, must be familiar with the laws of balance. An actor ignorant of the laws of balance is less than an apprentice. For instance, the Kamerny Theatre director's[1] ignorance of biomechanics has had the most dismal consequences. Neither fencing nor acrobatics have helped him; he has succeeded merely in making a cult out of the dexterity of tailors and cobblers.

How do we set about moulding the new actor? It is quite simple I think. When we admire a child's movements we are admiring his biomechanical skill. If we place him in an environment in which gymnastics and all forms of sport are both available and compulsory, we shall achieve the new man who is capable of any form of labour. *Only via the sports arena can we approach the theatrical arena.*

Every movement is a hieroglyph with its own peculiar meaning. The theatre should employ only those movements which are immediately decipherable; everything else is superfluous . . .

Consider Pushkin: 'Inspiration is as necessary in geometry as in poetry, but ecstasy is not necessary.' Ecstasy is the notorious inner experience, the 'authentic emotion'; it is the system of my teacher Konstantin Stanislavsky, who, by the way, will probably abandon it very shortly. We need not ecstasy but excitation, based firmly on the physical premise.

[From a report of the same lecture in *Teatralnaya Moskva*,
Moscow, 1922, no 45, pp. 9–10.]

[1] Tairov.

Bubus, the Teacher, 1925.

Bubus, the Teacher, 1925.

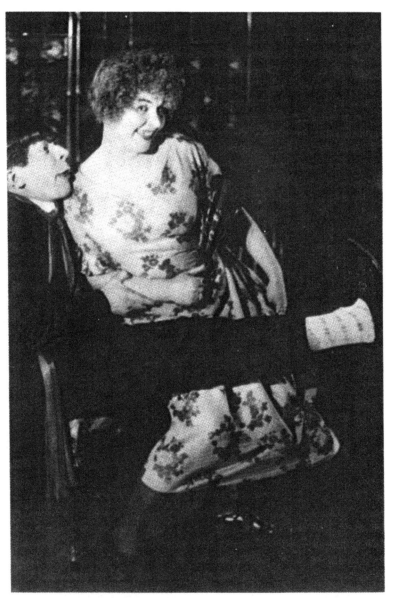

The Warrant, 1925. Sergei Martinson and Zinaida Raikh.

The Warrant, 1925. (Meyerhold seated bottom right.).

An actor must possess the capacity for *Reflex Excitability*. Nobody can become an actor without it.

Excitability

Excitability is the ability to realize in feelings,[1] movements and words a task which is prescribed externally.

The manifestation of excitability

The co-ordinated manifestations of excitability together constitute the actor's performance. Each separate manifestation comprises an *acting cycle*.[2]

Each *acting cycle* comprises three invariable stages:

1. INTENTION.
2. REALIZATION.
3. REACTION.

The intention is the intellectual assimilation of a task prescribed externally by the dramatist, the director, or the initiative of the performer.

The realization is the cycle of volitional, mimetic[3] and vocal reflexes.

The reaction is the attenuation of the volitional reflex as it is realized mimetically and vocally in preparation for the reception of a new intention (the transition to a new acting cycle). . . .

> [Meyerhold, V. M. Bebutov and I. A. Aksyonov,
> *Emploi aktyora*, Moscow, 1922, pp. 3–4.]

NOTE   Apart from the two reports of Meyerhold's lecture in *Ermitazh* and *Teatralnaya Moskva*, his only substantial published pronouncement on biomechanics is contained in his review[4] of Tairov's book, *Zapiski Rezhissyora* ('A Director's Notes'), which largely reiterates what is printed above and furthers his polemic against what he saw as the studied balleticism of the Kamerny Theatre.

Meyerhold delivered a second public lecture on biomechanics in October

---

[1] The term 'feelings' is used in the strictly technical sense with no loose, sentimental connotation.
The same applies to 'volitional'. The word is used to exclude on the one hand the 'inspirational' method of acting (and the systematic use of narcotic stimulants), and on the other the method of 'authentic emotions' (the hypnotic conditioning of the imagination) . . . [Meyerhold's note.]

[2] Literally 'element of acting'. [Translator.]

[3] 'Mimetic reflexes' comprise all the movements performed by the separate parts of the actor's body and the movements of the entire body in space. [Meyerhold's note.]

[4] Published in *Pechat i revolyutsia*, Moscow, 1922, no 1, pp. 305–9.

1922 which, like the first, was followed by a display of exercises by his pupils. Shortly afterwards, in an article entitled 'Biomechanics according to Meyerhold',[1] Ippolit Sokolov dismissed Meyerhold's claim to the invention of biomechanics, referring to 'over 100 major works on the subject', most notably Jules Amar's *Le Moteur humain et les bases scientifiques du travail professionnel* (Paris, 1914). Furthermore, he claimed that Meyerhold's exercises were either physiologically unsound and 'downright anti-Taylorist' or simply rehashed circus clowning.

Meyerhold answered his critic in a lecture entitled 'Tartuffes of Communism and Cuckolds of Morality'. Judging from the one brief résumé published,[2] he made little attempt to refute Sokolov's charges, saying that his system had no scientific basis and that its underlying theory rested on 'one brochure by Coquelin'. He must have meant Constant-Benoît Coquelin's *L'art et le comédien* (1880) or *L'art du comédien* (1886),[3] in which the remarks on the dual personality of the actor are strikingly similar to Meyerhold's formulation $N = A_1 + A_2$.

Meyerhold's own writings show that as early as 1905 his production methods were shaped by a preoccupation with mime and movement. With the opening of his Studio in 1913 came the opportunity to explore the formal discipline of the *commedia dell' arte*, as well as the conventions of the Oriental theatres. It was at this time that he laid the basis for what later became called 'biomechanics'. One of the Studio's 'comédiens' recalls:

. . . from the exercise 'Shooting a bow' there developed the étude, 'The Hunt', and then a whole pantomime which was used to train every 'generation' in the Studio. A whole series of exercises and études became 'classics' and were used later in the teaching of biomechanics.[4]

Similarly, Valery Bebutov says that Meyerhold based the exercise 'The Leap on to the Chest' on his observations of the Sicilian actor, Giovanni Grasso, who visited Petersburg before the First World War.[5]

Thus Meyerhold derived his exercises from various sources, refining them and adding new ones during his first year at the State Theatre Workshop until they numbered about twenty. As he said to Harold Clurman in 1935, 'each exercise is a melodrama. Each movement gives the actor a sense of performing on the stage.'[6]

---

[1] *Teatr*, Moscow, 1922, no 5, pp. 149–51.

[2] *Teatr i Musyka*, Moscow, 1922, no 7, 23–24.

[3] For an English translation of Coquelin see *Actors on Acting* (editors: T. Cole and H. K. Chinoy), New York, 1949, pp. 195–206.

[4] Alexei Gripich, 'Uchitel stseny' in *Vstrechi s Meyerholdom*, cit., p. 125.

[5] V. Bebutov, 'Neutomimy novator' in *Vstrechi s Meyerholdom*, cit., p. 76. (For an illustration of this exercise see the photograph facing p. 160.)

[6] Harold Clurman, 'Conversation with Two Masters' in *Theatre Arts Monthly*, New York, 1935, November, p. 874.

Erast Garin, one of Meyerhold's pupils in 1922, describes the exercise 'Shooting a bow':

An imaginary bow is held in the left hand. The student advances with the left shoulder forward. When he spots the target he stops, balanced equally on both feet. The right hand describes an arc in order to reach an arrow in an imaginary belt behind his back. The movement of the hand affects the whole body, causing the balance to shift to the back foot.

The hand draws the arrow and loads the bow. The balance is transferred to the front foot. He aims. The bow is drawn with the balance shifting again to the back foot. The arrow is fired and the exercise completed with a leap and a cry.

Through this, one of the earliest exercises, the pupil begins to comprehend himself in spatial terms, acquires physical self-control, develops elasticity and balance, realizes that the merest gesture − say with the hand − resounds throughout the entire body, and gains practice in the so-called 'refusal'. Thus, in this exercise the 'pre-gesture', the 'refusal', is the hand reaching back for the arrow. The étude is an example of the 'acting sequence' which comprises intention, realization and re-action.[1]

Emploi aktyora ('The Actor's Emploi') was published by the State Higher Theatre Workshop, and is an attempt to define seventeen male and seventeen female types according to their physical characteristics and vocal ranges. Each emploi is accompanied by examples of suitable roles drawn from a wide range of dramatic literature: classical and modern, Russian and foreign.[2]

Whilst honouring the traditional notion of emploi, Meyerhold reserved the right to interpret it freely. For instance, in the 1930s he said:

It is not true that the modern director has no need to take account of the actor's emploi. The question is what use he makes of it. Here's a paradox for you: I need to know who is the juvenile lead in my theatre so as never to cast him as a juvenile lead. I have often noticed that an actor blossoms out quite unexpectedly in a part where he has to struggle to subdue his natural characteristics. They are still there, but they act as a kind of accompaniment to the character he has created. There is nothing more tedious than a provincial heroine playing Katerina.[3] The fascination of Komissarzhevskaya lay in her playing of heroines without being

[1] Erast Garin, 'O Mandate i o drugom' in *V strechi c Meyerholdom*, cit., pp. 322−3. For a detailed exposition of Meyerhold's biomechanical 'études' see Mel Gordon, 'Meyerhold's Biomechanics', *The Drama Review*, Vol. 18, No. 3 (T−63), pp. 73−88.
[2] For a translation of *Emploi aktyora* see Marjorie Hoover, *Meyerhold − The Art of Conscious Theatre*, University of Massachusetts, 1974.
[3] In Ostrovsky's *Storm*.

at all the heroine type. Unfortunately, the nature of actors is such that when they are type-cast they usually stop working and assume that their voice and appearance will see them through. In order to spur an actor into action you sometimes need to set him a paradoxical task which he can manage only by discarding his normal criteria. In my experience this method of casting nearly always justifies itself. . . .[1]

---

2. The Magnanimous Cuckold

After the closure of the Theatre R.S.F.S.R. No. 1 we were left without a theatre and began to work on the problem of productions without a stage.

This was strongly reflected in the nature of the production on which we were engaged at the time. We never did have much money, and at that time we had none at all. The entire production of *The Magnanimous Cuckold* cost 200 roubles at the present rate. We were forced to put it on at the Nezlobin Theatre, where the stage was cluttered up with their gold-painted sets and hung from top to bottom with canvas flats. For us, clearing all that trash off the stage was fun, but at the same time exhausting work; naturally, the Nezlobin stage-crew was conspicuous by its absence and our entire company had to cope with the Herculean task during a break in the final rehearsals.

The production was intended to furnish the basis for a new style of acting and a new kind of setting which broke away from the conventional framing of the acting area with wings and a proscenium arch. The aim was to lay every line of the setting completely bare, and the device was pursued to the limit of schematization. We succeeded in implementing this principle totally.

At the same time, the success of this production signified the success of the new theatrical philosophy on which it was based; now there is no doubt that the entire 'Left Theatre' not only dates from this production but to this day bears traces of its influence.

The fact that the stylistic extremes displayed by this production – although they frightened a section of critical opinion – were greeted *with delight* by the widest possible audience, proved that an urgent desire for

[1] Recalled by Alexander Gladkov in 'Meyerhold govorit', *Novy mir*, Moscow, 1961, no 8, p. 232.

just such a theatrical style was felt by this new audience, which regarded the theatre as one of the many *cultural* conquests of the Revolution. With this production we hoped to lay the basis for a new form of theatrical presentation with no need for illusionistic settings or complicated props, making do with the simplest objects which came to hand and transforming a spectacle performed by specialists into an improvised performance which could be put on by workers in their leisure time.

The subsequent development of our work has shown that the declared aim of this production was essential and that the whole course of modern stagecraft is leading to this end as inevitably as the advance of modern society in general.

['Kak byl postavlen *Velikodushny rogonosets*' in *Novy Zritel*,
Moscow, 1926, no 39, p. 6.]

3. Pre-acting

The actor's work consists in the artful juxtaposing of acting and pre-acting.

In the Russian theatre, the famous actor Lensky (1874–1908) was a master in the art of pre-acting. In the part of Benedict (in Shakespeare's *Much Ado About Nothing*) he gave a classic demonstration of pre-acting, which was described as follows in *Russkie vedomosty*, 1908, no 241:

'Benedict emerges from his hiding-place behind a bush, where he has just overheard the conversation about his love for Beatrice which had been contrived especially for his ears. For a long time he stands staring at the audience, his face frozen in amazement. Then suddenly his lips move very slightly. Now watch his eyes closely: they are still fixed in concentration, but from beneath the brows imperceptibly, gradually, there begins to creep a triumphant happy smile; the actor doesn't say a word, but you can see that a great irrepressible wave of joy is welling up inside Benedict; his face muscles, his cheeks begin to laugh and a smile spreads uncontrollably over his quivering face; suddenly a thought penetrates his uncomprehending joy and in a final mimetic chord the eyes which until now have been frozen with astonishment light up with delight. Now Benedict's whole body is one whole transport of wild rapture and the auditorium thunders with applause, although *the actor has yet to say a single word and only now begins his speech.'*

Critics might argue that this is a perfectly normal instance of the spoken text being enhanced by mimetic embellishments. But note that we intentionally emphasized the last words of the quotation to stress the point at issue.

Pre-acting prepares the spectator's perception in such a way that he comprehends the scenic situation fully resolved in advance and so has no need to make any effort to grasp the underlying message of the scene. This was a favourite device in the old Japanese and Chinese theatres. Nowadays, when the theatre is once more being employed as a platform for agitation, an acting system in which special stress is laid on pre-acting is indispensable to the actor-tribune.

The actor-tribune needs to convey to the spectator his attitude to the lines he is speaking and the situations he is enacting; he wants to force the spectator to respond in a particular way to the action which is unfolding before him.

The actor-tribune creates his art not for art's sake; it is not even by means of 'art' that he desires to work.

The actor-tribune sets himself the task of developing scenic situations not in order to impress the spectator with the beauty of their theatricality, but like a surgeon whose task it is to uncover what lies within. The actor-tribune acts not the situation itself, but what is concealed behind it and what it has to reveal for a specifically propagandist purpose.

When the actor-tribune lifts the mask of the character to reveal his true nature to the spectator he does not merely speak the lines furnished by the dramatist, he uncovers the roots from which the lines have sprung.

If the actor-tribune is to spin from the inevitable tangle of a complex production a thread of clearly discernible propagandist intentions by acting not the situation but what lies at the heart of the situation, if he is to accomplish this new task, he needs to re-examine his technique and give back to the theatre what it lost during the period of reaction when it slid into the quagmire of *apolitical* chit-chat.

['Igra i predigra' in the brochure, *Uchitel Bubus*,
Moscow, 1925, pp. 14–16.]

Part Six

THE GOVERNMENT INSPECTOR

1926

IN HIS REVIEW OF *The Forest* the eminent critic Alexander Kugel wrote: '. . . amongst us there are still many who were brought up on the exemplary works of Russian creative literature, and we regard such treatment of our great poets as unexampled barbarism.'[1] The charge was not new: many critics had protested in similar terms against the outrages perpetrated on *The Storm*, on *Masquerade*, on *Tarelkin's Death*. But Meyerhold persisted in honouring Mounet-Sully's dictum, 'Chaque texte n'est qu'un prétexte',[2] claiming that '. . . the art of the director is the art not of an executant, but of an author – so long as one has earned the right.'[3] No production demonstrated this more thoroughly than *The Government Inspector* on 9 December 1926.

After the first performance of the play in April 1836, Gogol was so terrified by the outraged protests of conservative critics that he denied all satirical intent, saying, 'Put two or three rogues on the stage and everyone flies into a rage and cries "We are not rogues!" '[4] Rejecting this excuse as disingenuous, Meyerhold attached far greater significance to what Gogol said eleven years later in his *Author's Confession*:

In *The Government Inspector* I decided to gather into one heap everything rotten in Russia as I then saw it, all the injustices which are perpetrated in those places and in those circumstances where justice is most required of a man; I decided to hold up everything to ridicule at once.[5]

As Meyerhold's co-adaptor, Mikhail Korenev, said:

The theatre was faced with the task of making *The Government Inspector* an *accusatory production*. Needless to say, our target was not merely peculation in some miserable little town in the middle of nowhere which has never got on to any map, but as far as possible the entire Nicholayan era, together with the way of life of its nobility and officials.[6]

In the original Petersburg production the cast paid little attention to

[1] *Rampa*, Moscow, 5–10 February 1924, p. 7.
[2] Quoted by Valery Bebutov in *Vstrechi s Meyerholdom*, cit., p. 77.
[3] 'Meyerhold govorit' in *Tarusskie stranitsy*, cit., p. 306.
[4] Letter to M. P. Pogodin, 10 May 1836, in N. V. Gogol, *Polnoe sobranie sochinenii* (Izd. A.N.S.S.S.R.), Leningrad, 1940–52, vol. 11, p. 41.
[5] Ibid., vol. 8, p. 440.
[6] In *Gogol i Meyerhold* (sbornik statei), Moscow, 1927, p. 78.

Gogol's precise notes on character portrayal, transforming the play into a trivial farce with Khlestakov 'like some vaudeville rogue . . . the conventional swindler, that drab character who has appeared in exactly the same costume for the past two hundred years'.[1] It must have been harmless, because even the stolid Tsar Nicholas was vastly amused and instructed the entire Royal Family and Privy Council to see it.

The play fared little better in Moscow a month later – even though the great Shchepkin played the Mayor – and Gogol, deeply depressed, fled the country to return only occasionally over the next twelve years. He continued to work on the text, seeking to eradicate the farcical elements which he considered had contributed to the burlesque of the first production. The final version published in 1842 contains numerous amendments, notably the insertion of the epigraph, 'Don't blame the mirror if your own mug is crooked', and the Mayor's aside to the audience in the final scene, 'What are you laughing at? You're laughing at yourselves!' Although this version is now accepted as canonical, it was not performed until 1870, by which time, says Korenev:

> Tradition unwittingly or perhaps, on the contrary, with most cunning malice aforethought, [had] set *The Government Inspector* on the rails of vaudeville and simple rib-tickling comedy and obscured its social significance; in their customary interpretation, the characters scarcely ever rose above the level of the schematized masks of light comedy.[2]

But new efforts were made to define Gogol's dramatic style, leading to the emergence of two further schools of opinion at the beginning of the twentieth century. First, there was the 'neo-naturalistic' interpretation[3] which identified his theatre as the forerunner of the genre works of Ostrovsky, Sukhovo-Kobylin, Lev Tolstoy, Turgenev and others, and was exemplified by the Moscow Art production of 1908. Second, there were the attempts of the symbolists (notably Rozanov's *Legend of the Great Inquisitor*, Bely's *Gogol* and Merezhkovsky's *Gogol and the Devil*) to reinterpret *The Government Inspector* in the light of the writings of Gogol's late 'mystical' period, in particular the *Dénouement* to the play (1846), in which he represents it as an allegory of the Last Judgement with Khlestakov the personification of man's 'venal, treacherous conscience'. In 1908 Meyerhold expressed his admiration for Merezhkovsky's article,[4] and the manner of his work with Komissarzhevskaya suggests strongly that the

---

[1] 'Otryvok iz pisma k odnomu literaturu', 25 May 1836, N. V. Gogol, op. cit., vol. 4, p. 99.

[2] *Gogol i Meyerhold*, cit., p. 77.   [3] See p. 220 below.

[4] 'Iz pisem o teatre' in *Zolotoe runo*, Petersburg, 1908, no 7–9, pp. 108–10.

projected production of *The Government Inspector* at her theatre in 1907[1] would almost certainly have reflected the symbolist interpretation.

However, in 1926 Meyerhold rejected all such narrow readings, seeing the play as a unique synthesis of realism, hyperbole and fantasy, agreeing with Pushkin that the treatment was comic, but the over-all effect disturbingly lachrymose.[2] Years later, when charged with the lack of humour in his production, Meyerhold said:

> Gogol was fond of saying that funny things often become sad if you look long enough at them. This transformation of mirth into sadness is the conjuring trick of Gogol's dramatic style.[3]

The Government Inspector was perhaps the clearest and the most coherent realization of the style which in his crucial essay, *The Fairground Booth* (1912), Meyerhold defined as the 'tragic grotesque'.

II

In his earlier interpretations of the classics, Meyerhold, for all his startling innovations, had remained faithful to the printed text. Even in his 'montage' of *The Forest* he altered little of the actual dialogue and added nothing to it. But the breadth of his conception of *The Government Inspector* forced him to adopt an altogether freer approach. As Mikhail Chekhov wrote:

> He realized that to stage *The Government Inspector* and only *The Government Inspector* would be torment to himself with an unbearable vow of silence. *The Government Inspector* started to grow and swell until it split wide open; through the cracks there gushed a raging torrent: *Dead Souls*, *The Nevsky Prospect*, Podkolyosin, Poprishchev, the dreams of the Mayoress, horrors, guffaws, raptures, the screams of ladies, the fears of petty bureaucrats. . . .[4]

As a foundation for his grand design, Meyerhold took the first draft of the play which dates from 1835. He restored the scene in which Anna Andreevna boasts to her daughter of the Cavalry Captain driven to despair by her flashing eyes;[5] the character of the N.C.O.'s wife who wanted to raise her skirts to show Khlestakov the bruises she received from the Mayor's flogging;[6] the comic dialogue where Khlestakov tries in vain to penetrate Doctor Hübner's German in order to extract a bribe from him.[7] He introduced isolated lines from *The Gamblers*, *Marriage* and *Vladimir of the Third Degree*, together with unmistakable touches from the Petersburg stories. On the departure of Khlestakov and Osip at the close of Act

---

[1] Nikolai Volkov, op. cit., vol. 1, pp. 304, 311–14.　　[2] Cf. p. 220 below.
[3] 'Meyerhold govorit' in *Tarusskie stranitsy*, cit., p. 305.
[4] *Gogol i Meyerhold*, cit., p. 85.　　[5] N. V. Gogol, op. cit., vol. 4, pp. 105–6.
[6] Ibid., pp. 323–6.　　[7] Ibid., pp. 317–18.

Four the theatre was filled with the ghostly jingling of harness bells, reminding the audience of the flight of Chichikov's celestial troika at the end of the first part of *Dead Souls*.

The majority of the amendments seemed to contradict Gogol's own revisions of the play, restoring its farcical elements; but this was thoroughly consistent with the satirical style perfected by Meyerhold in earlier productions, which employed pantomime and visual 'business' to bring out the true significance of the action and the performer's attitude towards it. Thus the absurdity of Anna Andreevna's amorous reminiscences about the Cavalry Captain was demonstrated by the sudden materialization of a succession of adoring young officers from behind furniture and out of cupboards, brandishing bouquets and histrionically committing suicide. Thus Khlestakov claimed that he lived 'to pluck the flowers of pleasure' (Act Three, Scene Five) and immediately relieved himself of a gobbet of phlegm. Thus during the drunken recital of his Petersburg exploits he idly drew Anna Andreevna's entranced little finger to his lips on a teaspoon.

The merest commonplace action was transformed into a studied pantomime: the ruminative, unison puffing of long pipes at the opening meeting, the elaborate toilette of the Mayor before setting off for the inn – even the proffering of bribes to Khlestakov – all assumed the precision of a familiar ceremony which exactly conveyed the ossified daily round of petty officialdom.

III

Meyerhold's portrayal of character was far removed from the traditional 'humming and hawing idiots dressed up to look more idiotic still'.[1] For his visit to Khlestakov in his rat's nest under the stairs of the inn, the Mayor was arrayed in an ornate shako and voluminous cloak, looking like some august field-marshal from the glorious campaign against Napoleon. The transformation of Anna Andreevna from the accepted stereotype was even more striking (due in part, it has been suggested, to Meyerhold's desire to display the charms of his wife, Zinaida Raikh, to best advantage). Gogol's 'provincial coquette, not quite beyond middle age, educated half on novels and verses in visitors' books and half in fussing over the pantry and the maids' room . . .' became a society beauty with a lustrous black chignon, and shoulders of gleaming alabaster rising from the rich silks which swathed her voluptuous figure. However, as Andrei Bely points out,[2] she was a creature straight from Gogol's own imagination, one of the ladies

[1] *Gogol i Meyerhold*, cit., p. 79.   [2] Ibid., pp. 27–29.

from the town of N. who so excited Chichikov's erotic fancy at the Governor's ball in *Dead Souls*.[1]

Even so, just as in Gogol, this was hyperbole with a purpose. Whether all this finery represented a true picture of remote provincial life was beside the point; what it did represent was the bombastic Mayor and his feather-brained wife as they pictured themselves in their social-climbing dreams. When finally the subterfuge was exploded the Mayor lost his wits, to be removed raving in a strait-jacket by his own cloddish policemen; Anna Andreevna was borne away senseless on the shoulders of her faithful entourage of subalterns, like some fallen Racinian heroine. To such heights had their deluded fantasies soared that this grotesquely tragic end seemed fitting, even inevitable, and the audience had no need of the Mayor's chilling whisper 'What are you laughing at? You're laughing at yourselves!' to freeze the smiles on their faces. Farce turned into nightmare as the church bells, ordered to celebrate Maria Antonovna's betrothal, boomed louder and louder, police whistles shrilled, and a disembodied Jewish band sent the guests on a frenzied gallop through the auditorium. Simultaneously, a white screen rose in front of the stage, bearing the fatal announcement of the true inspector's arrival and then slowly disappeared aloft to disclose life-size terror-stricken effigies of the townspeople – condemned to eternal petrifaction.

What of Khlestakov, the engineer of this whole nightmare? Meyerhold drew attention to his affinity with the card-sharper, Ikharyov, in *The Gamblers*,[2] but he gave him as many more aspects as he had once identified in Harlequin and Don Juan.[3] Leonid Grossman describes his first entrance:

> He appears onstage, a character from some tale by Hoffmann, slender, clad in black with a stiff mannered gait, strange spectacles, a sinister old-fashioned tall hat, a rug and a cane, apparently tormented by some private vision. He is a flâneur from the Nevsky Prospect, a native of Gogol's own Petersburg. . . .[4]

And he has a double, an 'officer in transit' (sprung from Khlestakov's passing reference in the original text [Act Two, Scene Three] to an infantry captain who had fleeced him at cards in Penza) with a pale lugubrious visage and a cynical daring reminiscent of Lermontov's Pechorin. He is Khlestakov's taciturn accomplice in every enterprise. At the inn he sets to work marking a pack of cards, and immediately Khlestakov's air of distraction vanishes and he, too, becomes a sharp-witted swindler. On the way to the Mayor's (Act Three, Scene Five), Khlestakov borrows his companion's imposing fur-collared cape and tall shako, and 'Before our

---

[1] *Dead Souls*, part 1, chapter 8. [2] See p. 220 below.
[3] See pp. 131–3 above. [4] *Gogol i Meyerhold*, cit., p. 42.

very eyes this timorous little fop, this most servile of civil servants is transformed into the phantasmagorical figure of the impostor'.[1]

The pair of them dance a quadrille with Anna Andreevna and her daughter, Maria: whilst Khlestakov plays the love-smitten gallant to mother and daughter in turn, his double looks on with a disdainful sneer, revealing the whole tawdriness of these amorous manoeuvres.

The 'officer in transit' was, on the one hand, 'a mystical representation of everything which took place behind the scenes of Khlestakov's soul',[2] and on the other 'an animated piece of furniture',[3] ready to provide the accessories for every transformation, an attentive ear for a soliloquy – even an occasional phrase on the rare occasion when words failed his garrulous companion.

Khlestakov had a different mask for every situation: Nevsky flâneur, ingenious card-sharper, timorous clerk, imperious general, adroit adventurer. He was all of these plus a Russian Munchhausen who elevated the lie to an art form. Yet on the words, 'Well how are things, Pushkin, old friend?' (Act Three, Scene Six), he lapsed into the melancholic reverie of a solitary poet, and for a fleeting moment one was vouchsafed a glimpse of Gogol himself. Much was made of Meyerhold's 'mystical' interpretation of Khlestakov, but a thoroughly rational justification for it is supplied by Gogol himself:

> In a word, [Khlestakov] should be a type containing traits to be found scattered in a variety of Russian characters but which happen here to be combined in one, as is often the case in nature. There is nobody who for a minute – or even for a number of minutes – has not changed or does not go on changing into a Khlestakov, although naturally he is reluctant to admit it. We even make fun of this habit – but only, of course, when we see it in someone else. Even the smart guards officer, even the eminent head of the family, even our friend, the humble man of letters, will sometimes turn into a Khlestakov. In short, there's hardly a single man who won't become him at least once in his lifetime – the only point is that he'll change back again and carry on as though it never happened.[4]

If everyone is something of a Khlestakov, then surely it was anything but 'mystical' of Meyerhold to depict in him something of everyone.

As a counterweight to the unrelieved corruption of the townspeople and the fiendish machinations of Khlestakov, Meyerhold interpreted his valet, Osip, as a vigorous positive character. Rejecting the traditional picture of the scrofulous drunken rascal, he made him a red-cheeked country lad who

[1] Anatoly Lunacharsky, *O teatre i dramaturgii*, Moscow, 1958, vol. 1, p. 402.

[2] Dmitri Talnikov, *Novaya reviziya Revizora*, Moscow–Leningrad, 1927, p. 52.

[3] A. Lunacharsky, loc. cit.

[4] 'Otryvok iz pisma k odnomu literatoru', cit., p. 101.

sang traditional folk-songs and emanated robust common sense. The text of his reminiscences of Petersburg (Act Two, Scene One) was not changed, but he was furnished with the audience of a charwoman (from *The Gamblers* – see p. 221 below) who pealed with laughter throughout; like the 'officer in transit' and Anna Andreevna's young officers – to say nothing of Doctor Hübner and his ministrations to the Mayor in Act One (see pp. 223–5 below) – the charwoman both served a practical theatrical purpose (by helping to avoid the outmoded soliloquy) and accentuated the irony of the dialogue (Osip's contempt for Petersburg society). But further to that, her laughter served as a coloratura accompaniment to Osip's tenor recitative: one instance of the production's musical conception which is dicussed below.

IV

Meyerhold's version of *The Government Inspector* was considerably longer than the original, and his extensive use of pantomime and *tableaux vivants* made it longer still. In his customary manner he divided the play into fifteen titled episodes, a sequence of fifteen separate vignettes which followed the chronological sequence of Gogol's plot.

Meyerhold wanted to use elaborate settings to evoke the atmosphere of the 1830s, but without recourse to the lengthy scene changes which are inimical to the psychological effects of montage. Accordingly, he devised a method of kinetic staging,[1] similar in principle to the double revolve in *The Warrant*.

The stage was enclosed by a semicircular, imitation polished mahogany screen containing a series of eleven double doors (plus two more at either wing), surmounted by a dull green border and with three large suspended green lights. The centre section of the screen opened to admit a tiny truck-stage (about 4.25 metres × 3.5 metres) which rolled silently forward on runners to face the audience with actors and setting ready assembled. At the end of the scene the screen reopened and the truck retreated, to be replaced by another similarly prepared. All but four scenes were played on these trucks, with the inn scene ('After Penza') alone lowered from the flies. The remainder occupied the full stage area, with the final 'grand rond' overflowing into the auditorium. Dobchinsky's headlong tumble down the stairs of the inn continued right out of sight into the orchestra pit – a 'mise hors scène', as Eisenstein called it.[2]

[1] The settings were executed by Dmitriev and Shlepyanov according to Meyerhold's plans.

[2] Sergei Eisenstein. *Izbrannie proizvedeniya v shesti tomakh*, Moscow, 1964–1971, vol. 4, p. 148.

The full stage was used to striking effect in the episode entitled 'Procession' (Act Three, Scene Five) when a tipsy Khlestakov in voluminous cloak steered an erratic course the length of a balustrade with a sycophantic *corps de ballet* of town dignitaries matching his every stagger. In 'Bribes' (Act Four, Scenes Seven to Eleven) the wooden screen was transformed into a cunning 'bribe machine': as Khlestakov lay stupefied on the empty stage in a flickering half-light, eleven hands, seemingly conjured up by his drunken imagination, materialized simultaneously from eleven doors and apprehensively tendered eleven wads of banknotes which Khlestakov pocketed with the mechanical gestures of a clockwork doll.

Each scene on the truck-stage glided forward from the gloom like the reincarnation of a long-buried past, an exquisitely composed engraving projected out of its gleaming mahogany frame; a long pause was held for the image to register, then the tableau came to life. Sergei Radlov describes the scene where Khlestakov drunkenly expatiates on his Petersburg exploits:

> Crystal sparkles, blue and translucent; heavy silk, gleaming and flowing; the dazzling black hair and dazzling white breast of a grand stately lady; a dandy, drunk as only a Hoffmann could imagine, romantically gaunt, lifts a cigar to his languid lips with the movement of a somnambulist. A silver bowl filled with pieces of fat, succulent watermelon. Enchanted objects, wobbling slightly, float from hand to hand, passed by servants in a trance. Huge splendid divans, like elephants carved from mahogany, stand poised in majestic slumber. What is this – *Caligari* in slow motion by some lunatic projectionist?[1]

To some casual observers the profusion of lifelike detail seemed to suggest a rapprochement with Moscow Art naturalism, but in truth the picture was anything but naturalistic. The pot-belly of a wardrobe, the voluptuous curve of a Récamier couch, the deep rose-patterned back of a divan: they were all subtly exaggerated to enhance the poses of the characters and to impinge more firmly on the retina of the spectator.

Above all, the truck-stage afforded no space for ill-considered, 'inspirational' movement. With as many as thirty characters pressed together in a human pyramid, the merest deviation in timing or movement could destroy the whole ensemble. By this most practical device (inspired, it has been said, by the primitive wagon-stage)[2] Meyerhold compelled his company to exercise the self-discipline which had always been the ultimate objective of biomechanics and all the experiments which preceded the formulation of that system.

[1] Sergei Radlov, *Desyat let v teatre*, Leningrad, 1929, p. 148.

[2] Emmanuil Kaplan in *Revizor v Teatre imeni Vs. Meyerholda* (sbornik statei), Leningrad, 1927, p. 71.

V

The powerful atmosphere and the sense of period in Meyerhold's *Government Inspector* owed much to the complex musical score which accompanied the production. It included arrangements of works by nineteenth-century Russian composers, in particular romances by Glinka and Dargomyzhsky, and music specially composed by Mikhail Gnesin. Gnesin describes how the music heard during the ball celebrating Maria Antonovna's betrothal to Khlestakov (Act Five, Scenes Three to Seven) was based on the little Jewish bands which Meyerhold recalled from the balls and weddings of his youth in Penza.[1] It was the same music that Chekhov specified as an accompaniment to Ranevskaya's agony in Act Three of *The Cherry Orchard*.

Twenty years earlier, in his analysis of that same act (pp. 28–29 above) Meyerhold defined its musical structure in which the actual music was one element in an over-all rhythmical harmony designed to reveal the 'subtext' of the drama. Now he analyzed and interpreted *The Government Inspector* in precisely the same manner, exploiting to perfection the lessons he had learnt from Georg Fuchs and Adolphe Appia. More than anything, it was this concept of 'musicality' that set Meyerhold apart from every other stage-director of his time.

One example will suffice to illustrate his orchestration of Gogol's score:

Introduction. Dark. Somewhere, slow quiet music begins to play. In the centre of the stage massive doors swing silently wide open of their own accord and a platform moves slowly forward towards the spectator, out of the gloom, out of the distance, out of the past – one senses this immediately, because it is contained in the music. The music swells and comes nearer, then suddenly on an abrupt chord – *sforzando* – the platform is flooded with light in unison with the music.

On the platform stand a table and a few chairs; candles burn; officials sit. The audience seems to crane forward towards the dark and gloomy age of Nicholas in order to see better what it was like in those days.

Suddenly, the music grows quiet – *subito piano* – gloomy like the period, like the colours of the setting: red furniture, red doors and red walls, green uniforms and green hanging lampshades: the colour scheme of government offices. The music is abruptly retarded, then drawn out expectantly; everybody waits – on the stage and in the audience. Smoke rises from pipes and chibouks. The long stems 'cross out' the faces of the officials lit by the flickering candle flames; they are like fossilized monsters: crossed out and obliterated, once and for all. There they sit, wreathed in a haze with only the shadows of their pipes flickering on their faces; and the music plays on, slower and quieter as though flickering too, bearing them away from us, further and further into that irretrievable 'then'. A pause – *fermata*. And then a voice: 'Gentlemen, I have invited you here to give you some most unpleasant

[1] Mikhail Gnesin, *Statyi, vospominaniya, materialy*, Moscow, 1961, p. 198.

news . . .' like Rossini in the Act One *stretto* with Doctor Bartholo and Don Basilio, only there the tempo is *presto* whilst here it is very slow.

Then suddenly, as though on a word of command, at a stroke of the conductor's baton, everyone stirs in agitation, pipes jump from lips, fists clench, heads swivel. The last syllable of 'revizor' [inspector] seems to tweak everybody. Now the word is hissed in a whisper: the whole word by some, just the consonants by others, and somewhere even a softly rolled 'r'. The word 'revizor' is divided musically into every conceivable intonation. The ensemble of suddenly startled officials blows up and dies away like a squall. Everyone freezes and falls silent; the guilty conscience rises in alarm, then hides its poisonous head again, like a serpent lying motionless and saving its deadly venom.

The dynamics of this perfectly fashioned musical introduction (episode one – 'A Letter from Chmykhov') fluctuate constantly. The sudden *forte-fortissimo* of the Mayor's cry 'send for Lyapkin-Tyapkin!' The terrified officials spring up in all directions, hiding their guilty consciences as far away as possible – under the table, behind each other's backs, even behind the armchair where the Mayor was just sitting. It is like a dance-pantomime of fright. The District Physician begins to squeal on the letter 'i', first a long-drawn-out whistle then jerkily on 'e' *staccato*, then the two 'notes' alternatively rising and falling, whilst the next lines are 'embroidered' on to this background. In orchestral terms, it is like a piccolo with double bass *pizzicato*, just like the comic scenes in Rimsky-Korsakov's *May Night*. A sudden screech *glissando* from the Doctor and a new 'dance of terror' begins. The plastic pattern of the characters' movements corresponds to the rhythmical pattern of their voices. Their brief pauses seem to foretoken the dumb scene of the finale.[1]

VI

There can be little doubt that Meyerhold's *Government Inspector* inspired a greater volume of critical literature than any other production in the history of the theatre.[2] Despite the violent criticism of its alleged 'mysticism', the attempts to discredit its author's political integrity, and the hysterical protests at the liberties taken with Gogol's hallowed text, the work was performed regularly up to the very day of the theatre's liquidation in 1938. Not only did it establish once and for all the creative autonomy of the stage-director, it gave rise to numerous 'reinterpretations' of Gogol and other Russian classics. Most notable amongst these was Shostakovich's first opera, *The Nose*, composed in 1928–9, when he was working at Meyerhold's theatre. The libretto is based on Gogol's story of the same name plus fragments from *Diary of a Madman*, *Dead Souls*, *Nevsky Prospect* and *Old-world Landowners* and has a similar episodic structure to Meyerhold's *Government Inspector*.

When the Moscow Art Theatre was preparing Bulgakov's version of *Dead Souls* in 1930, Stanislavsky took the production out of Vassily

---

[1] Emmanuil Kaplan in *Vstrechi s Meyerholdom*, cit., pp. 336–7.

[2] For a comprehensive bibliography see Sergei Danilov, *Revizor na stsene*, Leningrad, 1934.

Sakhnovsky's hands because he objected to its Meyerholdian 'symbolism'. It is Stanislavsky's version, staged finally in 1932 and virtually a polemic against *The Government Inspector*, which remains in the Moscow Art repertoire to this day.

---

1. Observations on the Play

When an actor starts work on a part his first task is to establish the emploi. But he cannot do this until he has identified the genre of the play: it could be a drama, a farce, a pastorale, a comedy, a tragi-comedy, a tragedy, a romantic tragedy, a realistic tragedy, and so on. These are subtle differences which he must be able to distinguish.

What is most amazing about *The Government Inspector* is that although it contains all the elements of those plays written before it, although it was constructed according to various established dramatic premises, there can be no doubt – at least for me – that far from being the culmination of a tradition, it is the start of a new one. Although Gogol employs a number of familiar devices in the play, we suddenly realize that his treatment of them is new.

This is also true of his portrayal of character. Khlestakov, for example, is taken to represent the traditional theatrical masks of the impostor and the fop. Gogol himself realized this; so should the actor who plays Khlestakov. But since we are dealing with a play which is more of an innovation than a culmination, the actor can immediately sever all links with masks of this kind – not only can, but perhaps *must* sever them. Once he does, he is bound to see the truth of this.

It seems to me that this is revealed in Gogol's *Departure of the Audience*.[1] What prompted him to write it? As I see it, a desire to make clear that *The Government Inspector* was an innovation rather than a culmination. You may say that he wrote it because he was dissatisfied with the way the play was performed, etc., but I maintain that he wrote it as an innovator who had discovered a new form. He was anxious to depict the critics of his play and to include a wide range of people in order to show that

---

[1] *The Departure of the Audience after the Presentation of a New Comedy*, a dramatized dialogue in one act, written in 1842.

219

the reason they were scandalized was because they had failed to grasp the true significance of what he had written.

Since we are dealing with a work which is not merely the culmination of a tradition, we must look at it afresh in order to discover the origins of later developments in Russian drama. Nowadays we know that certain of the writers who followed Gogol began to write in the new Gogolian manner, adopting his new dramatic method. Theatrical historians fabricated an entire school out of this movement, calling it 'neo-naturalistic' and claiming that it contained the key to the understanding of Gogol.

The question arises of the nature of Gogol's comedy, which I would venture to describe as not so much 'comedy of the absurd' as 'comedy of the absurd situation'. One needs to be as tentative as this because of the further question: Is it comic at all? I suspect that it is not. When Gogol read the first chapters of *Dead Souls* to Pushkin, Pushkin – who, after all, loved a good laugh – 'gradually became more and more gloomy, and finally was absolutely miserable'. When Gogol finished reading, Pushkin said in a grief-stricken voice: 'My God, how sad our Russia is!'[1] Gogol had achieved the desired effect: although the treatment was comic, Pushkin understood at once that the intention was something more than comic.

When I warn an actor of the danger of lapsing into abstractions, I forbid the very mention of masks because they are too risky. When you are dealing with this new form of drama which contains such precise references as the infantry captain from Penza or a feather fished out of the soup; when you are dealing with a text containing such concrete details, you must be scrupulous in your regard for them. This is why I say straight out – this is Khlestakov. Like a materialist, I talk in terms of concrete things.

If the actor wants to find out what kind of a man Khlestakov is, he must study the details of his biography. Perhaps he is a card-sharper out of *The Gamblers*, or an impostor who fancies a bit of a lark, or simply someone willing to try his luck. Or he may even be on a tour specifically to win money from people. Paradoxical as it may seem, I recently re-read *The Gamblers* and there I found the whole prescription for the part set out. In that play the characters meet simply in order to win money from each other. They all have marked cards and almost set up a press exclusively for the printing of marked packs of cards. Begging their pardon, one of them tells the rest that a really well-marked pack 'has a name just like a person: Adelaida Ivanovna'.[2] It seems to me that Khlestakov has a similar history.

[1] 'Chetyre pisma k raznym litsam po povodu *Myortvykh dush*', 3, N. V. Gogol, op. cit., vol. 8, p. 294.

[2] N. V. Gogol, op. cit., vol. 5, p. 76.

But if so, why doesn't he set to work straight away? Well, firstly because he has only just arrived, and secondly because you can't just break into a gallop from standstill. Clearly he is still finding his bearings: discovering the whereabouts of the club, looking up addresses, etc. Then suddenly he has a stroke of luck and he's off. He is taken for a government inspector, 'naturally does not fail to take advantage', and falls in with this new role. And since he is not forced to rely on cards (after all, he might merely earn a good hiding that way), he makes money with the greatest of ease.

This approach makes it possible for the actors to base all their movements, all their actions on the other works of Gogol, rather than study the conventions of the theatre of Gogol's day. We invented the Charwoman and then found a Charwoman in Gogol himself,[1] and she gave us a definite prescription for playing her. By re-reading Gogol's works, the actor discovers gestures and movements which he can incorporate in the lines of, say, Khlestakov. They will give him a firm foundation which will determine his stance, his gait, his mode of dress, and so on . . .

[Quoted in *Gogol i Meyerhold*, cit., pp. 80–82]

NOTE   These remarks to the cast of *The Government Inspector* were recorded by Mikhail Korenev at a rehearsal on 15 March 1926. Korenev assisted Meyerhold in his adaptation of Gogol's text.

---

2. Meyerhold at Rehearsal

ACT ONE (13 FEBRUARY 1926)

Meyerhold (to the Mayor). We'll go through the whole entrance[2] without words. Once we've agreed that the part should be played in strict time, I need to consider how to make it as easy as possible for the actor. He must be relieved of anything likely to prove a burden. You must get rid of that senile voice. Let him be made up to look fifty, but let the voice remain young. Let's consider the reason for this. It seems to me that in such

---

[1] *The Gamblers*, ibid., p. 70, Uteshitelny: 'And on the stairs some charwoman, an absolute fright . . .' In Meyerhold's production she sat guffawing next to Osip throughout his opening soliloquy.

[2] Scene One.

company, amidst such a gallery of idiots – after all, even the Commissioner is an idiot, and Luka Lukich, and the Judge, and the Postmaster: idiots the lot of them – in this assembly of absolute blithering idiots the Mayor can scarcely help standing out. He's a bit craftier and a bit cleverer, a man with a certain polish. It's possible that yesterday he visited another town, not the capital, of course, but if this is a district centre then perhaps the capital of the province. He has wormed his way into society, been around a bit. Everything indicates that he is head and shoulders above the rest. He exhibits a certain surface polish, although you'd never mistake it for education. What he says about the schoolmasters shows that he knows some history;[1] his remarks reveal at least a quasi-culture. But then what other kind of culture could it be there? His manner of speech has a certain fluency; he can construct a sentence much better than, say, Bobchinsky and Dobchinsky. Their brains function slowly, whereas he is relatively decisive; once he's made up his mind he doesn't waste words. He is a bit of an orator; he knows how to make a speech.

We must make him younger. Why has the Mayor always been played as an old man until now? Because he has always been played by veteran actors. Maksheev and Davydov, for instance, both played him when they were old men, and whenever younger actors are given the part, they all seem to copy Davydov. I don't know how Vladimir Nikolaevich [Davydov] played the Mayor when he was a young man at the Korsh Theatre in Moscow, but possibly even then he honoured tradition and played him as an old man. That is how all these tricks and inflections have grown up, the outcome of following the example of old men with big names.

Since you're young – after all, you're fifteen to twenty years younger than me – forget about that senile voice. Enunciate every word perfectly clearly. For the present don't groan; we can consider that later when the picture's clearer. Perhaps we'll give you an armchair to rehearse with straight away. Sit down, think, make yourself comfortable, then begin.

Before putting on his uniform, the Mayor is in a dressing-gown. Perhaps he's had a sleep after lunch and received the letter whilst still resting in his armchair; he's issued an order summoning all the departmental heads and then felt ill.

Give them the armchair from *The Forest*. He sits there, feeling ill. And give him a glass of warm water.

Mayor. Perhaps he puts on spectacles to read the letter?

Meyerhold. No, we don't want to complicate it. The letter without glasses. They'll hold a candle in front of him.

<hr>

[1] i.e. his references to Alexander the Great.

Question. So the act takes place in the evening?

Meyerhold. Yes, in the evening. We want it to be evening.

Dobchinsky. After dinner? That means Bobchinsky and Dobchinsky have spent the whole day running around the town.

Meyerhold (to Hübner). Here is a job for the Doctor. Get in his way – keep giving him teaspoonfuls of water to drink. Get in his way. And he must take it. He takes some, sometimes refuses, sometimes drinks, then takes the glass himself and takes a few gulps – it's the sort of mixture you can drink by the glass. And you must speak in German so that his lines become confused with yours. This will help him to overcome the difficulty. You will keep up the tempo. This is the great problem and you can help him maintain the pace. Once he is faced with an obstacle he will experience the desire to overcome it.

You can even speak loudly; let the audience hear you. Say something the whole time. Make it all *perpetuum mobile.* You speak German – after all, you are of German extraction!

Has anybody got a cloth or a scarf? (They bandage the Mayor's head.) There! Walk around him beating your breast, put mustard plasters on his feet to draw the blood away from his head. Can you think of something to say in German? Repeat some sentence or other.

Everybody close together. Nobody over there. Everyone seated. Enter the Mayor. But we'll begin from the stationary point after he has settled himself in the armchair. He groans. You (to Hübner) are preparing the mixture and generally fussing around. After the Mayor has said a few lines, begin to dose him.

When everybody says 'What, an inspector! it mustn't be in unison. Some say 'in-spec-tor'. There must be a variety of logical intonations, some saying it quickly, others dragging it out. [p. 21.][1]

'Well I never!' etc. – very quick. Very quick reaction, no need to say it in character. Even if you do, the audience won't be able to tell who's speaking. They sit jammed together on a divan, almost ten of them. You should hide your individual characteristics. The audience won't notice who is Ammos Fyodorovich, who is Artemy Fillipovich, who is Luka Lukich – they all speak at once. Blurt the words out.

Avdotya[2] takes no part in this. She is on her knees, tickling the Mayor's heels. Mishka holds the candle and the letter. Perhaps the Mayor has

---

[1] Page numbers refer to the Marsh and Brooks translation, Methuen, London, 1968. For ease of reference, this translation is quoted here.

[2] The Mayor's housekeeper, who does not appear onstage in the original play, but who is mentioned by Bobchinsky (p. 29) and later by Anna Andreevna (p. 36).

given him them to hold. *Meyerhold* (to the Mayor). Groan. A groan will help to heighten the atmosphere, then straight after the groan, the line: 'There you are. Now you know.' [p. 22.]

Mayor in the armchair. Mishka, Avdotya, Hübner by him. By the way, that'll help to give the impression of a generalissimo lying there. Like the tsar of the town. *Meyerhold* (to Ammos Fyodorovich). 'Anton Antonovich, it's my belief there's more to it than that . . .' [p. 22.]: there should be more 'for your ear alone' in the intonation. I don't know how it'll sound on stage. More confidential, as though whispering in his ear. He's not pondering but rumour-mongering. Then you can speed it up.

Meyerhold (to Hübner). Every time you react the same to any note of alarm. You soothe the Mayor: 'Sein Sie ruhig!' and at the same time seem to be reproaching the others. Alarm will harm the patient. I don't know what, but say something both to them and to him. This irritates the Mayor and his irritation gives him a chance to quicken the tempo. The Doctor somehow contrives to admonish each one in turn whilst continuing to attend to the Mayor. This is very complicated; we need the advice of a specialist. 'Warum sprechen Sie so?' – something like that. Hübner is an enormous part, bigger than the Mayor. Ammos Fyodorovich to Hübner: 'Don't you . . .', Hübner gets in his way. (to the Mayor) 'Specially you, Artemy Filippovich!' and so on – blurt it out suddenly, all in one breath. [p.22.] (to Hübner). As soon as he hears his name he says: 'Das habe ich schon gesagt.' [p.23.]

(to the Mayor). Make your remarks to the Judge extremely irritated, then the tempo will be right. 'Anyway I only mentioned . . .' down to 'under divine protection'. – cut. [p. 24.] It slows down the action. It's nice, but it's only padding.

We'll do it like this. We'll have you (the Mayor) sitting half-turned towards them, so that every time you escape from Hübner there is someone for you to turn to. 'And you, Luka Lukich . . . your teachers.' [p. 24.] You rise, kneeling on the armchair. You draw yourself up, then let your expression take full effect. Then you'll hit off the right expression automatically. When you draw yourself up, Hübner takes off your trousers and takes advantage of the temporary change in your position to apply the mustard plasters. I've put all this in to boost the tempo.

'There's that one——' [p. 24] – not too loud, quickly so that it's lighter, more transparent. Luka Lukich replies briskly. The Mayor speaks, but Luka Lukich does not stop; he says 'But what can I do', or something similar. [p. 25.]

Schools Superintendent stand so that you can see the Mayor. Make sure

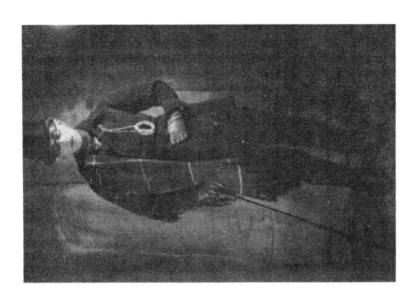

(a) Meyerhold and Erast Garin modelling a pose for the Dumb Scene.

(b) Garin as Khlestakov.

The Government Inspector, 1926.

(*a*) Episode Six: 'The Procession'.

(*b*) Episode Five: 'Filled with the tenderest love' (Zinaida Raikh as Anna Andreevna).

The Government Inspector, 1926.

the audience hears 'You were both wide of the mark'.[1] The Mayor speaks exasperatedly. He is exasperated because they have missed the point and are making a joke out of it. They have got out of hand, as it were.

The Mayor not only beckons to the Postmaster, but leans on him and the Doctor to raise himself up. He speaks confidentially, but quickly and loudly so that he is audible. Understand? Confidentially but extremely hurriedly. [p. 26.]

Meyerhold (to the Mayor). Grip him (the Postmaster) tight round the neck, then it'll be easier for him to break free, and all the time Hübner is growling in German: 'Dieser Postmeister . . . Gott!'

Meyerhold (to the Postmaster). As though saying 'Here we are, just let me see, just let me see.' [p. 27.] Rummages in his pockets, which are full of letters. He's a walking cupboard. Then slow down the tempo, make a great business out of it. Give him a whole pile of letters to rehearse with, so that he can keep on pulling them out and sorting through them until he finds the right one.

Meyerhold (to the Mayor). It is better to be on your feet by 'that door's going to open and . . .' [p. 28]; you go off, leaning on the Doctor and then come on again without the compresses.

The Doctor will be very useful in maintaining the proper tempo. It's better like that, absolutely clear.

ACT ONE (4 MARCH 1926)

Meyerhold (to the Mayor). Excellent, it's coming on. You've caught the Mayor's sharpness and given the lines an appropriate sub-text; one can sense the italics, the odd barbed word here and there. That's a great advance. It means you have reached a stage from which further improvement will be easy. But you'll need to make it lighter now; at present it's still a little ponderous, although in the first part especially you've got the right amount of sharpness, bite and clarity of diction. You're not even an old man any more; you've overcome that senile mumbling which was spoiling the effect the whole time. Now the voice is young and sometimes there's even a suggestion of Polish clarity and lightness, which is fine because it's no coincidence that his name, Dmukhanovsky, has a Polish ring to it.

At present the groaning sounds rather false. Of course, that will disappear as you begin to vary it from place to place. Then what will probably happen is that after each groan the text will sound different; in places they

[1] Omitted by Marsh and Brooks; should follow Judge's line 'just what I said!' (p. 26).

225

will even give a suggestion of tiredness. The groans determine the music of the words or, more precisely, the timbre of the text. And these fluctuations are what your interpretation will consist of. He will clutch at some part of his chest, say his heart, and his pulse will begin to flutter. The audience must realize that the groans are not mere conventions but that there really is something wrong with his heart. He should groan and clutch at his heart in such a way that the audience will be afraid that he is on the point of having an apoplectic fit. It should be really frightening.

Now some details which can be given added meaning. 'Of course the porter should be encouraged to keep poultry . . .' and so on [p. 23.] – you're saying it in parentheses and your voice is tending to drop. It doesn't help to put it in parentheses; better take it quickly to avoid the drop in the voice. Keep in your mind the words 'it's not the thing' and pronounce the preceding words not by lowering your voice, not as though in parentheses; rather, they should serve as a springboard before the words 'not nice'. If he has got 'it's not the thing' in his mind from the very beginning, then the whole speech will convey the idea. He should be thinking all the time 'to Hell with him' and hating him really. The whole time the Mayor must make sure the text keeps moving forward. Now the part will come much more easily.

The scene of the Mayor and the Postmaster. 'We're the ones who'll get more than we bargained for, not the Turks. Read this!' [p. 26.] The Mayor must definitely hand the letter to the Postmaster, and the Postmaster should scan it quickly with a practised eye. After all, you know how to read letters quickly: it's your speciality. You just pause, and then you've read it. Then – 'That's different . . .' meaning 'if what's written here is true'. The line must be motivated, otherwise it's meaningless. And the pause gains significance by the Mayor approaching the Postmaster and dropping his voice to a confidential whisper. He has to alter the tone of his voice, make it more intimate, more insinuating, because it would be difficult for him to come straight out with something like 'unseal the letters'. And it gives the audience a rest. The Mayor speaks very softly, quickly, in a monotone. If you are whispering in someone's ear, you don't indulge in all sorts of melodious embellishments. Let it be barely audible so that the audience has to strain to catch what he is saying. It'll be a rest for you as well as for the audience. And on 'you'd be amazed what you can learn' [p. 26] the Postmaster adopts the same tone. Then he rummages amongst his letters and offers one to the Mayor. The Mayor eyes it stupidly, but his thoughts are on the Inspector, on the letter he has received. The Postmaster thrusts it into his hands, pointing at it and saying 'don't just look at it'. Let him wave it under his nose and let's not have the usual description. Here the actual text doesn't matter. The description of the ball is always read out in the same way, but let's skip through it softly. And then, as though saying, 'well, what are you gawping at! If you don't want to, I'll read it!' he snatches the letter from him. Let there be some business here.

The Judge is coming in wrongly here. He should elbow his way into the centre of the group and plant a furry little slobbering puppy on top of the pile of letters. Then, muttering, he catches hold of it and demonstrates that it's a bitch: 'sister to that splendid hound . . .' [p. 27.] This is an amusing, purely physiological scene like some veterinary laboratory when they're operating on glands and everybody looks on and joins in. They watch closely as he lays the pup on its back and parts its legs – they all have a good look to make sure for themselves. A puppy in a laboratory – we'll work on it.[1]

'Good God, who cares about your free shooting, today of all days' [p. 27] – there's no need to say it, better to mime it. 'The door might open any moment . . .' – say it as though realizing that this lot are absolutely hopeless; you might as well leave them to it – and then he thrusts the puppy at you. I'll tidy it up in a few places and then the actual *mise en scène* should be fine. I'll return to the Mayor later.

Now Artemy Filippovich. Good, your opening lines are splendid. [p. 22–23.] That sweetness is fine, like running treacle, it conveys the idea of 'strawberry'[2] perfectly. Later on I'm not so sure. It's not right, because in their exchange Artemy Filippovich and Ammos Fyodorovich get very agitated. [p. 31–32.] Don't stick rigidly to the text. 'Come on, come on, Ammos Fyodorovich . . .' etc. – The lines should come in a stampede. Play it as a pointless quarrel. Let the audience get the impression that they are squabbling irritably without either knowing why. The Mayor has thrown everyone into a panic and they are all peevish like people who have just been woken up. They are just like Oblomov,[3] who was always irritable when obliged to do anything. Here it doesn't matter if the audience doesn't catch every line so long as they hear 'Well, to hell with you!' The line about the Judge and Solomon [p. 32] should also have a touch of malice. The dialogue should have a kind of a beat to it so that it is alternately audible and inaudible. Gogol won't turn in his grave over that. There should be a turmoil: a kind of all-prevailing exasperation – 'an und

---

[1] The business with the puppy was invented by Meyerhold.
[2] His surname, 'Zemlyanika', means literally 'strawberry'.
[3] The slothful hero of Goncharov's eponymous novel.

für sich', as the Germans say. It is a monologue and there is no audible dialogue, just a sort of growling.

Meyerhold (to the Judge). 'And ever since he's smelt a bit – *pause* – of vodka.' Otherwise it will sound literary, not conversational. He doesn't intend to say it at first – only 'he's smelt a bit'. Then he feels obliged to add 'of vodka', so that it comes out separate from the rest. I don't know how you should say it. You know best, but don't bother about it now, otherwise the line will lose its spontaneity.[1]

You reply 'Depends what you mean by "sin"', A.A.' when the Mayor says angrily 'That's the way the good Lord made us. Voltaire can say what he likes . . .' [p. 24.] When you say 'Depends what you mean . . .' – you should be thinking already about the 'shawl', but you're making him think of it suddenly; the audience should be prepared for it. The two of them should be getting at the same thing. You laugh, but there's no need to. Break off before 'a shawl' – then thrust.

Meyerhold (to the Mayor). And you don't respond to this immediately. In fact, first you're confused and then: 'but I go to church every Sunday'.[2] Almost as if you were recounting an anecdote: 'but you stole my cigar-case'. See what I mean, Judge?

Now, Luka Lukich, with our interpretation of the Mayor, you're getting it wrong. You should counter agressively with 'But what can I do? . . .' He must be agressive, attack, like someone who dismisses your criticism and then abuses you: 'What's it got to do with me? It's all *their* fault'. The whole time you must attack him. Whenever the Mayor says anything you butt in with something like 'Well, what do you expect me to do?' each time with a different intonation, but always very formal. He has a formal manner and speaks well, but without any real animation. 'I wouldn't want my worst enemy to work in education' [p. 25] should suggest that it's hopeless trying to do anything with teachers. Give the impression that this gang of teachers is to blame for everything.

The Mayor quiet, but you (Luka Lukich) again agressively, and again your leitmotiv: 'Well what do you expect me to do with them?' He has quietened down, but you are still pursuing him: 'What can I do, they're nothing but a gang of ruffians'. Now the Mayor has recovered, but you notice nothing; you're in a frenzy. He just says: 'Oh God! Oh God!' and goes away.

It's very good how the scene with Bobchinsky and Dobchinsky [pp. 28–31] is developing all the time instead of remaining fixed. Usually the

[1] Marsh and Brooks, p. 24: '. . . and he's smelt of vodka ever since.'
[2] In Gogol follows 'I am firm in my faith, at least' (ibid., p. 24).

scene is fixed and that's that, but here it's still growing and gathering fresh nuances.

When Dobchinsky says – 'an unexpected . . . occurrence', you are stylizing it, but it really is 'unexpected' ('occurrence' should be almost inaudible), there is no need to stylize it.[1]

Mayor – 'My heart's all of a flutter'[2] – slight groan. The groan is physiologically determined. 'My heart's all of a flutter'. He feels a pain in his heart and he must register it immediately.

Bobchinsky. 'As soon as I had had the pleasure of leaving you.' Stress 'leaving' not 'you'.

Rastakovsky must be on stage. Both Rastakovsky and Korobkin. 'To see' – he searches for the person and then finds him. He can't find someone who's not there. He might be put off if he has to say 'To – ' into thin air – the intonation will be wrong. So we'll have Korobkin on stage. [p. 28.]

Dobchinsky. 'Near the stall where they sell hot pies.' [p. 29.] Bobchinsky looks angrily at him and repeats 'Near the stall . . .' – and Dobchinsky completes the phrase. On all three occasions the same trick. Three times Bobchinsky angrily begins a phrase, each time and Dobchinsky finishes it off: 'To fetch a keg – of French brandy.' 'Quite well dressed – but not in uniform.'

Meyerhold (to Bobchinsky). 'I know you – one of your teeth.' You're putting 'I know you' in parentheses, but it should have an exclamation mark. 'One of your teeth has a whistle'[3] – don't underline 'has a whistle'. Don't make it so literary: rap it out. You are saying 'inspector' very hurriedly instead of announcing it. Enunciate it – 'in-spec-tor'. Again the pronunciation should suggest the italics.

The second part of the act is much weaker than the first. Probably because we haven't any policeman yet.

Svistunov, you're answering like a countryman, not like a townsman. [p. 32.] Even if he is from the country he will have acquired a military bearing from his training. He is a country lad who has become militarized in the town. Work on it. Answers a little more precise: 'By no means', 'Just so'. You should be precise in everything, but that's the fault of the production at the moment, not yours.

Mayor. Tell me, Vsevolod Emilevich, how can I issue commands at varying distances?

[1] Marsh and Brooks, p. 28: 'Something really unexpected!'
[2] Ibid., p. 28: 'You've got our hearts in our boots . . .'
[3] Ibid., p. 30: 'Ever since you lost that tooth you've talked with a whistle . . .'

Meyerhold. We'll simply make sure they're at varying distances from you. You should command, not shout like you did today, but that's only temporary, I know. It's a good thing you've got rid of that traditional quavering voice.

You've got the harshness, the scathing tone splendidly. The first part is fine. And the abrupt, puppet-like gestures are coming. They won't detract from the impression of abnormality. It will be better when it is less forced. It's hard, but once we get the lightness the abnormality will come. All your groans are on the same note, but once you learn to vary them and introduce nuances the impression of derangement will be there. And it won't stand out so sharply. The groans will be more fully motivated and the artificiality will go.

Mayor. But is this quiet tone of voice to Luka Lukich right? [p. 25.]

Meyerhold. Of course: you exchange roles here. You quieten down and Luka Lukich puts pressure on you.

You mustn't forget that once you've built up the entire part – including the monologue in Act Five, the whole tonality will alter. If you overlook the development of the part and its culmination in Act Five, there is a risk of giving everything away in Act One. You should develop it gradually, otherwise it will explode and there will be nothing left but Act One.

It is a considerable achievement to have established the complete tonal range of the character, but once the whole part is clear we shall find that everything leads up to the climax of the Act Five monologue. The way you talk to Khlestakov in Act Two will indicate how you should go mad in Act Five. Your behaviour when Khlestakov is lying about Petersburg, and when you and Anna Andreevna seem to have achieved all you desire – these scenes are decisive and once you have got them right you will know how to speak the Act Five monologue.

[*Teatr i dramaturgiya*, Moscow, 1934,
no 2, pp. 40–42.]

NOTE Recorded at rehearsal by Mikhail Korenev on 13 February and 4 March 1926. Not all the details mentioned here by Meyerhold were retained in the eventual production.

Part Seven

'AN ALIEN THEATRE'

1927-1940

AFTER *The Warrant* in April 1925, two seasons passed without a single production by Meyerhold of a Soviet play. Whilst Soviet society had outgrown the need for blatant propaganda pieces, no dramatist was yet writing with the social insight or poetic inspiration which Meyerhold demanded. A new play by Mayakovsky, *A Comedy with Murder*, was promised for April 1926, but never completed,[1] and plans to stage a dramatic adaptation of Bely's novel, *Moscow*, were abandoned. The one work which fired Meyerhold's imagination during this period was Tretyakov's *I Want a Child*, a controversial examination of traditional attitudes towards love and sexual impulses with the heroine 'an agronomist who relieves her sexual tension by giving birth to a baby, whilst paying due regard to the demands of practical eugenics'.[2] Having accepted the play in 1926, Meyerhold tried for almost four years to secure the censor's approval of the text. In view of the controversial subject, he proposed to stage it in the form of an illustrated discussion which the spectators would be free to interrupt. In keeping with this conception, El Lissitsky designed a setting which embraced the entire interior of the theatre, completely obliterating the division between stage and audience. So complex was the project that Meyerhold decided to postpone it until the rebuilding of his outmoded and inadequate theatre. This he never lived to see and a production was lost which, to judge from the model and photographs which survive, would have exemplified the spatial and functional concepts of constructivism to a degree which the theatrical work of Popova, Stepanova and Shestakov never did.

Such was the repertoire crisis at the Meyerhold Theatre in the late twenties that Meyerhold himself staged no new work to mark the tenth anniversary of the October Revolution. The best the theatre could offer was *A Window on the Country* (8 November 1927), a 'political review' in the style of *Give us Europe* produced by twelve of Meyerhold's pupils. Aimed at propagandizing the drive to modernize agriculture, it comprised

[1] See N. I. Khardzhiev, 'Zametki o Mayakovskom' in *Novoe o Mayakovskom* (*Literaturnoe nasledstvo*, vol. 65), Moscow, 1958, pp. 400–1.
[2] S. M. Tretyakov, quoted by A. V. Fevralsky in Sergei Tretyakov, *Slyshish, Moskva?!*, Moscow, 1966, p. 198.

a series of jejune sketches of peasants engaged in their traditional tasks and pastimes, alternating with filmed illustrations of the latest technological achievements.

Eventually the lack of suitable new plays compelled Meyerhold to return to the classics, this time *Woe from Wit*, Griboedov's satirical portrayal of Moscow society in the 1820s. The production was a reinterpretation in the manner of his *Government Inspector*, and was inspired by a letter from Pushkin to Bestuzhev (January 1825), in which he wrote:

> Who is the intelligent character in *Woe from Wit*? answer: Griboedov. And do you know what Chatsky is? A passionate, honourable, decent young fellow who has spent some time in the company of a very intelligent man (namely, Griboedov) and has absorbed his thoughts, his witticisms and his satirical remarks. Everything he says is very intelligent, but to whom does he say it? Famusov? Skalozub? The old Moscow grannies at the ball? Molchalin? That is unpardonable. The first test of a man's intelligence is his ability to recognize whom he is dealing with and to avoid casting pearls before such swine as Repetilov.

Accordingly, Meyerhold's aim was to set Chatsky apart from the rest of society and relate him to the young radicals of the Decembrist movement with whom Griboedov himself had been in sympathy. The text was extensively cut and rearranged in order to minimise Chatsky's rapport with Famusov, Sophie, Molchalin and the rest, and when he did speak to them, it was often whilst improvising on the piano. The music was designed to reflect the various aspects of his character: Beethoven – his militant reforming zeal; Mozart – his Byronic weltschmerz; Bach – his exalted humanity; John Field – his tender dreams of Sophie. During the ball scene he was seen in the adjacent library declaiming the inflammatory verses of Pushkin and Ryleev to a group of fellow Decembrists.

On the other hand, the characters of Famusov and Sophie were purged of all ambivalence so as to sharpen the social conflict. Famusov was depicted in lecherous pursuit of Liza, and Sophie involved in a dubious relationship with Molchalin. The dialogue was punctuated with such gratuitous action as dancing lessons, shooting practice and a game of billiards, all with the same ironical purpose as the pantomime and gymnastics in *The Forest*. The main feature of the setting was a supposedly practicable construction by Shestakov which, in fact, was little used in the production. The most memorable moment was the slander scene when thirty-two guests, seated bolt upright at a long table directly facing the audience, slowly relayed the rumour of Chatsky's madness to the accompaniment of a tranquil Field nocturne. With the appearance of the solitary figure of Chatsky in front of the table, they all raised their napkins as though in self-defence, hissing menacingly like cornered snakes.

The production, which had its première on 12 March 1928, was given the more unequivocal title of Griboedov's first draft of the play, *Woe TO Wit* – in other words, 'woe to him who is uncautious enough to exercise his intelligence'. As Meyerhold himself admitted, the adaptation was not a success, suffering from 'false academicism' and a disproportionate emphasis on certain episodes. He later called it the 'Petersburg version', in order to emphasize its affinity with his pre-revolutionary work, and in September 1935 produced a second version, the 'Moscow version', which was dedicated both to the pianist, Lev Oborin (the original dedicatee), and to the Chinese actor, Mei Lan-fang, who had recently visited Russia and whose style Meyerhold held up as a model to his actors. It is this dedication which provides the clue to the production's comparative failure: the cast of the richest verse play in the Russian language were exhorted to emulate the plastic skills of the greatest living exponent of Chinese dance-drama.

In July 1928, Meyerhold and Zinaida Raikh left the Soviet Union on holiday and spent the next five months in France. At that time audiences at his theatre had dropped to less than three-quarters capacity. This was due largely to the staleness of the repertoire, which contained such well-worn favourites as *The Forest*, and a revival of *The Magnanimous Cuckold* with Raikh replacing Babanova as Stella. With the failure of *Woe to Wit* and *A Window on the Country*, the theatre's financial position was precarious. Scorning all available Soviet plays except the controversial *I Want a Child*, Meyerhold preferred to wait for the new works promised by Erdman and Mayakovsky, and sought to bridge the gap by arranging a season for his theatre in Paris. But Glaviskusstvo, the newly formed state authority controlling all the arts, twice ordered him to discontinue negotiations and even threatened to close his theatre if he failed to return and improve its position. After a violent controversy which split even the ranks of Glaviskusstvo, a special government commission was formed to investigate the theatre's affairs. It condemned Meyerhold's negligence, but recommended a subsidy to cover outstanding debts and running costs for a further two months up to the end of November, delaying its final decision on the theatre's future until his return. The recommendations amounted to an ultimatum, which possibly was motivated by the fear that Meyerhold was considering following the example of Mikhail Chekhov, the actor and artistic director of the Second Moscow Art Theatre, who had decided to emigrate in August 1928.

Rather than risk losing his theatre, Meyerhold abandoned plans for a tour and returned to Moscow on 2 December 1928, having been ordered by his French doctors to rest until then. Far from admitting his own financial negligence, he straightway complained of the state of the old Sohn Theatre (where only 150 out of 390 seats in the circle were usable) and demanded more storage and rehearsal space. On this, he said, depended the repertoire for the season, which he hoped would include *I Want a Child*, Erdman's *Suicide* and Selvinsky's *The Second Army Commander*.[1]

However, the first new production turned out to be *The Bed Bug*, which Mayakovsky read to the company for the first time on 28 December. Announcing his plan to stage it as quickly as possible, Meyerhold declared 'The repertoire crisis has been completely overcome (as least for the present). The theatre's confidence in the foremost experimental dramatist of the Revolution remains steadfast.'[2] After little more than a month's rehearsal, the play was presented on 13 February 1929.

In terms of theatrical innovation, *The Bed Bug* was one of Meyerhold's least significant productions. The first half, which culminates in the hilarious nuptials of the lapsed party member, Prisypkin, and the manicurist, Elzevira Renaissance, was played as a caricature of petit-bourgeois manners in the same style of vaudeville grotesque as Erdman's *Warrant*. At the suggestion of Mayakovsky, who once again worked more as Meyerhold's co-director than his assistant, the young 'Kukriniksy' cartoon group were invited to design the settings, costumes, and make-up. Nearly all the costumes and properties were bought over the counter in Moscow shops in order to demonstrate the pretentious ugliness of current fashions and the all too discomfiting topicality of the satire (rammed home at the final curtain by the de-frosted Prisypkin's joyful recognition of a whole audience of fellow bourgeois). Part Two, set in 1979, was designed by the constructivist artist, Alexander Rodchenko; but his vision of a disciplined, scientific Communist future was so lifeless and hygienic that the spectator was hard put to decide where the parody really stopped.

The music was composed by the young, little-known Dmitri Shostakovich and, as he recalls,[3] based on the marches of fire-brigade bands much admired by Mayakovsky. Its strident cacophony was less to the taste of most critics; R. Pelshe wrote:

---

[1] For an account of Meyerhold's abortive attempt to stage *The Suicide* see E. Braun *Meyerhold: A Revolution in Theatre* (London, 1995), pp. 269–272.

[2] Ibid., 28 December 1928, p. 4.

[3] See V. Katanyan, *Mayakovsky-literaturnaya khronika*, 3rd ed., Moscow, 1956, p. 369.

. . . we recommend Comrade Shostakovich to reflect more seriously on questions of musical culture in the light of the development of our socialist society according to the precepts of Marxism.'[1]

Despite widespread criticism, particularly of the contributions of Rodchenko and Shostakovich, *The Bed Bug* was a huge popular success, due largely to the inspired portrayal of Prisypkin by Igor Ilinsky. For another season at least, the Meyerhold Theatre was safe.

With the steady consolidation of Soviet power, dramatists began to explore more complex forms than the crude placard-drama. On the one hand there were essays in satire such as Erdman's *Warrant* and Mayakovsky's *Bed Bug*; on the other, there were the first attempts to develop a form of tragedy consistent with the principles of Marxist dialectical materialism. Notable amongst these were Bulgakov's *Days of the Turbins* (1925), Trenyov's *Lyubov Yarovaya* (1926) and Ilya Selvinsky's *Commander of the Second Army* (1929).

The Second Army Commander is set in the Civil War and revolves around the conflict between Chub, a partisan leader of peasant origin thrown up by the masses, and Okonny, an army clerk and one time book-keeper who sees in the Revolution the means to self-realisation and glory. More an epic poem than a play, it was staged by Meyerhold (first performance: Kharkov, 24 July 1929) in a static, almost hieratic manner, reminiscent of Verhaeren's *Dawn*. The acting area was enclosed by a lofty wooden screen which functioned as a sounding-board rather than representing any discernible location. Against it, a flight of steps descended from stage-left to right in a gradual spiral. At one point the Battle of Beloyarsk was described by a commentator whilst a refrain in mazurka time was chanted by the entire company. Both commentator and chorus used megaphones which, like the masks in Greek tragedy, amplified their voices to awesome power.

Meyerhold once more used real objects for their associative power (this time even a real horse); but as a conscious revolt against the prevalent genre representation of the Civil War period he made every character like the resurrected hero from some remote legend. Boris Alpers wrote at the time:

If you removed their Caucasian hats and their sheepskin jerkins, you would find half-severed skulls, cloven heads, gaping breasts, torsos disfigured with a five-pointed star.
That is why they stand motionless holding their tall lances; that is why they move with such a slow and measured tread, the imprint of some strange reverie on every face.[2]

[1] *Sovremenny teatr*, Moscow, 1929, no. 15, p. 235.
[2] *Novy zritel*, Moscow, 1929, no 40, p. 4.

Like Erenburg and Faiko before him, Selvinsky resented Meyerhold's free interpretation of his work and claimed that he 'debased it to the level of primitive agitation',[1] but even so he confessed himself entranced by many of the effects which were achieved, and has since conceded the considerable influence of the production on his later work.[2] Having turned his hand to tragedy for the first time since *The Dawn* (1920), Meyerhold had again upheld his right as a creative artist and succeeded in setting an example for dramatists to follow.

On 16 March 1930 Meyerhold presented his version of *The Bath House*, Mayakovsky's 'drama in six acts with circus fireworks'. In 1927 the Fifteenth Congress of the Soviet Communist Party had called for an all-out campaign against bureaucracy in order to speed the process of 'socialist reconstruction', and this was the Meyerhold Theatre's second response, the first being the production of Bezimensky's satire, *The Shot*, by a group of his pupils in December 1929.

Mikhail Zoshchenko describes Mayakovsky's first reading of the play to the actors and Artistic Soviet[3] of the Meyerhold Theatre on 23 September 1929:

> The reading was a triumph. The actors and writers laughed uproariously and applauded the poet. They grasped the point of every single phrase. I have seldom seen such a positive reaction.[4]

But the Central Committee for Repertoire Control failed to share their enthusiasm; it considered the satire far too provocative and demanded numerous cuts and amendments before it passed the text for performance. This was hardly surprising, for at that time some influential critics were suggesting that satire did nothing but harm the cause of socialism, and that art should depict only 'real life'.[5] It is precisely this attitude that Mayakovsky lampoons in the third act of *The Bath House*, where the arch-bureaucrat, Pobedonossikov, and his retinue have just seen the play, failed to recognize themselves in it, and now instruct the director on the theatre's proper function:

[1] Quoted by O. Litovsky in *Sovremenny teatr*, Moscow, 1929, no 40, p. 540.

[2] Cf. Ilya Selvinsky in *Vstrechi s Meyerholdom*, cit., pp. 387–96.

[3] From 1927 onwards 'artistic soviets' were set up in all theatres. Their function was to supervise the selection and presentation of plays. In most cases, the chairman was nominated by the Party.

[4] In the introduction to *Almanakh estrady* (ed. Zoshchenko), Leningrad, 1933.

[5] Cf. V. Blyum, 'Vozroditsya li satira?' in *Literaturnaya gazeta*, Moscow 1929, no 6, p. 3.

In the name of every worker and peasant, I [Pobedonossikov] beg you not to disturb my peace of mind. An alarm clock? perish the thought! Your job is to beguile my eye and ear, not assault them . . . .
We need to rest after the discharge of our official obligations. Back to the classics! Study the great geniuses of the accursed past.

When they are all ejected from the Phosphorescent Woman's time-machine which bears away the inventor and his proletarian friends to a Communist future in the year 2030, Pobedonossikov cries to the hack painter, Belvedonsky:

Artist, seize the opportunity! Depict a real, live man as he is mortally insulted!

It was a jibe at 'real-life' realism and its leading practitioners, the Association of Proletarian Writers (RAPP), who were the sworn enemies both of Meyerhold and Mayakovsky.

Meyerhold and Mayakovsky had already come under heavy fire from RAPP when they staged *The Bed Bug*. Now the bombardment was resumed even before the Moscow premiere of *The Bath House*, ensuring that the play opened in an atmosphere of mistrust and hostility.[1] RAPP critics saw it as a malicious misrepresentation of Soviet officialdom, and its presentation a regression to the heavy-handed knock-about style of the early twenties. In so far as it is possible to tell from photographs and the few objective accounts published, the production does seem in some respects to have resembled the 1921 version of *Mystery-Bouffe*. Once again the 'clean' were portrayed as a series of preposterous grotesques, whilst the 'unclean' were an ill-differentiated series of komsomols in uniform blue overalls whose rhythmical vigour recalled *The Magnanimous Cuckold.* Zinaida Raikh as the Phosphorescent Woman appeared in a gleaming flying helmet and an alluring close-fitting space suit.

The young architect, Sergei Vakhtangov (son of the director), designed a setting which featured a towering scaffolding with a series of steps and platforms. In a number of scenes a huge screen in the form of a venetian blind with each slat bearing a political slogan was lowered from the flies. The walls of the auditorium, too, bore rhyming slogans by Mayakovsky, broadcasting the policies of the theatrical left and ridiculing the bureaucrats, the censor, RAPP, the critics, and the Moscow Art Theatre.

Like Lissitsky's visionary project for *I Want a Child*, this spectacle

[1] See V. Pertsov, *Mayakovsky v poslednie gody*, Moscow, 1965, p. 324.

'with circus and fireworks' threatened to burst the tottering walls of the aged Sohn Theatre; it demanded the grand multiple stage, the total theatre, which Meyerhold was then planning.

Whilst conceding its imperfections, Meyerhold regarded *The Bath House* as the best of his four productions of Mayakovsky.[1] Nevertheless, it was coolly received by the public, possibly because it seemed like a throwback to the agitatory clichés of the early 'twenties, possibly (as recent Soviet critics have suggested) because its style was ahead of its time. In any case, poor attendances compelled the theatre to drop the production. It was a loss that hit Meyerhold hard, but far greater was the loss of Mayakovsky himself, who committed suicide on 14 April 1930 at the age of 36. So close were the two — both as men and as artists — that to read Mayakovsky today is to sense the true atmosphere of Meyerhold's theatre. There were many reasons for Meyerhold's troubles in the thirties, but as significant as any was the loss at their very outset of his truest friend and ally, the only living dramatist he ever treated as his equal.

Early in 1930, Meyerhold was finally granted permission to take his theatre abroad on tour. They left Moscow shortly after the premiere of *The Bath House* and spent six weeks in Germany, visiting Breslau, Berlin and Cologne. The repertoire consisted of *Roar, China! The Government Inspector*, *The Forest* and *The Magnanimous Cuckold*. The company arrived in Paris in May and gave ten performances there, starting on 16 June. With the exception of *Roar, China!* the plays presented were the same. The opening performance of *The Government Inspector* was the occasion for a vociferous demonstration by a section of the Russian émigré community, which protested at Meyerhold's 'mutilation' of Gogol. But nevertheless, that opening night at the modest little Théâtre de Montparnasse was a triumph. Ilya Erenburg recalls:

> There was Louis Jouvet, Picasso, Dullin, Cocteau, Eluard, Derain, Baty . . . And when the performance ended, these people, gorged with art — one would have thought — and in the habit of carefully measuring out their approval, rose to their feet and united in an ovation.[2]

At the end of June the company returned to Moscow, while Meyerhold and Zinaida Raikh remained in France on holiday until September. According to the artist, Yury Annenkov, who knew him well from his Petrograd days, Meyerhold was thinking seriously of going to work in America at

---

[1] 'Meyerhold govorit' in *Novy mir*, Moscow, 1961, no 8, p. 224.

[2] Ilya Erenburg, 'Lyudi, gody, zhizn in *Sobranie sochineniy v 9 tomakh*, vol. 8, Moscow, 1966, p. 340.

The Government Inspector, 1926. Episode Fourteen: 'A Fine Celebration!' (Right: Pyotr Starkovsky as the Mayor and Zinaida Raikh as Anna Andreevna.)

(a) The 'Petersburg Version' (1928). The calumny scene.
Garin as Chatsky (foreground).

(b) The 'Moscow Version' (1935). Tsaryov as Chatsky (extreme right).

Woe to Wit.

that time but was persuaded by Raikh to return to Moscow first. Certainly, in a letter to Annenkov dated 6 September 1930, Meyerhold writes: '. . . Soon to Moscow. Then to New York (November 1930)'.[1]

The true burden of Meyerhold's *Reconstruction of the Theatre*, published in 1930, was his reiteration of the principles of the popular theatre and his call for a revival of spectacle to expose the tedium of so-called 'real-life drama'. This he could not achieve in practice without the support of like-minded dramatists; but Mayakovsky was dead, and any return to the classics risked the charge of escapism.

When Meyerhold staged Vsevolod Vishnevsky's *The Final Conflict* (7 February 1931), he believed that he had discovered a playwright capable in time of replacing Mayakovsky. The work defied categorization: it began with an elaborate production number which parodied the Bolshoi's version of Gliere's ballet, *The Red Poppy*, a ludicrously idealized picture of life in the Red Navy. This was interrupted by sailors appearing from the audience and promising a real story of naval life. There followed a series of loosely connected episodes contrasting the adventures of debauched 'anarchist' sailors on the spree in Odessa with the cultured atmosphere of the seamen's club. In the finale a detachment of twenty-seven frontier guards and sailors held a beleaguered frontier post on the first day of an imagined future war. Machine guns fired blanks directly at the spectators, artillery thundered from the back of the theatre, searchlight beams darted, and on cue an actress planted in the audience was convulsed with sobbing. As the last survivor gasped away his life, a radio receiver blared out a trivial song by Maurice Chevalier. Summoning his remaining strength, the sailor painfully chalked on a screen:

$$162,000,000$$
$$-27$$

$$161,999,973$$

demonstrating the value of the sacrifice and the will of the rest of the Soviet people to fight on. His task accomplished, the sailor died with a smile on his lips – then immediately stood up, advanced to the forestage and said: 'Men and women – everyone who is ready to join in defence of the U.S.S.R. – stand up!' The audience stood to a man, but as one critic sourly observed they would have stood after Glinka's *A Life for the Tsar*.

[1] Yury Annenkov, *Dnevnik moikh vstrech*, New York, 1966, vol. 2, pp. 85–87 (with a facsimile reproduction of Meyerhold's letter).

For all its incoherence and crude effects, *The Final Conflict*, with its combination of burlesque, low comedy, genre realism, melodrama and tragedy, was the style of popular theatre which Meyerhold was striving for. However, the collaboration with Vishnevsky broke down when they disagreed violently over the interpretation of his next play, *Fighting in the West*, and it was Tairov, so despised by Meyerhold, who directed Vishnevsky's most celebrated work, *An Optimistic Tragedy*, when it was staged at the Kamerny Theatre in 1933.

Yury Olesha's *List of Benefits* (4 June 1931) was remarkable for being one of Meyerhold's very few 'chamber works', a production in which he made no attempt to stretch the resources of the traditional stage. The play tells the story of a fictitious Soviet tragic actress, Yelena Goncharova, who finds her creativity stifled by 'rectilinear, schematized plays devoid of imagination'; she emigrates to Paris, the city of her dreams, only to find herself propositioned by lecherous impressarios and invited to perform pornographic sketches in a music hall. Disenchanted and filled with remorse, Yelena joins a demonstration of unemployed workers at the barricades and is killed by a shot from a White émigré.

Meyerhold was responsible for the inclusion in the play of certain incidents from the biography of Mikhail Chekhov, which the actor had recounted to him in Berlin a year earlier.[1] The story of Yelena Goncharova contains much that typifies the dilemma confronting many Russian artists in the twenties and thirties. Ideologically ambivalent, it was far from the affirmative statement demanded by orthodox critics and did little to help the reputation of Meyerhold or his theatre.

In October 1931 the old Sohn Theatre was closed for renovation, leaving the company homeless until it moved into the Passage Theatre (now the Yermolova) in Summer 1932. The time was spent on tour, first in Leningrad and later in Tashkent, no new productions being staged.

Originally, Meyerhold was allocated money only for essential repairs to the existing theatre; but he wanted nothing less than a completely new building, designed to his own specification. This he announced only after demolishing the old building, calculating that the state would finance his new project rather than tolerate a ruined theatre in the very centre of Moscow. This assumption proved correct, but it led to endless delays and the building was only just approaching completion when the Meyerhold Theatre was liquidated in January 1938. In consequence, Meyerhold was

[1] See Nikolai N. Chushkin, *Gamlet-Kachalov*, Moscow, 1966, pp. 257–9.

compelled to spend the final years of his life struggling to overcome the inadequacies of a theatre which was inferior even to the ramshackle Sohn. The Passage was a miserable little box which was as much responsible for the gradual stagnation of the company's repertoire as the tenets of socialist realism or the mediocrity of contemporary dramatic literature.

The new theatre on Mayakovsky Square was designed by Sergei Vakhtangov and Mikhail Barkhin under the direct supervision of Meyerhold. It took the form of a steeply raked, horseshoe-shaped amphitheatre seating 1,600 spectators. The thrust stage was pear-shaped (approximately 24 metres deep and 7.5 metres at the widest point), with two revolves (the smaller downstage), both of variable level. There was no fly tower, scene changes being carried out on lifts beneath the stage. The entire auditorium was covered with a glass canopy with provision for stage lighting from above. Immediately behind the stage was a wide arc of dressing-rooms affording direct access on to the acting area. Directly above them was an orchestra gallery. To either side and to the rear of the main revolve there were gaps wide enough to allow the passage of motor vehicles. A configuration closer to a conventional proscenium stage could be obtained by installing portable seating downstage, up to the forward edge of the main revolve.

After Meyerhold's death the theatre was extensively modified by another architect and opened in October 1940 as the Tchaikovsky Concert Hall. Since then, it has been used only occasionally for dramatic productions.[1]

Estranged from Vishnevsky and despairing of finding any other Soviet dramatist worthy of production, Meyerhold commissioned the young novelist Yury German to adapt his novel, *Prelude*, for the stage. The production at the Passage Theatre (28 January 1933) exhibited all Meyerhold's impeccable style and sense of theatre, but it was modestly conceived and of historical significance only in so far as it was the last work by a Soviet author to be shown publicly at the Meyerhold Theatre.

At the party purge of his theatre carried out later that year, Meyerhold showed no signs of committing the anticipated act of contrition; on the contrary, he attributed his alleged shortcomings to external circumstances, excusing himself by saying:

> I cannot represent the great advances of socialist reconstruction with plywood scenery. I need new technical resources in a new building. The problems facing the theatre are problems of technology.[2]

[1] For an account of the project by the architects see *Theatre Quarterly*, Vol. II, No. 7, pp. 69–73.

[2] Reported by M. Gliarov in *Rabis*, Moscow, 1933, no 11, pp. 34–35.

Meanwhile, he once more sought refuge in the classics. Late in 1932 he revived his production of *Dom Juan* at the former Alexandrinsky (now Pushkin) Theatre with Yury Yuriev again playing the lead. Soon afterwards he staged *Krechinsky's Wedding*, by Sukhovo-Kobylin, at his own theatre (14 April 1933), and invited Yuriev to play Krechinsky.

By comparison with Meyerhold's earlier versions of the Russian classics, *Krechinsky's Wedding* was exceptionally restrained; the settings were simple, with lighting the predominant means of expression. Pride of place was given to the minutely studied performances of Yuriev and Igor Ilinsky (who played Rasplyuev). Ilinsky writes:

> . . . with this production, Meyerhold undoubtedly advanced a further step towards profound psychologism and inner development of character.
>
> A new period seemed to have begun at the Meyerhold Theatre. A departure from the familiar Meyerhold of sensational bluff, the urge to shock and scandalize . . .[1]

Yury Bakhrushin recalls Meyerhold saying some time after the liquidation of his theatre:

> Anyone who saw *The Forest, The Government Inspector, Woe to Wit* and *The Lady of the Camellias* knows how I changed direction. My last two productions, *Natasha* and *How the Steel was Tempered*,[2] were conceived quite differently: purely realistically.[3]

Even so, in 1937 Meyerhold was still showing visitors round his practically finished new theatre, enthusiastically describing his plans for *Boris Godunov*, and *Hamlet* – possibly with settings by Picasso.[4] One wonders how 'realistic' his work would have been, once away from the confines of the Passage and out on the deep arena of the grand auditorium on Maya-kovsky Square.

Dumas's melodrama, *The Lady of the Camellias*, which was presented at the Meyerhold Theatre on 19 March 1934, seemed a curious, not to say hazardous choice; Meyerhold explained it in an interview with Harold Clurman:

> I am interested in showing the bad attitude of the bourgeoisie to women. Marguerite is treated like a slave or a servant. Men bargain over her, throw money in her face, insult her – all because they say they love her. I was interested to show this because we, too, in the Soviet Union, have had a wrong conception of love and of women. Our attitude has been too biologic [*sic*] . . .[5]

[1] Igor Ilinsky, op. cit., p. 244.   [2] Neither was shown publicly.

[3] *Vstrechi s Meyerholdom*, cit., p. 589.

[4] According to Alexander Gladkov, Meyerhold discussed this project with Picasso in Paris in Summer 1936 ('Iz vospominaniy o Meyerholde' in *Moskva teatralnaya*, Moscow, 1960, p. 365).

[5] Harold Clurman, 'Conversation with Two Masters', cit., p. 874.

But perhaps Yosif Yuzovsky was closer to the truth when he imagined Meyerhold saying:

> I no longer desire ascetic self-denial of my heroes, my settings, and my costumes. I wish my spectator joy; I want him to possess the world of beauty which was usurped by the ruling classes.[1]

The production was perhaps a gesture of abdication, an admission of weariness after years of struggling to extract something of worth from the contemporary Soviet repertoire. But above all, Meyerhold desired to see his beloved Zinaida in the part of Marguerite Gautier. He openly admitted that his conception of Marguerite was based on the performance of Eleonora Duse whom he had seen in his early days in Petersburg. Even so, Meyerhold's was far from a traditional interpretation; Leonid Varpakhovsky, who worked with him on the production, writes:

> Instead of the feverish flush, the weak chest and the coughing, all suggesting sickness and a sense of doom, there was recklessness, gaiety, eagerness, energy, no hint of illness.
> Once more one found oneself recalling Meyerhold's words: 'In order to shoot an arrow, one must first draw the bowstring' . . .
> To indicate the illness of the heroine from the very beginning. Meyerhold made Kulyabko-Koretskaya (who played Marguerite's companion) follow her closely, holding a warm shawl as though trying to prevent her catching cold.[2]

Many critics complained that Meyerhold, after all his 'reinterpretations' of the Russian classics, did not lay a finger on Dumas's highly questionable text. This was not true: his stage version included additional material from the original novel, as well as fragments from Flaubert and Zola;[3] although this is not to say that the ideological balance of the play was significantly altered.

The action was transposed from the 1840s to the late 1870s, which, according to Meyerhold, 'offer a more expressive stage of this particular phase of bourgeois society'.[4] It was also the age of Manet, Degas and Renoir: their works – particularly Renoir's – were carefully studied and copied in the scenery, properties, costumes, and even the actors' movements.

The basic settings were simple and flexible, consisting largely of screens and drapes, but the properties were all exquisite period pieces, each serving a specific function and each made to register with the aid of spotlighting. In one act Meyerhold employed his favourite device of the staircase, this

---

[1] Yosif Yuzovsky, *Zatem lyudi khodyat v teatr*, Moscow, 1964, p. 40 (first published in *Literaturny kritik*, Moscow, 1934, no 6.)
[2] *Vstrechi c Meyerholdom*, cit., p. 476.
[3] Alexander Gladkov in *Vstrechi s Meyerholdom*, cit., pp. 500–1.
[4] See p. 275 below.

time a graceful spiral in wrought iron. The limitations of the cramped box-stage were minimized by setting the scenes at a sharp angle to the proscenium line, thereby giving the spectator the impression of watching from the wings. Most of the actors' movements, following the line of the setting, were diagonal, ensuring the spectator a three quarters-view which was more plastic and free from masking, even in extreme close-up. Thus, the production was conventionally representational yet conceived in the three-dimensional terms more commonly associated with the open stage.

Meyerhold's letters to Shebalin bear eloquent witness to the role of music in the production, and require no elucidation.

Zinaida Raikh was a born Marguerite. So often Meyerhold had been accused of distorting his productions for her benefit, but on this occasion her grace, beauty, and stage presence made *The Lady of the Camellias* the one unquestionable public triumph of the Meyerhold Theatre in the thirties – despite the predictably sour response from the majority of critics. In the same year a dramatic adaptation of Balzac's novel, *A Bachelor's Establishment*, was presented by the Vakhtangov Theatre. But the ironic advice given to visitors was: 'if you want Balzac go to Meyerhold, you'll see Dumas fils at the Vakhtangov.'[1]

After eighteen years devoted exclusively to drama, Meyerhold returned to the opera in 1935 when he produced Tchaikovsky's *Queen of Spades* for the Maly Opera in Leningrad (première – 25 January). In Meyerhold's opinion, the libretto by Tchaikovsky's brother, Modest, was a crude distortion of Pushkin's text, wholly motivated by his desire to gratify the prevailing taste for cheap romantic spectacle. Accordingly, he set out 'to saturate the atmosphere of Tchaikovsky's wonderful music . . . with the ozone of Pushkin's even more wonderful tale',[2] enlisting the aid of a young poet, Valentin Stenich, to compose a new libretto.

At the suggestion of the Director of Imperial Theatres Modest Tchaikovsky had moved the period of the opera from the 1830s back to the last years of Catherine the Great's reign which, it was felt, afforded greater opportunities for elaborate costumes and spectacle. To avoid the social anachronism of Hermann, a poor officer of the Engineers, consorting with the nobility, he was transformed into an Hussar. But this completely obscured a crucial point in Pushkin's story: the Countess exemplifies the hereditary society from which Hermann feels excluded; to penetrate it he needs the wealth which only luck at cards can bring him. He pursues Liza

[1] Samuel Margolin in *Molodaya gvardia*, Moscow, 1934, no 8, p. 131.
[2] p. 278 below.

not because he loves her, but because through her he can discover the secret of the fatal three cards. Liza kills herself because she realizes this, not because Hermann has killed the Countess.

Meyerhold restored the action to the 1830s and made Hermann once more Pushkin's poor Engineers officer, emphasizing his isolation by making him a brooding solitary of the kind who had dominated so many of his earlier productions. Ivan Sollertinsky described him as 'a remarkable synthesis of the unbridled romantic hero, the "young man of the nineteenth century" consumed with Napoleonic ambition, demonic passions, the melancholy of Childe Harold, and the introspection of Hamlet . . .'[1] Meyerhold himself compared him to Lermontov's Pechorin and Pushkin's Yevgeny in *The Bronze Horseman*.[2] Stenich based his libretto on the poetry of Pushkin and his pleiad, in places incorporating actual fragments of their verses, elsewhere retaining Modest's original text. Inevitably the result was uneven, and few critics conceded any stylistic improvement. However, as Meyerhold shows, the new plot was far closer to Pushkin, with Liza assuming a role properly subordinate to the central Hermann-Countess conflict. The figure of the 'Stranger' who stepped forward to take up Hermann's fatal challenge[3] was an invention of Meyerhold, a typical Hoffmanesque flourish which stirred memories of the infernal emissaries of his Petersburg days. Scenes included simply for the adornment of the Imperial stage – such as the opening in the Summer Garden and the Russian dances performed by Liza's friends – were removed entirely, whilst the ball was staged as a series of intimate tableaux designed to reveal Hermann's fluctuating emotions (see pp. 285–6 below).

The settings were broadly representational, with properties employed with the same expediency as in *The Government Inspector* and *The Lady of the Camellias*. The production was remarkable for the care with which soloists and chorus alike were rehearsed. Meyerhold describes his new approach to the problem of music and movement compared with his previous operatic work:

> Whereas in *Tristan* I insisted on the actor's movements and gestures synchronizing with the tempo of the music and the tonic scheme with almost mathematical accuracy, I tried in *The Queen of Spades* to allow the actor rhythmical freedom within the limits of the musical phrase (like Chaliapin), so that his interpretation, whilst remaining dependent on the music, would have a contrapuntal rather than a metrically precise relationship to it, sometimes even acting as a contrast, a variation, anticipating or lagging behind the score instead of simply keeping in unison.[4]

[1] *Sovetsky teatr*, Moscow, 1935, no 1, p. 12.
[2] Quoted by G. Lapkina, *Na afishe-Pushkin*, Leningrad-Moscow, 1965, p. 55.
[3] See p. 288 below.   [4] 'Meyerhold govorit' in *Tarusskie stranitsy*, cit., p. 307.

There are precise illustrations of this principle in Meyerhold's synopsis of the production which is included below.

The one almost universal criticism was that the new libretto deprived Tchaikovsky's score of much of its thematic logic, particularly in the exposition of the Hermann-Liza relationship. Certainly, if one imagines the Summer Garden music transposed to the scene at Narumov's house (see p. 282 below), one sees the logic of such complaints. However, the achievements were considerable, considerable enough for the Maly to invite Meyerhold to direct Moussorgsky's *Boris Godunov* the following season,[1] considerable enough for Stanislavsky to invite him to work at his Opera Theatre in 1938. After Meyerhold's rehabilitation Shostakovich wrote:

> In my opinion, his production of *The Queen of Spades* was a remarkable achievement of the operatic theatre, and I consider that it should be revived.[2]

To mark the seventy-fifth anniversary of Chekhov's birth, the Meyerhold Theatre staged three of his vaudevilles: *The Jubilee*, *The Bear* and *The Proposal*, under the collective title *33 Swoons* (25 March 1935). According to Meyerhold, there are no less than thirty-three occasions in the course of the three plays when a character swoons. Each swoon was played as a distinct 'jeu de théâtre', accompanied by special 'swoon music' brass for the men and strings (for the ladies). Convinced that Chekhov's characters are more than mere two-dimensional figures in a humorous anecdote, Meyerhold resorted to a device which Chekhov employs constantly in his full-length plays: he equipped them with an abundance of hand-props, which they were obliged 'to master', and in so doing betray their emotions. Unfortunately, all this business, plus the repeated bouts of neurasthenia culminating in fainting fits, deprived the production of all pace, the paramount requirement of the vaudeville. Speaking of *The Proposal*, Meyerhold admitted, 'Chekhov's light, transparent humour was crushed beneath the weight of our theories and the result was a disaster.'[3]

Sadly, this untypical production was to prove the last new work ever to be seen by the public at the Meyerhold Theatre. At the beginning of 1936 the campaign against formalism in the arts took an ominous turn. Immediately following the denunciation of formalism by Zhdanov before an assembly of the Supreme Soviet, there appeared in *Pravda* two editorial articles condemning the productions of Shostakovich's opera, *Lady Mac-*

---

[1] The production was never started.

[2] 'Dumy o proidyonnom puti' in *Sovetskaya musyka*, 1956, no 9, p. 12.

[3] 'Meyerhold govorit' in *Novy mir*, Moscow, 1961, no 8, p. 228.

beth of Mtsensk, and his ballet, *The Clear Stream*.[1] The works were removed forthwith from the repertoire. At the end of February, Mikhail Chekhov's former theatre, the Second Moscow Art Theatre, was liquidated on the command of the Supreme Soviet and the Central Committee of the Communist Party.

With few exceptions, stage-directors took the first available opportunity to confess their past aberrations and affirm their faith in socialist realism. On 14 March 1936 Meyerhold delivered a lecture in Leningrad entitled 'Meyerhold against Meyerholditis': far from admitting his mistakes, he accused his imitators of propagating 'meyerholditis', the plagiarization and indiscriminate application of his formal devices with no comprehension of their logical motivation. Furthermore, he boldly defended Shostakovich against the attacks in *Pravda*.[2]

Simultaneously, a conference of 'workers in the arts' was convened in Moscow to discuss the implications of the attacks on Shostakovich and the later articles condemning formalism which had appeared in *Pravda*. Meyerhold was the target of many assaults, notably from the principal speaker, Johann Altman (the editor of *Teatr*), and Radlov and Okhlopkov, two of the directors he had charged in Leningrad with 'meyerholditis'. He replied on 26 March 1936, and as the transcript of his speech shows (pp. 289–98), he yielded absolutely nothing to his critics. Indeed, his words were tantamount to a rejection of socialist realism and the official interpretation of the term 'formalism'. No one who heard it could have missed the withering sarcasm behind Meyerhold's remarks on simplicity in art, or have failed to be shaken by the fine arrogance with which he asserted his creative independence. At a time of craven hypocrisy and self-humiliation, his public declaration of artistic integrity was almost without parallel.

Following charges in the official press that his was the only theatre in the entire Soviet Union without a single Soviet play in its repertoire, Meyerhold considered staging first an updated version of *The Bed Bug* and then a dramatic adaptation of Nikolai Ostrovsky's novel, *How the Steel was tempered*. The Mayakovsky project was quickly abandoned, whilst a further year passed before *One Life* (as the Ostrovsky was retitled) was ready for rehearsal. After a revival of *The Government Inspector* in April 1936, the second half of the year was devoted to rehearsals of Pushkin's *Boris Godunov*, for which Prokofiev composed the music. Virtually every scene was rehearsed, but the production outgrew the Passage' stage

---

[1] 'Chaos in place of music' (28 January 1936); 'Balletic fraud' (6 February 1936).
[2] Published in *Vsevolod Meyerhold – Ecrits sur le théâtre*, vol. iv (trans. B. Picon-Vallin, Lausanne, 1992), pp. 30–47.

and finally was laid aside to await the opening of the new theatre.

In Autumn 1937 Meyerhold started to rehearse *One Life* with the intention of presenting it to commemorate the twentieth anniversary of the October Revolution. The production was ready, but the Supreme Committee for the Control of the Arts demanded extensive amendments before authorizing its performance. The anniversary date passed and work was still in progress when on 17 December 1937 *Pravda* published an article by the Committee's president, Platon Kerzhentsev, entitled 'An Alien Theatre'.[1] In the crudest terms, it condemned Meyerhold's entire career, and concluded: 'The systematic deviation from Soviet reality, the political distortion of that reality, and hostile slanders against our way of life have brought [his] theatre to total ideological and artistic ruin, to shameful bankruptcy.... Do Soviet art and the Soviet public really need such a theatre?'

By now, the answer to this question was clearly considered beyond debate. On 8 January 1938, after a morning performance of *The Government Inspector*, the Meyerhold Theatre was liquidated and the rewriting of Meyerhold's biography began. The theatre's repertoire for the final week tells its own story: *The Government Inspector, The Lady of the Camellias, Woe to Wit, Krechinsky's Wedding, The Forest.*

Just two months later all Moscow was astounded to hear that Stanislavsky had invited Meyerhold to become his assistant at his Opera Theatre. How did this reconciliation of seeming opposites come about? Stanislavsky was not moved by compassion alone: despite the popular conception of their complete incompatibility, the relationship, though distant, had never been marred by the acrimony which separated Meyerhold and Tairov. Neither ever questioned the other's integrity, and Meyerhold never lost an opportunity to express the love and gratitude he felt for his first and only teacher. For many years the two scarcely met, but from 1936 onwards a distinct rapprochement was observed.

It is not clear to what extent the rapprochement was artistic as well as personal. The teachings of Stanislavksy's latter years did show a far greater concern with the physical aspects of acting,[2] but this was motivated by his desire to achieve a total understanding of the acting process – it led to no radical change in style, no perceptible difference in the outward appearance of the production.

Meyerhold's late work may have seemed noticeably more 'realistic', but

[1] 'Chuzhoy teatr.'

[2] Cf. K. S. Stanislavsky, *Building a Character* (trans. Elizabeth Hapgood), London, 1950. Robert Lewis, *Method – Or Madness?* New York, 1958.

it was still conceived in terms of external, visual *irony*: there remained the olique comments on the character and the situation offered by settings, objects, lighting, music, other characters – and from the actor himself. All this remained essentially *non-realistic* and consistent with the Meyerhold tradition.

On 7 August 1938, Stanislavsky died. Yury Bakhrushin, at that time his deputy at the Opera Theatre, recalls that shortly before his death he said: 'Take care of Meyerhold; he is my sole heir in the theatre – here or anywhere else.'[1] two months later Meyerhold became the Opera's artistic director.

Prevented by failing health from leaving his home, Stanislavsky had entrusted the rehearsals of his last production, *Rigoletto*, to Meyerhold. The opera had its première on 10 March 1939, and it was intended that Meyerhold should prepare his own production of *Don Giovanni* for the following season.

Then on 13 June 1939 the All-Union Conference of Stage Directors opened with an address by Andrei Vyshinsky, Vice-President of the Soviet of People's Commissars. Two days later, Meyerhold participated in the debate on the main speeches. Until recently the contents of his speech have remained in dispute, and it was not until 1991 that the verbatim text was finally published in Russia.[2] This full version tallies with extracts that had appeared in *Teatr* in February 1974 and once and for all exposes as a fabrication the frequently cited version that Yury Yelagin, an emigré musician, claimed to have reconstructed from notes that he took at the conference.[3]

Sadly, what Meyerhold actually said bore no resemblance to the brave words that Yelagin attemped to inscribe in legend. His speech was miserably deferential, rambling and inconclusive, but even so, it fell far short of what the platform clearly expected of him and in his concluding remarks the chairman Khrapchenko said 'Comrade Meyerhold ... said nothing about the nature of his mistakes, whereas he should have revealed those mistakes that led to his theatre becoming a theatre that was hostile towards the Soviet people, a theatre that was closed on the command of the Party.'[4]

By this time, however, Meyerhold was back in Leningrad, where he was directing a display of physical culture by students of the Lesgaft Institute.

[1] *Vstrechi s Meyerholdom*, cit., p. 589.
[2] *Mir Iskusstv: almanakh* (eds. M. Katovskaya & S. Isaev), Moscow, 1991.
[3] Yury Yelagin, *Temny Geniy (Vsevolod Meierkhold)*, New York, 1955.
[4] *Mir Iskusstv*, cit., p. 461.

On 20 June 1939 he was arrested by the NKVD and brought to Moscow where he was placed in solitary confinement in the Lubyanka prison. On the night of 14 July Zinaida Raikh was savagely murdered in their Moscow flat. Of all the property there, only a file of papers was taken. The assailants, described officially as 'thugs', were never caught. Shortly afterwards, the flat was requisitioned by the NKVD, divided up and handed over to Beria's secretary and his chauffeur and family.

Recently published official records have confirmed that over a period of several months Meyerhold was subjected to brutal interrogation.[1] Finally, he signed a false confession, admitting to collaboration with British and Japanese intelligence and to involvement with Trotskyist elements. However, he soon withdrew this confession and made one final plea for clemency to Molotov, Chairman of the Soviet of People's Commissars. His appeal was rejected and on 31 January 1940 he was taken from the Butyrka Prison to the cellars of the Military Collegium of the Soviet Supreme Court close to Red Square. There his summary trial was held in secret with no witnesses, no defence counsel and no right of appeal. Sentenced to death, he was shot on 2 February and his body was removed to an unknown place.

For the next fifteen years all mention of Meyerhold's name was suppressed in the Soviet Union, and it was two years after Stalin's death in 1953 before the first steps were taken to secure his rehabilitation. Finally on 26 November 1955 the sentence pronounced in 1940 was officially quashed and the lengthy and still hazardous process of Meyerhold's artistic rehabilitation began, headed with great courage and tenacity by his granddaughter, Maria Valentei. That process culminated in 1995 with the opening of the International Meyerhold Centre in Moscow. It was not until 1991 that the location of Meyerhold's grave was reported by a journalist working for the newpaper *Vechernyaya Moskva*. A search of the recently opened KGB archives had revealed that following his execution Meyerhold's body was cremated and the ashes deposited in 'Common Grave No. 1' in the Moscow cemetery of the Don Monastery, together with those of countless other victims of the Stalin terror. A recently erected monument bears the inscription 'Here lie the remains of innocent victims of political repression who were tortured and shot in the years 1930–1942. To their eternal memory.'[2]

[1] See especially *Teatralnaya zhizn*, 1989, No. 5 and 1990, No. 2; *Ogonyok*, April, 1989; *Teatr*, January, 1990.

[2] For a fuller account of the final months of Meyerhold's life see Edward Braun, *Meyerhold: A Revolution in Theatre* (Methuen, 1995), pp. 291–308. (previously published in *New Theatre Quarterly*, February 1993.)

1. The Reconstruction of the Theatre

Comrades – when we come to discuss the influence which the modern revolutionary theatre can exert upon the spectator at a time when its own organizers have still to agree on the precise form it should take, we must not overlook a single aspect of it, particularly in view of the need to take account of the demands both of our Party and of the new spectator. Once the theatre is regarded as a means of agitation, it follows that the first concern of all those concerned in the theatre is the clarity of the message conveyed from the stage; the spectator will want to know precisely why a play is being performed and what the director and actors are trying to say in it.

We can induce the spectator to join us in examining a wide range of topics presented as a debate, but employing dramatic situations and characters. We can persuade him to reason and to argue. This ability to start the spectator's brain working is just one of the theatre's properties. But it has another, quite different property: it can stimulate the spectator's feelings and steer him through a complex labyrinth of emotions. Since the theatre has the power to stimulate the emotions as well as the intellect, it follows that it is wrong for a play as a work of art to limit itself to sheer rhetoric, employing raisonneurs and indulging in dialogues borrowed from the so-called 'conversational theatre'. We reject such a theatre as a mere debating chamber. I could recite this lecture to piano or orchestral accompaniment, leaving pauses for the audience to listen to the music and digest my arguments; but it would not transform my lecture and you, the audience, into a dramatic performance.

Since a dramatic performance depends on laws peculiar to the theatre, it is not enough for it to appeal purely to the spectator's intellect. A play must do more than prompt some idea or depict events in such a way as to invite automatic conclusions. Actors do not perform simply to demonstrate the idea of the author, the director or themselves; their struggles, the whole dramatic conflict has a far higher aim than the mere exposition of thesis and antithesis. It is not for that that the public goes to the theatre.

My principal aim today is to try to resolve the confusion which to this day is troubling the theatrical front. In trying to do this, I shall refer to events abroad as well as in the Soviet Union; I must consider not only our world but the world at large. The masses, hungering for spectacle as well as bread, want entertainment which appeals to the heart as well as the intellect, which engages them totally. For this reason our theatre managers and directors must aim to make their productions sparkle with interest and variety. The aim of the theatrical powers that be is to provide as much variety as possible, and for this reason they must try whenever possible to employ every art form.

There was a time when Wagner's idea of a new theatre which would be a dramatic synthesis of words, music, lighting, rhythmical movement and all the magic of the plastic parts was regarded as purely utopian. Now we can see that this is exactly what a production should be: we should employ all the elements which the other arts have to offer and fuse them to produce a concerted effect on the audience.

The theatre which relies on the rhetoric of raisonneurs, which is purely agitatory and thus anti-artistic has long since been exposed as a harmful phenomenon. Other theatres have been successfully propagandist by actually silencing the actor at the play's climax, introducing music to heighten the tension (e.g. *Bubus, the Teacher* by my theatre and *Days in the Melting Pot* by the Leningrad Young Workers' Theatre).[1] You must regard the dramatic theatre as a musical theatre as well. In taking advantage of every possible technical advance, the theatre cannot afford to ignore the cinematograph; the action of the actor on stage can be juxtaposed with his filmed image on a screen.

Alternatively, we might see the dramatic theatre transformed into a kind of revue in which the actor appears now as a dramatic artist, now as an opera singer, now as a dancer, now as an equilibrist, now as a gymnast, now as a clown. Thus, by employing elements of the other arts the theatre can make the performance more diverting and deepen the spectator's comprehension of it.

The tedious division of a play into acts leads to a static drama which is no longer acceptable. Nowadays, we must divide the play into episodes or scenes as in Shakespeare or the traditional Spanish theatre. It was in this way that they overcame the inertia brought about by the pseudo-classical unities of time and action.

Drama is entering a new phase; we are developing a new theatrical genre which focuses attention on the struggle between the theatre and the cinema. In Western Europe and America there are considerably more cinemas than dramatic theatres and opera houses, and statistics show that in Germany and America the cinema is attracting far greater audiences than any other type of theatre. As a result, some people are saying that

[1] *Days in the Melting Pot* by N. Lvov, produced in April 1928.

the theatre and the opera have yielded first place to the cinema. It is interesting to trace the course of the struggle for supremacy.

The cinema has now reached its zenith. One fine day when cinemas were still attracting huge audiences cinema managers began to sense that the public was becoming dissatisfied. People wanted to see more than just a dumb show and film-makers were forced to look beyond the limitations of existing cinematic techniques. How much longer would it be before the dumb began to speak? This cinema technique followed the course which the public dictated. In order to compete with the theatre, with live actors, means were discovered of furnishing the screen with dialogue, and the result was the talking film. Should one interpret this as a victory for the cinema over the theatre? To me, it is a surrender of the cinema's position. What can compare with the freedom of the cinema? It can shift the scene from one country to another, change night into day in a flash, achieve marvels of transformation, dazzle with acrobatic tricks. Yet all this was still not enough to keep the spectator enthralled: he wanted words, and without them he became bored. Eventually, he insisted on his dumb idols' bursting into speech.

Has it not struck you that from the moment the film began to talk the international power of the screen began to diminish. A Chaplin, who today is understood not only in America but in the Netherlands and the U.S.S.R., becomes incomprehensible the moment he starts to speak English. A Russian peasant will refuse to accept Chaplin as an Englishman. Only so long as he limits himself to mime does Chaplin remain familiar and comprehensible. That is why we regard this achievement of the cinema as a surrender of its position. But what victories, we are asked, can the theatre claim to its credit?

The theatres which exist in our country at the moment are not the ones we are sure to get sooner or later. Up to now we have been in no position to finance cultural projects, but obviously it is our intention to build new theatres and to vacate those which we inherited from the age of imperialism, nobility and private ownership. In those days they built box-stages designed to foster illusion, stages for plays during which the spectator could relax, take a nap, flirt with the ladies, or exchange gossip.

We who are building a theatre which must compete with the cinema say: let us carry through the 'cinefication' of the theatre to its logical conclusion, let us equip the theatre with all the technical refinements of the cinema (by that I don't mean simply the erection of a cinema screen on stage). Give us the chance to work in a theatre incorporating modern

255

techniques and capable of meeting the demands which our conception of the theatrical spectacle will create, and we shall stage productions which will attract just as many spectators as the cinema.

The revolution in the form and content of the modern theatre is being delayed only by the lack of funds to re-equip our stage and auditorium.

We must consider the demands of the contemporary spectator and think in terms of audiences not of three to five hundred (the proletariat is not interested in so-called 'intimate' or 'chamber' theatres) but of tens of thousands. Consider the packed crowds at football, volley-ball and ice-hockey matches: soon we shall be presenting dramatized sporting events in the same stadia. The modern spectator demands the kind of thrill which only the tension generated by an audience of thousands can give.

Nowadays, every production is designed to induce audience participation: modern dramatists and directors rely not only on the efforts of the actors and the facilities afforded by the stage machinery but on the efforts of the audience as well. We produce every play on the assumption that it will be still unfinished when it appears on the stage. We do this consciously because we realize that the crucial revision of a production is that which is made by the spectator.

The author and the director regard all the work which they carry out on a production simply as preparation of the ground on which those two vital theatrical forces, the actor and the spectator, will work daily in the course of the performance. The author and the director provide no more than the framework, and it must not cramp or hinder the actor and the spectator, but encourage them to work harmoniously together. We directors and dramatists know that what we prescribe during rehearsals is only an approximation: the final realization and consolidation of the production is carried out by the audience in co-operation with the actor. Hence the number of 'revisers' must be huge; the revision must be carried out by a mass audience.

It is just the same in the cinema. The spectacular films made in Hollywood are subjected to similar revision before they are released to the general public. Before the general release, a completed film is exposed to the impromptu criticism of a large cinema audience. After the audience has entered the cinema the advertised film is replaced by the film on trial. There are a large number of studio representatives present to record the verdict of the audience, which is unbiased and not specially selected like the audiences at theatre premières. Thus, a random 'mass audience' acts as the judge of the film on trial. The representatives watch the audience

(a) The sentries.

(b) Account of the Battle of Beloyarsk.

The Second Army Commander, 1929.

El Lissitsky's
projected setting for
I Want a Child,
1926–30
(model
reconstruction).

closely and observe which passages are greeted enthusiastically and which passages drag. Afterwards the film is revised, and only then is it released to the general public.

What kind of theatre do we envisage for the presentation of the new spectacle? First of all, we must remove the boxes and abolish seating in tiers. The only design suitable for a performance created by the combined efforts of actors and spectators is the amphitheatre, where there is no division of the audience into separate classes dependent on social standing and financial resources.

Also, we must destroy the box-stage once and for all, for only then can we hope to achieve a truly dynamic spectacle. By making the stage machinery sufficiently flexible to present a series of rapidly changing scenes, we shall be able to abolish the tedious unity of place and the compression of the action into four or five unwieldy acts. The new stage will have no proscenium arch and will be equipped with a series of platforms which can be moved horizontally and vertically to facilitate transformation scenes and the manipulation of kinetic constructions.[1]

Each actor will appear in a whole range of parts. It is not right for one part to be overloaded with material while others contain so little that they can be left to inexperienced extras. In the new theatre there will be no extras. There are no bad parts, only bad actors. Any part becomes important if it is played by a good actor. Famous actors would be glad of the opportunity to play seven, even ten parts during the course of a production, switching character by changing masks and by other simple means.

People are only just becoming aware of the struggle being waged between the cinema and the theatre. What will the outcome be? Clearly, the theatre is unlikely to lose ground: it is on the point of gaining the advantages of a stage with such technical advantages that it will be able to embark with confidence on a fight to the death. The theatre has already initiated the process of 'cinefication' and is certain to pursue it still further. But the cinema, I am afraid, is bound to encounter the obstacle which I have already mentioned: one fine day the actor in talking films will realize that he is losing his international audience and will want to revert to the silent film.

Whenever we try in our theatres and opera houses to build the kind of constructions suited to the revolutionary content of the plays demanded by the new proletariat, we encounter vast problems because the theatre has yet to be industrialized. At present, we cannot afford to rebuild our stages, and technically they are far from perfect. Even so, by using kinetic

[1] Cf. the description of the new Meyerhold Theatre on p. 243 above.

constructions to 'cinefy' the stage,[1] we have already scored a number of victories over the cinema. Three working-class districts in Leningrad now possess comfortable theatres with large capacity-amphitheatres (unfortunately, their stages are still equipped in the old style).

When I was in Italy two or three years ago I was amazed at the lack of a true theatre in a country which once sustained such a lofty dramatic culture, a country which once witnessed the great art of improvisation in full flower, the bitter struggle between those two eighteenth-century dramatic masters, Goldoni and Gozzi, and the dazzling rise of the puppet theatre (surviving to this day in some parts). I wondered why this should be. I know the Italian traditional theatre well, having learnt as much from it as from the Japanese. Its roots are sound, but no organization has taken the trouble to care for the tender shoots and prevent the roots from withering. If you think that traditions survive without attention you are wrong – they need watering just like a bulb under cultivation. It is ridiculous to expect a tradition to flourish by itself; culture doesn't function like that. Anybody who is familiar with the history of the Italian theatre knows what a bitter struggle Gozzi had with Goldoni when they quarrelled over the need to revive the ancient tradition of the mask in Italian comedy. In his battles with Goldoni Gozzi placed his trust in the masses, in popular taste, and in the needs of the contemporary Italian audience; furthermore he assembled a troupe of actors ready to fight with him to preserve the lusty traditions of the theatre. But then his campaign to revive the masks the people loved so much suffered a series of setbacks; Goldoni triumphed once more, and the popular theatre went into decline.

The old traditions have been hidden away and there is nobody to restore them to the light. After Goldoni, anarchy prevailed, an anarchy which was stimulated afresh by the Futurism of Marinetti. Remember his famous slogan: 'Down with tradition! Burn down the museums and abolish every link with the past. Let us create a new art, divorced from the past.'

The Italian people, who thrilled to the dramatic fairy-tales revived by Gozzi and paid no heed to the scorn of the followers of Signor Chiari[2] and Signor Goldoni, have the same attitude towards the theatre today as they had then.

But *the public* demands spectacle. Remember the well-known formula

[1] i.e. in *Give us Europe*, *The Warrant*, and *The Government Inspector*.
[2] Pietro Chiari (1711–85). Venetian dramatist and rival of Goldoni in the field of the *commedia erudita*. He was attacked by Gozzi for his ponderous, elevated style.

'bread and circuses': it is as valid today as it ever was. The demand for spectacle persists, and to satisfy it the priests have taken to the stage. It is the Catholic Church which is keeping alive the traditions of the Italian theatre.

At this point it is interesting to recall a story told by Gozzi in the introduction to his 'fiabe', *The Snake-Woman* (first performed by Sacchi's[1] troupe at the St Angelo Theatre in Venice on 29 October 1762):

'Scene five, act two of this tale – writes Gozzi – is one of those inventions which solemn newspaper scribblers and authors of witless satire call trivial nonsense.

'The play is full of miraculous happenings, so in order to save time and money and to save the troupe enacting a whole host of miracles with which, nevertheless, the spectator must be acquainted, I was obliged to bring Truffaldino on to the stage masquerading as a ragged newspaper vendor to render a brief account of the miracles, illustrating his narrative with various tricks.

'Sacchi came on as Truffaldino in a short ragged cloak and dirty cap; he had a huge armful of printed leaflets and proceeded to impersonate one of those loafers, recounting the news in a few words and inviting the public to buy his sheets for a halfpenny apiece.

'These unexpected scenes were performed by Sacchi with that grace and accuracy of portrayal which invariably guarantee his success; the house shook with unabating gales of laughter and coins and sweetmeats were showered from the boxes in exchange for a single leaflet.

'Such a seemingly trivial invention, fully justified by the absolute freedom of interpretation which my tales invariably permit, was properly appreciated by people of discernment. The scene initiated a chain of events, rumour of which spread throughout the town, exciting everyone's curiosity and desire to witness the spectacle.

'When the newspaper vendors heard of the scene's success, they gathered at the entrance to the theatre with piles of old mildewed leaflets bearing no relation whatsoever to the play; as the audience emerged from the theatre they shouted themselves hoarse, proclaiming the great events depicted in *The Snake-Woman*. Under the cover of darkness they sold innumerable leaflets and then adjourned to the tavern to drink Sacchi's health. The whole affair excited the sort of gossip which ensures the success of a comedy troupe.

[1] Antonio Giovanni Sacchi (1708–88). He and his company performed Gozzi's 'fiabi' with great success in Venice from 1761 to 1765.

'If one takes the disreputable, expands it and presents it faithfully in the theatre, thereby exciting the public's interest, the disreputable is disreputable no longer, but becomes a useful and diverting invention. If you doubt its power to divert, ask the public; if you doubt its usefulness, ask the actors: you will soon see that it accords with Horace's precept.'[1]

By employing this theatrical device, Gozzi succeeded in bridging the gap between the stage and the street.

Nobody since — either in the nineteenth century or in our day — has tried or, at least, tried successfully to create a theatre to answer the demands of the Italian people. Who, then, has satisfied the unique craving of the Italian people for the *theatrical* theatre, for the outdoor theatre, for the powerful impact of dramatic ritual?

Who? — The Church.

The Vatican has become a laboratory for research into the art of production. Of all theatre-directors, the Pope is the most inventive, the most ingenious.

Even now, as I sit checking this summary of my lecture, the newspaper contains a report of widespread anti-semitic disturbances which have turned into an organized Jewish pogrom. But take note: 'On the eve of the disturbances in Lvov there were organized Catholic processions.'

It's clear enough: in 1849 Pius IX in his encyclical condemning socialism proclaimed the primacy of the Pope as a shield against 'the enemies of God and mankind'; then in the 1860s, whilst condemning naturalism, rationalism, socialism and liberalism, he even declared himself unable to come to terms with 'progress and modern civilization'.

Now the Catholic Church has offered its hand to Fascism. With their religious processions and their Fascist rallies, these two organizations are unrivalled in their restoration of the traditional devices of the street theatre — not only in Italy but in every country which has given the Catholic Church free reign.

Our clergy have only recently seen the advantages of new methods based on theatrical practice to hoodwink the uninformed elements of the population; as witness this interesting account given at the fourth atheist congress of the Moscow region:

'The priests are transforming the church into a place of enticing amusement. The sexton has been replaced by a choir, the choir by an orchestra; distinguished artists are invited to sing to harmonium or organ accompaniment. The priests scorn neither the guitar nor the violin, and in the

[1] Horace's precept: 'miscere utile dulci' (mix the useful with the pleasant.)

Northern Caucasus and the Ukraine even the accordion is creeping into church services.'

The stage-director can learn just as much by wandering about the streets of a town when he's on holiday as he can by spending hours bent over books and illustrations in libraries and museums. If he wants to put an edge on his observations, he should plunge headlong into the hurly-burly of the streets rather than potter around the gardens of theatrical culture.

When I was in Italy I soon realized that here was a country with a remarkable theatre, a theatre endowed with an astonishing 'director', a theatre on which masses of money are lavished, a theatre of extraordinary power, a theatre of impressive ceremony, a theatre with a unique flavour. No theatre can hope to compete against such odds; hungry for spectacle, the population greedily snaps up the bait dangled before it. I say the 'population' intentionally, implying the mass of the people without any social distinction. The Pope, that theatre manager and artistic director in the Vatican, occasionally puts on a show of such opulence, and staged with such theatrical skill that even the most confirmed atheist comes running to see it. I mean the ceremonial appearances of the Pope, the religious processions, the grandiose illuminations and firework displays; I mean all those barriers erected to control both the masses straining to kiss the hand of the Pope and the masses straining anxiously to keep as far away from him as possible. In one such day everybody is caught up in the sensational spectacle, rather like the very rare occasions here – perhaps once in two or three years and then, for some reason, only in Leningrad – when a mass performance is organized in which not only the actors but the masses, too, are direct participants. In Rome the crowds are drawn irresistibly to the Pope's spectacles, to see in motion a machine which is controlled by masters of the theatre who understand the power of spectacle.

How can the directors of the Italian theatre hope to compete with spectacles of this kind? Who wants to visit a run-down little theatre at the dead-end of some back street with room for no more than a hundred or, at most, a thousand spectators?

The time has come to put on spectacles for audiences of at least ten thousand. The modern spectator wants not only to enjoy the performance, he longs for the grand scale. He gets the same sensation from the roar of tens of thousands massed in a stadium as a child in Novorossisk who leans backwards against the north-east wind, held up at a thirty-degree angle to the ground.

After examining the attendance figures for theatres and other forms of entertainment published in the Berlin newspapers, Alexei Gvozdev concludes that the contemporary spectator in the West has no interest in chamber performances and is being lured into the big luxury cinemas. The statistics quoted in his article 'Abroad (reflections on Western topics)' in *Zhizn iskusstva*[1] indicate that the growth of big luxury cinemas in modern towns is increasing. Cinemas are steadily increasing in quantity as well as in size. The constant flow of cinema spectators is reaching vast proportions: people arrive and leave and the crowds outside buzz with conversation, exchanging impressions and turning the streets into a sort of foyer.

If we consider the Italian theatre in the light of the modern spectator's requirements, we see that those who determine the course of the theatre (traditionalists, quasi-traditionalists; people preoccupied with stage lighting or acting styles, with the interrelation of the director and the designer, the director and the dramatist, the director and the actor, etc.) should all realize that the fundamental problem of today turns about a completely different axis. All those little laboratories working on the solution of this, that or the other problem: some find it, some don't, some blame the actor, some blame the director and the designer, some blame the repertoire.

But all these problems have gone by the board today. They all ignore the demands of the masses for a new type of spectacle; they ignore the need to establish new aims in the theatre, the need to examine the problems posed by the mass spectacle, the need to consider a new design of theatre.

It is clear that the fundamental desire of the masses is to pack into great stadia with room for tens of thousands. The Pope has recognized this desire, and obviously Mussolini does not intend to build either theatres or stadia now that the State has joined forces with the Church: he is quite happy to alternate his military parades with Catholic processions. He has no need of theatres when he has such a remarkable 'director' as the Pope.

In France they have neither a pope nor religious processions; religion has lapsed and people pay little attention to it. Speaking purely from my experience of French life as a tourist, bigotry and idolatry seem to be out of fashion there. But in France the theatre has another rival: the street itself. In France the masters of the plastic arts have assumed the position once held by the great Italian painters, sculptors and architects – which is the reason for the influx of art-lovers into Paris. In almost every street you will find traces of the influence of some famous painter or sculptor.

[1] *Zhizn iskusstva*, Leningrad, 1928, no 20, pp. 8–9.

They have produced, and continue to produce, at such a rate that art encroaches upon everyday life with amazing persistence and, willy-nilly, the taste of the French petty bourgeois is superior to the taste of the petty bourgeois in any other country. This taste is cultivated so tenaciously, so energetically, and so consistently that even in some mean little back street shop on the outskirts of Paris you will detect the influence of the plastic arts. Their influence is such that the most commonplace object is fashioned so as to be sure of attracting a purchaser. Every object bears the clear stylistic imprint of some renowned school or other, be it the Impressionist, the Pre-Raphaelite, the Cubist, the Surrealist, or simply the Realist school.

Not only everyday articles reflect this influence; you will see it in people's clothes, too – in the working-class quarters as well as in the fashionable districts. You may meet a man in the Place d'Italie or the Place Clichy, poorly dressed with his trousers coming through at the knees, a tattered jacket and a waistcoat with loose threads where the buttons should be; yet this man, a bricklayer perhaps, will be going to work wearing the most stylish necktie. Even in the working-class quarters the sight of such a jauntily worn necktie recalls a detail from Manet, Cézanne or some other great artist. Through your mind there passes a whole series of illustrious names who all exert a constant influence on the tastes of every conceivable class of Parisian society.

This influence is seen at its most striking in the streets; you will sense it immediately on the Fourteenth of July when everywhere is a scene of gay revelry. People emerge from the farthest recesses and everybody dances, young and old alike. Anyone who enjoys the streets, who enjoys feasting his eyes on shop-windows piled high with all kinds of everyday wares and artful trifles, anyone who enjoys the cafés which line the pavements, is unlikely to be moved by the polished art of the serious theatre. Unless the theatre shouts as lustily as the streets, it won't attract an audience for love nor money. The Parisian derives far more enjoyment from the fêtes and travelling theatres which perform from time to time in the various parts of the city than from anything the dramatic theatre has to offer. Whenever a famous artist is persuaded to create designs for the theatre, it invariably leads to great embarrassment. No self-respecting painter, sculptor or architect wants to work on the material of second-rate dramatists; and he doesn't want to work with second-rate directors and third-rate actors either. If in spite of this he still agrees to produce designs for the theatre, he will simply toss it the leftovers from his own ample table. Artists cannot get enthusiastic over the theatre.

On the other hand, a piece of glassware (France is particularly advanced in this field) appeals as strongly to the eye of a French worker as it would to a bourgeois or the most thoroughgoing snob from New York. The worker is amazed at the way nature has been harnessed to produce such an object, but when he goes to the theatre everything strikes him as dull and trivial. He would gladly desert Louis Jouvet and Gaston Baty for a little boulevard theatre where he can see aspects of his own everyday life depicted in some ingenuous farce; there he can appreciate every line, because only yesterday on the Place d'Italie he himself was engaged in a kind of performance. There is an intriguing tradition of song-writing amongst the workers: one of them will compose some ditty and print it roughly himself; another, who is a good accordion-player, works out an accompaniment; a third plays the drums. In the evening the author-performer goes to one of the busy squares and strikes up his song, accompanied by the accordionist and drummer. Then he will persuade the crowd which has gathered round to learn the song, enthusiastically encouraging latecomers to join in with the others who are all singing harmoniously together from the sheets of music they have bought for a couple of sous. Isn't there something of the open-air theatre in this?

Why should he go to the theatre if his eye is not overwhelmed with the beauty of the sets, if there are no brilliant illuminations, none of the fairy-lights of the multicoloured carousel, if there is nothing in the dialogue to equal the everyday banter he exchanges with his wife and neighbours? Thus, a gulf opens up between the needs of high society and the working man, between what the theatre and the street have to offer.

It reminds me of a director who once caused such a stir here with his paradoxical books and articles on the theatre: Yevreinov. I recall his eccentricity, his desire to dramatize life. I should have thought that he would find it easy enough to realize his dream in a town like Paris where the dramatization of life seems such a practical possibility. He need only go to the Place d'Italie, join the workers in their self-composed songs and set about directing them. It's a pity that he's not prepared to move out of the émigré quarter of Passy into a working-class district.[1]

This, then, is what strikes you first when you travel around France or Italy on holiday: you are forced to the conclusion that in such countries the theatre has no chance whatsoever of flourishing, nothing new to say; it has far too many powerful competitors.

But, comrades, if you are in France or Italy and you begin to consider what is happening here, a completely different picture emerges. You think of all the intriguing experiments which are being performed in the

[1] Yevreinov emigrated to Paris in 1925.

264

Soviet Union, and from a distance you see them in a new light. You realize why all those Frenchmen, Italians, Dutchmen, Danes, Swedes and Americans engaged in the theatre take the trouble to come here, and why they follow so avidly everything which we are doing. They are trying to solve the mystery of the theatre's high standing in the U.S.S.R. One has only to consider the aspects of our culture which excite their curiosity to understand why it is from us of all people that they want to borrow.

At this point, I feel I must digress and re-examine some of the conclusions reached by Gvozdev in his article in *Zhizn iskusstva*. He quotes statistics for America and Germany, but I must say he seems to have given this vastly important question insufficient attention; he has, so to speak, steered clear of the most dangerous waters.

To assert that on a world front drama is surrendering its position to revue, variety and the cinema strikes me as completely fallacious. How can one possibly conclude from audience figures for Berlin and New York alone, or from the growing demand in the capitalist cities of the West for light entertainment (mainly for variety, operetta and revue), that dramatic art as a whole is on the point of collapse?

Unfortunately, there is one set of statistics which for some reason Gvozdev has chosen to overlook, but which he cannot afford to overlook if his analysis is to be anything but purely superficial.

'The artistic activities of clubs and reading-rooms in the U.S.S.R. continue to expand rapidly. According to the figures for one month in 1927 the number of artistic groups in clubs and reading rooms amounted to approximately 15,000. Membership of these groups exceeded 285,000. During this single month these groups presented more than 33,000 productions which were seen by more than 7 million spectators.'[1]

Not only in France but in Germany and in America, too, the natural element of the masses is the street. As far as their theatrical needs are concerned, the masses are like a ship with neither rudder nor sails. So confused is the spectator that he has lost himself in a wood consisting of just three trees: fêtes, cinema and variety. The street itself is a stage, the spectator – an actor; but both lack the firm direction of an authoritative organization to transform them into true theatre. Consequently, the French worker falls under the influence of bourgeois fashions in apolitical art and is readily corrupted by boulevard dance-halls, by funfare amusements on fête-days (the tradition of the show-booth is dead), by cafés-chantants, by displays of nudity in variety theatres.

[1] Source not quoted.

265

Here in the U.S.S.R. we can derive satisfaction from the fact that the increasing total of drama circles is yielding a vast number of amateur actors capable of performing not only on our club stages but also in our mass demonstrations. But more important than this is that by encountering more and more creative works, new in form and strong in ideological content, the masses are indulging in that creative revolutionary activity of which Lenin was such a passionate advocate. By exploiting their innate possibilities they are satisfying what Karl Marx regarded as a fundamental precept of Communism.

Since the masses provide the main impulse in our country's struggle to equal and overtake the leading capitalist countries, it is vital that they possess the well-being which is afforded not only by congenial labour conditions (socialist rationalization) but by properly organized leisure as well. In its turn, leisure should be devoted not only to sleep but equally to 'ventilating the brain'; all neuropathists stress the importance of this and prescribe laughter as a cure for nervous disorders.

We do not regard the dramatic activities of the masses as a means of swelling our own ranks; we have no wish to turn the whole population into one vast army of thespians. The theatre is being transformed into a bridgehead for the conquest of the new man; the theatre gives balance to the training curriculum. Before he can achieve total mastery over the forces of nature the new man needs the flexibility which comes from leisure time spent in club theatres, in sports stadia and in parades on revolutionary holidays. It is here, in fighting for the cultural revolution, that the creative initiative of the masses will come to full flower.

'The fate of the theatre is being decided not in the West but here.' To Gvozdev, this statement is no more than a 'half-truth', and he considers it wrong to disregard what is happening in the theatre 'in countries with advanced technology'.

But we in our turn think it is impossible to draw any conclusions about the state of the dramatic theatre simply on the basis of Western European and American statistics, taking no account of Soviet statistics at a time when our theatrical experiments in the professional (not to mention the amateur) field are exerting an enormous influence on American, on Western European, and even on Eastern theatre practice.

At present, while the foundations of capitalism in the West are secure, it seems quite natural that most of the fifty-one theatres in Berlin should be devoted to farce, light comedy, operetta and revue, and that only a small number (ten altogether) still present serious drama. But will this situation persist after the foundations of capitalism have collapsed? Certainly not.

Are there the same opportunities for experiment here as there are in the theatre of Piscator (much admired by Gvozdev), who, 'not shrinking from a rapprochement between the theatre and the cinema, *does not insist* on the unconditional primacy of the actor in the theatre, and considers that *modern technique can also fill the role of the actor*'? (My parentheses – Vs. M.)

Bravo Piscator, for finding in the architect, Walter Gropius, such a talented collaborator!

Bravo Gvozdev, for reiterating their belief in the need for close co-operation in the modern theatre between the director and the engineer-architect! But damn it! What rubbish Gvozdev talks in the following passage from the same article:

'In the last century the theatre depended on the unity of the dramatist and the actor. But now the destiny of the theatre is ruled by those who are capable of transforming the actor's theatre into a theatre which can take advantage of the advances made in the industrial age.'

The fate of the theatre today depends as much on the unity of the dramatist and the actor as it ever did.

The more advanced technology becomes, the farther the spread of industrialization and the greater the range of machines at man's disposal, the more territory will be conquered by the theatre of word and movement (but always word and movement as one), by the theatre of drama (but always with music), by the theatre of high comedy, by the opera . . . . But not until capitalism is replaced by socialism will this theatre predominate over all others.

Gvozdev didn't take the trouble to compare the number of theatres and spectacles in Moscow with the number in Berlin. If he did he would see that there is good reason for the clamour of those Western theatre enthusiasts who are trying to dispel anxiety by enumerating the advantages of the serious theatre; he would see that their discourses on 'the aesthetics of the eternal art of the theatre' are no mere idle abstractions.

As regards Germany, Gvozdev would do well to concern himself less with the struggle between the cinema and the theatre and more with a deeper analysis of the rivalry between the Bühnenvolksbund and the Volksbühnenverein, the former being the dramatic voice of the Christian Nationalists of Southern Germany, and the latter that of the Social Democrats in the North. If he took the trouble to discover the true motives behind both organizations' attempts to gain control of the democratic element of the population, he might understand why the German masses choose 'to choke to death from an excess of undemanding operettas and variety shows rather than choke to death on the kind of art being churned out by the laboratories of the Social Democrat 'Kulturträger',[1] which is barely distinguishable from the art of the Christian Nationalists.

But why – to return to my previous argument – should the future of the theatre depend on the unity of the dramatist with the actor as it did in the last century? Why should the actor today still occupy the central position in the theatre? The explanation is that every single problem which concerns the modern theatre comes down to the same question: who is capable of rousing the audience's enthusiasm and what means should he employ? If the modern theatre is to justify its existence, it must not purvey some pointless commercial fiction: it must inspire the audience to leave the performance determined to tackle the task of construction with renewed vigour.

Our resolute advance along the road of socialism is being obstructed by those weak elements of humanity which readily succumb to such vices as oblomovism,[2] Tolstoyan non-resistance to evil, hooliganism, alcoholism, religious stupefaction, counter-revolutionary provocations. . . .

Strange to say, there are 36,805 religious organizations in the R.S.F.S.R. The total of religious communities has almost doubled since 1922–3. Sectarian communities of every description are springing up: Evangelists, Christians, Baptists, Tolstoyans, Adventists, Dukhobors, and the rest. Their influence extends to no less than 1,700,000 of the country's youth.

If you read the daily papers you will see that almost every day the malevolent and resolute kulak delivers yet another stab in the back to a Communist, a peasant correspondent, or some other representative of Soviet power. If we compare this with what passes for real life in our contemporary theatre, we are forced to admit how woefully remote from life our theatre is.

We have already renounced the apolitical theatre and learnt to react quickly to momentous political, economic and cultural events in our country (sabotage in the coal-mines, the problems of demobilization, the class war in the villages, the fight for the emancipation of women); but who knows how to stage productions which imbue the spectator with that vigour which seems to us the best means of defending the more vulnerable elements of the population against the poison gases of the clerics and the kulaks, against the decadent opiates of the urban bourgeoisie? If we really want the theatre to play its part in the cultural revolution by providing

[1] In German in the text.
[2] Slothful apathy, the malady of the hero of Goncharov's novel, *Oblomov*.

the antidote to these ills, we must rely on the actor: the actor working in collaboration with the dramatist.

Now that the tempo of the cultural revolution is directly related to the tempo of the five-year plan, we cannot remain indifferent to the ills of those amongst us who are hindering our progress towards socialism. The problem is not that our dramatists have failed so far to tackle such themes as the fight against anti-semitism, alcoholism and sectarianism; rather, it is that we have not yet decided how best to deploy the forces at the theatre's disposal in order to help conquer these reactionary evils.

The sectarians have begun to oppose us with the heavy artillery of agitation. They are driving the waverers relentlessly into their own counter-revolutionary camp; they are concentrating on those who still remain sceptical about our final assault on the barricades which year after year are raised by our foes at home and abroad to bar our advance to a socialist world.

Once we grasp this, we can appreciate the full magnitude of the task confronting the theatre. We can see now that all those thundering broadsides of ours were just so many blank charges: all those speeches à thèse, those attempts at 'agitation', so often dull and sometimes just plain stupid; those schematized types, signalling their characters as though by semaphore: one signal for the virtuous 'reds', another for the evil 'whites'.

And what about all those scenes in so-called revolutionary plays depicting 'the decline of Europe'? Has it not struck you that the reason for their success is their blatant disregard for the directives of the Glavrepertkom?[1] Dramatists and directors present a picture of 'decadence' in the hope of disgusting the audience. But far from being disgusted, the spectator falls into raptures over the 'delights' before him: he enjoys watching unclothed women dancing the foxtrot, he enjoys listening to jazz. And why does he enjoy it? Surely because the so-called 'positive' scenes are full of dreary raisonneurs; there's not one single character who radiates the fervour demanded by such subjects as socialist reconstruction.

The theatre is faced with a new task. The theatre must work on the spectator in order to awaken and strengthen in him a militancy strong enough to help him conquer the oblomovism, manilovism,[2] hypocrisy, erotomania and pessimism within himself. How can we acquaint the manual labourers of socialism with the full magnitude of the revolution?

---

[1] 'The Central Committee for Repertoire Control.' The official organ of state censorship for the performing arts, established in 1923.

[2] Deluded complacency, from the character, Manilov, in Gogol's *Dead Souls*.

How can we imbue them with that 'life-giving force' (to quote Comrade Stalin) which will carry the masses forward to a world of new revolutionary creative effort?

How indeed, if not through the theatre?

And once again the actor stands out as the main transmitter of the invigorating shock. But what must we do to make this shock effective, to help the actor transmit it to the audience? Above all, we must strengthen those elements of the production which strike directly at the spectator's emotions.

In the light of present conditions we must take down that old slogan which has been so violently distorted by the more diehard of our critics. I mean: 'Down with beauty in the theatre!' When we started to build stage-constructions in place of old-style sets we thundered: 'Down with beauty!' We meant that painted designs pandered to the snob with his own peculiar conception of the function of the theatre; to such spectators painted sets seemed indispensable.

The modern spectator, who developed his own sense of style during the struggles of the Revolution and has shown himself quite ready to accept the extremes of stylized production (he has become familiar with stylization through watching productions at the Meyerhold Theatre and theatres of that type, as well as club performances at which he can experience the impact of a theatre employing the most primitive means) – the modern spectator finds constructions wholly convincing.

Now that the taste of the mass spectator has become far more sophisticated, we must think in terms of more complex musical spectacles. So surely it is time we reconsidered the slogan, 'Down with beauty'. By employing a good sound construction (as a convenient platform for acting) we do not free ourselves from the obligation to construct it beautifully. When Ford markets a good sound automobile he also tries to make it look beautiful, even if his conception of beauty is different from, say, that of the 'World of Art'. We must realize that the beauty of Ford's car is a direct outcome of its efficiency and reliability.

Today's aesthetic must take account of the new standards which have been created by new social conditions. The art of today is different from the art of a feudal or bourgeois society. We must understand clearly what we mean by beauty and reject all beauty that is not utilitarian. We need beauty today as much as we ever did in order to counteract the effects of the 'oblomovism' whose roots are spreading rapidly through our society. And now that the kulaks are putting out even stronger roots in our villages, now that the Church is ensnaring our youth, it is time we all told the so-called 'Kulturträger'[1] of the theatre to make still greater efforts to help our art flood the country with beauty.

All of us, dramatists, directors and actors, must not lose sight of the fact that the priests are employing propaganda weapons borrowed from the arsenal of the arts. The Commissar for the Arts should engrave this on his memory and bear it in mind every time he considers cutting the grants to theatres for new productions.

The contemporary theatre is faced with so many new tasks, yet we are doing so little. Society is quite prepared to mobilize vast forces to overcome alcoholism, because it knows that if it doesn't win alcoholism will do vast and irreparable damage to our country. Society recognizes the soil which nourishes anti-semitism and such-like abominations.

Meanwhile the First Art Theatre puts on *Blockade*.[2] The apparent success of this production cannot obscure its underlying poverty. When our army crosses the stage with red banners flying, the scene is greeted with applause. That's fine – but as I follow the course of events on stage closely, an ear cocked to the inner pulse of the play, I am left completely unmoved by the stirring sounds of this martial music. When I observe the deep imprint of scepticism and Chekhovian decadence in the other scenes (where there is no Red Army procession to sustain them), when I see this entire production designed simply to wring a sentimental tear from the audience, then I know that the theatre of pre-revolutionary despair lives on in the First Art Theatre. It is still infected by the malaise of that decadent intelligentsia which was ridiculed so brilliantly in Chekhov's plays.

The interpretation of revolutionary material like *Blockade*, *The Flaming Bridge*[3] and *Whoopee, we're alive!*[4] is completely devoid of the inspiration which the contemporary audience needs. There is nothing inspiring in the way the Civil War is depicted and it would come as no surprise if the entire audience said at the final curtain: 'Thank goodness those times are past.'

The audience of today must be shocked into realizing that there are battles still to be won, that the time is not yet ripe for a summing-up, that we have no right to assume that the horrors of the Civil War are a thing of the past.

We must choose dramatic subjects, plots, and characters which will

[1] In German in the text.
[2] By Vsevolod Ivanov; produced by Nemirovich-Danchenko in 1929.
[3] By Boris Romashov; staged at the Maly Theatre in 1929.
[4] By Ernst Toller; staged at the Theatre of the Revolution in 1928.

make the theatre tremble with the sheer joy of living. That is something which neither the cinema nor the theatre has succeeded in doing. Take the film *New Babylon*:[1] the scene showing 'the decline of the bourgeoisie' is enough to make a pornography connoisseur's mouth water; yet the sequences showing the Communards are shot against a background of fog, gloom, and mire. It makes you wonder whatever happened to the spirit which inspired the 'Internationale', the infectious joy and enthusiasm which fired the speeches of the Commune leaders and sustained the revolutionaries throughout the days of unremitting labour which followed.

Although the work of Sergei Eisenstein (a master of the cinema) is far superior to anything which the 'Feksy'[2] have produced, even his *October*[3] makes the mistake of failing to show 'the starlit sky', the dreams which are just as much a part of revolution as the blood.

Eisenstein ignores 'the dream' which helps mankind 'shoulder formidable and exhausting tasks in the arts, the sciences and everyday life, and carry them through to their conclusion'. As Pisarev[4] once wrote, 'even the vast distances separating the dream from reality become tolerable if the dreamer really believes in his dream, if he always looks hard at life and measures what he sees against his castles in the air'. (Lenin put this theory into practice.)

The internal construction of Eisenstein's film is quite remarkable and reflects the deepest integrity; yet one gets angry when watching it: how is it that the director failed to include any sequences depicting the revolutionary's dream? Had he considered this theme, he might have revealed that heroism which in all true revolutionaries is coloured with a certain 'romanticism'.

I am sure that this occurs because workers on the theatrical and cinematic fronts simply refuse to take account of the demands of the moment. Nowadays there is no longer any need for plays or films about revolution which depict moaning women tearing their hair as they do in *New Babylon*. Why on earth are revolutionaries shown so rarely – if at all – going into battle with smiles on their faces? The sight of a revolutionary smiling in the face of death is completely unknown both in the theatre and in the cinema. There is not one revolutionary play or film with a character whose face lights up with simple, almost childlike joy at the

[1] Made by Grigory Kozintsev and Leonid Trauberg and released in 1929.
[2] Members of the 'Factory of Eccentrism' group. See p. 187 above.
[3] Released in 1928.
[4] Dmitry Pisarev (1840–69), Russian critic.

(a) Igor Ilinsky as Prisypkin.   (b) Alexei Temerin as Bayan.

The Bed Bug, 1929.

(c) Zinaida Raikh   (d) Maxim Shtraukh
as the Phosphorescent Woman.   as Pobedonossikov.

The Bath House, 1930.

The Bath House,
1930.

moment of greatest adversity. Lenin could always summon up a smile when the fight was hardest.

This smile is what is lacking. It is what we need to brighten plays consisting of one hundred per cent ideology. The audience gets bored and it is not surprising that sceptics begin to moan about 'the same old ideology.'

This is what we've come to: thanks to our appalling lack of subtlety, we are gradually allowing a weapon, which was once so powerful, to slip from our grasp.

Consider *Whoopee, we're alive!* Such an invigorating title, but I couldn't bear to sit it out and left a third of the way through. The stage is filled with mental patients beating their breasts, and when a Communist does come on you can hardly distinguish him from the gangsters amidst the confusion of obscure effects in the style of Leonid Andreev. *Whoopee, we're alive!* remains no more than a title on a screen; the actual production is more like 'Whoopee, a jump backwards' – backwards into the world of Leonid Andreev and his rejection of the Revolution.

This is the reason why some comrades are crying out: 'Enough! Let's give this so-called ideology a rest; let's have a little music, a little light – anything you like, but for goodness' sake entertain us with this art of yours; revive us for the battle to come! No more gloomy colours! No more horrors!'

We must find some new tonality. But how can we find it while the critics go on praising Vsevolod Ivanov for his *Blockade*, and the director of *Whoopee, we're alive!* By comparison, the plays of Vladimir Mayakovsky and Nikolai Erdman are splendid; with their poetry and their satirical wit, they attack the weakest points of our society without driving the spectator to despair.

We must reconstruct the theatre in such a way that the spectator is presented not with unadorned facts but with a revolutionary form through which he can absorb powerful revolutionary content, dazzling in its variety and its complexity. But this reconstruction is bound to be a lengthy, arduous task, which will entail the equally lengthy and arduous process of rooting out the remains of petit bourgeois ideology. For this reason, we feel that the problem of transforming our way of life is closely related to the problem of establishing the theatre at the very heart of our way of life.

The theatre which strikes us above all as moving in the right direction is the Young Workers' Theatre (T R A M). Although it still copies all the devices of such stylized theatres as the Meyerhold Theatre, it remains new and valuable because its actors see themselves as active members of a society faced with the daunting task of rooting out petit bourgeois ideology and establishing socialism in its place.

[Published as *Rekonstruktsia teatra*,
Leningrad-Moscow, 1930.]

NOTE   The published text was based on three lectures given by Meyerhold in Leningrad, Kiev and Kharkov in 1929. His militant tone was appropriate to the spirit of the times: 1929 was the first year of Stalin's first Five Year Plan; with the launching of this shock programme of industrialization and agricultural collectivization, the relative tolerance of the NEP period was succeeded by a ruthless onslaught on the surviving dissident elements in Soviet society. The arts were called upon to participate in this campaign.

However, many of Meyerhold's remarks in this piece are patently *pro domo sua*: the advocacy of spectacle, music, and the devices of the traditional popular theatre is not only an affirmation of long-held convictions, it is also an apologia for the style of the new theatre he was then planning, a style hardly consistent with the dictates of Socialist Realism; his reference to cuts in state subsidies for the arts could easily be interpreted as an allusion to his own recent financial crisis; in praising Mayakovsky and Erdman he is championing satire at a time when the very existence of such a genre in a socialist state is being questioned by orthodox critics; he ridicules the schematization of conventional Civil War dramas precisely when he himself is staging Selvinsky's *The Second Army Commander*, a tragedy whose equivocal protagonists were widely condemned as ideologically ambiguous and even anti-Soviet.

---

2. The Lady of the Camellias

[Extracts from two letters to the composer, Vissarion Shebalin.]

Vinnitsa, 24 June 1933.

. . . We have decided to transpose Dumas's play from the 1840s to the end of the 1870s. We are watching the play's characters through the eyes of Edouard Manet. In order to interpret the author's ideas more emphatically, and in view of the sharpened ideas which are carried through the entire composition of our production, it seems to us that the 1870s offer a more expressive stage of this particular phase of bourgeois society.

It is not Weber's *Invitation to the Valse* or the *Fantasia* of Henri Rossellen that excites Marguerite Gautier. Instead, we choose a period when the can-can was in full bloom. And the valse – the smooth, limpid, modest, naïve valse of Lanner, Glinka, Weber merges into the voluptuous, spicy, flamboyant valse of Johann Strauss. Decadence proud of itself. (The splendid traditions of Flaubert, Stendhal and Balzac are left far behind: lonely Maupassant runs away from Paris and the Eiffel Tower.) The cabaret, flourishing in the midst of Paris's decay, sends forth a flood of scabrous little songs, of diseurs and diseuses, overflowing not only the stage but the salon, scattering indecencies without lyricism. (Flaubert said, 'Any indecency may be tolerated if it is lyrical.')

The Kingdom of Mistinguette. New family 'morals' oblige one to have a 'friend'. 'Mistress' becomes the market name for the new type of Parisienne. Youth displays itself in all its splendour at the Bal Quatz Arts, where alcove debauches develop into open orgies.

This is the atmosphere in which Marguerite Gautier perishes.

We are sending you under separate cover a copy of the play in which all points affecting music and chronometry are indicated. Here are some details and general comments:

Music for the first act

1, 2, 3 – Varville is at the piano (Varville is in the army, perhaps a major, obviously an habitué of the music halls, a balletomane, cynical but courteous): (1) he picks out a tune (*Madame Nichette*, etc.), then sings, accompanying himself; (2) once seated at the piano, he strikes up a march, then, later (3) a chansonette of some contemporary star.

(Note: As we had little music for rehearsals, we have been using any *pas de quatre* in 12:8 time.)

4 – Two valses: (*a*) a rather crude, provocative valse (Saint-Gauden improvises a lyric for it on the name Amanda, vocalizing with it, twisting the name in and out of the simple rhythms); (*b*) a limpid, tender valse, notably more graceful than the first and conveying the feeling (since this is Armand's theme) that the pianist has caught the very moment when love enters the lives of Armand and Marguerite.

5 – A frivolous ditty for Prudence, very short.

6 – A little song for another guest (a professional diseuse).

7 – A melodramatic musical background, against which Prudence recites

from a 'blood-and-thunder tragedy' (Voltaire or Racine?). Prudence, in a purple robe, stabs with a dagger the nearest handsome young man at the supper table, who collapses laughing.[1]

8 – Gaston, who frequents cabarets and is a friend of La Camille, tries out the piano with a few bars of a polka.

9 – Gaston then fires away at a nasty song with short couplets and a refrain (must be completely vulgar).

10 – Valse *con brio, bravado*, devil knows what: for a dance (vertical formation).

11 – Finale of first act, a carnival scene in the spirit of the Quatz Arts Ball, has three phases: (*a*) carnival *espagnole*.[2] All wear sombreros, mantillas, mantles, etc. Spain – dry yellow colours – sultry ardour – Toledo. The music is harsh (something like Glinka's *Aragon Jota*). On the stage an orchestra of noises – somebody strumming a guitar, another whistling into a bottle, others striking glasses, etc. This noise-orchestra is supported by the real orchestra. Naturally the noises are organized and interwoven contrapuntally, the whole producing a cacophonous texture. Everything is done by the real orchestra, while the actors hold property instruments.[3] (*b*) The Spanish carnival melts into a stormy, typically French can-can. The actors throw off their mantles, and everything suddenly glitters nakedly. Plunge into an orgy. The audience must get the impression that there is going to be a hellish night, a terrific orgy. (*c*) We must have a small chorus (for *tutti*) of Normans and Bretons, in dialect.[4] They sing an artless naïve ballad, which is the introduction to the final scene. They wear Spanish costumes, but their song is native and rural.

Music for later acts
Here are only a few pointers now. We will send fully worked-out details later:

1 – In Act Three we are introducing a wandering musician, walking from one village to another, playing a bag-pipe or some such rural instrument. We may even show him on the stage as a lay-figure.

2 – In Act Four, we will have a can-can and a mazurka. Wild dancing backstage, indicated not only by the music but by the china rattling in the cupboards.

3 – And a valse.

[1] Later omitted or transformed. [Translator]
[2] Later omitted or transformed. [Translator]
[3] Later omitted or transformed. [Translator]
[4] Transformed into a valse, echoed in the fourth act. [Translator]

Odessa, 16 July 1933.

. . . 1 – Act Four begins with music. A can-can (or galop) begins before the light comes up (or, as we used to say, before the curtain is raised). The character of this short introduction must be reminiscent of a traditional operetta finale in a scheme such as this:

8 beats: forte: major key; 16 beats: piano: major key; 8 beats: forte: major key; 16 beats: piano: minor key; 8 beats: forte: minor key; 8 beats: piano: minor key; 8 beats: forte: major key; 16 beats: piano: major key; 8 beats: fortissimo: major key.

You hear the music from behind the scenes, giving you the impression that several rooms separate us from the orchestra and that the intervening doors are being constantly opened and shut. Before the music has ended, it has served as a background for the first scene of this act. Length: 1 minute, 10 seconds.

2 – Between 'give me another ten louis-d'or' (followed by a short pause) and before Gaston compliments Olympia on her 'charming party', a mazurka (*brillante*), chic, danceable, with sharply accented impulses. Length: 1 minute, 30 seconds.

3 – Valse: dashing, nervous. Against this background, the scene between Armand and Prudence. Length 1 minute, 50 seconds.

4 – Second valse. This should be tender and lyrical. It begins at the end of Gustave's speech 'Injury to a woman . . .' Length: 2 minutes, 50 seconds.

5 – Supper-music: 'music for dessert'. Very graceful. Ice cream-cakes of different colours, garlanded with fruits, are served. You feel like saying: Shall they play a scherzo? No! Yes, a scherzo! No, not quite that. More expressive. Sober, with an undercurrent of a lyrical beat. Ah, how expressive music can be! This music should be divided into parts. It is a whole play in itself. Expressively tense (saturated with subtle eroticism). It should not soften the scene. On the contrary, it should be intensified, growing into a powerful finale, where Armand throws Marguerite to the floor, bringing everyone on to the stage as he throws the money in Marguerite's face. No longer is this a scherzo. Everything has gone wrong. Someone has put his foot in the ice-cream cake. Length: 3 minutes, 10 seconds.

Dear Vissarion Yakovlevich, you know better than I do what is needed. No one ever responds as satisfactorily as you do. We love you very, very much, both as a composer and as Vissarion Yakovlevich.

277

Greetings to both of you from both of us.

(Vs. Meyerhold)

[First published under the title
'Meyerhold Orders Music' in *Theatre Arts Monthly*,
September 1936, pp. 694–9.]

·NOTE   The above translation was made by Jay Leyda from the original letters, which have never been published in Russian. Mr Leyda has kindly agreed to its republication here.

3. The Queen of Spades

Where is the spirit of Pushkin to be found in Tchaikovsky's *Queen of Spades*? In the *mise en scène*? In Modest Tchaikovsky's libretto? Where?

To saturate the atmosphere of Tchaikovsky's wonderful music for *The Queen of Spades* with the ozone of Pushkin's even more wonderful tale – that was the task undertaken by the Leningrad Maly Opera under the musical direction of Samuel Samosud.

At one time Pushkin's *Queen of Spades* was generally considered as something quite distinct from Tchaikovsky's opera. Opera companies performing the work did nothing at all to disturb this ambivalence in the mind of the audience. The more enlightened members of the opera-going public derived the greatest pleasure from Tchaikovsky's music, whilst invariably asking in perplexity, 'But where does Pushkin come in?'

When we came to 'pushkinize' *The Queen of Spades* we started by exposing the librettist Modest Tchaikovsky: that lackey of the Director of Imperial Theatres, Monsieur Vsevolozhsky. Our principal motive in this was to restore the reputation of Peter Ilich Tchaikovsky, who, thanks to this brother, was left sitting between two stools. All the time he was composing the score his thoughts were concentrated on Pushkin's story, yet he marred the work by heeding the advice of Modest and the Director of Imperial Theatres.

Furthermore – and this became our main concern whilst composing the new *mise en scène* and libretto – we wanted to restore Pushkin's reputation.

How is it possible that all the most popular interpreters of Hermann have portrayed him so that not one single gesture, not one single movement, not one single phrase has suggested any of the numerous motifs in which Pushkin's inspired *Queen of Spades* abounds?

Take the epigraph to chapter five:

'That night the late Baroness von V. came to me. She was dressed all in white and said: Good evening, Councillor!' (Shvedenborg.)

Anyone thinking of staging *The Queen of Spades* should take this epigraph to the fifth chapter as the epigraph to the whole story. For therein lies the key. Read it more carefully: it is a combination of the elements of fantasy and reality – the very combination which terrifies a reader most.

In previous productions of *The Queen of Spades* the dead Countess has always appeared in a shroud. With her appearance – of course, the *deus ex machina*! – the director sets in motion the whole machinery for the manufacture of theatrical horrors, which is calculated to reduce even the least sophisticated spectator to laughter. Such directors either cannot or will not accept that the theatre is quite capable of depicting the horrific in the most naïve, the most simple manner. By using the simplest devices the horrific becomes even more horrifying; it is horror of an altogether different order.

The ghost as a distinct emploi merits a study to itself; but at all cost it must be treated as an emploi in its own right. This is not the place for such specialized digressions, but let us examine the subject for a moment on a non-theoretical level by describing two scenes where ghosts appear. One is from Shakespeare's *Hamlet*, the other from Calderon's *Constant Prince*.[1]

Seashore. Sea mist. Frost. A chill wind chases silver waves up on to a sandy, snow-free beach. Hamlet, wrapped from head to foot in a black cloak, is waiting for the Ghost of his Father. He looks impatiently out to sea. The minutes drag unbearably. Peering into the distance, Hamlet sees his Father (the Ghost of his Father) amidst the waves breaking on the shore; he is emerging from the mist, dragging his feet with difficulty from the clinging sandy bottom of the sea. He is clad from head to foot in silver: silver cloak, silver chain-mail, a silvery beard. Water is frozen on to the chain-mail and on to his beard. He is cold and he moves with difficulty. He reaches the shore and Hamlet runs to meet him. Hamlet pulls off his black cloak to reveal silver chain-mail. He wraps his father from head to foot in the black cloak and embraces him. During the brief scene we see

---

[1] Produced by Meyerhold at the Alexandrinsky Theatre in 1915.

the father in silver and Hamlet in black, then the father in black and Hamlet in silver. Having embraced, father and son leave the stage.

The important thing here is that the ghost of Hamlet's father is capable of shivering and of displaying affection, of breathing heavily from exhaustion and of embracing tenderly. The ghost might respond with a smile when his son wraps him in the cloak. He is a ghost on whose cheek a tear of gratitude freezes.

It is a different matter with Calderon, but again there is a ghost.

A battlefield. Fernando has just been slain in battle and comes on to a completely empty stage as a ghost, crossing from one side to the other. Instead of wearing a shroud or a winding-sheet (the sort of costume in which he might have been dragged from the grave), he is dressed as Fernando, the warrior. But Calderon adds one single detail: in Fernando's hand he places a taper, a lighted wax taper. Carrying this taper, the ghost crosses from one side of the stage to the other, moving silently. The actor continues to play the same part: just as he played Fernando in life, so he plays him in death.

I have quoted these two examples in order to show the error made in productions of *The Queen of Spades* where the entire machinery of the theatre is set in motion in order to frighten the spectator when the ghost of the Countess appears to Hermann in his room in the barracks. They wheel on the Countess on some sort of platform, make her appear in the costume she was wearing in her grave, use trick lighting – all to show that here on the one hand is the real world and here are living people; but here on the other is a being from the other world, here is an apparition. Thus they distort the whole fabric of Pushkin's story in which fantasy is purposely interwoven with reality.

We must give a straight answer to the question: Did Tchaikovsky write his *Queen of Spades* according to the libretto of his brother, Modest, or did he write it in spite of it? On 28 March 1888 Peter Ilich wrote to Modest:

'Forgive me, Modya, but I do not regret abandoning my intention to write *The Queen of Spades*. After the failure of *The Enchantress*, I wanted revenge and was ready to grasp at any plot; I resented not writing. But now all that is past. I am definitely going to write a symphony, and I shall not write an opera unless I find a subject to inspire me. I am not moved by the subject of *The Queen of Spades* and I might write it just anyhow.'

This quotation will certainly amaze anyone who is familiar with that profoundly felt, highly emotional work, *The Queen of Spades*. Just imagine, there was a time when Tchaikovsky had no desire to write an opera based on Pushkin's story. But the mystery is solved when we read this further quotation from a letter of Peter Ilich in the following year (18 December 1889):

'I have decided to decline all invitations both here and abroad and go to Italy for four months in order to rest and work on my new opera. I have chosen the subject of Pushkin's *Queen of Spades*.'

From our experience of the theatre we know that whenever the best actors and directors are attracted irresistibly to a work and dream of devoting themselves undividedly to it, they usually just curl up into a ball, terrified of starting the work which so excites them. I am convinced that this is because the creative fire is starting to burn inside them.

From Tchaikovsky's letters we know that he was in tears as he finished the pages recounting Hermann's fate; he wept again when he was finishing the opera and whenever he played over those pages to his friends on the piano.

Peter Ilich kept careful watch on Modest's work for the three years preceding his letter from Tiflis. In one letter he writes:

'Three years ago my brother, Modest, started writing a libretto based on *The Queen of Spades* at the request of a certain Klenovsky, and in those three years he has gradually composed a most successful libretto.'[1]

He kept an eye on his brother's work without ever seeing the actual manuscript; the reason he kept an eye on it was because it was *The Queen of Spades*. Once he remarked, 'I have resented not writing it myself.'[2]

Now let us see the involved and tragic fate of the master, from under whose very nose they tried to snatch this wonderful subject.

Peter Ilich begins to write *The Queen of Spades*. How does his work go whilst he is in Italy? Anxiously, under great strain, and very quickly. He writes the first scene in feverish haste. For the second scene there is no plot. He sends letter after letter to his brother, saying: 'Look, I'm already finishing; you may be too late.' His brother sends Scene Two. After the composition of Scene Two, further letters and telegrams back and forth: 'Come on, send more quickly.'

Whilst he is waiting for material Peter Ilich takes up his own pen, writing: 'Meanwhile I am writing odd phrases, but when I get yours I'll set them to music, or perhaps you'll accept mine.'[3]

[1] To Nadezhda von Meck, 17 December 1889.
[2] To Modest Tchaikovsky, 28 March 1888.
[3] Paraphrase from letter to Modest Tchaikovsky, 12 February 1890.

In composing the opera, Tchaikovsky was obviously guided to a certain extent by his brother's libretto. He had to use this libretto because it was Modest Tchaikovsky who had been commissioned as librettist by the Director of Imperial Theatres. This same Vsevolozhsky went so far as to issue a whole series of instructions (horror of horrors!) to the librettist; the latter wrote one scene of which Peter Ilich wrote: 'I have composed the intermezzo precisely according to your Excellency's wishes.'[1] It is not ·difficult to spot these absolutely worthless, loathsome and tasteless passages in the libretto; they are typical of the age of Alexander III, the most tasteless epoch of the whole nineteenth century.

But there can be no doubt that Tchaikovsky retained his own conception of Pushkin's *Queen of Spades* whilst writing his opera. If we examine the work closely, we find that Tchaikovsky has realized Pushkin's conception with the same means that the great master himself employed. Yet it remains his own creation, leavened with the yeast of Pushkin's imagination and inspired by Pushkin's own characters and ideas.

Consequently, we set about achieving a rapprochement between Pushkin and Tchaikovsky on the basis of the musical score; on the definite assumption that Modest's libretto and *mise en scène* should be replace with a new libretto and a new *mise en scène*.

This we did to the extent permitted by Peter Ilich himself. For instance, in a letter of 3 August 1890 to the Grand Duke Constantine he writes: 'What you say about the opening scene in the Summer Garden is absolutely true. I, too, am very much afraid that it might turn out rather like some trivial operetta.'

Do you remember this famous scene with the Summer Garden full of wet-nurses? To start with, the wet-nurses are allowed on to the stage, then when it is time for the soloists to sing they are asked to leave the Summer Garden; when the soloists are finished they are allowed back again. Tchaikovsky's prognosis that it 'might turn out rather like some absurd operetta' proved only too correct.

But let us look at Pushkin's *Queen of Spades*. The story begins: 'They were playing cards at the home of Narumov, an officer of the Horse Guards.' We listen to the music: there is absolutely nothing which specifically suggests either wet-nurses or children. So we reason as follows: since it is not reflected in the music, let us try to get closer to the events described by Pushkin.

This is how we begin: a view with beautiful wrought-iron gates, typical

[1] To Ivan Vsevolozhsky, 26 March 1890.

of old Petersburg. Against this background Hermann stands silent, motion-less. And that is all.

The scene quickly changes. Suddenly, the view and the railings are gone. We see a room at Narumov's. Just as in Pushkin: 'Once they were playing cards at the home of Narumov, an officer of the Horse Guards.' On the table stands a girl in travesty, surrounded by hussars holding glasses brimming with wine. The girl sings the song which in Modest Tchaikovsky's libretto is sung by the children: 'We've all joined up to scare our foes. Hurrah! Hurrah! Hurrah! . . .' The song has new words.

This short scene is followed by a scene between Hermann and Tomsky which is also very short. Then another, again short: officers at cards; two or three short lines convey the course of the game; we see one happy gambler, one unhappy. Hermann stands alone, following the game from a distance. One is reminded of Pushkin's lines: 'Night after night, Hermann followed the vicissitudes of the game with feverish trepidation.'

As I said, these two scenes are separated by the Hermann-Tomsky scene, and here I must stop to explain how we arrived at the scene of Hermann's first entrance.

There was a fine musician and teacher called Dalcroze. He is well known as the inventor of the system called 'eurhythmics'. Unquestionably, his work was most valuable. But alas, what happened? Dalcroze's invention was seized upon by opera singers. 'If we synchronize our movements with the music, then everything will be quite simple' reasoned operatic direc-tors and singers contentedly.

So you just listen to the loud parts and ignore the rest. What is this – music or anti-music? In my opinion, anti-music, because all music is based on rhythm, the task of which is to conceal the regular metrical divisions. Movement in unison with music creates a new kind of 'Vampuka',[1] but it is still 'Vampuka'. We are trying to avoid this metrical unison of music and movement. We are aiming at a *contrapuntal* fusion of the two ele-ments.

The oboe begins to play a melody unrelated to Hermann; he enters, walks two to three paces forward, then stops abruptly, leaning against a pillar. Silence. Tomsky addresses him: 'What's wrong with you, my friend?' Hermann replies.

After the duet between Hermann and Yeletsky (in our version Yeletsky is a lucky gambler) the scene changes. Characters walk about the stage,

---

[1] The title of an operatic burlesque by Vladimir Erenberg produced at the Distorting Mirror in Petersburg in 1909. Subsequently 'vampuka' became an expression of ridicule embracing all absurd operatic clichés.

throwing on cloaks, pulling on gloves and buckling sabres. Black cloaks, white gloves, gleaming sabres. Cloaks on, they step into the street to be greeted by a chill wind and the bleak Petersburg scene which is to serve as the background to Tomsky's ballad. The mood of *The Bronze Horseman*.[1] When the sound of distant thunder is heard the audience is prepared for it: it seems somehow inevitable, not the work of some *deus ex machina*.

The Quintet won't do. Odd remarks are exchanged about some Countess or other. The theme of the Countess seems to arise quite by chance. They talk about the Countess as though the conversation had no bearing at all on the central plot. It is somehow fortuitous. It is the same in the music.

Here, it is important to deploy the characters in order to stress the solitude of Hermann amongst the other officers. This has never been done successfully before.

The ballad which Tomsky sings to the officers elicits no reply from them. Their ironic attitude towards the ballad must be emphasized. They accept it as an anecdote, a joke which they are rather inclined to ridicule. This attitude of theirs to the ballad is stressed throughout. Against the background of a delicately wrought gate stands the solitary Hermann. He reacts to the story differently. This is the crucial scene which anticipates the subsequent theme of Hermann's isolation.

Now the scene with Liza. A set of rooms which we see arranged vertically. Downstairs an entrance hall. The windows seem to look on to one of the Petersburg canals. From the hall a staircase leads up to Liza's room; a second staircase leads to the music room, where there is a harpsichord. The windows of the music room look on to the hall.

Through the windows of the music room we see Liza and Polina standing by the harpsichord, where a guest is playing; they hold music from which they are singing. After their duet, Liza goes to her room. Polina hardly notices Liza's going, picks up another sheet of music and begins to sing a romance. Against the background we see Liza wandering unhappily about her room, as though unable to stand still. Polina finishes the romance, realizes that Liza is not herself, and leaves with the accompanist.

As Liza stands alone, singing her unhappy solo, Hermann crosses the forestage past the railings of the canal. The forestage is in semi-darkness, and Liza's room is brightly lit. Hermann's silhouette passes behind the windows; seeing one of them half-open, he enters the hall. The moment

[1] Pushkin's narrative poem set in Petersburg.

when he enters the hall coincides with a chord in the orchestra (here one may observe Dalcroze's law), and then immediately two parallel movements occur: Hermann runs from the window towards Liza; Liza runs away from Hermann to her room. Hermann follows her quickly.

There follows a second chord. Hermann enters Liza's room. In both these instances (the entry through the window and the entry into Liza's room) we agree with Dalcroze. Here unison is quite appropriate.

The Ball scene. The Ball is included at the instructions of His Excellency, the Director of Imperial Theatres, M. Vsevolozhsky. We know this from the letters of Peter Ilich. Vsevolozhsky could not imagine an opera house without all its attendant opulence and a cast of hundreds lounging about the stage, impeding the action. Hence the host of extras which, like the wet-nurses, has to be removed from the stage for no conceivable reason.

Since the command for a ball emanated from Vsevolozhsky, let us try to get rid of all these superfluous characters. We're not interested in costume displays. At our ball we have a small number of actors who move around very little; they look bored, in accordance with the production's intention. Without disrupting the continuity of the scene, we use a series of special small drapes to isolate various intimate scenes instead of herding crowds on and off the stage. We construct the intimate scenes in such a way as to draw the spectator's attention to that which is significant.

In the past the audience has usually lost track of Hermann at the ball and so the thread of his life has been broken. But I make a special effort to include him in every scene. The whole time the spectator follows the conflict of Hermann's emotions. He gets a clear picture of his ambivalence: one moment he is yearning passionately for Liza, the next he is drawn to the green baize of the gaming-table. If the ball is allowed to become a mere protracted interlude, the spectator loses the thread of the action.

As an example let us take Yeletsky's famous romance. It happens like this: we see a part of the music room at the ball; the romance is sung not by Yeletsky but by an 'Unknown Guest'. However, while the romance is being sung, the audience is witnessing Hermann's torment on the other side of the stage. We need the romance to reveal Hermann's state of mind.

This is followed by the famous intermezzo; it is sung by amateur singers, holding music and singing not in Russian but in Italian.

For the first time, the music room is revealed in its entirety to show the guests being entertained with a pantomime in the style of Jacques Callot. During the performance of this pantomime we witness the following scene. On the forestage sits the Countess with Liza next to her. During the pantomime in which the plot revolves around a note which the heroine, Smeraldina, gives to the hero, Tartaglia, we see Hermann, sitting behind Liza, press a note into her hand. Smeraldina passes the note to Tartaglia at the same time as Hermann passes his note to Liza. The episode is reflected as though in a mirror.

The Countess's bedroom. In the centre of the stage, the Countess's room. This room, which resembles a mausoleum of the Directoire period, is bounded by a staircase running in a spiral from left to right. To get to Liza's room Hermann has to climb to the upper landing. The wall bounding the staircase is hung with a host of portraits of eighteenth-century ladies and generals. Passing Liza's door, Hermann goes up to the portrait of the Countess as the 'Venus of Muscovy'.

When a little later the Countess stands by the fireplace and sings a French romance we see her in precisely the same pose as the portrait on the upper landing. This is her first appearance; in the scene with Liza her voice is only heard offstage.

The Countess is portrayed as she is in Pushkin. In spite of her age she still follows fashion: at 89 she dresses like a fashionable lady in her thirties. We show her as an old woman trying to hide her years. She doesn't walk like Baba-Yaga;[1] we've taken away her stick and she is neither bent nor palsied. Even in the grave she will lie elegantly. At the ball she holds herself erect. 'Who are those people? What are they dancing?' She feels young as she watches the younger generation. As in Pushkin, she wears a yellow gown. She beautifies herself with the help of rouge and ceruse. That is how she makes her entrance, and how she addresses her hangers-on: 'I don't need your flattery.' The audience hears the voices of her entourage offstage behind the doors opening on to the corridor. The Countess enters, attended by a single maid.

Before the Countess's entrance, Hermann descends the staircase and hides beneath the stairs so as not to meet her. He watches her enter and listens to her romance. He is burning with impatience to discover what he came for. When the Countess falls asleep he hides behind the screen in order to appear before her later. Hermann moves unhurriedly and conceals himself. The rhythm of the music, not the way he moves, expresses his internal agitation.

He handles the entire scene with the Countess most carefully, for fear of terrifying her even further. His every movement demonstrates his efforts to calm her. Only once, when he goes over to the fireplace, does he

[1] The witch in Russian folk-tales.

286

strike a threatening pose (in this scene there are a number of poses which suggest a comparison between Hermann and Napoleon).

The Countess raises her fan, as though trying to shield her face from the pistol which Hermann has yet to draw; when Hermann says 'you are old' the fan falls from her hands. She drops the fan and moves towards the door. Hermann continues his aria and does not notice her. He is in a state of delirium. The Countess tries unsuccessfully to open the door. Then Hermann runs to the door as though afraid of her escaping. The Countess moves downstage, seeking to take refuge in Liza's room, but collapses on to a chair half-way.

Hermann runs up to her: 'Tell me! Tell me!' Seeing her sitting stubbornly silent, he decides to resort to the pistol. He draws it and adopts a menacing pose, aiming at the Countess. She cries out, but does not fall.

Hermann approaches her: 'Enough of this childish behaviour! Are you going to name the three cards – yes or no?' Then silence. It is like a chorale suddenly bursting forth then ceasing abruptly. The Countess falls to her knees. We make sure her fall does not coincide with the chord in the orchestra, so that it takes place in silence. First the fall, then the chord.

But I think that's enough examples.

We have not adhered pedantically to Pushkin; rather we have extracted that which conveys the essence of his story.

We have examined the music afresh. All those separate set-pieces, arias, duets and choruses which until now have always been studied and rehearsed so lovingly: they are not just a series of isolated islands; the bridge passages are equally important. By devoting particular attention to these bridge passages, we have succeeded in imbuing the opera with the spirit of Pushkin's *Queen of Spades*.

Try studying the music depicting the behaviour of the incidental characters, try using this music to bring them to life, and you will find that they are by no means superfluous. They are of the greatest significance. The beginnings of superb melodies, isolated phrases which have never before caught the ear, are to be found in these totally neglected passages, until now regarded as merely transitional.

Stage action is used specifically to accentuate the underlying elements of the score, to make the audience listen to what it has always ignored in the past. The stage gesture is, so to speak, an extension of the musical gesture. The stage gesture accentuates the musical gesture.

One needs to consider the specific properties of the music and to understand what a 'free interpretation' of it means. This is both very important and very dangerous, because what appears to be a free interpretation may in fact be merely slavish. The only way the director can achieve true freedom is by penetrating to the absolute foundations of the music, the very heart of the movement contained within it. If we agree that the *mise en scène* is essential to the revelation of a work of art in all its true profundity, then for goodness' sake, let us not be content with half-measures. The director must aim not for mere prettiness, he must exploit the *mise en scène* in order to reveal the sub-text, what lies concealed between the lines.

Down with music and movement in unison, down with those laws of Dalcroze which demand a triplet for every triplet, a fermata for every fermata.

You should begin by establishing a single broad line of stage movement, and only start to embellish it when you have a firm foundation. You should measure stage movement in musical form – and vice versa.

The thoughts of the characters should follow the thoughts of the score.

Final scene. Hermann stakes such a huge sum of money that he cannot get the notes out of his pocket; he has to chalk the amount on the table. The others are afraid to play with him, many back away and he is left almost alone. He issues a general challenge.

A character steps forward who has not appeared before. I call him 'The Stranger'. He steps forward and announces: 'I will play . . .' He comes up to the table and starts to deal. But whilst the Stranger is approaching the table and all attention is fixed on him and Hermann, the yellow-clad figure of the Countess materializes unnoticed at the table; she sits with her back to the audience, following the cards.

Hermann cries :'My ace!' . . . A long pause. Then the silence in the orchestra is broken not by the Stranger but by the Old Woman saying 'Your Queen loses.'

'Hermann shrieks: 'What Queen?' A further pause. Then again, the Old Woman: 'The one in your hand, the Queen of Spades.'

Pointing at the card, the ghost of the Countess staggers back slightly, as though about to fall. Hermann sees her in the same dress that she was wearing in the bedroom and falling just as she did when he pointed the pistol at her.

Blackout. Immediately a new setting: a ward in the Obukhovskaya Hospital with a bed jutting on to the forestage. Hermann is sitting on the bed. We hear the same music as we heard in the barracks before the appear-

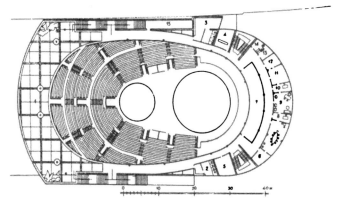

1. foyer, 2 and 3. lavatories, 4. stage director's office, 5. music library and instrument storage, 6. musical director, 7. orchestra, 8. typist, 9. theatre direction, 10. secretary, 11. technical director's office, 12. stage manager, 13 and 14. lavatories, 15. smoke-room (the third and final variant afforded access for motor vehicles on to the main revolve beneath points 2, 3 and 7).

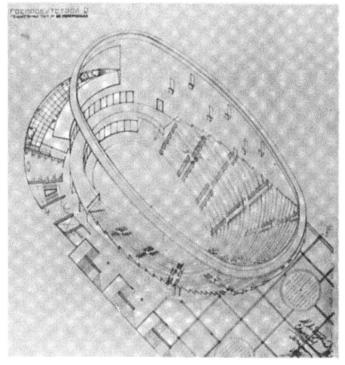

The new Meyerhold Theatre (second variant, 1932).
Architects: Mikhail Barkhin and Sergei Vakhtangov.

Meyerhold on the site of his new theatre, 1937–8.

ance of the Countess's ghost. Hermann speaks the same words that she spoke then, as though playing her role.

So ends Tchaikovsky's *Queen of Spades*. So ends Pushkin's *Queen of Spades*.

> [Published as 'Pushkin i Tchaikovsky'
> in *Pikovaya Dama* (*sbornik statei*),
> Leningrad, 1935, pp. 5–11.]

NOTE   The published text was based on a talk given by Meyerhold at the 'Masters' of the Arts Club', Moscow, on 17 November 1934.

4. A Reply to Criticism

The theatre world expects me to move on from criticism of other theatres and devote this speech to unsparing criticism of myself.

My entire artistic career, all my productions have been nothing but constant self-criticism. I never approach a new production without first shaking myself free of the previous one. The biography of every true artist is that of a man tortured ceaselessly by dissatisfaction with himself. The true artist becomes an artist not merely through using the gifts with which he has been endowed by nature, but also by dint of the colossal labour of perfecting those gifts. The artist becomes a true master by endless observation, reflection and study, by consolidating the basis of his philosophy. He does not divorce himself from reality, because he knows that he belongs to the society in which he lives and works, the society which is building the path to socialism. The life of that artist consists equally of the triumph he enjoys the day he applies the last stroke to his canvas and of the bitter suffering he endures the day after, when he recognizes the mistakes he has made.

Only the dilettante is pleased with himself the whole time and is never plagued with doubts. The master is unfailingly ruthless with himself; complacency and conceit are alien to him. But there are moments when an artist may seem complacent, self-assured and arrogant. At times Mayakovsky gave that impression, but his self-assurance was only put on as a kind of armour against the attacks of the conservatives. Mayakovsky's arrogance was as brittle as can be.

Should a master indulge in unrestrained self-criticism before the time is ripe? No, not before he is able to see straight. Some can see clearly very quickly, almost at once, whereas others take a long time to discover their mistakes. Clearly it is the same with critics; sometimes it is very difficult for them to get the measure of a living artist. Thus it may happen that a critic who wants to discuss my most glaring mistakes takes the book I wrote in 1913 and bombards it with long-range artillery. Possibly he is reluctant to risk firing at my current work – it is a moving target and he might miss. You expose the shortcomings of an artist, then tomorrow he is different and your exposure collapses like a house of cards.

The great critics have always succeeded in getting the measure of the artist of the moment. They are able to analyse his work because they are well armed with a firmly based philosophy. They can view the work of the artist from a great height. Belinsky, Chernyshevsky, Dobrolyubov – all the great names in the field of nineteenth-century criticism. We know other critics who committed themselves boldly to the attack because from the heights on which they stood they had a clear view of the works in question.

The Party has attached particular importance to our conference, so we have no right to waste time paddling in shallow waters; we must all become ocean-going vessels. We must pay the closest attention to all matters raised here, and if there have been any statements which have misled us in any way, then now is the time to discuss them.

I want to consider how we were confused by Radlov.[1] He spoke of the stage-director whose influence must be indiscernible in the production. What kind of a man is this, this director who craftily hides himself behind the scenes? Surely he displays a dangerous degree of 'Molchalinism':[2] 'he attends rehearsals', 'holds his tongue', 'is ready with a chair, picks up a handkerchief. . . ' No, the director must not be excluded from the mounting of the production. He must be the organizer; he must unite the collective, inspire it with his ideas. It is fine if the play has four characters and they are played by actors like Klimov, Ryzhov,[3] and so on. Obviously, with such a quarter, quintet or septet, the director needs only to attend rehearsals and hold his tongue because they understand everything per-

[1] Sergei Radlov (1892–1958), director of opera and drama, a pupil at Meyerhold's Studio 1913–17.

[2] From Molchalin in Griboedov's *Woe from Wit*, a character who achieves his ends through servile taciturnity.

[3] Actors of the Maly Theatre.

fectly. We recall such productions at the Maly, productions with Yerm-olova, Fedotova, Musil, Lensky, Leshkovskaya. What did the director do in those days? He took his seat at the director's desk, placed his watch in front of him, made sure the rehearsal began and ended on time and checked that the furniture was correctly positioned on stage.

Nowadays things have changed. After all, the director is given a mandate to produce by our Party and Government. Should he simply turn up at the theatre and hold his tongue? Radlov says: 'I hate a director who is constantly looking out from the wings and saying: that's my *mise en scène*; it was I who thought of that; it was I who mangled the author's text.' I saw Radlov's *Othello* at the Maly and I said: 'There's Radlov, there he is saying from the wings: That's my *mise en scène*, it was I who thought of that, I who mangled the author's text.' At that production I happened to be sitting next to an Englishman who had the English text with him. We talked together in German because I don't speak English. He was puzzled the whole time; he couldn't find his bearings at all. Clearly, Radlov had absolutely ruined the original text – so why does he blame others for doing the same?

Furthermore, Radlov says: 'Meyerhold should look for "meyerholditis"[1] in himself and not in others'. I am urged to talk more about myself and less about others. To this I would reply: both as an actor and as a director, my body is so covered with wounds from the critics' shafts that there doesn't seem to be a part left unscathed. Just look at theatre criticism from 1905 right up to the present day. Read what Blyum has just written in *Teatr i dramaturgia*,[2] or Talnikov in *Literaturny sovremennik*.[3] That's why I have to look for unscathed parts on Okhlopkov's body to aim at – after all, he and I are supposed to be one flesh. When I attack Okhlopkov, he is wrong to think that it is him I am attacking – I am attacking myself.

Okhlopkov was applauded for declaring that 'the division of a play into episodes hampers the development of character on the stage'. But surely Shakespeare did nothing but divide his plays into episodes. Did this stop him from portraying man in all his complexity? Certainly not!

Okhlopkov goes on: 'There are artists who use the pretext that there are no good modern Soviet plays to escape from reality.' Of course, he is hinting at me. The reason I am concentrating on the classics is precisely in order to render them accessible to the modern spectator. I adapt them in order to make them relevant in the context of the class struggle. What is there about this to suggest a retreat from reality? . . .

[1] See p. 249 above. [2] Moscow, 1936, no 3, pp. 70–74.
[3] Leningrad, 1936, no 2, pp. 183–212.

I wonder if Okhlopkov will recognize himself in this quotation from Goethe: 'Recently, I came across a pamphlet dealing with theories on the nature of colour: evidently the author had absorbed my ideas completely and based everything on them. I read the work with great pleasure, but to my astonishment discovered that he did not mention me once. Subsequently, the riddle was solved. A mutual friend came to see me and made the following admission: *the young author was anxious to make a name for himself with the work*, and quite rightly feared that he would suffer in the esteem of the scholastic world if he dared to substantiate his views by referring to me. The modest work was successful. Later, the shrewd author presented himself to me in person and expressed his apologies.'[1]

I should like to deal with one remark made by Comrade Altman[2] in his speech devoted to me. Comrade Altmann said: 'Some plays Meyerhold rewrites completely, others he leaves in their original form.' As an example of the latter category he cites *The Lady of the Camellias*. This remark of Comrade Altmann does not correspond to the facts. I altered *The Lady of the Camellias* extensively, but I managed to do it so cunningly that the stitches are not readily discernible.[3] It's no wonder that I was attacked by a section of the French press. They didn't like my adaptation because it is differently motivated from Dumas's original play.

Then Comrade Altmann said that it is a cold production which leaves modern youth unmoved. I have not had time to read all the letters I have received from a wide range of comrades about this production. I will limit myself to a short extract from the letter of a group of Red Army soldiers in Moscow:

'You have reminded us once more that women are still not free from slavery, that we are still faced with a stern battle for the emancipation of women in five-sixths of the world, a battle to exterminate one of the most shameful manifestations of capitalism – prostitution.'

. . . Now about the three Pioneers who were bought tickets for *Woe to Wit* by Comrade Pashennaya.[4] She seems to me to have been copying the émigrée-mothers in Paris, anxious for the safety of their children, who

---

[1] Meyerhold is suggesting that Okhlopkov's productions at the Realistic Theatre reveal his influence. Okhlopkov worked as an actor with Meyerhold prior to becoming artistic director of the Realistic Theatre in 1930.

[2] Johann Altmann, at that time editor of *Sovetskoe iskusstvo*, later of *Teatr*.

[3] Cf. p. 245 above.

[4] Vera Pashennaya (1887–1962), actress at the Maly Theatre and director of its Studio.

had bought tickets for our production of *The Government Inspector* on tour there in 1930. The following was overheard at the box-office: 'We are going, but we shan't permit our children to see it.' They realized that in our production the spectator could sense between the lines of the text – in every gesture, in every trick of staging – our hatred for the society which was overthrown by the October Revolution.

. . . Tairov says: 'Levin[1] is a Communist' – as though a Communist is incapable of writing a bad play; as though it is not possible for a Communist without realizing it, to use Soviet themes as a smoke-screen to hide his own mediocrity. Is that possible or not?

[Altmann: But it wasn't the case with Levin.]

But I am talking about this smoke-screen in two senses; I know for certain that in many theatres directors include plays with Soviet themes in the repertoire just for the sake of statistics and stage them any old how, whilst on other plays (plays 'dear to their hearts') they expend vast resources and energy.

Tairov himself has admitted that from 1929 to 1936 he produced only nine Soviet plays. He submitted himself to the most comprehensive, the most sincere self-criticism; he described all his voltes-face, but he failed to mention that he contrived to put on in rapid succession three plays which were subsequently removed from the repertoire.: *Natalya Tarpova*, *The Pathetique Sonata* and *The Conspiracy of Equals*.

Tairov revealed frankly, painstakingly, step by step, his idealistic tendencies and his mistakes. But how did it come about that in the period from 1920 to 1936 he repeatedly put on plays which held him in the thrall of idealistic philosophy? In theory he is constantly reforming himself, but in practice what do we find? In 1920 – Claudel's *Tidings brought to Mary*, in 1923 – Chesterton's *The Man who was Thursday*, then Marienhof's *Babylonian Advocate*, in 1925 – *Kukirol*, in 1925 – *Rosita*, in 1928 – *The Crimson Island*, in 1931 – *The Pathetique Sonata*, in 1934 – *The Heights of Happiness*.

It seems to me that were I, as the director of a theatre, to admit to my errors in theory, I should need before all else to revise my repertoire policy.

I have examined Tairov's work mainly because I wanted to examine myself, to see whether I am in the same position as Tairov. It is the most terrifying thing when one's theories do not correspond to one's practice. I have examined my repertoire and reached the following conclusion:

[1] Boris Levin (1898–1940), Soviet playwright. Tairov staged his *Motherland* at the Kamerny Theatre in January 1936.

Tairov has said that in his theatre there are two main tendencies, the harlequinade and the heroic; well, I consider that there is little wrong with these tendencies – but only so long as they are protected against Western European decadence. For therein lies the great danger.

I, too, have been exposed to many Western European influences, but they have simply bounced off me, because I have made a close study of our own folklore and have always heeded the pulse of popular creative art. I have found that this serves as an antidote. My slogan has been 'set your course by the art of the people'. Someone raised the question of the influence of professional art on non-professional art and vice versa. We must keep an eye open for any vigorous developments which can help us in our search for new means of dramatic expression.

[From the floor: When has that ever happened?]

I'll give some examples in answer to that question. Firstly, it happened in Ostrovsky's *Forest*. All the devices which appear to have shocked many people bear the imprint of vigorous, popular art. It is this which continues to sustain the play today.

We must examine every part of our work and if all the parts are sound, then the so-called 'leftist deviations' (which sounds almost paradoxical) should be left untouched. For example, the scene where Arkashka takes off his trousers and is left in his striped underpants (many respectable ladies and their daughters find this shocking) should be left in.

[From the floor: And the green wig?]

We have cut the green wig.

Even a production like *Tarelkin's Death*, despite the unsuccessful costumes which bear the stamp of Western European influences, can remain so long as we adapt characters like Raspluyev and Tarelkin to bring them closer to the modern spectator.

Let me quote the episode in *The Warrant* where the so-called 'hired Communists' appear (the organ-grinder, the lady with a tambourine and parrot, the acrobat); this scene owes its great effectiveness to the devices of the popular theatre from which it is constructed.

To help me assess my work, I check on the influence it has had on other sectors of the theatrical front. For instance, I consider that had we not included *The Magnanimous Cuckold* in our repertoire in 1922, some similar production would have had to be devised in order to rouse the theatre from its lethargy. Had I renounced *The Magnanimous Cuckold*, I would have 'throttled my own song', to quote Mayakovsky.

The Maly production of *Lyubov Yarovaya*[1] would never have been

[1] By Konstantin Trenyov. First performed at the Maly Theatre in 1926.

staged as it was, had we not previously put on *Magnanimous Cuckold*. And if I spoke of the provincialism exhibited by the Maly production, it is because the director could not see that the 'constructivist setting' (so-called) demanded a new style of make-up, new costumes and a new acting method to help the actors to break away from the slavish portrayal of real life.

Without our *Forest*, Konstantin Sergeevich Stanislavsky would never have produced his splendid *Fervent Heart*[1] at the Moscow Art Theatre. The great masters of the Art Theatre visit us and know how to avail themselves of our methods: they don't just borrow mechanically, but select on merit whatever they consider useful.

Yes, there are quite a few things to be learnt from us.

Take our production of Selvinsky's *Commander of the Second Army*. Wasn't that instructive? We managed to set the play firmly on its feet by employing the conventions of the Shakespearian theatre.

Comrade Vishnevsky worked with me on *The Last Decisive* – although it's true that later he repudiated it, just as he repudiated me. But that was when he was still in the clutches of R A P P.[2] When he came to write that fine film, *We from Kronstadt*,[3] our production of *The Last Decisive* (together with the film's director) was of great assistance to Vishnevsky; the scene in the play depicting the loss of 'Post No 6'[4] served as a kind of preliminary study for *We from Kronstadt*.

Why did I go to Leningrad to give my first lecture on the subject *Meyerhold against Meyerholditis*?[5] There are a great number of my pupils in Leningrad, and I wanted to get straight to the centre of the anthill, so to speak, where Comrades Fyodorov, Lyutse, Wiener, Kroll and others are at work. In Moscow I have fewer pupils but more imitators. And it is these imitators who are really destroying me. Take the Vakhtangov Theatre, for example: their *Hamlet* is very poorly digested Meyerhold.[6]

If you adapt an author, then you need to adapt him as we did in *The Forest* and *The Government Inspector*. You must stick to the fundamental ideological aims of the author. Gorchakov thought he would be crafty and work a few 'meyerholdisms' into his production of *Molière*,[7] but he made the mistake of working on material which was ideologically unsound. I shall ignore Volkonsky, who has wrought such havoc at the Maly Theatre; he is a typical pseudo-innovator.

[1] By Ostrovsky. Produced in 1926.
[2] The Russian Association of Proletarian Writers.
[3] Directed by Yefim Dzigan (1936).
[4] See p. 241 above.   [5] See p. 249 above.
[6] Directed by Nikolai Akimov (1932).
[7] By Mikhail Bulgakov (Moscow Art Theatre, 1936).

Let us now examine the theatrical policy pursued by the Theatrical Department of the Commissariat for Education when Comrade Arkadiev was Head of the Department. The Commissariat had no repertoire plan and no interest whatsoever in a repertoire policy. There was no differentiation between theatres and every theatre indulged in its own experiments. The result was total confusion.

The opening of every new studio was accompanied by the most extravagant claims for its director – and was quickly followed by his defamation. Theatres were allowed to pursue a policy of *laisser-faire*. Take the Theatre of Satire which was basically a good theatre. Then Blyum (an irresponsible critic) declared in some publication or other: 'There is absolutely no place for satire in the conditions of Soviet society.'[1]

The artistic director of the Theatre of Satire took heed of Blyum's declaration and began to wonder whether the Theatre of Satire should be transformed into a 'theatre of comedy'. Laughter was replaced by sneering, and the theatre began to look for the sort of author who in my opinion, should under no circumstances be allowed within its doors. For instance, Bulgakov has wormed his way in. Another is Prut, who, mark you, has written a play on the theme 'hands off other men's wives'. This just won't do. The artistic direction of the theatre should seriously consider restoring its collective with a course of Molière, Gogol and Saltykov-Shchedrin.

The People's Commissariat for Education was ineffective in the theatrical sphere largely because it did nothing but set theatres against each other; they were divided constantly by unhealthy rivalry and competition.

In a conversation with Clara Tsetkin, Lenin said: 'It is not important what art gives to a few hundred, even to a few thousand. Art belongs to the people; it must be comprehensible to the masses and loved by them.' The articles in the central organ of our party contain stirring demands for clarity and simplicity in our art.[2] We know that these articles are inspired by the same view of art as Lenin's. We know that the moment Comrade Stalin turned his attention to the artistic front he began to issue the most valuable instructions, calling on artists to abandon all fancy tricks and pursue the new course of Socialist Realism.

The most important thing in art is simplicity. But every artist has his own conception of simplicity. In his search for simplicity the artist must not lose his own identity.

Artists fall into two categories: the healthy and the sick. The latter class is described in such terms as 'absurdity in sculpture', 'leftist monstrosities', 'cacophonous architecture', and so on.

[1] See p. 238 above.   [2] *Pravda*. See pp. 248–9 above.

In studying the history of art we sometimes encounter phenomena which we have yet to examine with sufficient attention. Shortly before his death the late Academician Pavlov stated: 'I have explored the brain of the dog, now I am going to study mental defectives. But before we can study the normal man, we must first study the actor.' We who are employed on the theatrical front cannot afford to ignore this remark by Pavlov. We need to draw a few distinctions. Take Serov and Vrubel: Serov was a healthy man, whilst Vrubel was sick. They were both responsible for remarkable works of art; but had Vrubel been healthy, his work would have been even more remarkable.[1]

Often a sound artistic experiment gets mixed up with a pathological one. This is a problem for the critics, but we, too, need to know what to retain and what to reject.

The All-Union Committee on the Arts should consider the problem of experimental art. It should join us in eliminating from the arts formalism, naturalism and harmful leftism. But care must be taken not to throw away the baby with the bath-water. Our art of the theatre is most complex and we are obliged to cross-breed the most disparate elements in our productions. But we must make sure that we select objects worth cross-breeding. For example, a dramatist may have written a good play, but that does not mean that it will yield a good production for a given collective. The history of the art of the theatre abounds in fiascos which resulted from attempts to produce hybrids from incompatible elements.

For instance, the former Alexandrinsky Theatre failed to produce a successful hybrid from a company containing such artists as Davydov, Varlamov and Savina and a play such as Chekhov's *Seagull*. Yet what a success the play had when it was put on by the Moscow Art Theatre.

To return to the Maly Theatre, I consider that the system of guest directors suggested by Amaglobeli[2] would prove disastrous for the theatre. A theatre should have a strong artistic director with a strong will and a strong artistic policy, a director who is ready to devote attention to the schooling of his actors. The Maly Theatre will continue in a state of feverish confusion for as long as it continues to change its directors. The artistic director should select a sufficient number of assistants who are all capable of realizing a programme with a firm ideological basis.

. . . Why do I lay such stress on experimental work? When the articles appeared in *Pravda* many directors said: 'At last! Now our work will be much easier!' 'No deviations to left or right!' 'Forward nice and

---

[1] Mikhail Vrubel (1856–1910) died in a mental asylum.
[2] Artistic director of the Maly Theatre, 1933–6.

easy to the paradise of the golden mean!' 'Long live the golden mean!'

But it won't be like that at all. We are faced with a titanic struggle for worthwhile productions. There will still be the same exhausting experimental work. And this raises a question which demands a definite answer: should everyone be given the right to experiment?

To conclude my speech, I should like to touch on the question of form and content. Form and content are a union which demands the firmest cementing, which can be achieved only through the pressure of a living force – and that living force is the will of man (the artist). It is man who creates a work of art, it is man who plays the leading part in it, and it is man to whom it is presented.

In the true work of art, form and content are inseparable; that is what is so tantalizing for the creative artist! The artist experiences pure joy in the creative process when he steeps himself in the content of a work and finally discovers the appropriate form for it. Once he is convinced of the rightness of the form, he feels it pulsating with the true life of the content.

[*Teatr i dramaturgiya*,
Moscow, 1936, no 4, pp. 207–10.]

NOTE   An abridged transcript of Meyerhold's speech (edited by himself) to a conference of 'theatre workers' on 26 March 1936. Remarks of purely local interest have been omitted (indicated by a dotted line). For an account of the circumstances surrounding this speech, see pp. 248–9 above. See also Meyerhold's remarks on realism in his lecture, *Chaplin and Chaplinism* (pp. 322–4 below).

5. At the Stanislavsky Opera

. . . Concerning *Yevgeny Onegin*, I must say that some people here are wrong when they talk of preserving the basic principles of Konstantin Sergeevich, that is, his credo, his creative method. They are under the impression that it is actually possible to abolish something, to destroy a dogma. This is untrue.

Is it possible to interpret Stanislavsky's 'system' in this way? I think not. You should strive to isolate the spirit of his teaching, its kernel, its foundations. Once you have succeeded in this, you are free to build six columns instead of four if you wish – so long as you keep the same foundations. Then you will no longer be a pedant, and a mighty phenomenon like Konstantin Sergeevich will no longer be frozen in suspended animation.

I want to confront you with this thesis today because we need to agree on it. I have the impression (correct me if I am wrong) that when I was working on *Rigoletto*, even though I changed a great deal of Konstantin Sergeevich's *mise en scène*, I preserved the spirit of his work. I encountered no objection from the artists with whom I was working. Whenever I demonstrated some point to Orfenov, Bushuev or Borisoglebskaya there was no disagreement. From this I concluded that they felt quite at ease. There was no feeling of revolt, and they were in full accord with all my amendments because they realized that the essence of the work remained untouched.

I have been credited with scenes in the production in which I had no hand; I confess my guilt: I did nothing to such and such a scene; it remained completely untouched. Of course, I am only too pleased to be credited with work which I didn't do. But I didn't lay a finger on those scenes, so you can see the extent of our unanimity.

Konstantin Sergeevich was a progressive. In his last years particularly, his finger was most sensitive to our country's pulse. I discussed this with him more than once. It was not for nothing that he was honoured by the State, not for nothing that his jubilee was celebrated in such style by our Government and Party. Not only was he a remarkable artist, he was a remarkable citizen . . .

I have told you that I have no intention whatsoever of revising Konstantin Sergeevich's 'system'. On the contrary, you know the circumstances which led to my joining your theatre. I came here after the Party and the Government had drawn my attention to my mistake. I thought: why should I go to the Lensoviet Theatre? I will go to Konstantin Sergeevich and try to work with him. First of all it will be interesting to see what my long career as an artist has yielded – after all, not all my work has been worthless, there has been some good in it. I will offer Konstantin Sergeevich this small portion of good: here is this small portion of good, left over like ashes – the rest is dust. You can throw the rubbish away. Isn't it possible that you might find a use for the little which is left, Konstantin Sergeevich? But I'm cunning, I'll take something from you as well. A long time ago I learnt from you. We haven't met since then. I'll take something for myself.

Once I had a real discussion with him. He spoke for an hour and a half. Then it was my turn and I spoke for an hour and a half. Much of what I said was new to him and he said: 'I'm damned! Nobody at our theatre has worked on that!' And I listened to him and took in what he said. There was the sort of productive atmosphere which develops when two artists are comparing their experiences. When we read mathematical journals we see how mathematicians in New York and the Arctic work on the same problem and compare results through journals. 'Just look at that! Hell, that hadn't occurred to me and he's solved it!'

Konstantin Sergeevich said: 'Don't you want to reform me?' I said I wanted to reach agreement with him and he replied: 'I thought you were planning a revolt. I've taken over a Mozart-style auditorium. It would be a good idea to start staging intimate Mozart operas there. The productions there may be run-of-the-mill and cliché-ridden, but we'll blow some fresh air through the theatre.' He used to say: 'We'll perform without a front curtain. . . .' He said that just to please me.

This shows that Konstantin Sergeevich needed a rebel near him who was prepared to roll up his sleeves and work. He was a fine teacher, an artist endowed with great initiative. He loved art; it was his life. That's what he was like. But does that mean that we must preserve his four columns? To hell with them! I'm not going to start defending four columns with you. I'm used to being persecuted. You can persecute me from pillar to post and I may leave. But I'm not going to start preserving columns.

[First published in *Stanislavsky-Pisateli,
artisty, rezhissyory o velikom deyatele russkogo teatra*,
Moscow, 1963, pp. 68–70.]

NOTE   Extracts from a transcript of Meyerhold's address to the company of the Stanislavsky Opera Theatre on 4 April 1939.

Part Eight

THE CINEMA

IN 1912 MEYERHOLD WROTE:

There is no place for the cinematograph in the world of art, even in a purely auxiliary capacity. . . .
    The cinema, that dream come true of those who strive for the photographic representation of life, is a shining example of the obsession with quasi-verisimilitude.[1]

The following year, when he was in Paris for the production of D'Annunzio's *La Pisanelle*, he made the acquaintance of D'Annunzio himself, Guillaume Apollinaire and Edouard de Max.[2] As Jay Leyda suggests,[3] it may well have been they who persuaded Meyerhold to reconsider the artistic possibilities of the cinema. In any case, when in May 1915 he was invited by Pavel Thiemann to make a film for the Moscow company of Thiemann and Reinhardt, he accepted, albeit cautiously. In an interview he said:

First of all I must say that the technical aspect of cinematography is far more advanced than the artistic. My task is perhaps to discover unexplored techniques. First of all I want to study, to analyse the element of movement in the cinematograph.
    The screen demands its own actors. So often we have seen artists who are splendid in the theatre or opera prove themselves totally unsuited to the cinematograph. Their movements are either too free or too cramped, their gestures far too weighty. . . .
    In my opinion, it is a grave mistake to try to transfer dramatic or operatic works to the cinematograph. . . .
    My opinion of existing cinematography is totally negative. . . .
    It is still too early to say whether the cinematograph will become an art form in its own right or simply an adjunct to the theatre.[4]

At Meyerhold's suggestion, it was decided to make a film of Oscar Wilde's novel, *The Picture of Dorian Gray*. Meyerhold himself composed the scenario and the shooting was completed in rather less than three months. The part of Dorian was played by an actress and Meyerhold himself played Lord Henry Wotton.

[1] V. E. Meyerhold, *O Teatre*, cit., pp. 163–4 (see pp. 134–5 above).
[2] De Max, as well as the young Abel Gance, played in *La Pisanelle*.
[3] Jay Leyda, *Kino*, London, 1960, p. 58.
[4] *Teatralnaya gazeta*, Moscow, 31 May 1915, p. 7.

305

Alexander Levitsky, the foremost cameraman in Russia before the Revolution, worked on the film with Meyerhold, and, as both admit,[1] their collaboration was fraught with discord. The main trouble seems to have been Meyerhold's initial reluctance to concede the creative role of the cameraman, and his own slight appreciation of the practical difficulties of photography. For his part, Levitsky was astonished to be confronted for the first time with a series of sketches (prepared by Meyerhold and his designer, Yogorov) specifying the pictorial composition of each sequence, in which particular attention was paid to the disposition of colour masses and chiaroscuro effects. At that time, the normal practice in Russia was first to design a complete setting and then to shoot the entire scene against it from varying angles. Levitsky claims that much of what Meyerhold specified was impracticable, and indicates that it was himself who suggested the use of dissolves, close-ups, brief takes, even rudimentary montage, to make Meyerhold's inspiration viable cinematically.

Certainly Meyerhold was avid to utilize every means of expression the cinema had to offer, and in return he brought to it his own unique understanding of the dramatic power of rhythm and gesture. As Jay Leyda writes:

> Meyerhold's theories of actors' movement seem from today's perspective ready-made for an adolescent cinema, and were indeed later adapted by Kuleshov to film use.[2]
>
> [The Picture of Dorian Gray] was original and daring as few films before it or since have dared to be. Russian artists who saw it and then The Cabinet of Doctor Caligari a few years later in Europe tell me that if it had been shown abroad it would have surpassed Caligari's reputation as a heightening of film art. It was undoubtedly the most important Russian film made previous to the February revolution.[3]

In his authoritative book on the pre-revolutionary Russian cinema, Semyon Ginsburg goes so far as to say that '... Meyerhold was the very first in the history of the cinema to put forward the idea of the silent cinematograph as, above all, a *pictorial* art.'[4]

Keen to pursue his experiment, Meyerhold agreed the following summer to make a second film for Thiemann and Reinhardt, this time of Przybyszew-ski's novel, *The Strong Man*, in which he himself was also to play a secondary role.

[1] See A. Levitsky, *Rasskazy o kinematografe*, Moscow, 1964, pp. 78–106, for a detailed account of the film.

[2] Jay Leyda, op. cit., p. 59.

[3] Ibid., p. 81.

[4] S. Ginsburg, *Kinematografia dorevolyutsionnoy Rossii*, Moscow, 1963, p. 303

The Lady of the Camellias, 1934. Setting for Act One.

The Queen of Spades, 1935. The Countess' Bedroom in Act Three.

The Picture of Dorian Gray, 1915. Varvara Yanova as Dorian and Meyerhold as Lord Henry (scene from the film).

He chose a new cameraman, complaining that previously he had been held back by Levitsky's 'conservative ways'.[1] On this occasion the collaboration seems to have been far more harmonious and the film was finished by the end of August 1917. It was shown publicly in October, but understandably enough at that time, it attracted little attention and no substantial critical accounts appeared.

Meyerhold never directed another film, although various projects were mooted. At the end of 1925 it was announced that he had agreed to film John Reed's *Ten Days that Shook the World* for Proletkino,[2] but work was never started and three years later it appeared under the title *October*, directed by his former pupil, Eisenstein.[3]

Unfortunately, no trace of either of Meyerhold's films survives. However, in 1928 he played the role of the Senator in Protazanov's *White Eagle*, a copy of which is still preserved in the Soviet State Film Archive. It was Meyerhold's only appearance on stage or screen after the Revolution.

1. The Picture of Dorian Gray

There is no point in discussing the technical faults of the picture; they are obvious enough. I shall discuss it with a view to illustrating the principles underlying it. By studying the mistakes we have made in the past, we can establish the possibilities open to the cinematograph of the future.

In the theatre I have always striven to exploit fully all that the arts have to offer. That is why I used to have no great liking for the cinema; the basis of cinematography is photography, and photography in itself does not constitute an art form (admittedly, in any skill there is a level at which that skill may become an art form, but it is not art in the normal sense of the word). However, cinematography does not consist of photography alone: it contains other elements which combine with photography to

[1] *Teatralnaya gazeta*, Moscow, 7 August 1916, p. 15.

[2] *Novy zritel*, Moscow, 1925, no 18, p. 15.

[3] For a detailed account of Meyerhold's connections with the cinema after the Revolution see A. V. Fevralsky, *Puti k sintezu: Meyerhold i kino*, Moscow, 1978.

produce an art form. In the cinema we project on to a screen movement, juxtaposed surfaces, the dimension of time. Together, they constitute the necessary components for the creation of a work of art. Like a pianist, the actor on the screen can control the rhythm of his playing and emphasize that which is significant (this is where titles are most important). When an audience sits quietly in a darkened room watching a logical sequence of pictures divided up into a number of stages, it is immersed in an art form which is composed of acting, the interplay of surfaces, and the psychology of time. The fact that the actors are subordinated to a cameraman, whose task it is to ensure that the rhythm of the action is never broken, makes it possible to speak of the art of the cinema. The deployment of light and shade on the screen, the efforts of the photographer to achieve what they call an 'astonishing photo', his understanding of the negative, the limits of its sensitivity, force us to concede the possibility of virtuosity in this field.

When *The Picture of Dorian Gray* was made the director and the cameraman were in conflict. Both are to blame for the faults resulting from this conflict: once they disagreed the finished product was bound to be less than perfect. They disagreed over whose responsibility it was to light the picture. In the theatre it is the job of the designer, but in the cinema the camera is worked by the cameraman, so clearly he should control the lighting because he is better placed to determine the requirements of a particular scene. But whereas in a photographic studio it may be simply a matter of adjusting the curtains to admit the amount of light required, the cinema cameraman must be thoroughly acquainted with the conception of the designer and understand the point of the scenario. It is not enough merely to seek beautiful and pleasing effects.

Recently, more and more scenarios have been based on novels. In adapting a novel for the cinema, the problem lies in transferring to the screen not only the plot but the whole atmosphere of the work; somehow the screen must be permeated with the entire spirit of the novel. Nowadays, films are being made of Dostoevsky, Turgenev, Przybyszewski, Wilde, and so on. The manner in which the plot is realized on the screen should vary according to the author. The plot of a novel by Dickens should be filmed with an eye to the style of Dickens. If the cameraman disregards this when setting up the lighting, his task becomes simple; but in lighting first a picture by Wilde, then one by Dostoevsky, he should consult with the director and the designer in order to establish the extent to which his approach must vary.

In the cinema there is no scenery, but a series of surfaces, a number of screens, which can be arranged variously to create the desired mood. In *Dorian Gray* the scene in front of the poster, the scene by the fence, the scene where they carry the portrait upstairs, the scene in the opium den: they are all scenes of a single kind, the screens are juxtaposed in such a manner that they play a subordinate role. The play of light on the figures recalls the works of Hoffmann, in which everyday phenomena sometimes lose their familiarity and suddenly appear fantastic. The reader stops for a moment, amazed by the abrupt change of mood, the encroachment of the fantastic, and then rereads the page to discover where the shift occurred – the merging of the real with the fantastic.

The screens may be arranged in such a way that the spectator is forced to view the world through the eyes of the author. If you see a picture of an adulterer, you watch dispassionately, for it is merely a representation of life; but once some association or other is stirred within you, you begin to perceive the mood of the novel as it was conceived by the novelist or the director of the film.

The task of the actor is equally difficult. It is not merely a question of portraying a conventional young aesthete who reads recherché novels, surrounded by outlandish curios transported from India – that would be simple. We are faced with a man with his own psychology, his own peculiar conception of the world: he transforms even the simple act of smelling flowers into a cult and changes the orchid in his buttonhole to match his varying moods. This is not just another dramatic role, it embodies a particular kind of decadence, the peculiar exoticism of the author. Whoever plays the part must not so much act it as set it to music, get right under the skin of what needs to be expressed.

As regards the cameraman, he must understand his camera, not only from the purely technical aspect, but as a source of light in its own right – this is something cameramen overlook at present. They never experiment alone before starting to shoot with the director, designer and actors. But the cameraman should be able to handle his camera as precisely as a concert pianist plays his piano, familiar with all its possibilities and limitations. He should study the mysteries of light so that director and designer feel bound to seek his advice on the setting before they plan the *mise en scène*. There should be rehearsals between the three of them before the actors ever arrive on the scene. The cameraman should be able to spot mistakes on sight.

The actor should realize before he starts that a style of acting is required which is quite different from the theatrical style. Efforts are being made to reform the theatre, but the conflict has yet to be resolved. The question is whether 'to experience' a role or whether to demonstrate the experience to the spectator.

For the cinema artist, there should be no such question. The screen makes the difference between true and false acting absolutely clear. The leading role in *Dorian Gray* is played by Varvara Yanova, an actress trained in a school of dramatic art. She understands the art of the theatre, but her acting in this film is full of faults: in places she overacts and her characterization lacks subtlety. It was not until I met her again when making the picture based on Przybyszewski's *Strong Man* that I realized she had overcome the errors of the old school and had discovered the secret of the art of the screen. In the theatre of my dreams artists will perform without acting, delighting in the display of their technical virtuosity (that is, they will perform without living the part inwardly). Did you notice the actor who played Alan in the picture? One is struck by the correctness and the restraint of his acting. The reason is that he is not an actor but part-artist, and part-poet. He is a highly cultivated man who knows how to enter a drawing-room, how to hold himself, how to sit down, how to stand up. He measures his every step (it is this which reveals a person's upbringing). He uses his body, his every movement, to show himself off to the best advantage; he is full of self-assurance and beauty. His whole performance is on the formal plane, and he is not concerned with experiencing the states of mind of Alan. He enters confidently, secure in the knowledge that the public will admire the immaculate parting in his hair. When he reads the letter he has no need whatsoever to experience any emotion in order to sink into the armchair and express alarm by covering his face with his long, elegantly manicured hands. The spectator is alarmed, guessing that the matter relates to Sybil Vane, and the alarm conveyed by Alan as he reads the mysterious letter is sufficient to evoke a whole complex of psychological associations and emotions.

In the theatre, the effect produced by the play suffers greatly from the predilection of theatre managers for ham-actors rather than genuine artists. They overplay the tragedy of a part, recoil in terror, breathe heavily, take their time over killing a man, and commit many other similar errors of judgement. But all this is even more harmful on the screen, where every second you spend over an action seems somehow to double itself. The film affords a great deal of space to whatever is being photographed. Since the camera is so sensitive, acting must be kept to a minimum.

It is possible to play the same part twice and each time be mistaken over the effect one is producing. Once I played a scene in which I had no emotional sense at all of the tears I was shedding before the audience, and

I was convinced that I had given a wretched performance. The next time I played the scene I got so carried away that my eyes streamed real tears. Afterwards, I met a man who had seen both performances and I asked him for his impressions. He replied that the first time he was deeply moved by my performance, but the second time it had no effect on him at all. The effect does not depend on 'real' tears. A great artist retains control over himself even when tears do appear; he utilizes all technical means to show the tears to the spectator and thereby forces him to believe in the tears (it is irrelevant whether they are 'really' flowing or not). When I played the scene the second time the tears flowed, but I neglected the means I should have employed to make the audience believe in them, and so the effect was lost.

It is not just a question of mood. Often an inexperienced artist tries to persuade the cameraman to shoot a scene immediately because he feels in the right mood for acting. The cameraman begins shooting and the artist hastens to take advantage of his mood, completely ignoring *how* he is acting; the result is such a poor take that the cameraman thanks his lucky stars he wasted only seven, not twenty-five, metres of film. But then there are the actors like the one who played Alan, people well versed in life who prove to be amazingly controlled actors. It's all a question of rhythm of movement and action. It is this rhythm with a capital 'R' which places such demands on cameraman, director, designer and actors. We must remember that the screen is something suspended in time and space, and that the actor of the future must cultivate a sense of time. Sometimes in the middle of shooting the cameraman shouts 'Don't rush' or 'Quicker'. 'Quicker' means you must synthesize your gestures. 'Don't rush' meant 'Act calmly, watch your timing'.

One must develop an instinctive sense of time, the ability to judge whether you've been acting for one minute or seven. There is the case of the actor who took seven minutes over a speech. After a few performances, the director paid no further attention to him. However, when he watched the fifteenth or twentieth performance he found that the actor was taking not seven but twelve minutes. What went wrong? Apparently, with each performance the actor had discovered new meaning in the speech.

So you see how important rhythm is as a means of controlling one's performance. An instinctive sense of time, 'an ear for time', is of vast importance for the cinema artist. In swimming, all the right movements are quite useless if you lack the instinct to keep your body afloat; it is just as vital for the cinema artist to possess a sense of rhythm. In art intuition is of great importance. You can develop a sense of time gradually through exercises. You can use a clock to check the time taken to perform a scene in front of a mirror.

The cinema camera does not tolerate abrupt movements. It has its own secrets. Like a famous pianist who first plays a virtuoso passage slowly and deliberately, the cameraman must study the rhythmical intervals of a passage and point out the slightest deflection from the agreed tempo. Scriabin's secret lay not only in his fingers but in the animation of his whole body, the angle of his head, his manner of accentuation, his strict sense of rhythm.

Even a simple move from a door to a chair, from a chair on to the fore-stage has its own precise allocation of time. Turns, exits and entrances are particularly difficult on the screen. In the scene where Dorian gives the servant the letter, I asked him to start the gesture, then stop and hesitate slightly. In this way, the phrase 'Wait a moment' creates a psychological impression: the audience waits, wondering what will happen next.

When the studio set is ready the scene should be rehearsed with each section timed with a stopwatch. Then, if the actors are ready, you can begin shooting. The screen demands extreme discipline. The actor must not be afraid of light: he must always keep his eyes open so that they may be seen to be acting.

Titles play a most important part in a picture. It was a mistake to use Dorian's lines: 'Here is the first passionate love letter I have ever written in my life. Strange that my first passionate love letter should have been addressed to a dead girl.' Two sentences killed the powerful impression which would have been made by the one line: 'Strange that my first passionate love letter should have been addressed to a dead girl.'

Titles are used not only to explain what would otherwise remain obscure. The whole screen is constant movement. Sitting in a darkened room, we hear the whirr of the projector and it serves as a constant reminder of time; it makes us aware of our existence in the dimension of time. For this reason, the division of the picture into parts and then further into scenes has a definite significance. Titles should be inserted not only as a means of explanation (there should be a minimum of titles; the audience should be able to follow everything from the action alone and from the manner in which it is presented); titles should be used for the sake of the evocative power of the words. Whilst affording a rest from the picture, the title should grip the spectator with the point of the sentence.

In the theatre of the future the actor will subordinate his movements to rhythm; he will create a unique music of movement. When human movements become musical even in their form, words will be no more than an embellishment and only fine words will satisfy us.

[Published in *Iz istorii kino*, no 6,
[Moscow, 1965, pp. 18–24.]

NOTE   Transcript of a lecture delivered by Meyerhold in 1918 at the Studio of Cinematic Art of the Skobelev Committee.

---

2. Chaplin and Chaplinism

This is the first time that I have spoken on this most intriguing subject. It seems unlikely that I shall exhaust its possibilities today, for not only is it intriguing but also rather complex.

I feel it would be pointless to examine all Chaplin's works in chronological order and then extract some lesson from them. . . . I intend to approach the subject differently: having defined the quintessence of Chaplinism, I will go on from Chaplin to other masters of the cinema in order to reveal the common thread linking them all.

When I was introduced to you mention was made of the influence which I have had on various artists of the cinema. I think that I have had an influence on the cinema, but the last thing I want to do is to adopt the pose of some master whose influence has spread to every field of the arts. Certainly not. But when I speak of Chaplin and that magical art which we call 'Chaplinism', I am bound to consider the work of my own pupils. My primary task today will be to establish the resemblance, the astonishing resemblance, between the work of Chaplin and Sergei Eistenstein – however improbable that might seem at first sight.

All Eisenstein's work has its origins in the laboratory where we once worked together as teacher and pupil.[1] But our relationship was not so much the relationship of teacher and pupil as of two artists in revolt, up to our necks and afraid to swallow for fear of the disgusting slime in which we found the theatre wallowing in 1917. The theatre was sinking in a swamp of naturalism, feeble imitation and eclecticism, with even the

[1] See p. 187 above.

epigones imitating epigones. There was no music – either in the theatre or in the cinema. For all the inevitable incidental music, films were totally anti-musical. The music ground on, a combination of Tchaikovsky and Mozart, or Beethoven and Scriabin, but still there was no *music*. You could listen to the music by itself with your eyes closed and imagine the sequences on the screen following one another completely devoid of rhythm.

After that brief introduction, I will now give you a short chronology, emphasizing what I regard as the most vital and characteristic features of each period of Chaplin's work. To the majority of you who are familiar with Chaplin this may seem superfluous, but I cannot avoid it if I am to lay bare the roots of his great art.

The first period was his work at Mack Sennett's studio. At that time his clowning had not yet risen to the level of humour. It pleases me to use the term 'humour', because thanks to a number of works in the cinema, theatre and literature it has assumed a new profundity. Recent research into Pushkin has thrown new light on the true meaning of humour, and we no longer use the word as we did in our schooldays.

The clowning in Chaplin's early films had not yet risen to the level of humour; I mean the films made in 1915: *His New Job*, *Work*, *By the Sea*, *The Star Boarder*. Then came *A Night in the Show*, and anybody who has seen either this film or *Carmen* will have realized the artistic advance they signified. I would place *A Night in the Show* first, for in that film – as opposed to *Carmen*, in which the predominant mood is abstract tragedy – Chaplin clearly eliminated all excessive hyperbole and sheer knockabout comedy from his clowning. But, of course, this was only a cautious beginning.

In the films made in 1916, when Chaplin was working with Mutual, Griffith's former company, one sees the first traces of pathos (*The Adventurer*, *The Vagabond*). The hero of *The Vagabond* is perhaps Chaplin's first characterization of real depth. In this film one senses the emergence of the future Chaplin, the Chaplin with a predilection for monumental subjects.

What other new elements are there apart from pathos? Through the comedy one glimpses elements of tragedy. Equally significant is the absence of the acrobatic tricks which played such an important part in his earlier comedies.

As a teacher I began by employing many means of expression which had been rejected by the theatre; one of them was acrobatic training, which I revived in the system known as 'biomechanics'. That is why I so enjoy following the course of Chaplin's career: in discovering the means he employed to develop his monumental art, I find that he, too, realized the necessity for acrobatic training in the actor's education.

To return to Chaplin. He now began to use a new method of editing, involving a certain restraint in cutting. For the first time he used retardation. I am not talking about his skill as an actor: that is a purely natural talent, as astonishing as someone coming along to the opera and revealing that he was born with a perfectly trained voice. Chaplin was already an accomplished actor when he entered the cinema; his acting reveals not merely a thorough training but a bafflingly unique mimetic talent.

At that time he was trying to form his own group. Partners were chosen for him quite haphazardly, although he did play opposite some fine artists at a time when a distinct American comic tradition was already emerging in the cinema. He tried to assemble his own company within the studios where he was working, and over the years something approaching a company of his own did take shape.

I must say that I can trace no such concern for the collective in the films of our young directors. There is no attempt to assemble a regular ensemble, and the actor is for ever on the move: one day he's filming with the Vasilevs, the next with Kozintsev and Trauberg, the next with Eisenstein, and so on. As a theatrical observer of the cinema, I see our cinema actors being forced to live from one part to the next, from director to director. I get the impression that there is nobody in the cinema interested in forming his own ensemble.

In or shortly before 1918, Chaplin began to manifest a preference for quality rather than sheer output of films. At that time his clowning began to acquire increasingly deeper motivation based on the most scrupulous observation of reality. This is of extreme importance, because it determined the very basis of his comic technique. Henceforth, every single piece of clowning bore witness to his profound and painstaking observation of reality.

Then with United Artists, the company of Douglas Fairbanks, Mary Pickford and Griffith, Chaplin made his famous *Woman of Paris*. It marked a further step towards profundity. I would go so far as to say that in this film Chaplin revealed his personal philosophy for the first time; he widened the scope of his art and showed an interest not so much in the plot of the film as in its associations, the incidental thoughts stimulated in the mind of the spectator, which convey the underlying idea.

Then he dealt a final blow to his past, to the days when he relied on tricks alone. He condemned his own formalist period – rather as Meyer-hold condemned Meyerholditis. In *The Goldrush* he displayed a new aspect, he invested the character he was playing with such significance that he was now fit to rank alongside such literary masters as Balzac, Dickens and Dostoevsky. He crossed the Rubicon and became a master destined to create vast, monumental canvases like *The Circus* and *Modern Times*. Thus Chaplin achieved the position which he occupies today.

Now let me turn for a moment to Pushkin. His dramatic precepts will help us understand the underlying elements of Chaplin's art. Pushkin wrote: 'Drama originated in the market place as entertainment for the people. Like children, the people demand entertainment, action. . . . The re-enactment of the passions and outpourings of the human soul are an unfailing novelty to them, endlessly gripping, awesome and instructive. Drama became the master of man's soul and man's passions.'[1]

Where did Chaplin find the mask of 'Charlie'? He found it in the street. In Pushkin's account of the birth of dramatic art the emphasis on its market-square origins is most significant: when he speaks of the revelation of the human soul through drama, he automatically associates it with the common people, for whom his own plays were intended.

Once Chaplin spotted a London cabby, an old drunk with a swaying gait and ridiculous movements. Hans Siemsen recounts Chaplin's own story: 'I followed him and observed him. The fellow interested me, and he showed me the way to that character which I finally found within myself.'[2]

This 'blending' of the cabby with Chaplin was possible only because Chaplin made no attempt to 'requisition' him, but discovered him *within himself*. That is absolutely typical of Chaplin! It contains the clue to the solution of the problem of the mask in the cinema, which is a question of the greatest importance.

Why, in this dear country of ours, do we continue to tolerate comedy films which are absolute failures? Why, when these are the very films which our workers, peasants and soldiers need? I think the whole trouble lies in our failure to recognize the need to discover a mask 'within one-self' – perhaps a number of masks around which the screen-writer can construct a scenario. To make this clear, let me repeat Pushkin's formula: 'Drama became the master of man's soul and man's passions.' Without

[1] A. S. Pushkin, *Polnoe sobranie sochinenii*, Moscow, 1964, vol. 7, p. 213.
[2] Quoted by Henry Poulaille in *Charles Chaplin*, Paris, 1927, p. 8. But see Chaplin's own account in *My Autobiography*, New York, 1964, pp. 144–7.

these passions, without a human soul, dramatic art – in this case, comedy – has no power over the masses.

Let us consider what attempts have been made to create a mask in this fashion. Take Igor Ilinsky as Arkashka in Ostrovsky's *Forest*. Arkashka was a comic literary or theatrical literary role (literary in so far as it was based on Ostrovsky, and theatrical in so far as we introduced a number of elements inspired by Chaplinism), which was built up from various Chaplinesque devices. Taking this character as a starting-point, Ilinsky tried to transfer its Meyerhold-Chaplinesque elements to the cinema screen, and it proved disastrous. The reason is that as well as Chaplin there is a character called Glupyshkin.[1] Once you begin to play comedy with the mask of Glupyshkin in the back of your mind, you are doomed to failure. Always remember that even Harold Lloyd had his positive and negative sides, and the negative bore the imprint of Glupyshkin. The same was true of Max Linder; Glupyshkin was to blame for his bad side, too. Both on the stage and on the cinema screen it is these incursions of ‚Glupyshkin, these 'tricks of nature', which mar the consistency of high comedy.

It is no use looking for just any mask; we must discover the mask which is closest to us and closest to the people for whom the film is intended. I haven't brought this up simply for the sake of argument, in the hope that afterwards you will say 'That was a nice point Meyerhold raised', but because so often our comedies are ruined in this way without our troubling to discover the reason. 'So Ilinsky's failed again this year,' we say – and that's that. But we must study our failures, learn from them and then put our film companies right.

The mask which Varlamov discovered for himself reflected his own personality plus what he found in Ostrovsky. It was there that he discovered the 'merchant's mask'. In the most painstaking fashion he developed the right melodious voice for it, the right intonation and the peculiar brand of Slavonic humour.

Olga Sadovskaya discovered the same kind of mask at the Maly as Varlamov did at the Alexandrinsky; Blumental-Tamarina is in the same tradition. Sadovskaya was remarkable because she knew how to present *herself* as a mask.

Ostrovsky himself created not one but a whole series of dramatic masks which he skilfully employed in one play after another. Titus Titych[2] crops up in play after play, and Ostrovsky need hardly have bothered to change

---

[1] Literally, 'juggins'.
[2] A wealthy merchant in *A Hangover from Another's Carousing*.

his name each time. Balzac was not afraid to 'repeat' characters in several novels. Arkashka is another mask. If you were to ask which characters of Ostrovsky made the deepest impression on the minds of his contemporaries, obviously the answer would be Titus Titych and Arkashka.

Chaplin has not merely found the correct tone for the humorous genre, he has created high comedy. Once again, let me check my opinion with Pushkin. For some time now I have withheld every production from the public until I have checked it against Pushkin's observations.

'High comedy – says Pushkin – depends not only on laughter but on the development of character, and frequently comes close to tragedy.'[1] He wrote this at the end of the 1820s. Clearly it was a forecast, a vision of the great advances which high comedy was destined to make. We read Gogol's high comedy, *The Government Inspector*, in the light of Pushkin's precepts; in it we look for the tragedy as well as the laughter. Gogol himself spoke of 'laughter through tears', but Pushkin was even bolder, asserting that high comedy could verge on tragedy.

And what about the high comedy of Chaplin? What do we find in films like *The Gold Rush?* Comedy which rises to the level of harshness and grief. I have seen people wiping the tears from their eyes at these films. Yet one's first reaction to Chaplin is a smile.

Pushkin goes on to speak of 'the three strings of our imagination which the magic of the drama sets vibrating . . .'[2] Again there follows a formula which we can use to define the essence of Chaplin's art. What are the three strings which are set vibrating by the magic of the drama? Laughter, pity and terror. There is no question that in Chaplin's films we find genuine suffering, calculated to move the spectators to pity. Laughter, pity, terror – these three strings of our imagination all vibrate to the magic of Charlie Chaplin. One recalls his severe, sorrowful sense of comedy, his desire to arouse pity as well as laughter, and sometimes terror, too. When I apply the same formula to the work of Eisenstein, you will see that there, too, the three strings are present, but one is clearly dominated by the other two.

There is one more point I must make in connection with Chaplin's art. It is aimed particularly at those young directors whose work I know best and whose films I have grown to like. Chaplin is able to direct a film as though he himself were the author. I am not the first person to mention this quality, but I esteem it especially highly because in my experience –

[1] Pushkin, loc. cit.   [2] Pushkin, loc. cit.

at 62 I feel I can say this – I have found that the only productions of mine which remain in the repertoire to this day are those which I directed as though I was writing them. By this I mean penetrating to the heart of the dramatic material whilst adhering firmly to one's own principles. Kornei Chukovsky realized this: he once remarked that watching one of my productions was like reading a book.

I think it is true to say that we derive the same kind of pleasure from the great works of Chaplin as we do from reading a novel. It is easy to understand Chaplin if one remembers Dickens, Cervantes and parts of Balzac. Why should Chaplin evoke the same response as the great novelists? Because all his films are imbued with undeniable humanity and undeniable truth. And it is by no means easy to depict humanity and truth on the screen, except, of course, by employing isolated banal devices. There are many films which are lachrymose and sentimental, but they fail to arouse the kind of sympathy inspired by a truly honest, humane author.

The Kid has been aptly described as a folk novel. Certainly, it affected me like a novel or a popular melodrama designed to enlist sympathy by speaking up for the helpless. Chaplin protects the Kid and takes him around with him; he even enters into a professional relationship with him: Jackie breaks windows and Chaplin repairs them. But this is merely the comic situation; the mother's abandoning of Jackie and the final awakening of her conscience which drives her to reclaim him are elements of true popular drama reminiscent of a Harlequinade. Carlo Gozzi revived the popular theatre by restoring the favourite masks of Italian popular comedy. He took them and built up a whole repertoire of plays based on the plots of well-known tales. Observe the simplicity of their construction: the actor faces the audience and recounts the play as though it were a familiar folk-tale. It is a device which we would do well to copy. But haven't we used it already? What about the Vasilevs? Consider their *Chapaev*. Chapaev, of course, is just the sort of popular figure who rallies the masses because he is 'theirs', because we who lived through the 'Sturm und Drang' of the Civil War know what kind of a man Chapaev is.

. . . Whenever Pushkin's remarks on the drama are quoted, one should check his theories against scenes from Shakespeare. He, himself, used to check them against the devices employed in Shakespearian tragedy.

Henry Poulaille gives an accurate analysis of a number of situations in Chaplin's work by comparing Chaplin, the dramatist, with Shakespeare. Without repeating what Poulaille says, I should like to consider some aspects of Chaplin, the dramatist, from the same angle.

317

Shakespeare's plays are constructed in such a way that their unity is not immediately apparent: the characters in the opening scene do not behave and speak in order to prepare the way for the scene which follows; Scene Two follows 'of its own accord', determined by a rhythm prescribed by the author. *Boris Godunov*, based on Shakespearian principles, is constructed in the same way.

When we study *Boris Godunov* we are amazed above all by the extraordinary sense of timing with which one scene is made to succeed another. They seem to strike the ear rather than the eye, rather like a symphony in many movements (not three or four, but twenty-four), with each scene a further stage in a rhythmical progression.

Hence Pushkin is a poet, not just because he writes in iambic pentameters, but because, as well as observing the rules of poetic composition, he constructs a rhythmical progression, closing each scene with a distinct terminal effect (an effect which I mentioned in an earlier lecture in connection with the need for a dramatist to possess what might be termed an epigrammatic talent).

When we come to examine Eisenstein's pronouncements we shall see how he divides up everything into 'attractions' – that is, into episodes, each with an unfailingly effective conclusion. He constructs these episodes according to musical principles, not with the conventional aim of advancing the narrative. This may sound rather abstruse unless we understand the nature of rhythm. Rhythm occurs as the result of a picture having a rigid, harmonious overall plan. Eisenstein constructs a picture rhythmically, and it is by examining this aspect of his work that we discover his creative qualities.

Eisenstein achieves something on the screen beyond the bounds of story and plot, something beyond the action (which is vital to the theatre but dispensable in the cinema); he achieves it on the basis of laws unique to the cinema. I fear I may be misinterpreted when I say 'something beyond the action which is vital to the theatre but dispensable in the cinema.' This should not be taken too literally; it is not abstraction that I have in mind, but something that has been asserted by the cinema ever since Chaplinism first appeared, something which has been fostered by Eisenstein in particular. I mean the ability of the film to play on the spectator's power of association. You will find the same device in my work, for I have come to regard the *mise en scène* not as something which works directly on the spectator but rather as a series of 'passes', each intended to evoke some association or other in the spectator (some premeditated, others outside my control). Your imagination is activated, your fantasy stimulated, and a whole chorus of associations is set off. A multitude of accumulated associations gives birth to new worlds – whole films which have never got beyond the cutting-room. You can no longer distinguish between what the director is responsible for and what is inspired by the associations which have invaded your imagination. A new world is created, quite separate from the fragments of life from which the film is composed.

At this point I must refer to Gogol's observation on the nature of Pushkin's poetry, in which he stresses Pushkin's amazing ability to transform life itself into a beauty of profound significance. We must submit the poetry of Chaplin to the same scrutiny. What does Gogol say? 'It is not reality, bare and unkempt, which enters his poetry, but purity and artlessness elevated to such a height that, by comparison, reality itself appears as a mere artificial caricature.'

Exactly the same may be said of Chaplin's work. His pictures are never invaded by bare and unkempt reality. Chaplin invented a caricature appearance for himself: the shoes, the bowler hat, the funny old coat, and the wide trousers are like nothing on earth. But the life which he portrays is incomparably more caricaturish. Through his caricature he seems to stress the monstrousness of the world he is unmasking, with all its cruelty, the exploitation of man by his neighbour, the police state, and all the delights of the capitalist society in which Chaplin is working.

What prompted Eisenstein to divide his subject-matter into a series of attractions, each with a carefully contrived climax? He developed the technique whilst working at the Proletkult Theatre, but it originated when he was working with me in my theatrical laboratory on the Novinsky Boulevard in Moscow. We were looking for a new type of stage, free from anything which might get in the actor's way. Like myself, Eisenstein needs an arena, a platform, a theatre like Shakespeare's Globe. When interviewers question me about this stage without a stage which I am building, I simply answer that I want an arena in which we can put on everything from variety turns like the Überbrettl[1] to vast spectacles of Shakespearian dimensions like Pushkin's *Boris Godunov* or *Oedipus, the King*.[2] It will be possible to alternate these productions with gymnastic displays, ballet and folk-dancing, because there will be nothing to separate the spectator from the one thing which matters – the performer himself.

[1] See note on p. 136 above.
[2] For a description of Meyerhold's new theatre, see p. 243 above.

Consider the formidable convention which hampers the film director. He is hemmed in by that detestable rectangle, the screen; it can't be thrust apart, so he overcomes it by employing the art of montage to obliterate it from the spectator's consciousness.

But this is a field which has been far from adequately explored, so that unfortunately – recalling Platon Kerzhentsev's recent call for a return to the style of Repin, Shishkin and Surikov[1] – there is the serious danger that the cinema will fail to make the contribution it ought to make. Not enough attention is paid to cutting and the art of montage. There are secrets of the screen which we still have not probed deeply enough. One example is the varying of the shooting angle. Occasionally some anarchist of a cameraman suddenly starts experimenting with shooting angles and the results are incomprehensible. He selects an angle for the sake of some arbitrary lighting effect or simply in order to demonstrate his own originality. Let him take warning that when a culture of mankind grows at such a speed as ours today we judge cinematographers according to the use they make of the small area of the cinema screen. We are not likely to be fooled by simple changes in perspective; you can count every possible shooting angle on your fingers. Our cameramen should take a lesson from Giotto, who knew how to utilize every corner of a canvas measuring no more than a few centimetres.

It is infuriating to watch the work of those directors who like to cover as much of the screen as possible. In our attempts to formulate a new language of the cinema we should pursue Goethe's doctrine of self-restraint to the limit.

In his afterword[2] to Kaufman's pamphlet on the Japanese cinema Eisenstein reproduces a small drawing from a Japanese children's textbook. Why does he include this drawing? He instinctively senses the need to employ the 'convention of limitation' to stir the spectator's fantasy in the same way that the child's fantasy is stirred by the drawing.

Obviously, one needs to study not only folklore (like Ostrovsky) but also children's art, because a child is capable of utilizing a sheet of paper in a way which reveals profound principles. . . .

Let us go to our children and see how naïvely they draw, yet what great art they produce. Eisenstein tells an interesting story of a child illustrating the subject 'lighting the stove'. The child drew 'some firewood,

[1] i.e. a return to 'realism'. Meyerhold is referring to the attacks on formalism in *Pravda* (see p. 248 above). At that time Kerzhentsev was President of the Supreme Committee for the Control of the Arts.

[2] Published in English as 'The Cinematographic Principle and the Ideogram' in Sergei Eisenstein's *Film Form* (translated by Jay Leyda), New York, 1949.

a stove and a chimney. But in the middle of the room there was a huge rectangle covered with zigzags. What was it? Matches, apparently. The child drew the matches on a scale appropriate to their crucial role in the action he was depicting.'

In the lighting of a stove matches have a particular significance. This sudden use of disproportion for no apparent reason is quite common in art; it is also employed by those who call themselves cinema directors, only on a far more modest scale than in the child's drawing.

In order to understand what strikes us as so remarkable in the work of Chaplin, you need to understand a little of what is implied by the so-called system of biomechanics, which in our time has fascinated both Eisenstein and myself.

As a young man, Eisenstein studied a number of works on the movement and behaviour of man in space in order to consolidate his theoretical knowledge. This helped him to formulate a coherent system based on his work in our biomechanics studio between 1922 and 1924, the period of *The Magnanimous Cuckold, Tarelkin's Death* and *The Forest*. The object of our experiments was the maximum exploitation of the expressive power of movement.

This skill can be acquired from a study of Chaplin. His so-called 'momentary pauses for aim', that peculiarly static style of acting, the freeze – it all comes down to the expedient concentration of action. Observe how Chaplin deploys his body in space to maximum effect; study, as we do, the movements of gymnasts and blacksmiths.

When we build our Hollywood in the South, the cinema is sure to have its own actors, who will be incapable of acting in the theatre because the laws of the theatre are quite distinct from the laws of the cinema screen.

What is there in common between Eisenstein and Chaplin? The reason I ask this is not to throw light on Eisenstein, who is familiar enough to us, but rather to reveal certain aspects of Chaplin: his remarkable lapidary style, his laconicism, his invariable division of the film into episodes or, as Eisenstein would say, 'attractions'.

In what respects do Eisenstein and Chaplin differ? In Eisenstein the predominant element is tragedy; in Chaplin it is pathos. Pushkin called laughter, pity and terror the three strings of our imagination which the magic of the drama sets vibrating. In Chaplin laughter and pity take precedence, whilst terror remains muted. In Eisenstein pity and terror predominate over laughter. In Eisenstein the critical moments of the action are expressed through terror, reminding one of the paintings of

Goya, the horror in Balzac and Dostoevsky. Chaplin recalls Dickens or Mark Twain.

Both Eisenstein and Chaplin employ sharp, laconic imagery. It is with good reason that Eisenstein quotes Khitomaro's 'tanka', which he sees as the script for a montage:

> Silently flies
> The mountain pheasant,
> His tail drags behind.
> O endless night –
> To be spent alone.[1]

Given man's powers of memory, the existence of two facts in juxtaposition prompts their correlation; no sooner do we begin to recognize this correlation than a composition is born and its laws begin to assert themselves.

The celebrated formulae which were once flaunted by Eisenstein are rooted in profound principles, but as far as I can see, forgotten. And for some time now the articles on the cinema in *Kino* have contained the most incredibly tedious rubbish.

But it is a pity that the dispute between Pudovkin and Eisenstein over 'linkage' and 'collision' montage has been forgotten. In fact, it has had no discernible effect on any recent film at all. It strikes me that it would be worth devoting time and money to the study of 'linkage' and 'collision' montage. Eisenstein advocated the juxtaposition of two conflicting shots. My production of *The Forest* was constructed on exactly the same principle, on the conflict of episodes. The five acts of Ostrovsky's play were split into thirty-three episodes, each one conflicting with the next. Clearly, this method enables one to exert a far greater influence over the spectator.

. . . Let me return to the notion of realism. The realism of Chaplin and Eisenstein is quite different from the realism of Shishkin.[2] But that does not mean that it is less realistic, just as it is wrong to regard Kazakh art as lifelike and Chinese art as formalist. I consider this a fatal mistake which must be put right at all costs. Why do we assert so confidently that the art of the Chinese actor, Mei Lan-fang, which made such a deep impression on Eisenstein, is realistic?[3]

In any country art is accepted as realistic so long as it accords with

[1] For another translation see Frederick Victor Dickens, *Primitive and Mediaeval Japanese Texts*, Oxford, 1906. It is this version which is quoted by Jay Leyda, loc. cit.

[2] Ivan Shishkin (1832–98), Russian landscape painter.

[3] Mei Lan-fang visited the Soviet Union in 1935.

principles which are familiar to the people of that country. Are we right in regarding Egyptian art as formalist? It is often considered to be stylized, but the Egyptians regarded its conventions as indispensable. The Chinese understand what is performed on the Chinese stage; they can interpret the scenic hieroglyphics and have no trouble in comprehending the acting of Mei Lan-fang, because he speaks in a language which is customary in the art of his country and his people. Hence, there are no grounds for regarding him as a formalist.

Incidentally, on the subject of terminology, there is an episode in *Three Sisters* [Act Two] where one character says 'cheremsha',[1] another says 'chikhirtma',[2] and they spend a long time quarrelling over it without realizing that they are both talking about the same thing. We are often like that in our use of terminology.

When we see an exhibition of Repin, we call his paintings realistic. We can learn how to draw from Repin. But when it's a question of creating a new work of art, we don't copy Repin because our realism, *socialist* realism, cannot be a reproduction of his realism. Similarly, Repin's realism cannot be socialist realism. Hokusai gives the following formula: 'I can permit myself the luxury of ignoring the canons, because I have achieved complete mastery over the canons.'

In his early years Vrubel was the best pupil in the Academy of Arts, the best draughtsman. Nobody could paint as well as he, so he felt free to disregard the canons of the Academy. He did not want to use the realistic language associated with the old school; he thought progressively and wanted to free art from the dead hand of academicism. As invariably happens, he went too far and his work reflects a certain abnormality and morbidity.

The next stage after Repin is Serov; he is closer to us, so let us learn from him, too. Let us learn from both, but let us still create an art appropriate to our own time. We must master new advances, scale new heights; we must build on the art which already exists by seeking new means of depicting actuality; we must invent, develop the one form which alone will reflect the great epoch in which we are fortunate enough to be living.

What is it that determines the form of socialist realism on the cinema screen? What techniques do we need to master? What is the most vital factor in the transformation of the film into a work of socialist realism?

I will approach the solution to this problem in a roundabout fashion. The most important thing that needs to be said about Chaplin is that, above all, he speaks to us as a poet. Next he speaks as a citizen, because through

[1] A kind of wild garlic.   [2] A Caucasian dish of mutton.

all his work there runs a single thread: Charlie Chaplin, the defender of the weak. He speaks to us as a poet because in all his pictures, wherever there is laughter, wherever there is terror, wherever there is pity, we see the apotheosis of realistic art.

I consider that we should approach socialist realism armed with all the beauty, all the attributes of realism. Or let us say lyricism. How can we possibly make good films either for or about our Komsomols without lyricism? I have seen a series of films depicting cheery Komsomols; every single one has had the inevitable smile and curly locks of the 'muzhik'. But all these cheery youths together contain not a single drop of lyricism. . . . I was talking to Nikolai Ostrovsky about his book, *How the Steel was Tempered*. What he emphasized was not the battle scenes and all the other terrible events of the Civil War in which so much blood was shed before we emerged victorious from the death struggle, but the novel's lyrical basis, the sub-text which, in his opinion, runs through every page. And when we came to adapt the work for the stage[1] the most difficult problem was how to convey this lyricism. And don't forget: this is the Ostrovsky who cannot move, who must always lie on his back as though in a coffin. He is full of the most extraordinary *joie de vivre* – not the *joie de vivre* of a 'cheery youth' but of a soldier-lyricist, a citizen whose revolutionary fervour ranges over such a vast compass that only the exalted tone of the lyric can do it justice.

[Published in *Iskusstvo kino*, Moscow, 1962, no 6, pp. 113–22]

NOTE Transcript of part of a lecture delivered by Meyerhold on 13 June 1936.

The listener would have interpreted his remarks on realism in the light of the recent attacks on formalism in *Pravda* (see pp. 248-9 above).

[1] See pp. 249–50 above.

SELECT BIBLIOGRAPHY

What follows is a selection of the principal works devoted wholly to
Meyerhold or containing significant reference to him. Newspaper and
periodical articles are not included; for these the reader is referred to the
footnotes above. For a comprehensive bibliography, including the principal
periodical articles and an extensive range of background material, see
Béatrice Picon-Vallin, *Meyerhold* (CNRS, Paris, 1990).

ALPERS, B.V., *Teatralnye ocherki* (2 Vols), Moscow, 1977

ANNENKOV, YU., *Dnevnik moikh vstrech* (2 vols.), New York, 1966

BOGDANOV-BEREZOVSKY, V.M., *Vstrechi*, Moscow, 1967

BRAUN, E., *Meyerhold: A Revolution in Theatre*, London, 1995

CARTER, H., *The New Spirit in the Russian Theatre 1917–1928*, London, 1929

DANA, H.W., *Handbook on Soviet Drama*, New York, 1938

DANILOV, S.S., *Revizor na stsene*, Leningrad, 1934

DAVYDOVA, M.V., *Ocherki istorii russkogo teatralno-dekoratsionnogo iskusstva
    XVIII – nachala XX vekov*, Moscow, 1974

DEICH, A.I., *Golos pamyati*, Moscow, 1966

EATON, K.B., *The Theater of Meyerhold and Brecht*, Westport, 1985

EIZENSHTEIN, S.M., *Izbrannye proizvedenia v shesti tomakh*, Moscow,
    1964–1971

ERENBURG, I.G., *Lyudi, gody, zhizni*, Moscow, 1961

FEVRALSKY, A.V., 'Meierkhold i Shekspir' in *Vilyam Shekspir-issledovania i
    materialy*, Moscow, 1964

FEVRALSKY, A.V., *Pervaya sovetskaya piesa*, Moscow, 1971

FEVRALSKY, A.V., *Puti k sintezu: Meierkhold i kino*, Moscow, 1978

FEVRALSKY, A.V., 'Stanislavsky i Meierkhold' in *Tarusskie stranitsy*, Kaluga,
    1961

FEVRALSKY, A.V., *Zapiski rovesnika veka*, Moscow, 1976

FREEDMAN, J., *Silence's Roar: The Life and Drama of Nikolai Erdman*,
    Oakville – New York – London, 1992

GARIN, E., *S Meierkholdom*, Moscow, 1974

GINZBURG, S.S., *Kinematografia dorevolyutsionnoy Rossii*, Moscow, 1963

GLADKOV, A.K., 'Iz vospominaniy o Meierkholde' in *Moskva teatralnaya*, Moscow, 1960

GLADKOV, A.K., 'Meierkhold govorit' in *Novy mir*, 1961, No. 8, translated as 'Meyerhold Speaks' in *Novy Mir* 1925-1967 (ed. M. Glenny), London, 1972

GLIKMAN, I., *Meierkhold i muzikalny teatr*, Leningrad, 1989

Gogol i Meierkhold (ed. E.F. Nikitina), Moscow, 1927

GOLOVIN, A. YA., *Golovin: Vstrechi i vpechatlenia. Pisma. Vospominania o Golovine*, Leningrad-Moscow, 1960

GORDON, M. & LAW, A., *Meyerhold, Eisenstein and Biomechanics*, North Carolina & London, 1996

GVOZDEV, A.A., Teatr im. Vsevoloda Meierkholda (1920-26), Leningrad, 1927

HAMON-SIREJOLS, C., *Le Constructivisme au théâtre*, Paris, 1992

HOOVER, M.L., *Meyerhold - The Art of Conscious Theater*, University of Massachusetts, 1974

HOOVER, M.L., *Meyerhold and his set designers*, New York, 1988

HOUGHTON, N., *Moscow Rehearsals*, New York, 1936

HOUGHTON, N., *Return engagement, New York, 1962*

ILINSKY, I.V., *Sam o sebe*, Moscow, 1962

Istoria Russkogo dramaticheskogo teatra, Vol. 7 (ed. E.G. Kholodov), Moscow, 1987

Istoria Sovetskogo dramaticheskogo teatra, Vols. 1-4 (ed. K.L. Rudnitsky), Moscow, 1966-1968

Istoria Sovetskogo teatra, Vol. 1 (ed. V. Ye. Rafalovich), Leningrad, 1933

KHERSONSKY, KH.N., *Stranitsy yunosti kino*, Moscow, 1965

KLEBERG, L., *Theatre as Action*, London, 1993

KOMISSARZHEVSKAYA V.F. *Pisma aktrisy, vospominania o ney, materialy*, Moscow-Leningrad, 1964

KRASOVSKY, YU, M., *Nekotorye problemy teatralnoi pedagogiki, V.E. Meierkholda* (1905-07), Leningrad, 1981

LAPKINA, G.A., *Na afishe - Pushkin*, Leningrad-Moscow, 1965

LEACH, R., *Vsevolod Meyerhold*, Cambridge, 1989

LEVITSKY, A.A., *Rasskazy o kinematografe*, Moscow, 1964

LODDER, C., *Russian Constructivism*, Yale University Press, 1983

LUNACHARSKY, A.V., *O teatre i dramaturgii*, Vol. I. Moscow, 1958

MARKOV, P.A., *O teatre* (4 vols.), Moscow, 1974-76

Maskarad Lermontova v eskizakh Golovina, Moscow-Leningrad, 1941

MATSKIN, A.P., *Portrety i nablyudenia*, Moscow, 1973

MAYAKOVSKY, V.V., *Teatr i kino* (2 vols.), Moscow, 1954

MEIERKHOLD, V.E., *Perepiska*, Moscow, 1976

Meierkhold repetiruyet (2 vols. ed. M. Sitkovetskaya), Moscow, 1993

Meierkholdovskiy sbornik: vypusk pervy (2 vols., ed. A. Sgerel), Moscow, 1992

MEIERKHOLD, V.E., *Statyi, pisma, rechi, besedy* (2 vols.), Moscow, 1968

MEYERHOLD, V.E., *Ecrits sur le théâtre* (4 vols., trans. B. Picon-Vallin), Lausanne, 1973-1992

I. Nemirovich-Danchenko – Teatralnoe nasledie, Vol. 2, Moscow, 1954

PICON-VALLIN, B., *Les Voies de la Création théâtrale, tome 17: Meyerhold*, Paris, 1990

PETROV, N.V., *50 i 500*, Moscow, 1960

Pikovaya dama – sbornik statey i materialov, Leningrad, 1935

POZHARSKAYA, M.N., *Russkoe teatralno-dekoratsionnoe iskusstvo kontsa XIX, nachala XX vekov*, Moscow, 1970

POLOTSKAYA, E.A., 'Chekhov i Meierkhold' in *Literaturnoe nasledstvo*, Vol. 68, Moscow, 1960

REDKO, A.E., *Teatr i evolyutsia teatralnykh form*, Leningrad, 1926

RIPELLINO, A.M., *Il trucco e l'anima*, Turin, 1965

RIPELLINO, A.M., *Majakovskij e il teatro russo d'avanguardia*, Turin, 1959 (also published in French as *Maiakovski et le théâtre russe d'avant garde*, Paris, 1965)

RODINA, T.M., *Aleksandr Blok i russkiy teatr nachala XX veka*, Moscow, 1972

ROSTOTSKY, B.E., *O rezhissyorskom tvorchestve, V.E. Meierkholda*, Moscow, 1960

RUBTSOV, A.V., *Dramaturgia Aleksandra Bloka*, Minsk, 1968

RUDNITSKY, K.L., *Russian and Soviet Theatre: Tradition and the avant-garde*, London 1988

RUDNITSKY, K.L., *Meyerhold the Director*, Ann Arbor, 1981

SAYLER, O.M., *The Russian Theatre under the Revolution*, Boston, 1920

SCHMIDT, P. (ed.), *Meyerhold at Work*, Manchester, 1981

SITKOVETSKAYA, N.M., 'V.E. Meierkhold do Oktyabrya' in *Vstrechi s proshlym* (ed. N.B. Volkova and others), Moscow, 1972

SOLLERTINSKY, I.I., *Kriticheskie statyi*, Leningrad, 1963

Sovetskiy teatr: dokumenty i materialy – Russkiy sovetskiy teatre: 1917-21 (ed. A.Z. Yufit), Leningrad, 1968

Sovetskiy teatr: dokumenty i materialy – russkiy sovetskiy teatr: 1921-27 (ed. A. Ya. Trabsky), Leningrad, 1975

STANISLAVSKY, K.S., *My Life in Art*, London, 1980

STANISLAVSKY, K.S., *Sobranie sochineniy v vosmi tomakh*, Moscow, 1954–1961

STROEVA, M.N., *Rezhissyorskie iskania Stanislavskogo 1898–1917*, Moscow, 1973

TALNIKOV, D.L., *Novaya revizia Revizora*, Moscow-Leningrad, 1927

Teatralny oktyabr-sbornik I (ed. A.A. Gvozdev and others), Leningrad-Moscow, 1926

TRETYAKOV, S.M., *Slyshish, Moskva?!*, Moscow, 1966

Tvorcheskoe nasledie V.E. Meierkholda (ed. L.D. Vendrovskaya and others), Moscow, 1978

VAN GYSEGHEM, A., *Theatre in Soviet Russia*, London, 1943

VAN NORMAN BAER, N (ed.), *Theatre in Revolution: Russian Avant-Garde Stage Design 1913–1935*, London, 1991

VOLKOV, N.D., *Meierkhold* (2 vols.), Moscow-Leningrad, 1929

VOLKOV, N.D., *Teatralnye vechera*, Moscow, 1966

Vstrechi s Meierkholdom (ed. M.A. Valentei and others), Moscow, 1967

YURIEV, YU. M., *Zapiski* (2 vols.), Leningrad-Moscow, 1963

YUTKEVICH, S.I., *Kontrapunkt rezhissyora*, Moscow, 1960

YUZOVSKY, YU., *Razgovor zatyanulsya za polnoch*, Moscow, 1966

YUZOVSKY, YU., *Spektakli i piesy*, Moscow, 1935

YUZOVSKY, YU., *Zatem lyudi khodyat v teatr*, Moscow, 1964

ZAKHAVA, B.E., *Sovremenniki*, Moscow, 1969

ZHAROV, M.I., *Zhizn, teatr, kino*, Moscow, 1967

ZNOSKO-BOROVSKY, E.A., *Russkiy teatr nachala XX veka*, Prague, 1925

ZOLOTNITSKY, D.I., *Zori teatralnogo oktyabrya*, Leningrad, 1976

INDEX

Works are given under authors' names. Names are not indexed if they are mentioned only in passing. In general, aspects of the theatre are grouped under collective headings, e.g. 'Improvisation' under 'Actors and acting', 'Forestage' under 'Stage, forms of'.